Liberation without Violence:

A Third-Party Approach

Liberation without Violence:

A Third-Party Approach

EDITED BY

A. PAUL HARE and HERBERT H. BLUMBERG

REX COLLINGS • LONDON • 1977

This collection first published in the UK
by Rex Collings Ltd 69 Marylebone High St
London W1

© A. Paul Hare and Herbert H. Blumberg 1977

ISBN   0860   36   0237

Typesetting by Malvern Typesetting Services
Printed in Great Britain by
The Pitman Press, Bath

CONTENTS

ACKNOWLEDGEMENTS

Helpful corrections were noted by Dale Hess and Marion Hess, who read the text, and A. R. Tylecote and others, who read the bibliographic guide.

For permission to reprint material, we are grateful to the various authors and to: Arnold-Heinemann, Joan Daves, Dimension Books, Friends Peace and International Relations Committee, Friends Peace Committee, *Gandhi Marg*, Harper and Row, Orbis Books, *Peace News*, Princeton University Press, *Resurgence*, Sarva Seva Sangh Prakashan, Sheed and Ward and *Social Dynamics*. Details of publication are shown on the first page of each chapter.

PREFACE

The pages of *Liberation without Violence* have raised many questions in my mind. Let me mention some.

Can one really be a 'third-party' and 'nonpartisan' at the same time? I do not believe that there are people—except some exceptions, I suppose—who would intervene or interfere in conflicts between others, unless the conflict has some bearing on their *own* lives—physical or mental. Almost all the known cases of such third-party intervention show that the third-party did so because it had some sort of sympathy with one or both of the parties concerned, a sympathy which involved emotional or intellectual interests; the conflict threatened their (the third-party's) beliefs or ideologies; or the conflict threatened the peace of their locality, country or the world as a whole, which they believed would directly or indirectly affect them.

The examples of third-party role in the resolution of conflict given in this book have been very carefully chosen. In addition to some common features and categories they represent, these examples also show that each conflict has its unique history and that, in the efforts of resolving these conflicts, methods used were also different in different cases. For instance, while in the case of the Cyprus Resettlement Project most of the third-party team were unattached people (non-partisan), in the Nagaland crisis all three members of the team had sympathy and attachment with one or the other side of the conflict. One member was definitely on the side of the Nagas, another was an integral part of the Indian Government machinery, and the third—comparatively less attached, yet with an approach nearer to the Indian position than to that of the Nagas. It is perhaps this diversity in 'partisan-ness' which helped in keeping the balance rather than the non-partisan character of the Peace Mission as such.

In considering many aspects of conflicts and their possible resolution, the third-party has to be clear about its own position vis-à-vis the conflict, the conflicting parties, the historicity of the environment enveloping the conflict, and the tools available. This applies more sharply to those third-parties which seek *nonviolent* solutions of conflicts. There is one thing which should be fully understood, that conflicts can be aggravated and worsened if a so-called third-party acts in a paternalistic way. There can be a tendency among votaries of nonviolence to emphasize the need for avoiding-curbing-minimizing violence and forgetting the deeper issues involved or giving secondary place to the real and lasting solution of the problem. I wonder how non-partisan was the team which went to Wounded Knee. It is as clear as a crystal that the conflict between the native Americans and the white Americans is rooted in exploitation by the whites. I can not think of a white American who is aware of the facts of American history to consider this a conflict between *two* equals or *two* guilty parties. I know personally that the members of the third-party team to Wounded Knee were enlightened Americans. They were perturbed to see that the native Americans had taken to violence, so they decided to go to the spot and see if they could avoid or minimize the violent part of the conflict. They stood between the two belligerent parties.

One of the common and to some extent legitimate criticisms of such mediatory actions is that instead of helping to resolve the conflict they often prolong it, i.e. help to maintain the status quo. The question before a nonviolent activist is whether to act as an orthodox (totally 'non-partisan') third-party would or as one who not only sympathizes but also identifies with the exploited, and acts as a pressure on the exploiter to change its position, i.e. to give-in much more than the underprivileged can and should be expected to. The team which went to Wounded Knee had itself posed such questions. Now after three years of 'reflections' it will be good to know what answers they have been working out.

In the orthodox traditions of third-party functioning, particularly when the quality of being 'absolutely non-partisan' takes the top priority, the question of law and order becomes more important than the resolution of conflict, which can be possible only if the element of injustice involved is removed. In such cases the third-party, however impartial, would be seen with hostility by the genuinely grieved side of the conflict. On the other hand the privileged party will tend to take advantage of the so-called non-partisan-ness of the arbitrator. How should, then, the third-party function, so that its role as a go-between becomes effective while its own political position is not kept hidden from either the concerned parties or the general public?

When should one consider a conflict resolved? I divide conflicts into two categories. There are conflicts of which the roots do not lie in injustice or exploitation. Their causes can be (a) lack of information; (b) lack or breakdown of communication; (c) misinformation; (d) false fear, misunderstanding, etc. It could even be a result of a practical joke. Such conflicts need the totally impartial arbitrator. Once conflicts of this category are resolved they can be forgotten.

The second category is of conflicts which generally have some sort of chain reaction. Let us take an example. Nation A rules over nation B. B struggles and succeeds in getting rid of nation A. For a moment the conflict seems to have been resolved, but soon a new class of people emerges from within the country B. This class of people now plays the same role which once the country A had played—exploitation. That means the conflict had not ended with the overthrow of foreign rule. It only deepened and at the same time localized. The conflict was between the exploiters and the exploited and it is still the same. It only changed the actors. Some actors have changed roles and others have redefined their goals.

I conclude from this that if the character of a struggle (conflict resolution) and its methodology do not encourage and work out a process by which it is carried on to its second phase, then to the third, and so on, until the symptoms and the causes are totally removed, it can not be considered resolved. Gandhi's example here is relevant. He was not fighting the British as such. He was fighting the evils and their effects caused by a foreign rule. He often said that getting rid of the British rule was only a preparatory step towards the goal, which was revolution.

Another question is: whether, in regard to conflicts where one of the parties is more grieved than the other, the quality for the third-party of being non-partisan is more important than its integrity as one who is committed to social and economic justice and to liberation and who is an uncorruptable body? There is one thing which seems to me to be crucial. Anybody functioning as third-party has to be known to both the conflicting parties as well as to those members of the general public who may be interested in the conflict and its resolution—known by his or her service to the community and for human quality. The greatest authority one can have is that which is attained by genuine friendship and love of human life and its quality. In the Indian village the 'panchayat', 'the assembly of five wise men' used to handle almost all the conflicts within the village community. A 'panch' (one of the five) was known to every member of the community as a wise man and one who can be relied upon, i.e. one who knows things and one who is considerate yet unyielding to pressures from outside; one who will speak against injustice.

It is gratifying that Paul Hare and Herbert Blumberg have focused on these and many other questions by compiling this collection of essays. It is a significant step toward furthering the art of nonviolent conflict resolution. The importance of this book is in its dealing with concrete and specific cases. Many of these cases have previously been brought to the notice of the public, but to see those and several others tied together in a planned way is particularly valuable. I have no doubt that this work will encourage further study into the still little explored world of nonviolent conflict resolution.

DEVI PRASAD

INTRODUCTION

HERBERT H. BLUMBERG

We have gathered descriptions of a variety of cases in which people have effected social change nonviolently or have helped show how to do so. Much of the material on *liberation without violence* represents a kind of fusion of two topics: social change, which says something about the 'path' we are on (see, for example, Buckhout, 1972), and conflict resolution, which has to do with how to meet some of the difficulties that we encounter along the way (see for instance, Smith, 1971).

The material in this book has been divided into four categories, according to whether the liberating action is partisan or non-partisan, and according to whether it is mainly carried out by people from one nation or transnationally.

Within each category the cases are arranged approximately in order of date of occurrence so that it is possible to trace the influence of early events on those which followed. In some cases there is no direct connection while in others the same persons are involved or the participants consciously use a previous action as a model.

Following the review of case materials in this volume is a section that summarizes various theoretical analyses and applications which help us to understand how the changes were brought about. In addition, there is a bibliographic guide to further case materials and analyses.

Perhaps the world has an especially great need for disinterested people coming together from different countries and dedicated to resolving difficulties that transcend national boundaries. However, many individuals first develop enthusiasm for a particular cause within their own countries. 'Partisan national' activity seems more frequent than cases which are nonpartisan or transnational or both.

By *partisan* we mean that the people who are acting for change are not 'independent' but actively identify themselves with an oppressed group. However, we have chosen to call even these cases *a third-party approach* because the actors have enough detachment from their own causes to try in some sense to seek solutions which incorporate the needs of all parties.

PARTISAN NATIONAL CASES

The first two cases are of classic actions: the Salt Satyagraha (which was part of the Gandhian campaign in India) and Martin Luther King's description of action against segregation in Birmingham, Alabama (part of the movements against the oppression of black people in the United States).

Gandhi developed the technique of satyagraha while he was still in South Africa, and various campaigns took place in India before and during the 1920s, culminating in the Salt Satyagraha, which lasted for about a year, from March 1930. The method (not merely a method, but a way of being and acting—a 'nonviolent truth force') was effective against oppressive laws. The movement emphasized a small disciplined group but gained wide popular support.

The organization of Bondurant's outline of the campaign provides a fine general model for documenting social action. It is very much worth reading about the Salt Satyagraha to get some impression of a large-scale nonviolent campaign in its classically disciplined form. 'Disciplined' is not quite the right word, for it suggests something negative and imposed rather than a spirit shared by the participants in work, positive effort, and being able to do something they want or need to do. In any event, the remaining cases in this section show varied forms of nonviolent action in different national settings.

No one point marks the beginning of the current actions for Black liberation in the United States. Even in the 1940s protests took place against White-only facilities in Northern cities such as Philadelphia and also tests were made against segregated seating patterns on long-distance buses in some of the border states between North and South. Some of the important events after that: the 1954 Supreme Court decision on school desegregation, the start of the Mongomery bus boycott in 1955, and the start of the sit-ins in 1960.

The Mongomery, Alabama, bus boycott and the Birmingham actions are among the well known activities which Martin Luther

King helped to organize. The Birmingham campaign is described in King's account (excerpted in this book). The earlier Montgomery bus boycott is worth considering briefly, here, as background. One well-known action, in 1956, a little before the beginning of mass waves of nonviolent protest was the Montgomery, Alabama, bus boycott, which was ultimately successful, in which—after all possible negotiations to end segregated seating had failed —thousands of Black people joined in the campaign of walk- in rather than ride on segregated buses. King's approach was in terms of Christian love, the very opposite of 'Black people against White people'. At the regular mass meetings, with the hall filled and overflowing, there were prayers and song. A different minister spoke each week, urging the group to love rather than hate. Even after King's own home was bombed and a crowd of Black people gathered (police tried to disperse the crowd, but their presence made matters worse), King arrived, and his approach was to urge that violence be met with nonviolence and benevolence. So the nonviolent movement for civil rights, continuing into the 1960s, is or was consciously Christian and Gandhian: Christian in pattern and values, Gandhian in the method of its goal-directed force.

I think it worth pausing at this point to consider the distinction between (a) the question of whether everyone is getting a 'fair share' and (b) the issue of whether the thing being shared (and the means of achieving it) is itself in need of change. The first question has to do with the equitable distribution of power and resources, and it applies particularly to the materials just reviewed. The second question, related more directly to the materials which follow in this section, has to do with basic values and the way people relate to one another.

Now, as regards a fair share of power and resources, the complaint can be either than an alien or foreign power controls too much (e.g. Bondurant's analysis of the Gandhian campaign against British rule in India), or else that some domestic group have more than their fair share (which was the basis of the American civil rights movement). Clearly, all of the authors surveyed here would agree that whatever is available should be available to everyone. While human solidarity and nonviolence reflected the dominant values of the Indian and civil rights actions, the specific objectives had to do with allocation of resources and power.

Indeed, the American civil rights movement of the 1960s,

although it evolved pragmatically, wound up protesting against a veritable catalogue of inequities, where many people (primarily in the South) had been receiving less than their fair share simply because they happened to be Black rather than White: voting rights, access to public facilities (as in Alabama), housing, education, and employment opportunities. One did *not*, as the movement spread, hear too much questioning of the *value* of the things being sought—the American cultural emphasis on 'things' rather than 'being', the possible meaninglessness of even the unattainable jobs, and so on.

More recently, of course, there were feminist, Black, and gay groups among those opposing American military involvements in Vietnam. And many women's groups, for example, are concerned about *human* consciousness: concern is not *limited* to employment opportunities, wage inequities, nor other deprivations associated with the Western female role, but the worth of the many highly competitive male roles is also questioned.

The value of every institution is open to question—and this includes the institution of education. If various minority groups are not 'provided with' their fair share of education, it is important—but not sufficient—that this inequity be rectified. For according to one view, education is meaningful only if people themselves find it actively worthwhile.

The experience of Paulo Freire—who worked with illiterate people in Brazil and later Chile—is here relevant, although not included among the cases in this book. His basic orientation is described in the following paragraph:

> His early sharing of the life of the poor also led him to the discovery of what he describes as the 'culture of silence' of the dispossessed. He came to realize that their ignorance and lethargy were the direct product of the whole situation of economic, social, and political domination—and of the paternalism—of which they were victims. Rather than being encouraged and equipped to know and respond to the concrete realities of their world, they were kept 'submerged' in a situation in which such critical awareness and response were practically impossible. And it became clear to him that the whole educational system was one of the major instruments for the maintenance of this culture of silence. [Freire, 1972, p. 10; from the Foreword by Richard Shaull.]

Freire distinguished between the pervasive 'banking concept of education' and 'problem-posing' education. According to the banking concept, students are treated like initially-empty containers into which the teacher 'makes deposits'. In this analogy, students are an oppressed group who are slowly filled with lectures and texts supplied by bank-clerk teachers. By contrast, in problem-posing education there must be *dialogue* between people *teaching each other*. In Freire's method, the carefully identified generative themes that form the basis of a group discussion are supplied locally and thus draw on the needs and interests of the people themselves. I think that this is not to deny the value of traditional course content for those who want it as part of their education — but that cannot be the start, especially for oppressed people who are not interested.

Illich (1973a), like Freire, is concerned with education not in the narrow sense of 'schooling' but in the broadest sense of people learning and feeling what is important to their lives. He describes the economic absurdity, and impossibility, of providing lengthy compulsory curricula for everyone in even the wealthiest countries much less for everyone in the world. School should not have a monopoly on education and on the spending of educational funds, he feels; and prerequisite levels of schooling should be banned as job-qualification criteria. Meaningful education is viewed as having two components: (a) skill-learning, which is efficiently done with drills and from tutors who are already skilled and (b) inventive, creative behaviour, which most happily emerges from groups meeting around a problem of common interest. It seems implicit in Illich's proposals that the full range of educational opportunity must, in both theory and practice, be available to everybody, not just to a minority of the population.

In his discussion of convivial reconstruction, Illich (1973b) urges that a balance be sought, in society, between demand-creating tools and those which lead to creative self-realization. By tools he includes not only implements and machines but also systems such as telephones, roads, and schools. He argues that a society (be it capitalist or socialist) that is mainly geared to ever-increasing production will ultimately find its endeavours to be self-defeating.

The question that comes up: is there a *means for achieving* justice and peace that is consistent with its own objectives? Camara (an archbishop in Brazil) outlines a programme of action which incorporates nonviolence and trust for others in the collection, truth-testing, and dissemination of information to document injustice (such as enforced poverty and curtailment of free communications). His call is for something that sounds a bit like a group of 'Nader's raiders' (the American teams of volunteers who locate unfair practices regarding goods and services available to consumers), except that he proposes a collectivity of people with solidarity, specializing in the publicity of political and economic deprivations. He urges everyone to join in this decentralized campaign.

The writings of Freire and Illich are now widely known and available. An extract from Camara's work is included among the case studies to provide at least one extended example of programmes and strategies.

As an example of partisan national activity in a European context, we have included a description of how farmers in the Larzac plateau in France have been opposing the enlargement of a military camp.

One could try to imagine how each of the cases could relate to 'Strategy for revolution', which is part of a manifesto for nonviolent revolution drafted by Geory Lakey (1972) for War Resisters International. The strategy includes a description of five steps for the development of a movement:

1. *Conscientization,* which has to do principally with the value of a web of people understanding that they have needs in common. Of basic value is the development of political consciousness; the adaptive spread of information in conferences, newspapers, etc. Political eduction must itself be participatory and integrative (there is a large variety of training methods, including roleplaying and quick decision games—Olson and Shivers, 1970). The force of a positive movement does not end with everlasting protest but goes on to create visions of what the new society would look like.

2. *Building organizations.* A need is seen for counter-institutions to provide the information and services that are now lacking: people should live the new social patterns—the small affinity group can serve as the basic building block of mass movements. The force of the means must be consistent with the goals (that is, the movement itself must have egalitarian leadership); and the values to be sought should be practised from the start—i.e. non-sexist, non-racist, non-authoritarian.

3. *Confrontation.* A goal-directed campaign needs to be carried out over a period of time. 'Nonviolence' represents a basic

value—the best response to the violence of one's opponent is viewed as being nonviolent action. There is a need for a large organizational network of people so that, if some are arrested or killed, thousands more are ready to take their places. It is seen as helpful to begin with a symbolic, almost pictorial campaign (perhaps possible examples are the Gandhian march to the sea to prepare salt from seawater, in protest against the salt tax; the building of a chapel on the beach in Culebra in the path of navy target practice (see Part III, Partisan Transnational Cases); and the attempt to plant a 'life-affirming' tree on the grounds of Edgewood Arsenal as part of the campaign against research being carried out there on chemical and biological warfare).

4. *Mass non-co-operation* — failure to show solidarity with the old order. Various activities are named—economic tactics, political non-co-operation, and physical interposition. The basic value is to win people over rather than to perpetuate cycles of violence.

5. *Parallel government* — the people themselves set up institutions to shape their lives.

The statement of 'strategy for revolution' concludes with a discussion of nonviolence and the need for a transnational perspective.

NONPARTISAN NATIONAL CASES

Some distinction can be made between cases in which a nonviolent group are actually party to a dispute (that is, they are part of an oppressed group or acting in solidarity with one) and cases in which they intercede as a *third-party*, either mediating between the two sides or otherwise providing generally-helpful goods or services. Actually, the two categories are separated by a spectrum of gradations rather than a sharp line, and even in the third-party cases the nonpartisan group may feel that one side are more the oppressed victims than the other, but nonetheless the nonpartisan group are not particularly identified as being part of either side (or any side, if there are more than two).

I think that in all of the cases, the basic values and guiding force for what we are calling the 'nonviolent group' are essentially the same, but the content of what they are doing turns out to be different in the two categories of cases. (Compare for example, the

partisan salt march with the nonpartisan Shanti Sena services.)
Now in both sections, the values are anti-oppression; they include
an empathy or awareness of the needs of *all* parties, and they
operate under a kind of 'force for truth and love' — which, at least in
principle, is hard to disagree with — and involves being active and
taking the initiative rather than passively sitting by. In the partisan
cases the main activity seems to be building and co-ordinating a
programme of liberation. However, in the nonpartisan cases, the
main job is to find out what help is needed and then to try providing
it, enabling others to join in as well.

Before we review here the actual cases, and see how various
services are provided, it may be useful to digress briefly to consider
the nature of human aggression, since this has some bearing on the
kinds of help that can be provided. We can look at questions of
instinct, motivation, reinforced learning, and social diffusion. I
think that Montagu (1968) has compellingly cited evidence to refute
the view that people are by instinct aggressive animals (or indeed
that many animals are commonly violent). If one nevertheless clings
to the view of natural aggression, one is still faced with the tasks of
(a) helping to build a society which at once restrains our 'violent
instincts' and at the same time permits us maximum freedom and
(b) helping to clean up after the wars and riots which do occur.

For motivation, a number of paradigms are relevant, but let us
single out the well-established frustration-aggression hypothesis
(Dollard, et al., 1961): that people have a variety of needs
—hunger, thirst, sexuality, achievement, affiliation, curiosity,
and so on—and there is sort of a hierarchy of various ways
to fill these various needs. But when everything else fails,
aggression is one possible response to frustration of a need. This
means that, sometimes, if there is some felt need that is not being
met, then it may look as if people are being naturally aggressive,
but what must be done is to see what the need is and whether in fact
it can be met. In this case, the third-party service is to work against
institutionalized poverty or injustice, or whatever else is thwarting
people's needs from being satisfied, and thereby prevent riots before
they occur, so to speak.

As regards reinforced learning, once a violent response is
initiated the recipient may well respond aggressively, and the
confrontation can escalate. As we shall see in some of the Indian
riot examples, the initial violence can come from a small number of

provocateurs, or from a misunderstanding, and once the cycle starts, it can almost carry on of its own accord, and people can get into the habit of responding violently. Here, there are a number of things that can be done. Osgood (1962) suggests a series of graduated peaceful initiatives to de-escalate a conflict, and while his suggestion is that the initiatives be made by one of the opposing parties, they could also be made by a third-party force. Where no one cleaned up debris after some of the Hindu-Moslem riots in India, and members of the Shanti Sena went in and started to do so, people from both sides joined in, and while there were some difficulties, at least it was getting done. What can really be effective are institutionalized peaceful patterns for conflict resolution. The examples cited are often labour-management disputes, which may go through a historical period of violent opposition, but which can be completely alleviated by procedures such as voluntary binding arbitration — where arbiters in labour disputes can be so much a part of the everyday society that one does not even think of them when it comes time to list creative third-party forces. Indeed, anything that has the effect of *breaking the chain of responses,* of violence reciprocated by more violence, will be of value. A large literature is devoted to such suggestions (see, e.g. Smith, 1971) — for instance, fractionating the conflict (viewing it on a smaller perspective and breaking it into smaller, manageable issues) and translating issues of 'values', on which people are reluctant to compromise, into issues of concrete disparities.

Finally, we learn that behaviour typically spreads through the social network, regardless of whether the innovative behaviour is doctors prescribing a new drug or demonstrators trying out a revised form of social protest (cf. Blumberg, 1968). So if you have finished helping out in one community after a riot and you are looking for something more to do, it is a reasonable guess that some of the same conditions may exist in nearby towns, and it would be worth seeing whether there are potentially explosive situations to be dealt with. Also, rumours spread through the social system and become unimaginably distorted and, though this sounds like a small thing, really can cause tremendous misunderstanding and violent outbreaks. So another third-party service is one of listening to all sides, and having reliable information and spreading the truth, through newsletters or other media.

Let us turn at this point to some of the actual cases of

nonpartisan national activity. Desai describes activity of the Shanti Sena, who for the most part are informal groups from the Gandhian ashrams, devoted to peaceful social action. Two cases are described of members of the Shanti Sena going into towns, Ahmedabad and Bhivandi, after riots in about 1969. Because two examples are given (and more are in Desai's book from which they were excerpted), one can compare them and separate the specific from the general. The first step in any case is to *learn what help is needed*, and this might involve literally going door to door, talking with people, learning about the immediate situation. In the two Indian examples, most of the help appeared to relate to resources (scarcity of supplies and information) and to interpersonal relations. In the 'supplies' category are distribution of blankets, arranging for small loans to affected businessmen (hawkers and petty traders), arranging for the delivery and fair allocation of medical aid and food rations to refugee camps, and activity combining interpersonal relations with supplies (such as, organizing groups of widows to find homes and collect pension grants to which they were entitled). In the field of interpersonal relations, third parties can act as mediators, bringing together members of opposing sides who otherwise would not be in communication. One technique in one of the Indian examples was for members of one side to nominate people from the other side whom they would be willing to talk with (this was in the effort to foster discussion between leaders from both sides). Sometimes it is enough simply to pass on information: for instance, people hesitated to report the location of dead bodies for fear of getting involved in legal proceedings; but they could safely communicate to members of the Shanti Sena information to be relayed to the District Collector. In the other Indian example, weekend camps on living together were originally set up for staff but wound up with local people joining in as well.

The 'Friendly Presence' account provides more detail regarding the kinds of third-party services that can be offered and some of the issues involved. The setting was a three-day conference featuring Black Panthers in Philadelphia at a time when there had been a lot of hostility with the police. Unlike Desai's Indian accounts that described some of the things to be done *after* a riot, Lyle Tatum describes activity which could help *prevent* a situation from becoming explosive. In the event, the police kept their distance anyway, and no trouble broke out, but the account does show how one can prepare for difficult situatons. The kinds of help will of course be different for various circumstances, but in this case some of the services which were provided were: maintaining various tables as 'information desks' stocked with maps, minor first-aid supplies, and drinking water (and this also gives some rationale for being present), and to some extent providing food and accommodation for conference attenders (which raises the issue of how closely identified one can become with a particular side and still maintain one's third-party status).

Some of the steps are: to develop one's services in consultation with the people on all sides (or at the very least to inform people of one's intended action), to mobilize sufficient third-party force, to provide them with at least some training in crowd control (e.g. 'roleplays' were carried out, in which some of the third-party trainees took the parts of police and Black Panthers in confrontation, while others interposed themselves between the two groups), and then actually to arrange for the necessary supplies, transportation, and communications networks.

The paper about Kent State deals with a rally that took place a year after the May 1970 shootings, in which—following an antiwar protest—the National Guard had shot into a crowd of unarmed students, killing four, and at about the same time students had been shot and killed at Jackson State College in Mississippi under similar circumstances. In any event, this rally, a year later, took place partly to note the anniversary of the killings and partly as a further protest against the war (and against ROTC, which is essentially military instruction carried out on campus). In addition to providing an account of the rally, the paper includes Hare's description of how people can offer third-party services—as marshals trained in crowd control and as communications links between parties (e.g. among the students in the rally, the administration, and the police).

Finally, Jim Schrag provides an account of how third-party teams interposed themselves at Wounded Knee between members of the American Indian Movement and Federal forces.

PARTISAN TRANSNATIONAL CASES

One view of conflict resolution is that violence is less likely to occur where people have some common identity and goals. For instance, it would be rather difficult to imagine a violent conflict now between Surrey and Sussex, because they are somehow both part of England. By analogy, anything which gives us practice at transcending *national* boundaries would be to the common good. And it is viewed as especially desirable if a group working towards nonviolent liberation is itself transnational—that is, the teams contain people of different nationalities working side by side. Viewed from the outside it means that the team is not a group of Canadians or a group of South Africans carrying out some action, but a group of *people* doing so.

April Carter has provided an account of transnational protest against the testing of atomic weapons—in this case against the 1959 French tests in the Sahara, in Africa. The first matter was to work out a plan for the protest. There was to be a journey to the test site, and then an attempt at dialogue or at least physical presence—or to go as far as possible before being stopped. A couple of preliminary questions had to do with what route to take into Algeria (whether to start from Ghana or Nigeria or Morocco) and whether to ride on camels or in landrovers. One issue that developed centred on the fact that Africans were in the majority among those undertaking most of the journey but in the minority among those who were relatively more influential in making decisions. It turned out that the protest group were stopped in various attempts even to travel through French-controlled countries, but at least they gained a measure of publicity and support.

Once a transnational group or organization exists, then *particular* actions can be either partisan or nonpartisan depending on what the group does. In the case of the World Peace Brigade (WPB) and people connected with it, the work supporting socioeconomic programmes and nonviolent action in eastern-central Africa was partisan, while the cease-fire in Nagaland (East-India) was achieved and patrolled by WPB leaders as a nonpartisan effort. Charles Walker's paper is concerned with setting up in Tanzania (then Tanganyika) a centre for peace and nonviolent action and providing a delegation to an alliance of groups that were organizing a freedom march and possibly a strike if there were any threat to free elections in Northern Rhodesia (Zambia). Some questions of values are raised—for instance, the difficulty of finding a complex coalition that would agree on nonviolence, though nonviolence characterized both the centre itself and the commitment for the particular march. The main difficulty (though not insurmountable ultimately had to do with resources and supplies—assembling transportation, people, and money from a variety of different countries (and when the location is a remote or not-so-remote part of Africa, communication itself becomes unwieldy). Perhaps suprisingly, once there was a common commitment and sufficient resources, no special mention was made of interpersonal difficulties even with a multinational team. As far as having enough force for the march itself, it was called off, but for a positive reason—namely, success in negotiations aimed at new open elections. And there also remains evidence of people making later use of the nonviolent training and tradition that they received in this effort.

One series of actions took place during 1970 and 1971 on Culebra (a small island off of Puerto Rico), which the American navy, among others, had been using for target practice for several decades. The Navy was viewed as an alien force that had established targets by expropriating land near the beach and sometimes tearing down homes. The immediate objective was to get an end to the bombing and shelling, which was damaging the coastal terrain and disturbing the residents for many hours a day. The form of the nonviolent actions, at different times, was for people to be present on the beach, and/or in small boats on the water, in the areas where shelling was to take place. This physical presence did actually halt the target practice for various brief periods. The conflict was more clearly joined when a small nondenominational chapel was built on the beach, directly in the line of Navy fire. As a result of various factors, the firing ceased by the end of 1975.

The remaining partisan transnational account is of the sending of relief supplies into Bangladesh from 1971 onward. The three phases of Operation Omega have included: border crossings (carrying relief supplies); general reconciliation and reconstruction, with many cases of direct action; and people working in specific areas.

NONPARTISAN TRANSNATIONAL CASES

Aram describes some of the activities of a small transnational team of peace observers, patrolling a ceasefire along an Indian/Nagaland border. The excerpts deal with arranging to avoid violent confrontations in the course of demonstrations and elections. The team had some legitimate respected status from the viewpoints of both sides and could communicate with both. Some of the intricacies of such communication are described in the chapter.

In 'Youth responds to crisis' some steps are described in detail for setting up an educational Institute for Social Change — in this case, a single summer programme on Curacao, a Dutch island near Venezuela, where there had been some rioting and looting about a year earlier. The four steps are very simply: work out tentative plans for a programme, find funds and support, look for personnel, and carry it out. 'Get the plan, the money, the people, and then do it.' According to Hare's analysis these four steps correspond to functional problem areas which all developing groups must deal with. In the Curacao example, at least some attempt was made to realize two particular kinds of values: one, the Gandhian ideals; the other, participatory social science (where the view is that education cannot be imposed but must come from working with people themselves). Results can be difficult to interpret. For example, although Curacao is relatively wealthy, some poverty and unemployment contributed to its earlier difficulty, and a model survey of the labour force was part of the educational effort. Now, depending on your viewpoint and the nature of the survey itself, such work could be viewed either as mainly serving corporate interests, or as meeting needs of the people themselves, or both.

The project on Cyprus was interrupted by the 1974 military actions. At least it is of value that there are now more people with crucial experience in offering third-party services on Cyprus — that is, they are familiar with the Cyprus situation, and moreover they have had first-hand experience there in organizing for the implementation of a project to rebuild the homes of refugees who wanted to return to them (Turkish-Cypriot refugees, who were displaced by conflict a decade before in the early 1960s).

Whatever the final impact, the project did make it clear that a transnational team, with local co-operation and a majority recruited locally for the final work, can carry out useful third-party services in a nonpartisan fashion. That is, the action was most directly helping displaced Turkish-Cypriots (who could be viewed as an oppressed minority on the island), but the team were able to work openly with Greek and Turkish people on Cyprus at all levels from the top leadership to the people in the villages.

REFERENCES

Blumberg, Herbert H., 1968. 'Accounting for a nonviolent mass demonstration'. Pp. 475-91 in A. P. Hare and H. H. Blumberg (eds.), Nonviolent Direct Action: American Cases, Social-Psychological Analyses. Washington, D.C.: Corpus Books.

Buckhout, Robert (ed.), 1972. Toward Social Change. New York: Harper.

Dollard, John, Neal E. Miller, Leonard W. Doob, O. H. Mowrer and Robert R. Sears, 1961. Frustration and Aggression. New Haven: Yale University Press.

Freire, Paulo, 1972. Pedagogy of the Oppressed. Harmondsworth, Middlesex: Penguin.

Illich, Ivan D., 1973a. Deschooling Society. Harmondsworth, Middlesex: Penguin.

——, 1973b. Tools for Conviviality. London: Calder and Boyars.

Lakey, George, 1972. Manifesto for Nonviolent Revolution. London: War Resisters International (Fourteenth Triennial Conference, Sheffield). (Also in WIN, 1972 (November 15), 8 (Nov. 8). 5-28).

Montagu, M. F. Ashley (ed.), 1968. Man and Aggression. New York: Oxford University Press.

Olson, T. and L. Shivers, 1970. Training for Nonviolent Action. London: Friends Peace and International Relations Committee.

Osgood, Charles Egerton, 1962. An Alternative to War or Surrender. Urbana: University of Illinois Press.

Smith, Clagett G. (ed.), 1971. Conflict Resolution. Notre Dame, Indiana: University of Notre Dame Press.

PART I

Partisan national cases

1

THE SALT SATYAGRAHA*

JOAN V. BONDURANT

Note: The Salt Satyagraha was part of the year-long Civil Disobedience movement of 1930–1. The following outline touches upon the entire movement, although many of the details of that extensive struggle have been omitted.

DATES, DURATION, AND LOCALE

In its extended form, civil disobedience continued for about one year, from March 1930 to March 1931. The movement was national, with headquarters in Bombay. Satyagraha activities were launched in every province.

OBJECTIVES

1. *Immediate*: Removal of the Salt Acts. These statutes provided for a government monopoly of salt. Revenue realized from the Salt Tax amounted at this time to $25,000,000 out of a total revenue of about $800,000,000. These laws were held to work a hardship on the people, especially the poor, and to constitute the taxation of a necessity.

2. *Long-range*: The Salt Acts were chosen by Gandhi for contravention in a general civil disobedience movement because they not only appeared to be basically unjust in themselves, but also because they symbolized an unpopular, unrepresentative, and alien government. British official sources described the object of the satyagraha as 'nothing less than to cause a complete paralysis of the administrative machinery . . .' The ultimate objective of civil

*'The Salt Satyagraha,' in Joan V. Bondurant, *Conquest of Violence; The Gandhian Philosophy of Conflict* (Copyright © 1958 by Princeton University Press): pp. 88–102, and footnote p. 237; University of California Press, 1969, 1972). Reprinted by permission of Princeton University Press.

disobedience was complete independence.

SATYAGRAHA PARTICIPANTS AND LEADERSHIP

1. *Gandhi* and other leaders of the Indian National Congress.

2. *Secondary leadership*: In the opening phase, direct participation was limited to disciplined members of Gandhi's ashram at Ahmedabad, selected by Gandhi to make the march to the sea. They were described as 'soldiers who had been steeled to the disciplines and hardships which a 200 mile march on foot would necessarily entail on them'.

Prominent Congressmen served as organizers in other parts of India. Among these were Rajagopalachariar in Tamilnad, Vallabhbhai Patel for the whole of Gujarat, Jawaharlal Nehru in the United Provinces, Satish Chandra Das Gupta in Bengal, Konda Venkatappaya in Andhra, and Gopabandhu Chowdhury in Utkal (Orissa).

3. *Participants*: After the initial breach of the salt laws, Indians throughout the country participated.

4. *Characteristics of participants:* The official government report indicated that the majority of participants were Hindus, but that Muslims did take part, especially on the Frontier. Officials expressed concern that the 'Hindu mercantile and industrial community showed active sympathy' and financially supported the movement. Another 'unexpected' element among satyagrahis was a large number of Indian women. 'Thousands of them—many being of good family and high educational attainments—suddenly emerged from the seclusion of their homes and in some instances actually from *purdah,* in order to join Congress demonstrations and assist in picketing . . . .'

PARTICIPANTS AND LEADERSHIP OF THE OPPOSITION

1. *Officials* of the Government of India.
2. *Police,* both British and Indian.
3. *Units of the army.*

ORGANIZATION AND CONSTRUCTIVE PROGRAMME

1. *Role of the Indian National Congress:* This campaign was conducted as part of an over-all political movement for independence. It was a programme adopted by the largest political opposition party in India and so was planned in the light of the organization and constitutional make-up of the Party. The Congress Party delegated to Gandhi full power and responsibility for organizing and leading the campaign (by resolution, 21 March 1930).

2. *Succession of leadership:* Extensive powers were given to the president of the Congress (then Jawaharlal Nehru) to act on behalf of the executive committee in case it could not meet. The president was empowered to nominate a successor in the event of his removal from action; the successor, in turn, was to have the same power of appointment of a successor. Similar powers were given to provincial and local Congress chiefs.

3. *Khadi:* The wearing of hand-spun cloth was imperative for all satyagrahis—it became the uniform of the Congress and the movement.

4. *Other aspects of constructive work:* Welfare and self-sufficiency work was considered one of the ways in which the cause could be promoted. A satyagrahi should 'find himself in one of the following states', Gandhi instructed: '1. In prison or in an analogous state, or 2. Engaged in Civil Disobedience, or 3. Under orders at the spinning wheel, or at some constructive work advancing Swaraj'.

PREPARATION FOR ACTION

1. *Public opinion on Swaraj*: Prior to the launching of this campaign, the sentiment for full independence was developed through discussion and the deliberations of the Congress Party. On 26 January the Congress, meeting in Lahore, had pledged its members to 'carry out the Congress instructions issued from time to time for the purpose of establishing Purna Swaraj' (full independence).

2. *Training courses*: Volunteers for satyagraha undertook courses of training for direct action, especially in methods of controlling

large crowds. Satyagrahis drilled regularly, though they did so without arms.

3. *Planning for civil disobedience*: The salt laws were selected for contravention. Gandhi planned to lead a march to the sea where satyagrahis would, in violation of the salt monopoly, prepare salt from sea water. Vallabhbhai Patel was chosen to prepare the way for the proposed march. He proceeded along the route to be taken, advising people of the objectives of the movement, and instructing them in the principles of satyagraha. They were urged to undertake constructive work, to abstain from intoxicants, and to overcome untouchability. (On 7 March Patel was arrested.)

4. *The Satyagraha Pledge*: The All-India Congress Committee, meeting at Ahmedabad on 21 March 1930, drew up the following pledge to be taken by those volunteering for satyagraha:

(1) I desire to join the civil resistance campaign for the Independence of India undertaken by the National Congress. (2) I accept the Creed of the National Congress, that is, the attainment of Purna Swaraj (complete independence) by the people of India by all peaceful and legitimate means. (3) I am ready and willing to go to jail and undergo all other sufferings and penalties that may be inflicted on me in this campaign. (4) In case I am sent to jail, I shall not seek any monetary help for my family from the Congress funds. (5) I shall implicitly obey the orders of those who are in charge of the campaign.

PRELIMINARY ACTION

1. *Notice of civil disobedience:* Through the Congress independence resolution adopted at Lahore, subsequently advertised and discussed widely, the intention of the Congress party to agitate for independence, if necessary through civil disobedience, was made known.

2. *Gandhi's letter to Lord Irwin, the Viceroy*: On 2 March 1930, Gandhi apprised the Viceroy of the satyagraha plan and reviewed the grievances of the people. Nonviolence, he wrote, could be 'an intensely active force'. It was his purpose, he told the Viceroy, 'to set in motion that force, as well against the organised violent force of the British rule as the unorganised violent force of the growing party of violence. . . . The nonviolence will be expressed through Civil Disobedience, for the moment confined to the inmates of the Satyagraha Ashram, but ultimately designed to cover all those who

choose to join the movement with its obvious limitations'.

3. *The ultimatum*: In his letter, Gandhi urged a negotiated settlement, barring which, he would lead a satyagraha movement. He further stated the exact day upon which he would proceed, with co-workers, to disregard the provisions of the Salt Acts. 'It is, I know, open to you' he told the Viceroy, 'to frustrate my design by arresting me. I hope that there will be tens of thousands ready, in a disciplined manner, to take up the work after me, and, in the act of disobeying the Salt Act, to lay themselves open to the penalties of a Law that should never have disfigured the Statute Book'. He would, Gandhi said, welcome further discussion, and his letter was in no way a threat but a 'simple and sacred duty peremptory on a civil resister'. A young Englishman (Reginald Reynolds) who had joined the ashram was selected to deliver the letter.

ACTION

1. *The march to the sea*: On 12 March, Gandhi and his co-satyagrahis left Ahmedabad for Dandi on the sea coast. He urged villagers along the way to pursue constructive work, to remain nonviolent, and to participate in the civil disobedience following the initial breach of the law at Dandi. The march was considered a form of penance and discipline for the beginning of civil disobedience. It also dramatized the issues and attracted nationwide attention.

2. *The opening of civil disobedience*: The satyagrahis reached Dandi on 5 April. The following morning, after prayers, they proceeded to the beach where they prepared salt from sea water, thus technically breaking the salt laws.

3. *Gandhi's statement to the press*: Upon breaking the law, Gandhi declared that it was then open to anyone who would take the risk of prosecution to manufacture salt wherever he wished. Villagers were to be instructed concerning the meaning of the salt tax and directed in methods of preparing salt.

4. *Issuing of leaflets*: Instructions concerning the manufacture of salt were published in the various parts of the country.

5. *Response from the people*: 'It seemed as though a spring had been suddenly released,' Nehru wrote. Everywhere people began to make salt. They collected 'pots and pans and ultimately succeeded

in producing some unwholesome stuff, which we waved about in triumph, and often auctioned for fancy prices'. The main thing, Nehru continued, was to commit a breach of the 'obnoxious Salt Law . . . As we saw the abounding enthusiasm of the people and the way salt-making was spreading like a prairie fire, we felt a little abashed and ashamed for having questioned the efficacy of this method when it was first proposed by Gandhiji. And we marvelled at the amazing knack of the man to impress the multitude and make it act in an organised way'.

6. *Hartal*: Throughout the country, shops closed in response to arrests of satyagraha leaders.

7. *Resignation of offices*: Headmen in villages and subordinate officers resigned in large numbers in sympathy with satyagraha.

8. *Symbolic acts:* In many parts of India dramatic demonstrations were conducted. In Bombay an 'effigy' of the Salt Acts was thrown into the sea as a symbol that British law was dead in the land.

9. *Succession in leadership*: Jawaharlal Nehru was arrested on 14 April and was succeeded by his father, Motilal Nehru. In other places, leaders of the satyagraha were replaced by appointment following the arrest of the initial leadership. Gandhi, arrested 5 May, was replaced by Abbas Tyabji.

10. *Non-payment of taxes*: In some areas, as in Bardoli, a programme of non-payment of taxes was undertaken.

11. *Action to control rioting*: Leaders attempted to preserve the nonviolent character of satyagraha. In response to the outbreak of riots in Karachi and Calcutta, Gandhi announced: 'If nonviolence has to fight the people's violence in addition to the violence of the Government it must still perform its arduous task at any cost.' (17 April.) Gandhi later (26 April) announced that if satyagrahis who followed him did not fulfill the basic conditions, he himself would practice satyagraha against them.

12. *Gandhi's second letter to Viceroy*: The Government, in a sort of non-co-operation of its own, refused to arrest Gandhi early in the campaign. The first week of May he explained in a second letter his next move—he would set out for Dharsana where the Government operated a large salt works. There he would demand possession of these works. It would be possible, he said, for the Viceroy to prevent this 'raid' in one of the following three ways:

(1) by removing the salt tax; (2) by arresting me and my party unless the country can, as I hope it will, replace every one taken away; (3) by sheer goondaism [hooliganism] unless every head broken is replaced as I hope it will be.

13. *Raids on salt works*: Following Gandhi's arrest on 5 May (just after midnight), volunteers, led by Congress notables, marched to occupy the salt depots. Fresh volunteers stepped in as others were struck down by the police. Organized first-aid units worked to revive victims.

14. *Non-violent persuasion of police*: Throughout the attack upon the satyagraha raiders, volunteers refrained from striking back or even from deflecting blows. They rushed onto the salt pans, wave upon wave. Where they could, they pleaded with the police to join them. Incidents were reported of policemen refusing to continue the assault. An American journalist, Negley Farson, recorded an incident in which a Sikh, blood-soaked from the assault of a police sergeant, fell under a heavy blow. Congress first-aid volunteers rushed up to rub his face with ice . . . .' he gave us a bloody grin and stood up to receive some more. . . .' The police sergeant was 'so sweaty from his exertions that his Sam Browne had stained his white tunic. I watched him with my heart in my mouth. He drew back his arm for a final swing — and then he dropped his hands down by his side. "It's no use," he said, turning to me with half an apologetic grin; "You can't hit a bugger when he stands up to you like that!" He gave the Sikh a mock salute and walked off.'

15. *Economic boycott*: When raids on salt works were halted upon the advent of the monsoon, civil disobedience took other forms including boycott of foreign-made products, especially cloth. Both cloth and liquor shops were persistently picketed.

16. *Disobedience of ordinances*: As the campaign proceeded, special ordinances designed to suppress publicity and control assembly were promulgated by the Government. These were consistently disobeyed in a general movement to the jails.

17. *Continuing activities*: The extensive campaign continued throughout the year and involved many manifestations of non-co-operation and civil disobedience.

18. *Culmination of the movement:* A settlement was reached following talks between Gandhi and the Viceroy, and the Gandhi-Irwin Agreement was published on 5 March 1931.

REACTION OF OPPONENTS

1. *Arrests*: Initially, the Government avoided making mass arrests, partly in response to the 'jail-courting' aspects of satyagraha. Finally, however, thousands of satyagrahis were arrested including hundreds of prominent Congress leaders.

2. *Police action*: From the respective statements made on opposing sides of the movement, it is clear that the police reacted with determination and force. The official report does not acknowledge police excesses. Many non-Indian witnesses, however, testified to the contrary. The biographer of Lord Irwin notes that 'the European Sergeants, provoked and overworked, did not always seem inclined to restrain their men.' Gandhi, in his letter addressed to the Viceroy, asserted that 'the rank and file has been often savagely and in some cases even indecently assaulted.' An American journalist, Webb Miller, reported that after one raid on a salt depot he counted, in a hospital, 320 injured, 'many still insensible with fractured skulls, others writhing in agony from kicks in the testicles and stomach . . .'

3. *Determination of the Government*: The Viceroy, addressing both Houses of the legislature on 9 July (1930), asserted that the mass action was 'nothing but the application of force under another form, and, when it has as its avowed object the making of Government impossible, a Government is bound either to resist or abdicate'. He concluded that the government must 'fight it with all our strength'.

4. *Special ordinances*: In an attempt to control the situation, the Government issued numerous ordinances including those providing for press censorship and suppression of objectionable printed matter. In places a ban was placed upon wearing of the white Gandhi cap.

5. *Viceroy announced Round Table Conference plans*: Lord Irwin announced (12 May) that steps were being taken to arrange a meeting in London of representatives to consider constitutional reforms for India.

6. *Continuing repression of agitation:* Throughout the early months of 1931 civil disobedience was met by arrests, firings, *lathi* charges, and other police force.

7. *Gandhi-Irwin Agreement*: Final settlement following talks between Viceroy and Gandhi.

8. *Fulfilment of the Gandhi-Irwin Agreement,* including repeal

of ordinances and release of satyagrahi prisoners.

RESULTS

1. *Modification of salt regulations*: The immediate objective of the salt satyagraha which opened the overall civil disobedience movement was, to a large extent, realized. The salt laws were not repealed, but a new official interpretation was effected in the settlement agreed to by Gandhi and Lord Irwin. That interpretation specified that 'For the sake . . . of giving relief to certain of the poorer classes,' the Government would 'extend their administrative provisions, on lines already prevailing in certain places, in order to permit local residents in villages, immediately adjoining areas where salt can be collected or made, to collect or make salt for domestic consumption or sale within such villages, but not for sale to, or trading with, individuals living outside them.'

2. *Other provisions of the Gandhi-Irwin Agreement*: According to the settlement arrived at in discussions between Gandhi and the Viceroy, the Government agreed to the following action: (1) Amnesty to persons convicted of nonviolent offences in connection with civil disobedience, (2) Withdrawal of the restraining ordinances, (3) Restoration of confiscated, forfeited, or attached properties, and (4) Administrative concession to make salt in certain areas.

In return, civil disobedience was to be ended and, in particular, the following activities discontinued: (1) Organized defiance of the provisions of any law, (2) Movement for non-payment of land revenue and other legal dues, (3) Publication of news-sheets in support of civil disobedience, and (4) Attempts to influence civil and military servants or village officials against government or to persuade them to resign their posts.

3. *Constitutional reforms*: The settlement included a statement that in further discussions on constitutional reform, representatives of the Congress would be invited to participate, and that in the deliberations of the next Round Table Conference, such questions as federation, reservation of subjects (e.g. defence, external affairs), financial credit, and position of minorities would be included.

SUMMARY ANALYSIS OF THE
SALT SATYAGRAHA

During 1930-1, satyagraha was employed throughout India to advance the cause of Indian independence. Thousands of localized campaigns in the over-all civil disobedience movement involved hundreds of thousands of persons, many of whom adopted satyagraha as a temporary expedient without fully understanding its basic philosophy. Nevertheless, the movement remained, for the most part, nonviolent. The opening campaign led by Gandhi in the march to the sea provided a model of adherence to basic principles and brilliance of strategy. An outstanding characteristic of the other campaigns during these months was the assertion of strong and effective leadership by hundreds of provincial and local Congressmen.

As for the elements of true satyagraha, all are to be found in the Salt Satyagraha. The immediate objective was the removal of laws which worked a hardship upon the poor. The Salt Acts, establishing a government monopoly over a food necessity, symbolized the further injustice—the subjugation of India by a foreign power. It therefore became the duty of the satyagrahi to disobey the unjust salt laws and to cling to the truth understood to be the right of the Indian people to manufacture salt as they chose. The further truth implications were understood to lie in a people's right to self-government.

The volunteer satyagrahis who initiated the salt campaign rigorously abided by the principle of nonviolence. During the later raids on the salt pans, some satyagrahis destroyed property by cutting wire and otherwise pulling down the fences surrounding the salt works. Gandhi himself did not lead the raids in which property was destroyed, and he might well have restrained property destruction or considered it a weakness in that phase of the campaign. Some satyagrahis justified the destruction of fences to gain access to the salt pans by arguing that the salt works were public property and should be made available to all citizens. There is no evidence, however, that any physical injury was inflicted by satyagrahis upon their opponents. Violence was, indeed, at work in the successive raids on the salt pans—but it was violence inflicted by police forces upon satyagrahis, many of whom sustained grave and agonizing injury. Wave upon wave of satyagrahis responded to the attack, their action remaining nonviolent but nonetheless aggressive. They retaliated, not with violence, but with the several persuasive tactics at their command.

Self-reliance characterized the conduct of the satyagrahis. They signed a pledge to offer civil resistance without expectation of material help for themselves or their families. Again, organized propaganda was published and distributed in the form of bulletins and leaflets, and publicity was further supplied by the press throughout the country in detailed reporting of satyagraha activities. Suppression of satyagraha propaganda and censorship of the press served to extend the opportunities for contravention of the law.

Initiative was retained by the satyagrahis throughout this civil disobedience movement. That action which centred upon contravention of the Salt Acts, progressed from the initial march to the sea and the first production of contraband salt to the subsequent seizure of salt from government depots and the spread of salt-making. Action then extended into the realm of economic boycott accompanied by picketing of cloth and liquor shops. Direct action was not undertaken until every effort had been made for an honourable settlement through negotiation and appeal to the Viceroy. The demand of the satyagrahis that Indians should be free to manufacture salt at will, was at no time relaxed. However, Gandhi remained ever ready to negotiate with the government for a settlement.

This satyagraha proceeded through the early steps of attempted negotiation, of agitation and demonstration, and the issuing of an ultimatum. The opponent was kept informed of intention and procedure. When the settlement was finally effected, following discussions between Gandhi and the Viceroy, the immediate objective — redress of grievances arising from the Salt Acts — was to a substantial degree realized even though the Acts themselves were not abolished. The long-term objective of *Swaraj* (independence) was, of course, not at once achieved. However, the Gandhi-Irwin Agreement provided that the Congress should participate in the second Round Table Conference to consider constitutional questions involved in the advancement of India along the road towards full independence.

REFERENCES

The data for this outline were abstracted from the sources listed below plus: *Congress Presidential Addresses*; *The New York Times*, for this period; *Young India*, for this period; and correspondence between the author and R. R. Diwaker, Pyarelal (Nayyar), and R. R. Keithahn.

Bernays, Robert, 1932. Naked Faquir. New York: H. Holt.

Bolton, Glorney, 1934. The Tragedy of Gandhi. London: Allen & Unwin.

Coupland, Sir Reginald, 1944. The Indian Problem: Report on the Constitutional Problem in India. New York: Oxford University Press.

Cumming, Sir John (ed.), 1932. Political India, 1832-1932, A Co-operative Survey of a Century. London: Humphrey Milford.

Diwakar, R. R., 1946. Satyagraha: Its Technique and History. Bombay: Hind Kitabs.

Farson, Negley, 1937. 'Indian hate lyric'. In Eugene Lyons (ed.), We Cover the World [by fifteen foreign correspondents]. New York: Harcourt, Brace.

Gregg, Richard B., 1938. The Power of Non-Violence. (Rev. Ed.) London: Routledge.

India, 1932. India in 1930-1: A Statement Prepared for Presentation to Parliament in Accordance with the Requirements of the 26th Section of the Government of India Act (5 and 6 Geo. V, Chap. 61). Calcutta: Government of India Central Publishing Branch.

Johnson, Alan Campbell, 1941. Viscount Halifax, A Biography. London: Robert Hale.

Miller, Webb, 1936. I Found No Peace: The Journal of a Foreign Correspondent. New York: The Literary Guild.

Mitra, Nripendra Nath (ed.). 1930 & 1931. The Indian Annual Register. (1930, Vols. I and II; and 1931, Vols. I and II.) Calcutta; Annual Register Office.

Nehru, Jawaharlal, 1942. An Autobiography. New Edition. London: John Lane the Bodley Head.

Sitaramayya, B. Pattabhi, 1935. The History of the Indian National Congress: (1885-1935). Madras: Working Committee of the Congress.

Sondhi, G. C. (ed.), 1948. To the Gates of Liberty: Congress Commemoration Volume. Calcutta: Swadesh Bharati.

2

NEW DAY IN BIRMINGHAM, ALABAMA*

MARTIN LUTHER KING, JR.

[After the successful demonstrations by Blacks in Birmingham, Alabama in 1963, Martin Luther King concluded that nonviolent direct action had established itself as a method of social change. In his book *Why We Can't Wait* he said, 'The victory of the theory of nonviolent direct action was a fact. Faith in this method had come to maturity in Birmingham. As a result, the whole spectrum of the civil rights struggle would undergo basic change. Nonviolence had passed the test of its steel in the fires of turmoil. The united power of southern segregation was the hammer. Birmingham was the anvil.' (p. 46.)

From 1957 through January 1963, while 'Bull' Connor, Commissioner of Public Safety, and other citizens of Birmingham were still claiming that the 'Negroes were satisfied', seventeen unsolved bombings of Black churches and homes of civil-rights leaders had occurred. One threat to the reign of White supremacy was the Alabama Christian Movement for Human Rights (ACHR) organized by Reverend Fred Shuttlesworth as an affiliate of the Southern Leadership Conference (SCLC) headed by King. In 1962 the ACHR began negotiations with representatives of the business community. However, little progress was made until the SCLC staff joined in the protest, first waiting for the results of a political campaign in which 'Bull' Connor and Albert Boutwell (a moderate by comparison) were two of the contestants for the office of Mayor. King's description of the action after the election is given in the following account.]

On Wednesday, 3 April 1963, the Birmingham *News* appeared on the stands, its front page bright with a colour drawing showing a golden sun rising over the city. It was captioned 'New Day Dawns

*From pp. 55-62, 105-9, 111-12 in *Why We Can't Wait* (hard covered ed.) by Martin Luther King, Jr. Copyright © 1963, 1964 by Martin Luther King, Jr. By permission of Harper & Row, Publishers, Inc. Reprinted by permission of Joan Daves.

for Birmingham', and celebrated Albert Boutwell's victory in the run-off vote for Mayor. The golden glow of racial harmony, the headline implied, could now be expected to descend on the city. As events were to show, it was indeed a new day for Birmingham; but not because Boutwell had won the election.

For all the optimism expressed in the press and elsewhere, we were convinced that Albert Boutwell was, in Fred Shuttlesworth's apt phrase, 'just a dignified Bull Connor'. We knew that the former state senator and lieutenant governor had been the principal author of Alabama's Pupil Placement Law, and was a consistent supporter of segregationist views. His statement a few days after election that 'we citizens of Birmingham respect and understand one another' showed that he understood nothing about two-fifths of Birmingham's citizens, to whom even polite segregation was no respect. Meanwhile, despite the results of the run-off, the city commissioners, including Bull Connor, had taken the position that they could not legally be removed from office until 1965. They would go into the courts to defend their position, and refused in the interim to move out of their City Hall offices. If they won in court (and conflict in the laws of Birmingham made this theoretically possible), they would remain in office for another two years. If they lost, their terms would still not expire until 15 April, the day after Easter. In either case, we were committed to enter the situation in a city which was operating literally under two governments.

We had decided to limit the first few days' efforts to sit-ins. Being prepared for a long struggle, we felt it best to begin modestly, with a limited number of arrests each day. By rationing our energies in this manner, we would help towards the buildup and drama of a growing campaign. The first demonstrations were, accordingly, not spectacular, but they were well organized. Operating on a precise timetable, small groups maintained a series of sit-ins at lunch counters in the downtown department stores and drugstores. When the demonstrators were asked to leave and refused, they were arrested under the local 'trespass after warning' ordinance. By Friday night, there had been no disturbances worth note. Evidently neither Bull Connor nor the merchants expected this quiet beginning to blossom into a large-scale operation.

After the first day we held a mass meeting, the first of sixty-five nightly meetings conducted at various churches in the Negro community. Through these meetings we were able to generate the power and depth which finally galvanized the entire Negro community. The mass meetings had a definite pattern, shaped by some of the finest activists in the civil-rights movement. Ralph Abernathy, with his unique combination of humour and dedication, has a genius for lifting an audience to heights of enthusiasm and holding it there. When he plants himself behind the lectern, squat and powerful, his round face breaking easily into laughter, his listeners both love and believe him. Wyatt Walker, youthful, lean and bespectacled, brought his energetic and untiring spirit to our meetings, whose members already knew and admired his dedicated work as a behind-the-scenes organizer of the campaign. There was a special adulation that went out to the fiery words and determined zeal of Fred Shuttlesworth, who had proved to his people that he would not ask anyone to go where he was not willing to lead. Although for the first week I was busy on matters that prevented my taking an active part in the demonstrations, I spoke at the mass meetings nightly on the philosophy of nonviolence and its methods. Besides these 'regulars' local speakers appeared from time to time to describe the injustices and humiliation of being a Negro in Birmingham, and occasional visitors from elsewhere across the country brought us welcome messages of support.

An important part of the mass meetings was the freedom songs. In a sense the freedom songs are the soul of the movement. They are more than just incantations of clever phrases designed to invigorate a campaign; they are as old as the history of the Negro in America. They are adaptations of the songs the slaves sang—the sorrow songs, the shouts for joy, the battle hymns and the anthems of our movement. I have heard people talk of their beat and rhythm, but we in the movement are as inspired by their words. 'Woke Up This Morning with My Mind Stayed on Freedom' is a sentence that needs no music to make its point. We sing the freedom songs today for the same reason the slaves sang them, because we too are in bondage and the songs add hope to our determination that 'We shall overcome, Black and White together, We shall overcome someday'.

I have stood in a meeting with hundreds of youngsters and joined in while they sang 'Ain't Gonna Let Nobody Turn Me 'Round'. It is not just a song; it is a resolve. A few minutes later, I have seen those same youngsters refuse to turn around from the onrush of a police dog, refuse to turn around before a pugnacious Bull Connor in command of men armed with power hoses. These songs bind us together, give us courage together, help us to march together.

Toward the end of the mass meetings, Abernathy or Shuttlesworth or I would extend an appeal for volunteers to serve in our nonviolent army. We made it clear that we would not send anyone out to demonstrate who had not convinced himself and us that he could accept and endure violence without retaliating. At the same time, we urged the volunteers to give up any possible weapons that they might have on their persons. Hundreds of people responded to this appeal. Some of those who carried penknives, Boy Scout knives—all kinds of knives—had them not because they wanted to use them against the police or other attackers, but because they wanted to defend themselves against Mr Connor's dogs. We proved to them that we needed no weapons—not so much as a toothpick. We proved that we possessed the most formidable weapon of all—the conviction that we were right. We had the protection of our knowledge that we were more concerned about realizing our righteous aims than about saving our skins.

The invitational periods at the mass meetings, when we asked for volunteers, were much like those invitational periods that occur every Sunday morning in Negro churches, when the pastor projects the call to those present to join the church. By twenties and thirties and forties, people came forward to join our army. We did not hesitate to call our movement an army. But it was a special army, with no supplies but its sincerity, no uniform but its determination, no arsenal except its faith, no currency but its conscience. It was an army that would move but not maul. It was an army that would sing but not slay. It was an army that would flank but not falter. It was an army to storm bastions of hatred, to lay siege to the fortresses of segregation, to surround symbols of discrimination. It was an army whose allegiance was to God and whose strategy and intelligence were the eloquently simple dictates of conscience.

As the meetings continued and as the battle for the soul of Birmingham quickened and caught the attention of the world, the meetings were more crowded and the volunteers more numerous. Men, women and children came forward to shake hands, and then proceeded to the back of the church, where the Leadership Training Committee made an appointment with them to come to our office the following day for screening and intensive training.

The focus of these training sessions was the socio-dramas

designed to prepare the demonstrators for some of the challenges they could expect to face. The harsh language and physical abuse of the police and the self-appointed guardians of the law were frankly presented, along with the nonviolent creed in action: to resist without bitterness; to be cursed and not reply; to be beaten and not hit back. The SCLC staff members who conducted these sessions played their roles with the conviction born of experience. They included the Reverend James Lawson, expelled from Vanderbilt University a few years back for his militant civil-rights work, and one of the country's leading exponents of the nonviolent credo; the Reverend James Bevel, already an experienced leader in Nashville, Greenwood, and other campaigns; his wife, Diane Nash Bevel, who as a student at Fisk had become an early symbol of the young Negroes' thrust towards freedom; the Reverend Bernard Lee, whose devotion to civil rights dated back to his leadership of the student movement at Alabama State College; the Reverend Andy Young, our able and dedicated programme director; and Dorothy Cotton, director of our ongoing Citizenship Education Program, who also brought her rich talent for song to the heart of the movement.

Not all who volunteered could pass our strict tests for service as demonstrators. But there was much to be done, over and above the dramatic act of presenting one's body in the marches. There were errands to be run, phone calls to be made, typing, so many things. If a volunteer wasn't suited to march, he [or she] was utilized in one of a dozen other ways to help the cause. Every volunteer was required to sign a Commitment Card that read:

I HEREBY PLEDGE MYSELF—MY PERSON AND BODY—TO THE NONVIOLENT MOVEMENT. THEREFORE I WILL KEEP THE FOLLOWING TEN COMMANDMENTS:

1. MEDITATE daily on the teachings and life of Jesus

2. REMEMBER always that the nonviolent movement in Birmingham seeks justice and reconciliation—not victory.

3. WALK and TALK in the manner of love, for God is love.

4. PRAY daily to be used by God in order that all [women and] men might be free.

5. SACRIFICE personal wishes in order that all [women and] men

might be free.

6. OBSERVE with both friend and foe the ordinary rules of courtesy.

7. SEEK to perform regular service for others and for the world.

8. REFRAIN from the violence of fist, tongue, or heart.

9. STRIVE to be in good spiritual and bodily health.

10. FOLLOW the directions of the movement and of the captain on a demonstration.

I sign this pledge, having seriously considered what I do and with the determination and will to persevere.

Name_____

Address _____

Phone _____

Nearest Relative _____

Address _____

Besides demonstrations, I could also help the movement by: (Circle the proper items)
Run errands, Drive my car, Fix food for volunteers, Clerical work, Make phone calls, Answer phones, Mimeograph, Type, Print signs, Distribute Leaflets.

ALABAMA CHRISTIAN MOVEMENT FOR HUMAN RIGHTS

[Since some of the local supporters felt the protest was badly timed, King conducted a one week speaking tour of local groups which transformed the mood within the Black community to one of faith and enthusiasm. There followed lunch counter sit-ins, marches, and a boycott of the white business centre. Purposefully failing to obey a court injunction King led a demonstration and was placed in jail. After eight days he was released on bail. Hundreds of high school children were now enlisted to join the ranks. 'For the first time in the civil-rights movement', King notes, 'we were able to put into effect the Gandhian principle: "Fill up the jails".' (p. 98.) On 2 May more than 1,000 young people demonstrated and went to jail. At the height of the campaign there were over 2,500 demonstrators in jail at one time, a large proportion of them young people. King continues the account:] . . .

With the jails filling up and the scorching glare of national disapproval focused on Birmingham, Bull Connor abandoned his posture of nonviolence. The result was an ugliness too well known to Americans and to people all over the world. The newspapers of 4 May carried pictures of prostrate women, and police bending over them with raised clubs; of children marching up to the bared fangs of police dogs; of the terrible force of pressure hoses sweeping bodies into the streets.

This was the time of our greatest stress, and the courage and conviction of those students and adults made it our finest hour. We did not fight back, but we did not turn back. We did not give way to bitterness. Some few spectators, who had not been trained in the discipline of nonviolence, reacted to the brutality of the police by throwing rocks and bottles. But the demonstrators remained nonviolent. In the face of this resolution and bravery, the moral conscience of the nation was deeply stirred and, all over the country, our fight became the fight of decent Americans of all races and creeds.

The moral indignation which was spreading throughout the land; the sympathy created by the children; the growing involvement of the Negro community—all these factors were mingling to create a certain atmosphere inside our movement. It was a pride in progress and a conviction that we were going to win. It was a mounting optimism which gave us the feeling that the implacable barriers that confronted us were doomed and already beginning to crumble. We were advised, in the utmost confidence, that the white business structure was weakening under the adverse publicity, the pressure of our boycott, and a parallel falling-off of white buying.

Strangely enough, the masses of white citizens in Birmingham were not fighting us. This was one of the most amazing aspects of the Birmingham crusade. Only a year or so ago, had we begun such a campaign, Bull Connor would have had his job done for him by murderously angry white citizens. Now, however, the majority were maintaining a strictly hands-off policy. I do not mean to insinuate that they were in sympathy with our cause or that they boycotted stores because we did. I simply suggest that it is powerfully symbolic of shifting attitudes in the South that the majority of the white citizens of Birmingham remained neutral through our campaign. This neutrality added force to our feeling that we were on the road to victory.

On one dramatic occasion even Bull Connor's men were shaken. It was a Sunday afternoon, when several hundred Birmingham Negroes had determined to hold a prayer meeting near the city jail. They gathered at the New Pilgrim Baptist Church and began an orderly march. Bull Connor ordered out the police dogs and fire hoses. When the marchers approached the border between the White and Negro areas, Connor ordered them to turn back. The Reverend Charles Billups, who was leading the march, politely refused. Enraged, Bull Connor whirled on his men and shouted:

'Dammit. Turn on the hoses.'

What happened in the next thirty seconds was one of the most fantastic events of the Birmingham story. Bull Connor's men, their deadly hoses poised for action, stood facing the marchers. The marchers, many of them on their knees, stared back, unafraid and unmoving. Slowly the Negroes stood up and began to advance. Connor's men, as though hypnotized, fell back, their hoses sagging uselessly in their hands while several hundred Negroes marched past them, without further interference, and held their prayer meeting as planned.

One more factor helped to encourage us in the belief that our goals were coming within reach. We had demonstrated in defiance of a civil injunction. For this act of disobedience, we had been cited for contempt. In Alabama, if you are cited for criminal contempt, you serve five days and that is the end of it. If you are cited for civil contempt, however, you figuratively hold the jail-house keys in the palm of your hand. At any time, if you are willing to recant, you can earn release. If you do not recant, you can be held for the rest of your natural life.

Most of the demonstrators had been cited for criminal contempt. About ten of us, however, all leaders of the movement, had been cited for civil contempt. When we were first placed under this charge, I am certain that the Birmingham authorities believed we would back down rather than face the threat of indefinite imprisonment. But by the time we appeared in court late in April to answer the charges, all of Birmingham knew that we would never recant, even if we had to rot away in their jails. The city thus faced the prospect of putting us into jail for life. Confronted with the certain knowledge that we would not give in, the city attorney undoubtedly realized that he would be sentencing us to a martyrdom which must eventually turn the full force of national public opinion against Birmingham.

Abruptly the tactics were reversed. The civil-contempt charge was changed to the less stringent criminal-contempt charge, under which we were swiftly convicted on 26 April. In addition, the judge announced that he would delay sentence and give us about twenty days to file an appeal. At this point there was little doubt in our minds that Birmingham's bastions of segregation were weakening.

[Throughout the campaign the SCLC leaders had been seeking to negotiate with the city leaders. Now on 4 May, the Attorney General in Washington dispatched Burke Marshall, his chief civil-rights assistant, to seek a truce. Meetings were held with the Senior Citizens Committee to lay the groundwork for agreement. Meanwhile, for several days violence swept through the streets of Birmingham. Eventually an agreement was reached that facilities would be desegregated, Blacks hired on a nondiscriminatory basis, all those in jail released on bond or on their own recognizance, and a public communication link between Black and White groups established. King continues the account:] . . .

Terrified by the very destructiveness brought on by their own acts, the city police appealed for state troopers to be brought into the area. Many of the White leaders now realized that something had to be done. Yet there were those among them who were still adamant. But one other incident was to occur that would transform recalcitrance into good faith. On Tuesday, 7 May, the Senior Citizens Committee had assembled in a down-town building to discuss our demands. In the first hours of this meeting, they were so intransigent that Burke Marshall despaired of a pact. The atmosphere was charged with tension, and tempers were running high.

In this mood, these 125-odd business leaders adjourned for lunch. As they walked out on the street, an extraordinary sight met their eyes. On that day several thousand Negroes had marched on the town. The jails were so full that the police could only arrest a handful. There were Negroes on the sidewalks, in the streets, standing, sitting in the aisles of downtown stores. There were square blocks of Negroes, a veritable sea of black faces. They were commiting no violence; they were just present and singing.

Downtown Birmingham echoed to the strains of the freedom songs.

Astounded, those businessmen, key figures in a great city, suddenly realized that the movement could not be stopped. When they returned—from the lunch they were unable to get—one of the men who had been in the most determined opposition cleared his throat and said: 'You know, I've been thinking this thing through. We ought to be able to work something out.'

That admission marked the beginning of the end. Late that afternoon, Burke Marshall informed us that representatives from the business and industrial community wanted to meet with the movement leaders immediately to work out a settlement. After talking with these men for about three hours, we became convinced that they were negotiating in good faith. On the basis of this assurance we called a twenty-four-hour truce on Wednesday morning.

That day the President devoted the entire opening statement of his press conference to the Birmingham situation, emphasizing how vital it was that the problems be squarely faced and resolved and expressing encouragement that a dialogue now existed between the opposing sides. Even while the President spoke, the truce was briefly threatened when Ralph and I were suddenly clapped into jail on an old charge. Some of my associates, feeling that they had again been betrayed, put on their walking shoes and prepared to march. They were restrained, however; we were swiftly bailed out; and negotiations were resumed.

After talking all night Wednesday, and practically all day and night Thursday, we reached an accord.

3

ACTION FOR JUSTICE AND PEACE*

HELDER CAMARA

GANDHI, FAILURE OR PROPHET?

If one takes Gandhi as the prototype of the leader of active and courageous nonviolence, now is the time to ask: 'Gandhi, where is the victory?'

In the short term, Gandhi seems to have failed. What, truly, are the prospects for his teaching, both in the underdeveloped countries and in the developed countries?

Here, in our opinion, are the Gandhian possibilities in the Third World. For truth and liberating moral pressure to be a real alternative to armed revolution, it seems essential that the established regime should have a minimum of respect for the rights of man, notably for freedom of expression. It is furthermore necessary that no totalitarian methods should be established to falsify truth, and no physical or moral tortures.

If a member of the movement, acting in agreement with the principles and methods of peaceful violence, is put in prison, one of the resources of the movement should be to gather dozens, hundreds, thousands of fellow members who would also agree to give themselves up at the same time at the gates of the prison, declaring their solidarity with their outraged brother or sister. This would clearly cause a sensation. And through the accounts of the newspapers, radio and television, and through the press agencies,

*Reprinted by permission from *Spiral of Violence*, London: Sheed and Ward, 1971, 45–51, and 56–59. From *Spiral of Violence* by Dom Helder Camara. Published by Dimension Books, Denville, NJ—reprinted with permission.

Reprinted by permission from *The Desert is Fertile*, London: Sheed and Ward, 1974, 1–3, and 43–6. And by permission of Orbis Books, Maryknoll, New York.

Reprinted by permission from *Helder Camara's Latin America* by Betty Richardson Nute, (Non-Violence in Action Series), Friends Peace and International Relations Committee 1974 (pp. 1–3).

Reprinted by permission from *Church and Colonialism*, London: Sheed and Ward, 1969, 131–9. From *The Church and Colonialism* by Dom Helder Camara. Published by Dimension Books, Denville, NJ—reprinted with permission.

the movement would obtain national and international recognition.

But, in the underdeveloped countries, authoritarian regimes easily take control under the pretext of safeguarding 'the social order' from attack by subversive elements or communists. Moreover, the press, radio and television only transmits what favours the regime and it is obvious that it will not venture to reflect liberating moral pressure.

Worse still: the communications media find themselves obliged to spread lies or distortions of the facts, directly and sometimes officially communicated by the information services.

Informers are encouraged. Moral and physical torture is employed as a scientific method of wresting confessions from the 'subversive' elements, or those supposed to be such. Instead of innocence being presumed until a crime is proved, the crime is presumed, and even if suspects are freed, through total lack of evidence against them and through the presence of indisputable evidence in their favour, no open and frank acknowledgement of the error committed is ever obtained.

How can moral pressure be brought into action in order to stir consciences as a preliminary condition for a change of structures—if access to the newspapers and magazines, to radio and television, is forbidden, without formal prohibition, but by secret but effective order, in the name of national security? How can liberating moral pressure be brought into action if meetings and gatherings are prohibited in public places, and if conferences behind closed doors draw suspicion both on the speakers and the participants?

Furthermore, one of the most terrible weapons of the authoritarian regimes is to spare the great leader and seize the humble collaborators, who are without inner assurance, without moral resistance, insufficiently prepared to be able to face complex, malicious and treacherous interrogation.

When Gandhi went on a hunger strike, the whole world was grieved and there was no empire, however powerful, capable of resisting the moral pressure which arose from the four corners of the earth. But let us suppose that the established regime had left Gandhi without a voice, had placed his closest and dearest collaborators in prison, that it had spread about them the worst slanders (for example that they informed against their comrades, that they were afraid and had admitted their participation in subversive movements, that they abandoned Satyagraha . . .) what would the apostle of nonviolence have been able to do?

One might think of having recourse to leaflets and manifestos: but those who handed them out would be placed in prison and tortured as dangerous agitators, those who printed or stencilled them would be beaten and their machines destroyed.

It is obvious that, among the simple people and those who are just beginning to become aware of things, the news of prisons and above all of tortures leads to fear and flight from the Movement. Use the pulpit? Surely priests acting in this way would not be understood by the majority of the faithful, who would reproach them with straying from their evangelical mission and accuse them of engaging in politics.

It is clear that anyone who, in proclaiming the Gospel, demands justice as condition of peace, risks imprisonment; if a foreigner, the person will be expelled.

More serious still for the priest than being put in prison is *not* being put in prison, but seeing in prison, all around, militant laypeople who have simply echoed the evangelical message.

In such a climate, is it not obvious that the young above all are going to abandon the violence of the peace-lovers, go underground and try to prepare for armed revolution?

Now we repeat again and again: if Vietnam proves that even a first-class power cannot defeat guerrilas if it does not have the support of the local population, it also proves that the greatest heroism in the world cannot stand up to a first-class power except when it can count on another supporting it from behind. Do not let us deceive ourselves. The socialist empires, whether of Soviet or Chinese allegiance, are just as cold and insensible as the capitalist empires towards the underdeveloped countres' hope for total development. The capitalist empires, with their affirmations of sacrifice for the free world, of defence of private enterprise, of safeguarding order from subversion and chaos, are in fact defending their political prestige and the economic interests arising from it; they are indeed at the service of economic power and the international trusts. The socialist empires for their part are hard and intransigent, they do not allow pluralism, they impose dialectical materialism, demand blind obedience to the party, set up a regime of total and permanent insecurity and fear, just like the fascist dictatorships of the extreme right.

What would Gandhi say, what would he advise the Third World to do, faced with the situation of humanity one hundred years after his birth?

THE LESSON OF HALF-FAILURE

[Dom Helder Camara's own response to the question concerning the Gandhian response to problems of the Third World is summarized in the first few pages of Camara's book of prose and poetry, *The Desert is Fertile* (1974:1-3).]

The world is so complicated that it would be ridiculous to try and produce a formula applicable to all situations, races, countries and continents. But there are problems overriding this diversity which face humanity as a whole, although of course they occur in varying forms and degrees.

Is there anywhere in the world free from injustice, inequality, and division? Is there anywhere where injustice is not the primary violence breeding all other violence? Where violent protest against injustice, taking to the streets, does not threaten public order and the security of the state? And where it does not meet with violent repression by the authorities?

Almost everywhere there are many, particularly among the young, who have come to believe that the only way to do away with injustice is to rouse the victims of injustice, the oppressed, and organize them to fight for better days.

There are also many who want a juster and more human world but do not believe that force and armed violence are the best way of getting it. Those who choose active nonviolence — the violence of the peaceful — do not need religion or ideology to see that the earth is ruled today by powerful combines, economic, political, technocratic, and military alliances. How would it be possible to beat these lords of the earth in armed combat when they have as their allies arms manufacturers and war-mongers?

The difficult question then arises: what can be achieved by nonviolence? Do the nonviolent realize that the need is not just for a few small reforms but, in both the developed and the underdeveloped countries, the transformation of the political, cultural, economic and social structures?

Yes. The nonviolent do not in the least underestimate the difficulty of the task. If I may speak personally, I could mention my own half-failure, which forces me to struggle on and offers me new hopes.

I dreamt for six years of a large liberating moral pressure movement. I started Action for Justice and Peace. I travelled half the world. I appealed to institutions, universities, churches, religious groups, trade unions, technicians' organizations, youth movements, etc. After six years I concluded that institutions as such are unable to engage in bold and decisive action for two reasons: they can only interpret the average opinions of their members, and in capitalist society they have to be directly or indirectly bound up with the system in order to survive.

Of course I was not able to visit the Eastern blocs. But if we condemn the serious failings in the capitalist super-states like the US and the EEC, we must likewise condemn the communist super-states, the USSR and China. And although it is still possible to denounce these failings in capitalist countries, it is not possible in Moscow or Peking.

And although I now realize that it is virtually useless to appeal to institutions as such, everywhere I go—and intuitively I include the East—I find minorities with the power for love and justice which could be likened to nuclear energy locked for millions of years in the smallest atoms and waiting to be released.

OBJECTIVES AND OUTLOOK

[The objectives and outlook of the Action for Justice and Peace are given in *Spiral of Violence* (Camara, 1971: 56-9).]

Action for Justice and Peace is self-explanatory: its aims are announced in its name:

—*Action*: not just speculation, theory, discussion, contemplation;

—*Justice*: there are injustices everywhere; everywhere there is need for justice;

—*Peace*: justice is the condition for peace, the path, the way. It is only through justice that a true and lasting peace will be achieved.

All those who, all over the world, hunger and thirst after justice, are invited to march together:

—*the oppressed* who suffer injustice, those of the underdeveloped countries, and also those in the underdeveloped strata of the rich countries;

—*those who* belong to the privileged classes of the poor countries or the rich classes of the rich countries but *no longer accept injustice* and acknowledge it to be violence No. 1;

—*the technologists,* who are best placed to understand the gravity of the ever-widening gulf between the developed world and the underdeveloped world and who, by nature and by profession, prefer liberating moral pressure to bloody violence;

—*those who,* having opted for bloody and armed violence, *are beginning to wonder whether the violence of the pacifists is not the true solution;*

—*those who* still are, or who were until yesterday, the authorities, and who have answered violence with violence (indeed even with torture), but who now *understand the urgency of the violence of the pacifists in demanding justice* without falling into armed violence and hatred.

All those who, all over the world, hunger and thirst after justice and accept the invitation to march together in the Action for Justice and Peace must know:

—that the AJP is not and never will be a political party;

—that it does not belong in any way to one person, one party, one country, one culture or one religion;

—that it is a gathering of people of good will convinced that only the roads of justice and love lead to true peace, who are resolved to exercise liberating moral pressure to obtain justice and help humanity to free itself from hatred and chaos.

Within his or her own religion, each person will discover the necessary impulse to give himself or herself entirely to justice as condition of peace.

Alongside the development of Action for Justice and Peace, it will one day be necessary to collect from the sacred books of all the religions the exhortations, precepts and prayers which speak about peace and justice, and similarly the examples of the great models in the various religions. For some religions the word 'justice' always presupposes such virtues, and is in fact a synonym for holiness.

As for peace, it is well-known that there can be instances of false peace, with the same deceptive beauty as stagnant marshes in moonlight. The peace which speaks to us, which moves us, for which we are prepared to give our lives, presupposes that the rights of all are fully respected: the rights of God and the rights of people. Not just the rights of some people, a privileged few, to the detriment of many others: the rights of each person and of all people.

ABRAHAMIC MINORITIES UNITE![1]

If you feel you belong in spirit to the family of Abraham do not wait for permission to act. Don't wait for official action or new laws. The family of Abraham is more a spirit than an institution, more a life style than an organization. It requires the minimum of structure and refers merely to several general principles.

The minimum of structure: anyone who feels he or she belongs to the family of Abraham should not remain alone. Make an effort to find someone, near at hand or further away, who already belongs to this family or who could belong. Make contact. How? That depends on the situation. The essential thing is to get out of isolation. There are no rules about the formation of groups, number of members, form that meetings should take. You are sisters and brothers meeting to help each other fight discouragement, and develop the necessary faith, hope, and love.

The first thing to do is to look and listen, get information on the situations in which the Abrahamic minorities could be involved. Won't that be a big job? No. Any members of the Abrahamic minorities can find out about what is happening around them, in the neighbourhoods where they live or at work.

One must discover where the worst injustices are, the worst exhibitions of selfishness, from the local to the international scale. All members of the family of Abraham, according to their opportunities, will be able to get much more detailed and human information than can be gathered from the official statistics.

In under-developed countries the Abrahamic minorities must try to find out and understand what is involved in a sub-human situation. 'Sub-human' is an explosive word. Take it in detail. Find out about housing. Do the places where some people live deserve to be called houses? Do they afford the necessary minimum of comfort to a human life? How many people are there per room? Look at the water, drains, electricity, the floor, the roof. Investigate clothing, food, health, work, transport, leisure in the same way. Pictures can be helpful. Take photographs and so on. But you must also turn to statistics to discover whether this is an isolated case or the general condition. You should ask the right questions. With work, for example, does it pay a living wage sufficient to support a family, is employment guaranteed or are there frequent redundancies? Are trade unions encouraged, tolerated, interfered with, forbidden? What are the apprenticeship conditions? the sanitary conditions? holidays? retirement provisions? Are the laws on social conditions kept? Are human beings treated with respect?

This sort of inquiry could of course arouse suspicion, and that could have unpleasant consequences. But it is necessary to find out what the real situation is in conditions of internal colonialism.

What other way is there of becoming convinced and of convincing others of the huge gap between those who operate and those who suffer from an almost feudal situation in which the masses have no voice and no hope? Such information would not aim at inciting anger and rebellion but at providing a solid argument for the necessity to change the structures.

We should not forget the extreme cases where it would be necessary to prove that an apparently patriarchal regime is in fact a cover for absolute dominion over life and death, for a master who can give and take at will, allow or forbid the provision and maintenance of houses, the cultivation of a small strip of land and the keeping of a few cattle, literacy, trade unionism etc.

How are we to find out about the price paid by sweated workers, slaves innumerable, for profits to those who put their money in foreign banks in secret numbered accounts?

How can we find out about abuses of economic power on the national and international scale? Where can we find figures for what official statistics do not disclose, for the illegal export of profits that are blood, sweat and tears?

Must we repeat it? Such information does not aim to provoke hatred or subversion. Its aim is to supply liberating moral pressure. For many, this in itself is dangerous and subversive. But one day it will be understood that this violence of the peaceful is greatly preferable to the explosion of armed violence.

LATIN AMERICA'S MARTIN LUTHER KING

[Betty Richardsaon Nute describes the launching of the movement for Action for Justice and Peace in *Helder Camara's Latin America* (1974:1-3).]

The frail little man with the eager, almost impish smile, steps briskly on to the harshly lit balcony, his long black cassock moving with his step. He joins an animated group of actors, singers, reporters, nuns, priests, and stands against the wall, alive with excitement, while below in the big patio, the crowd continues to gather. In twos and threes they come, some 3,000 of them, peasants and townsfolk, church people and lay, to help launch a movement 'for justice and peace'. It is 2 October 1968 in Recife, Brazil, and the vibrant little figure at the centre of the action is an archbishop; he is Dom Helder Camara, that leader of the poor and downtrodden whom some call the 'Martin Luther King of Latin America' '

Action indeed it is, in all its dynamism and simplicity, this launcing of a movement — no academic session, but rather, in the literal meaning of the word, a demonstration. In the flickering lights a group of young actors begin to declaim:

> Peace is our ideal, but not a false peace . . . not the deceitful peace that conceals injustice and rottenness.
>
> . . . Forty-five million Brazilians—half the population—do not have 36 new cruzeiros (just over $3) a month to live on . . .
>
> . . . Out of 100 Brazilian families 70 do not receive even the minimum wage . . .
>
> . . . Appearances of order and peace hide terrible injustices and undermine peace . . .
>
> . . . Is it subversion, is it communism, to open people's eyes to these truths?
>
> . . . The great masses of landless people do not know how to read and cannot vote. The powerful are masters of the political structures and do not allow the application of the laws that affect their privileges.
>
> . . . We want schools that free everyone from the slavery of ignorance, unemployment, hunger and fear.
>
> . . . These misfortunes . . . are caused by the unjust structures that must be changed without delay.
>
> . . . We are not opposed to progress. But we want progress to serve everyone, not merely a group that is constantly smaller and richer.
>
> . . . Pope Paul VI has well said: 'The earth was given to all, not

merely to the rich.' Surely this is not communism. It is the voice of the Pope.

The audience well knows the bitter lot of the poor in North East Brazil. The statistics reflect the harsh reality of their daily struggle for life: annual per capita income $40; seventy per cent of the population illiterate; infant mortality fifty per cent;[3] so little to eat that most fall 1,200 calories or more below minimum subsistence.[4] In a sort of rhythmic chant the actors carry the people with them. From all sides come applause and whistles.

They ask us how we expect structures to be changed without violence . . . And we answer with another question: 'Do you remember that the all-powerful slave-owners in Brazil were unable to prevent the 13th of May?[5] . . .' We now seek the liberation of native-born slaves . . .

And then the actors step back and Dom Helder speaks, the loud, warm impassioned voice that issues from his frail body filling all space. In a fragment of time he is one with his audience, telling them how each one can work for liberation by making people aware that they can control their own lives. It is important not to rush into a decision to work for liberation in the heat of emotion, he says, but to give it careful thought. There will be a course of instruction, followed by the signing of a pact, then work in teams of five to fifteen people; the struggle calls for courage, the courage of David facing Goliath, armed only with a slingshot and five stones; faith in God, trust in truth, trust in justice, trust in the good, trust in love.

Dom Helder Camara, Archbishop of Recife and Olinda, champion of the poor, keeps presidents awake and has caused the transfer of two generals in three years. On the day of the 1964 coup he is said to have met with outgoing President Goulart in the morning and with the head of the incoming junta, General Castelo Branco, in the afternoon, and to have been received with equal respect by both.[6]

'So when he takes the stands he does, he can afford to do so because the powerful protect him?' people may ask. The answer is clearly No, for powerful interests, such as individual landowners in the North East, use every weapon against him they feel they can. 'They' call him a communist, have murdered his secretary and several of his aides, bombed his house several times, and threaten his life sometimes nightly over the telephone. Most agree that what opens the doors of government for him is first and foremost the transcedent power of his personality, his wonderful ease of relationship. He himself says that as a churchman he can afford to say things which it is dangerous for others, including his aides, to say.

If one had to sum up Dom Helder in one word it might well be 'simplicity'. A friend captures much of the essence of the man as he describes his patience, his humility, his enjoyment of the most ordinary things, his celebration of each new day as a holiday. 'He combines in a unique way both intense suffering and a spirit of joyous abandon, . . . wrapping his immense goodness and power in an impish human smile.'[7]

SOCIAL SITUATION

[Camara's movement for Action for Justice and Peace centred on three sectors of society: the student world, the labour movement, and above all, the church. As an example of the work done by members of this movement we include part of a document published by the Catholic Workers' Action (ACO) of north-east Brazil on 1 May 1967. It is an inquiry into the social situation of the North-East, conducted by the ACO and published under the patronage of its archbishop, Dom Helder Camara, who was its inspiration (Camara, 1969:131-9).]

This document is born of the anguish and sense of responsibility of a group of workers in the North-East, engaged in the Catholic Workers' Action, after an analysis of the situation of the working classes of the region said to be 'in full development'.

It is not directed to any person or group in particular, but to all who have a share of the responsibility, who have 'eyes to see and ears to hear' and a heart to love. It is directed to every person of goodwill, rich or poor, ruler or subject, employer or worker, employed or unemployed, Christian or non-Christian, believer or atheist. It is directed, in particular, to the North-East, and to those of the North-East who are involved in the situation of misery and underdevelopment.

The document does not present detailed, concrete solutions, because the mission of the ACO is essentially evangelical. The object is first of all to stir the conscience by means of truth, because without truth authentic dialogue is impossible. In presenting the truth, it is our intention to challenge all people to a courageous dialogue which will lead to concrete solutions.

Although the cases quoted are isolated, they indicate a general situation of lack of respect for humanity, and they have been chosen almost at random from a large volume of facts gathered throughout the whole of the North-East, from Maranhao to Bahia. Anything which could identify persons or undertakings is generally avoided, because the purpose is only to draw out the significance of the attitudes.

They are attitudes which cry out for modification. It is our hope that this document may help the reader to discover new values and to acquire a permanent attitude of concern for justice and respect for the dignity of humanity. We have all co-operated in this work and are responsible for it.

THE WORKER IN THE DEVELOPING NORTH-EAST

The Brazilian North-East is currently the centre of the attention of the American continent, not only on account of the concentration and gravity of the socio-economic problems, but principally because it is here more than anywhere else in Latin America that planned development is being experienced at its most consistent and rational. While retaining the characteristics of an under-developed region, the North-East has expanded economically more than any other area of Brazil, due principally to heavy investment in electric power, roads, irrigation etc., and to an aggressive policy of industrialization, encouraged by a com-bination of fiscal incentives and capital aid.

One of the characteristics of the North-East is the abundance of available labour, residing in huts in the great human agglomerations of the larger cities and forming quarters which have risen spontaneously and increase day by day in proportion to the flow of migrants from the inland to the coast. These quarters are to be found all over Latin America, and are given various names—*alagados* in Recife, *favelas* in Rio de Janeiro and S Paulo, *malocas* in Rio Grande, *alagados* or *invazao* in Bahia, *vila miséria* in Argentina, *invasión* or *tugurios* in Colombia, *barriada* in Peru, *quilombo* in Panama. They are concentrated in great contingents of unemployed in the North-East. They are men and women with large families, mostly unskilled, who are badly-paid, under-paid, or simply unemployed.

In Recife, the capital of Pernambuco, the phenomenon is more manifest than in other places, and it has more serious consequences on account of the fact that Recife is the pole of major attraction for immigrants because of its greater social progress, both economic and cultural. More than thirty per cent of the total population of the state of Pernambuco is concentrated in the so-called 'greater Recife', which comprises the capital and four zones on the periphery, and represents only 1.5 per cent of state territory.

What is called 'available and cheap labour' is nothing other, therefore, than an immense legion of under-employed or unemployed, without qualification or opportunity for work. In 1965, we were informed by SUDENE [Centre for the Development of north-east Brazil] that there were more than one million unemployed in the great urban zones of the North-East.

These details and figures show, in some way, the reduction of the worker of the North-East to marginal status in the development drive which is going on in our region. The technicians examine the index of global expansion, they pursue economic goals, they are concerned with estimates and incidence of investments and then they display the graphs which mathematically reflect the rhythm of our region's enrichment. But perhaps they do not notice the criminal contradiction which they are helping to construct: in the measure in which the wealth of the region increases with development, the number of 'marginals' increases with development, the number of 'marginals' increases also, of those who do not participate in this wealth, who do not benefit from this development. The analysis of the reality and the plans are elaborated in inaccessible offices, by men who, by reason of their professional formation, approach the most painful phenomena with the cold objectivity of technology. What do they know of the worker? Have they any concern to harmonize development techniques with the demands of social justice?

On the other hand, what do the workers know of the industrial development plans of the region? Who has ever explained to them the significance of modernizing production processes? They understand nothing of the importance of specialist labour in development. They scarcely know anything about development.

In raising these problems, the ACO does not take up a position against development. In the 'Manifesto on the Situation of the Workers in the North-East' (March 1966), the ACO affirmed that 'only development can create the structural conditions which will make possible the welfare of all'. But as the manifesto also stated, 'the various stages of development must consider people in relation to themselves and to the society in which they live, not only because people are the primary goal of development, but also because they must be its principal agents by their conscious participation in the economico-social changes.'

For a human and social point of view, what is happening in the North-East is a distortion of the true object of development, which is the advancement of 'humanity and all people', to quote François Perroux, one of the most quoted theorists in the whole country, including the North-East.

The effects of development fall most frequently on the workers of the North-East affecting their lives and their mentality by the suffering and hopelessness which arise as a consequence of the distortions which progress is generating in our region.

Development is a cycle of conflicts. Conflicts between governments and undertakings, between progressive and conservative undertakings, between old interests and new, internal and external structures, etc. And workers are victims of these conflicts, because they have no defence, they have no preparation for defending themselves. Thus, while it is affirmed that 'the North-East is the most expanding region of Brazil', the working class of the North-East suffers an expanding misery which can be described as follows:

1. lower wages which are contrary to law;
2. a progressive increase of unemployment and under-employment brought about by industrial modernization;
3. a general climate of exploiting the worker;
4. a growth in incidence and cunning in the violation of labour laws;
5. the absence of any policy of creating more jobs, resulting in a progressive widening of the gap between the supply of new jobs (very small) and the supply of labour (very great).

We are witnessing, in the North-East, the substitution of a feudal structure by a capitalist structure, and as active Christians we cannot do other than manifest a profound fear at the materialist way in which capitalism tackles its problems, without concern for people, who can be used simply as figures in the planning statistics.

This fear grows from day to day as we see the symptoms of an economy characterized by the employment of capital to greatest advantage and by the liberal pragmatism which makes profit the primary goal. Large private groups, natives and foreigners, are set up in the region to take over the direction of the regional economy; the dominant economic concepts in the industrialization process are almost exclusively based on the laws of supply and demand; the determining factor in the great sectoral reforms (sugar cane, textile industries, etc.) is the fluctuation in the markets dominated by national and international capitalism.

SUDENE, which bears the responsibility for regional planning, uses as the principal instrument of development a combination of stimuli to industrialization, which only concern the interests of capital and are specially suited to large financial undertakings, in other words to the great economic groups. As a consequence, there is a tendency which could become irreversible towards a concentration of wealth in the hands of those who are already wealthy.

Meanwhile the workers of the North-East continue to be treated as 'available cheap labour', without any possibility of negotiating their labour hire in a highly technological industrialization, because:

1. The work factor has a limited place in the production process which is being set up, in which the machine substitutes for the person with greater efficiency.

2. The jobs which are created demand, in most cases, a specialist qualification which the worker of the North-East does not possess, for lack of opportunity.

In view of the inevitability of this type of industrialization, which does not solve the unemployment problem and therefore does not create the possibility of a just distribution of wealth, it would be legitimate to hope that SUDENE already had policies and means for correcting tendencies in regional development, which leave people at the margin of the process.

But this is not the case. In agriculture, for example, which occupies seventy per cent of the population of the North-East, there is a situation of misery and hunger and injustice and, what is more serious, no prospect of immediate improvement. The development programmes for zootechnics are too timid or simply deceptive. And the reason for this seems to be a lack of courage in making radical reforms which will change the archaic structure so that production may increase and the rural worker may have access to the land. What is being done is almost exclusively to the benefit of the great landowners for whom the financing systems function. The small farmers, without credit, without technical assistance, without the means of trade expansion, usually lose their profit to the middle-person and to the speculator and often enough fall into the cycle of misery.

In consequence the great mass of rural people, our brothers and sisters in the country areas, suffer all sorts of injustice, the greatest and commonest of which is the lack of regular work, and this leads them to accept every type of exploitation practised by the employers, or to emigrate to the urban centres in search of opportunities denied to them by agriculture. It is this emigrant mass which expands the borders of the slums and forms the 'available cheap labour' which acts as a bait for southern and foreign business people.

The lot of the city workers is no different from that of the land workers, because unemployment, injustice and exploitation unite them in the same drama and because both are victims of the same errors, the same omissions, the same distortion of economic planning. They are immersed in illiteracy, in humiliating housing conditions, in begging, in endemic diseases, in infant mortality, in violated dignity, in malnutrition; they have no schools for their children, there is no life in their trade unions, they are unemployed, they have no social welfare, and they lack leadership. In brief, they are to be found in the margin of progress. Their hope too lies in integral solutions which will give to economic development the social dimension which is demanded by human dignity.

As Christians studying the problems of the working class of the developing North-East, the members of the ACO keep in mind the teaching of Pope John XXIII in *Mater et Magistra*:

Social progress must accompany and be joined to economic development in such a way that all social categories may benefit from the increase in the national income. Care must be taken therefore, and serious efforts must be made to see, that there is no increase in the economic and social imbalance, but rather that it should diminish as far as possible.

It follows from this that the economic wealth of a people does not result only from the global abundance of goods, but still more from its just and effective distribtuion, which must ensure the full personal development of the community members, because this and this alone is the goal of the national economy.

The members of ACO, studying and gathering together in this document the contemporary problems of the working class in the North-East, especially as regards the lack of respect for human dignity, do so with the sense of responsibility which derives from complete acceptance of the further teaching of *Mater et Magistra*: 'Let every citizen feel responsible for the realization of the common good, in all the sectors of national life'. But they accept it principally in order to fulfil their proper mission, which is to evangelize. Evangelization must be tied to life, because only in that way is it possible to reach the whole person, body and soul. Our example is Christ, who always joined to the work of evangelization an attention and concern for people, healing the sick, multiplying the loaves, changing water into wine.

[As an epilogue we include a poem by Camara which gives further evidence of the similarity between his approach and that of Gandhi (Camara, 1974:21-2)]

Become an expert

Become an expert
in the art
of discovering the good
in every person.
No one
is entirely bad.
Become an expert
in the art
of finding the truthful core
in views of every kind.
The human mind
abhors total error.

REFERENCES

Camara, Helder, 1969. Church and Colonialism. London: Sheed and Ward.

——, 1971. Spiral of Violence. London: Sheed and Ward.

——, 1974. The Desert is Fertile. London: Sheed and Ward.

de Broucker, Jose, 1970. The Violence of a Peacemaker. New York: Orbis.

Nute, Betty Richardson, 1974. Helder Camara's Latin America. London: Friends Peace and International Relations Committee.

NOTES

1. *The Desert is Fertile* (Camara, 1974:43-6). [At several places the original English translations of Camara (1969, 1971, and 1974) showed male pronouns and nouns which have here been edited for general applicability.]

2. This description is based on the account given by de Broucker (1970:65).

3. See MacEoin, Gary, *Revolution Next Door*, Holt, Rinehart, Winston, New York, 1971, p. 31.

4. The United Nations considers 2,600 to be the minimum number of calories necessary for subsistence. According to figures quoted in *Time* magazine, March 25, 1974, the average calorie intake in North East Brazil has now declined to 1,323 per day.

5. May 13, 1888, is the date when slavery was abolished in Brazil.

6. The writer recalls the first occasion, in the early 1960s, when Dom Helder's influence with the powerful in government came to her attention. Church World Service, for whose Latin America programme she was then responsible, was having trouble getting certain shipments of medical and other supplies into Brazil duty-free. Just when the difficulties seemed greatest, she arrived in Rio on a field trip. 'Don't worry about the shipments,' she was told, 'Archbishop Camara (then Archbishop of Rio) is seeing President Kubitschek this morning and will get our Protestant shipments cleared along with the Catholic ones.' She has since met Dom Helder personally on several occasions.

7. Richard Shaull in his foreword to de Broucker's *The Violence of a Peacemaker* (1970).

4

THE BATTLE OF LARZAC*

ROGER RAWLINSON

Since October 1970 the peasant farmers of the Larzac plateau in Southern France have been opposing the extension of the little-used army camp at La Cavalerie. The camp site covers 7,500 acres and would be extended to 42,500 acres. The Agricultural union, the Save Larzac committee, the industrial unions, the teachers union political parties, and the Chamber of Commerce have all protested at the decision of M. Debré, the Minister of Defence.

A delegation from the Larzac was received by the Minister of Defence on 10 November 1971. Debré made it plain that he would not change his decision. He proposed setting up a Planning Commission which would discuss ways in which the Camp extension plan would be carried out. This in no way met the objections of those directly concerned. Only two peasants from the Larzac were on the Commission when it sat for the first time on 18 November. Other members represented the Administration, the Army, the local Councils and the trade unions. The terms of reference of this working party were limited at the outset to: 'Suggesting different boundaries to those proposed on condition that the area of the Camp extension should remain at about 14,000 Hectares (34,580 acres)', 'To prepare a programme of reorganization and re-equipment for the Larzac enterprises concerned'. Therefore, the farmers, the Union representatives and the Chairman of the Save Larzac Association refused to attend the second meeting of the Commission.

In the meantime the more militant peasants set out to reinforce the current of sympathy which was running in their favour. The Save Larzac Association published a full page advertisement in the national newspaper *Le Monde*. The satirical political paper *Le*

*Reprinted by permission from *Resurgence*, July-August 1975, 6 (No. 3). 18 20: and September-October 1975, 6 (No. 4), 12 14. (Part 1, not reprinted, appeared in *Resurgence*, May-June 1975, 6 (No. 2), 18-22). *Resurgence* is located at Felindre, Crymych. (Dyfed) Wales.

Canard Enchaîné with a readership of three-quarters of a million had already taken up the story. A national Save Larzac Co-ordination Committee was set up bringing together over 250 organizations representing a wide variety of interests.

The authorities still attempted to minimize the extent of the take-over. The minister insisted that only seventeen farms (later he said twenty-three) would be affected. The boundaries of the camp extension were drawn in such a way as to exclude some of the farm buildings and the land around them giving the impression that they could still carry on with a reduced area of pasture. The army promised that access to pastureland would be allowed to farmers and the public during a part of each month. M. Debré promised improvements for the region, a roof would be built over the municipal swimming pool at Millau.

In December 1971 the TV programme Hexagone was to deal with the role of the army in the life of the nation. A number of farmers from Loire-Atlantique discussed with a group from Paris. The peasants of the Larzac also participated but the programme was pre-recorded and the Larzac peasants' contribution failed to appear on the screen.

THE PEASANTS AND THE ARMY

The Larzac peasants' gradual change of attitude to the army must be seen against the background of France, the first country to adopt universal military conscription. Ever since the Revolution it has been part of French society and military service is accepted by the majority of citizens as a democratic duty to be proud of.

The existing Camp started in 1902 as a training establishment for reservists. (All ex-conscripts are called up for a short period each year.) The reservists, often older family men, were popular with local people and spent their money in shops and cafés. Nowadays the Camp is used as a shooting range by conscripts who are less interested in making local contacts. The total Camp area covers 7,000-acres but only 500 acres belongs to the Army. The rest is Common land under the jurisdiction of the Parishes and sheep are sometimes allowed to graze there. Hamlets and farm buildings in the area are now in ruin having been used for target practice. Trees have been uprooted and the soil churned up. This wanton destruction of property was the first thing which turned the farmers against the Army. The damage to land and crops outside the area also contributed to this feeling. The unilateral decision by the Minister of Defence, his failure to keep promises, false Government propaganda, all helped to foster a spirit of anti-militarism. Then the peasants met the 'Nonviolents' as they call them and they began to question the nation's defence policy and even the need for Armed Forces.

LESSONS OF CANJUERS

A delegation from the Save Larzac Association visited the plateau of Canjuers in Provence where 85,000 acres had been taken over by the army. As in the case of the Larzac, assurances had been given that neither agriculture nor tourism would suffer. However, none of these promises had been kept. There was no question of the flocks being allowed access to pasture land. Nothing had been done to find an alternative livelihood for those evicted. The parish of Comps was about to lose its Post Office and Police Station and the village of Broves had been wiped off the map. A scenic route leading to the Gorges de Verdon was subject to periodic closures at any time of the year.

A local man in a responsible position told the delegation, 'Our mistake was not to have hit hard enough at the beginning of the affair. We allowed ourselves to be outwitted.'

ACTIVE NONVIOLENCE

The struggle of the Larzac peasants entered a new phase in the spring of 1972. They had rejected violence because of their natural inclination and because they realized they needed the sympathy of the majority of their fellow citizens. Their anger with the army grew however as helicopters flying low over the flocks frightened the ewes sometimes producing abortions. As they shook their fists helplessly in the air they wondered what else they could do since lawful forms of protest did not seem enough.

On 1 March Lanza del Vasto, author and philosopher, Catholic disciple of Mahatma Gandhi and founder of the Community of the

Ark, gave some talks on active nonviolence in Millau, Rodez and Albi. This astonishing prophet in his long white cloak spoke of nonviolence as something natural and entirely compatible with the Christian religion. In 1936 Lanza del Vasto had travelled on foot through India, worn Indian clothes, and shared the life and hardships of pilgrims. He had worked at Gandhi's ashram where the Mahatma had recognized him as a devoted disciple. Lanza had told Gandhi of his desire to start a community in the west where there would be 'Politics without violence, a society without exploitation, religion without intolerance, love and truth in people's hearts, a return to the land and to simple living and craftsmanship'. Gandhi gave him a new name, Shantidas, meaning servant of peace. (See Lanza del Vasto, *Return to the Source.*) The community of the Ark was founded in 1944 and is now established in mountainous country south-west of the Larzac plateau. More than a hundred people, families and individuals, live in two hamlets La Borie and Nogaret. They are largely self-supporting and enjoy a simple peasant life style on their 2,000 acres of land. The Ark has many supporting groups and a few associated communities in different parts of France and abroad. Members of the community and their supporters have initiated and contributed to non-violent actions protesting against the use of torture in the Algerian war, against nuclear weapons and in support of French and Spanish conscientious objectors. They came to the Larzac as neighbours rather than as a group wishing to spread their own ideas about community life.

MOLOTOV COCKTAIL VERSUS GANDHI COCKTAIL

A week later the Catholic priest Abbé Jean Toulat, well known for his book, *The Bomb or Life?* talked to 1,500 people at a meeting in Millau. He argued that 'to prevent the army from taking root on the Larzac is to help peace. It is therefore a just endeavour . . . to Molotov cocktails you will prefer Gandhi cocktails—that is to say a mixture of truth, courage, love, humour and imagination. You will find forms of action which, while showing respect for people, will reach their hearts and force them to examine their consciences'.

On 11 March an Army charity ball was being held at the officer's mess at the Camp. On this cold rainy night about a hundred farmers gathered in the streets of La Cavalerie and after chaining themselves together started a march to the Camp. The police were there in force. Their vehicles were driven so close to the marchers that a man was forced onto the bonnet of a moving van. The demonstrators arrived in front of the mess and stood in silence while the Camp Commandant and a few officers came out to meet them. 'You are inside the Camp. I don't go to your homes when I am not invited so you must leave.' Silence. The officer's voice rose from the darkness: 'You are right to protest the expropriation of your land but you must protest to those above me. I have nothing to do with this.' Again silence. The ball went on but perhaps some consciences had been aroused. In this apprenticeship in nonviolence the peasants and their supporters had shown they could stand firm in the face of provocation.

SHANTIDAS FASTS

The Community of the Ark made careful preparations for their involvement in the Larzac Battle. The week after his talk at Millau, Shantidas announced to a meeting of farmers at La Cavalerie that he proposed fasting for two weeks on the Plateau. The peasants wholeheartedly agreed. Members of the Ark visited hamlets and farms to explain the meaning of this action.

On Sunday 19 March Shantidas took up his quarters at a farm at La Cavalerie which had been specially whitewashed and prepared, a small room with an open fire for him, a larger room for others who might join him, and a room with a display of photographs showing various aspects of the life of the Plateau, picturesque features, architecture, etc.

At nine in the morning and nine in the evening prayers were said followed by a talk. Every day a different group of four or five peasants took turns at fasting with Shantidas. A few young people outside the region also came, some to fast three days, others seven. In the evening extra people would arrive and discuss quietly and earnestly.

On Thursday, the fifth day, the local correspondents of the Parisian papers were received in the courtyard of the farm and, as the guns boomed in the background, Shantidas told them the full story. He said that the Ministerial decision could be contested on two grounds. First: because the Minister based his decision on an investigation which had been carried out years ago. He had been deceived. He was wrong in thinking the peasants would sell their land. Second: the Prefet had promised consultation and as long as this continued to be denied the liberty of French citizens was gravely affected.

THE MANIFESTO OF THE 103

On the tenth day (28 March) a list was published of the peasants directly concerned who had signed a pact binding themselves to refuse all offers for their land. The significant passage of this document reads as follows: 'We confirm publicly our opposition to the extension plan and, confident of our rights, we jointly pledge ourselves to reject all attempts at enticement or intimidation and all offers to buy our land on behalf of the Army, and offers of compensation.' They added that if any land were to come on the market they would purchase it. This Manifesto signed by 103 farmers out of a possible 107, made a big impression on public opinion.

Roger Moreau, one of the Companions of the Ark, explained the way it had happened: 'For a fortnight the peasants who had no idea what to do to defend themselves, sat in this very room around Lanza del Vasto who was fasting, and they meditated. It became a retreat. In this way their unity crystallized. They discovered this unity and out of it came the Manifesto of the 103. They took a joint pledge not to sell their land to the Army, and the group of the 103 was born that very moment, and so was their strength, I believe.' The 103 having now realized their unity and having accepted the weapon of nonviolence were henceforth to take full control of the Battle.

On that same day the Bishops of Rodez and Montpelier joined Shantidas and the others in the fast. At midday they celebrated mass together. The Protestant Minister of Millau read the lesson. The village church was full.

The same evening, Shantidas sent a letter to the President of the Republic. 'The people of the Larzac are determined to remain. The Minister has been deceived about the true state of affairs. Should an attempt be made to take the land by force thousands upon thousands of young and not so young people would peacefully prevent the operation.'

The following day television cameras appeared on the scene. That evening the true problem of the Larzac appeared on the regional channel and the following evening it was shown on all the national channels.

On 31 March some 3,000 'Marchers for Peace' arrived on the Plateau. They were mainly young people who had walked from Rodez from Montpellier and elsewhere. The peasants did their best to accomodate them in barns, others bivouacked wherever they could. Amongst them were Friends of the Ark, members of the peace Movement and left-wingers. They all converged on La Cavalerie, where they held open forums, gathered information from the peasants, prepared meals. Before breaking his fast at midday, Shantidas spoke a few words: 'The success of our struggle depends on unity and on fidelity to active nonviolence.'

'ET LE LARZAC'

A growing number of support groups were now active. At Reims the local group took advantage of the city's festivities in memory of Joan of Arc. The action began with a Referendum: 'Sheep or Tanks?' Carrying ballot boxes and distributing leaflets and voting forms, members of the group wandered through the streets of the 'medieval fair'. The following morning large crowds gathered in the Cathedral square to watch military and civilian ceremonies—Joan being presented to the City Fathers. Two people had climbed to the top of the Cathedral towers the evening before. As Joan appeared they unfolded a large banner 15 metres long on which appeared the words *'Et le Larzac?'* (What about the Larzac?). Fifteen young people suddenly jumped over the barriers, sat down in the middle of the Square and unfurled another long banner *'Et le Larzac?'* At Aurillac, the Prime Minister Pompidou was extolling the value of a return to the land—of young people remaining on family farms, when young workers and students just back from La Cavalerie took up a rhythmic chant of *'Et le Larzac, Et le Larzac . . .'*

Army activity increased and large numbers of Gendarmes were seen on the Plateau. A farmer's wife who had taken a short cut across the Camp (she had used this path for years) was detained for several hours and accused of spying. The 'Man from the Ministry', a certain M. Tournier, a person of undoubted charm and infinite patience, spent his time visiting the farms and villages of the Plateau and surrounding valleys. He would spell out the advantages of agreeing to sell land to the State but would not press the point. He always had something to offer. Here it might be a piped water supply, there a telephone, somewhere else a track would be tarred over. He would call on the Mayor of a village to talk of possible improvements and funds available from Government sources. Of course, all Mayors have projects in mind and in the highly centralized French system authorization for some schemes must come from Paris. He did have some success. He reported that, given time and providing that pressure was maintained, the population would become reconciled to the plan and most of the farmers would eventually agree to sell their land.

THE PRELIMINARY INQUIRY

The Minister of Defence announced on 26 May 1972 that an Inquiry would be held as a preliminary to declaring the Camp extension to be 'In the Public Interest'. 13,500 hectares (33,245 acres) would be acquired by the State for that purpose. The next day M. Sanguinetti of the Ministry of Defence, speaking to the Regional Council of the UDR [conservative political party], declared: 'If need be, expulsions will be carried out by force.' Fifteen to twenty thousand people gathered in Rodez on 14 July—French national day—and marched peacefully through the streets. There was a distinctly anti-militarist mood. Posters carried such slogans as 'Sheep not guns' or 'On the Larzac Debré wants to teach men to kill their brothers'. There were more than one hundred tractors—a striking answer to the Minister's assertion that only twenty farms were threatened by the extension.

The Preliminary Inquiry took place at the town hall of La Cavalerie between 16 and 30 October 1972. The whole procedure was carried out from start to finish in a highly irregular, not to say illegal, manner. Inhabitants of various parishes who wanted to object had to go to La Cavalerie to examine the files then return in person to deposit their complaints. Only two people at a time were allowed through the doors after checks by Officers of the Renseignements Gènèraux (Branch of the Police dealing with civilian intelligence). During the period the whole village was invaded by squadrons of mobile gendarmerie although there was no sign whatever of disturbances.

SHEEP GRAZE AT THE EIFFEL TOWER

During the Inquiry an action was carefully prepared in great secrecy by a few shepherds—like a commando raid, as one of them said. Sixty ewes, with 'Save the Larzac' marked on their fleece in blue dye, were loaded into a lorry and driven to the capital overnight. Contacts were waiting who alerted the press and the Broadcasting Corporation. The sheep began grazing on the Champ de Mars, the park at the foot of the Eiffel Tower, while the lorry was driven away. The shepherds were cheerful. When the Park Superintendent protested they pointed out the advantage of having sheep on his lawns: The grass was being cut and fertilized with natural manure—very expensive these days. The police wanted them to load their animals and go but the driver of the lorry 'must have gone away for a drink'. Eventually the lorry and its load was escorted out of the capital by police cars. On the same afternoon sheep appeared in Millau with SOS marked on their back. Both demonstrations were well reported in the press but nothing was shown on State-controlled television.

103 TREES

The Millau Municipal Council was expected to give its views to the Inquiry Commission, and on 27 October they met to consider a resolution which in effect asked the Government to create new employment and provide funds for improvements in the town. The peasants realized that the Mayor, M. Gabriac, and the Council were prepared to sacrifice the peasant families of the Larzac in return for promises which might not even be kept. The following day 103 Peasants gathered together to plant 103 pine trees to symbolize that they had roots on the Plateau and intended to stay.

In spite of all these efforts and overwhelming public support for the Larzac, the decree declaring the extension to be in the public interest was signed by the Prefect on 26 December ·1972. M. Debré announced it personally to the Senate. The three Inquiry Commissioners had been unanimous. They had merely ratified a decision already taken by their masters.

THE LONG MARCH

In the following ten days, arrangements were made. Twenty-six tractors with cabins were fitted out for the week-long journey to the capital. Each carried a panel with a symbolic fork entangled in barbed wire. Early in the morning of 7 January 1973 the convoy moved from the wintry sunshine of the Plateau down to fogbound Millau led by Elie Jonquet, fifty-nine, the eldest participant. They took a casket containing soil from the Larzac to be thrown into every river they were to cross. The column grew to seventy tractors since other peasants from the region insisted on accompanying their Larzac comrades. At Séverac-le-Chateau local supporters took over with their tractors. As they moved north it became a triumphant progress. Through the mountainous region of central France they were made particularly welcome by peasants who also had problems connected with the Government's neglect of their region. Everywhere along the route committees for the Defence of Larzac had worked hard to prepare for their reception. In the industrial city of Clermont-Ferrand people followed the tractor column through the streets; 2,500 people attended the evening meeting. At Nevers, M. Debatisse, President of the Federation of Farmers Unions declared his qualified support for the 103. 'Guard against being used for any other purpose than the defence of your own interests.' But the peasants in their talks to the public and statements to the press took quite a different line — the economy of the region and even disarmament were questions raised when they spoke of their struggle.

At Orleans a young Larzac peasant, Philippe Fauchot, from the collective farm of Les Beaumes, speaking to 4,000 people, said: 'I propose that real power should be given to the Regional Assemblies and that they should not merely have a consultative function which is always ignored. We cannot tolerate that the fate of the regions of

France should be entirely decided in the dusty offices of Paris — Yes to decentralization — Yes to federalism.'

The peasants were warned by officers of Civilian Intelligence that they would not be allowed to proceed further towards the capital. There was danger of traffic jams. Departure had been fixed for 5.30 a.m. Everyone was ready including the CRS (special Riot Police) who were blocking the entrance to the yard where the tractors were parked. Four hundred police were waiting in the streets. The peasants and local supporters decided to continue the march on foot. Headed by a band they marched out of Orleans accompanied by a large crowd. Local peasants on their tractors also joined them but the police stopped them from going any further. They were forced to go to Paris by train.

In Paris a large rally had been organized but was banned at the last minute by the police. However the object of the Long March had been achieved. The Authorities in the capital could be in no doubt as to the determination of the peasants to defend their land. A chain of support Committees all along the route had been tempered by their participation in the action and a further large number of people had been consciencized. 210,000 signatures had now been added to the Petition. Actions in support of the Larzac were taking place all over the country.

THE PEASANTS RETURN THEIR
MILITARY HANDBOOKS

For over two years the 103 had more or less kept within the law. Now a number of acts of civil disobedience were added to their repertory. About fifty peasants met at the Millau Post Office on 28 April 1973 to return their military handbooks which all conscripts are given when transferred to the Reserve. A letter was sent by each individual to explain his personal reasons for surrendering this document. These letters stated 'I do not want the Larzac to become a vast demonstration platform to show the people of the Third World the most efficient way to kill each other. It would be more honourable for France to teach and help them to live better and feed themselves better.' The peasants were prepared to take back their handbooks if the Government were to abandon all plans to extend the camp. Some sixty Larzac peasants returned their handbooks and similar actions were carried out by their supporters in different parts of the country. At Orleans twenty-one men, including eight priests, returned their documents and military medals. The peasants' documents were later sent back to them together with a letter explaining the gravity of the offence which might lead to withdrawal of civic rights. However, the handbooks were once again returned to the Minister with another protest letter.

BUILDING A NEW FARM

The 103 decided to build a new sheep farm or 'Bergerie' at the fourteenth century hamlet of La Blaquière. They visualized this project as a witness to the rightness of their cause and their determination to continue farming on the Plateau. Not surprisingly permission to build was refused by the Administration. The peasants went ahead. They raised money by donations and by selling Cement Coupons. Elie Jonquet, the oldest participant in the Long March to Paris stressed the symbolic nature of the action which was meant to preserve the land for peaceful uses. At the same time it would provide a living for two or three peasants who would run the farm on a collective basis. The 'Bergerie' was built of local stone in traditional style with stone arches to support the roof, a grain tower and a cistern. Throughout the summer volunteers from all over the country took turns at working on the site under the supervision of a skilled stone mason.

PEASANTS AND WORKERS:
LIP-LARZAC SAME STRUGGLE

In the course of their struggle the peasants were brought face to face with social and economic problems of other sections of society — industrial workers in particular with whom normally they have very little contact. A group of farmers were invited to the Samex factory in Millau. Samex is a firm which makes trousers. It employs 150 female workers, many of them very young, on a moving band production system. As a result of a speeding up of the production line and other unfair pressures the work force had gone

on strike with the support of their union. After a week the owner
had signed an agreement but at the same time, just before Easter
1972 he had sacked twenty-five of the women. The workers who had
occupied the factory premises now invited the farmers to come and
see for themselves. A farmer said afterwards, 'Very often we are led
to believe that working in a town is heaven. To us it appeared
frightening.' The following day they went round the farms
collecting food for the women. Peasants and workers realized that
their basic problems were the same in this neglected province: how
to retain their means of livelihood, improve conditions of work and
so remain in their own southern homeland.

A huge gathering of some 60,000 people took place on the
Plateau in August 1973. The initiative came from the Peasant-
Workers Movement, a left wing organization which defends the
interests of the small peasants. These are the peasants—the vast
majority—who have no capital and must rely on their work to make
a living. Like the Larzac peasants they receive no subsidies, they are
increasingly suffering loss of income and many are being forced off
the land. The big successful farmers on the other hand are financed
by the banks and the Government.

In their collaboration with the 103, the Peasant-Workers
Collective agreed to respect the nonviolent basis of the Larzac
struggle. Five rallying centres were arranged in different parts of
France. They took two days to make the journey, camping on the
way. Meetings had been arranged at appropriate halting places
where peasants are in conflict with the Authorities. The Western
March, for instance, starting from Brittany 800 strong, had grown
to 2,000 when they arrived near the military camp of Avon. The
peasants of the Avon-Fontrevault region have been resisting a take-
over of their land by the Army since 1956 and showed their
solidarity for the Larzac peasants from the start. The people from
the marches gathered on the Plateau on the Saturday evening at a
place called Rajal del Gorp—a kind of natural amphitheatre, a
spectacular ten-acre site dotted with bushes and strange shaped
rocks. This gathering brought together peasants and workers as
well as many people representing the nonviolent, Occitania, Left-
wing and Ecology movements. There was a strong contingent from
the Lip factory—a watch-making concern taken over by its workers
when about to be closed down, thus justifying one of the March's
slogans 'Lip-Larzac, same struggle'. Also present were delegations

from a number of nationalist movements: Breton, Basques, Reunion Islanders and even Northern Irishmen.

Each speaker saw the Larzac Battle as a symbol of the fight for justice and freedom. Antoine Richard, on behalf of the Peasant-Workers, said they would return to help the 103 if their land was expropriated. The Occitan representative accused the French state of 'the cultural genocide of a whole people who are rising up in socialism . . . It is by keeping the Larzac that we shall keep Occitania'. The workers of Romans, of Noguères, of Lip, the peasants of Fontevrault, of Nausac, all explained their particular struggle and stressed the importance of real solidarity between workers and peasants as expressed in this Festival. The last speaker, ex General La Bollardiere was just back from protesting at nuclear tests in Nururoa. He attacked French Defence policy and suggested nonviolent 'Combat' as an alternative. In the morning the forum continued and after lunch the whole crowd surged across the Plateau to the building site at La Blaquiere singing 'The Song of the Larzac'. The Lip workers left a present, a large clock, to be set in the wall of the Bergerie.

THE PLOUGHING OF UNCULTIVATED LAND

In the autumn the 103 mounted yet another imaginative action for which they were becoming famous. 460 landowners on the Plateau would have to give up their holdings if the camp were to be extended. Many of them were absentee owners who stood to gain a great deal since land values had risen considerably following the decision of the Government. People suspected that land speculators having inside information hoped to sell their holdings to the Government at inflated prices. One of the landowners M. Christian de la Malène, UDR deputy and former Minister had bought the Domaine of Baylet, 270 hectares of land within the parish of Nant in 1966. The 103 suddenly moved in on Friday 14 December and with the help of thirty tractors manured, ploughed, harrowed and sowed with rye a three hectares field which had lain fallow for many years. The whole operation was carried out in a day with great enthusiasm. It was also an occasion for a friendly get-together with a midday picnic under the shelter of a hedge around a large wood fire. The peasants stated to the press: '. . . This action does not constitute to our minds an attack on property. It should be interpreted as the will to restore value to land left uncultivated. Whilst many farmers cannot find land for themselves, whilst two-thirds of the World is undernourished, farmers like us cannot accept that land should deliberately be left lying fallow for speculative reasons . . .'

[As of the beginning of 1976, the extension has not been carried out. The army are still trying to influence public opinion and acquire the land. The farmers have so far been able to raise the money to buy what land has been offered for sale by some absentee owners, and they remain active in their campaign against extension of the camp.]

PART II

Nonpartisan national cases

5

INTERVENTION IN RIOTS IN INDIA*

NARAYAN DESAI

FOREWORD (BY A. PAUL HARE)

The problems faced by Indian society are real and require revolutionary solutions. The age-old inequalities in the social system persist: issues of caste, land tenure, cultural and religious strife. In September 1971 we saw the refugees, perhaps 8 million people, fleeing from an oppressive regime in East Bengal crowded into camps and makeshift shelters. A guerrilla force was operated in Bangla Desh, for months, but no political solution was in sight.

This series of essays by Narayan Desai provides a moving picture of the response of Gandhian workers to this revolutionary situation. It is a moving picture on two counts. First, the Shanti Sena (Peace Brigade) is continually developing new approaches and new responses in the face of a continually changing situation. Second, the thought and sight of men and women, with a great dedication to truth and a sense of love working towards a solution to these overwhelming problems, is moving indeed.

The process of revolution is usually assumed to require armed conflict. Power is presumed to grow only out of the barrel of the gun. Further, the violent struggle and the act of bringing down the old government and killing the leaders is thought to be liberating. 'The king must die' is an age-old cry. Some conflict between generations may always be present. But, unfortunately, the elimination of the old authority does not automatically ensure a new equalitarian society. A new tyrant may take the place of the old in the name of new slogans. Also the act of killing one's opponent is the ultimate form of dehumanization. One makes it clear that the opponent has no value for the new society and cannot possibly be

---

*Reprinted with permission from *Towards a Nonviolent Revolution*, Rajghat, Varanasi, India: Sarva Seva Sangh Prakashan, 1972, vii–ix, 29–48.

redeemed. The violent revolutionary is saying, in effect, 'I am not clever enough to change your mind, to win you over to the cause of the revolution, so I must kill you.'

Gandhi proposed a nonviolent revolution. It is based on two principles, *satya* (truth) and *ahimsa* (love). The search for the truth about human relationships includes not only what is true about the relationships between people today, but also what may be of people in the future when they have realized the new society. This new truth is to be found in concepts which provide more freedom for people than they presently enjoy; freedom to be more than masters or slaves, old or young, men or women. We see an example of the realization of this kind of truth at the end of the communal riots in Ahmedabad, described below, where Hindus and Muslims marched together shouting 'we may be Hindus and we may be Muslims, but we are all human beings'.

The principle of *ahimsa* is based on the assumption that love begets love and hostility begets hostility. Love also implies an equality in the relationships between the persons exchanging love. The person giving love demonstrates that he or she values the positive traits in other persons. The exchange of love provides the solidarity necessary for the new society to reach its goals.

Further, Gandhi stresses the importance of the relation between ends and means. Every revolutionary looks forward to peace in the new society but the violent revolutionary promotes a period of non-peace on the theory that only overt violence can sufficiently disrupt the old societal patterns. However, after the revolution, the violent revolutionary faces two tasks: (1) to overcome the destructive effect of violence and (2) to build the new peaceful society.

On contrast, the nonviolent revolutionary may still see a need to disrupt society, but the method of *satyagraha* is consistent with the goal of peaceful society. It can be used again if the social system becomes insensitive to the needs of the people. The nonviolent revolutionary is consistent in valuing human life *during* the revolution as well as *after* the revolution.

The Shanti Sena provides a cadre in the service of nonviolent revolution. Its approach includes turning violent conflict into nonviolent conflicts (as in the riot situations) and using protest for revolutionary change (as in *satyagraha*). In either event the task has just begun. The Shanti Sena continues to implement a programme for a new society that is based on a sense of the value of each individual, of equality in the control of community life, and of justice. The new society calls for a fair distribution of resources, direct and effective control of political processes by the people, appropriate distribution of leadership and other roles, and continuing process of combining the best of traditional values and culture with the search for truth.

The Shanti Sena emphasizes education and work with youth. Like all revolutionary groups, it looks to the youth to take up the vision and provide the energy to move forward towards the realization of the new society.

Narayan Desai, from his intimate association with ideas of Shanti Sena from its beginning and his intimate association with Gandhi, provides a unique perspective on the work of the movement. His accounts of Shanti Sainiks in riot situations, in rural communities and in relief work, provide vivid accounts of the many dimensions of nonviolent action. It is my hope that these accounts will inspire others to join in the work of the Shanti Sena to adopt these principles of nonviolent revolution to struggle for change in their own societies.

COMMUNAL RIOTS IN AHMEDABAD

Communal riots in Ahmedabad of September 1969 were the worst outburst of violence in a decade. They took toll of at least 2,000 lives and left stretches of urban Ahmedabad devastated by fire and rampage.

The tragedy of Ahmedabad provides an insight into the anatomy of communal riots.

First of all, there were the historical reasons. Although comparatively quiet during the intervening years, the city had two communal riots before independence. The nationalist Muslims, who had fought the communalists all their lives, were almost totally neglected after independence. What was worse, the communalist Muslims were admitted into the Congress, the ruling party. This had not only displeased the nationalist Muslims, but also enraged the Hindus. The Indo-Pak clash in the Runn of Kutch had inflamed some passions. The accidental death of Gujarat's Chief Minister during the war in 1965 provoked considerable communal fury. A right-wing Hindu party organized a statewide movement for the prohibition of cow-slaughter. It had its base at Ahmedabad. A large procession organized by the right-wing Muslims as a protest against the damage to the Al Aksa mosque in Palestine added some fuel to the fire.

With this background, Ahmedabad became a promising ground for the communalists. There was an inflammatory speech by a renowned Hindu political leader, who called himself a student of history. In the speech he suggested that the next attack on India from the Pakistan side would be along the Gujarat and Rajasthan borders. This gave some intellectual justification to the sense of insecurity and anger among Hindus.

Then there came two incidents of 'insulting religious books'. A police jeep seems to have hit a hawker of waste paper. Among the papers that tumbled down from his hand-pulled cart was a copy of the Holy Quran. There was resentment over this among the Muslim community and the police officer driving the jeep was immediately made to apologize. Soon after that, at a Hindu festival, a preacher was alleged to have been insulted by a Muslim police officer and the copy of the Ramayan from which the preacher was reciting on a microphone late in the evening, defying prohibitory orders to do so, was reported to have been trampled upon by the officer. No action was taken against this police officer until some Hindu monks went on a fast. The police officer was then dismissed. The Hindu majority thought that the delay in action was clearly an indication of the ruling party's partiality for Muslims.

The last straw came when at the Urs, a Muslim festival, some Sadhus pushing a herd of temple-cows through the crowd which had gathered for the Urs, had a row with some Muslims who were allegedly hurt by the startled cows. Some time after this incident, an angry mob of Muslims is said to have attacked the Jagannath temple, hurling rocks. There are many versions of this story. But, on the whole, it seems to be an incident of minor significance. No one was killed, nobody seriously injured, only the glass panes on the outside gaze of the temple were broken. Some leading Muslims of Ahmedabad apologized the next day. By then it was too late. The riots had broken out.

There seemed to be a pattern in the riots: history —rumours—first wave of attack, stray incidents of violence —second wave, immediate repercussions—third wave.

Rumours grew in intensity as they went on inflaming the situation. They started when some Hindus said that the attack on the temple was intended to dishonour the whole Hindu community. Then they said the temple cows were killed. Later on, it was given out that the Sadhus were killed and the temple images demolished and desecrated.

The rumours flourished even during the riots. Only they were much more rabid. Everything that was said was not only believed but rapidly exaggerated as it passed from mouth to mouth. The rumours which went well with the riots were of a different type. They said women had been molested and that there was large scale killing by Muslims on the other side of the city.

Parties of miscreants went round the city on foot, on scooters, in jeeps and in private cars, spreading these rumours. Of course, there was not the slightest truth in them. But the city, already scared, was prepared to believe almost anything. Some illegal pamphlets were published giving room to poisonous propaganda. A leading daily newspaper came out with a baseless story that women's breasts were cut in an area which was predominantly Muslim. The next day the Government compelled the newspaper to publish a denial of this news. But the damage was done. Indeed Muslim women were molested by members of wild mobs before the denial could be published in the newspaper.

Even the Government publicity machinery fell prey to the rumours. In one instance, there was a strong rumour in one part of the city that poison had been mixed in the milk supplied by Muslims. Unmindful of the fact that milk supplied to the city came from a thousand different sources and not one centralized dairy, the Ahmedabad station of All India Radio broadcast a warning asking the citizens not to drink milk. They did not have the balance of mind to remember the fact that a majority of the milk suppliers of Ahmedabad were Hindus! Needless to say that the fury of the mobs increased after this 'official' spread of rumours.

Violence increased from stage to stage in the first three waves of attack. Throngs of people went about from shop to shop and broke their locks. Another throng broke the bolted doors and entered the shops to plunder and ravage. In some places, the first wave of attack ended with arson. Several areas of the city were ablaze. The whole night the bewildered city watched the blood-red sky and listened to the pathetic screams of wretched innocent human beings.

The second stage began where the first had left off half-finished. The loot was more thorough, arson more widespread. The attacks were not restricted to shops and stray houses. Areas inhabited by the Muslim community were attacked on a mass scale.

It was at this second stage that the Special Reserve Police was called in by Government. It used force to disperse the crowds but not with much success.

The third wave of violence was the climax of the tragedy. Arson, looting, killings and assault on women went on in full fury. Whole areas of the city and some suburbs were turned into wreckage overnight. There were killings on a big scale. Some parts of the city looked like having been bombed in a war. The hospitals swelled with patients with serious injuries as also with dead bodies. Thousands of people were rendered homeless. Many were killed on the outskirts of the city while trying to escape.

The military was called at this stage. It took some time to decide who was really responsible for the maintenance of law and order — the civil authority or the military. This indecision gave the hooligans more time for their acts of cruelty.

Stray violence followed this stage of riots. There were incidents of stabbings and occasional explosions of bombs. But on the whole, the violence at this stage was more verbal than physical.

Ahmedabad did not have a well-organized Shanti Sena unit when the riots broke out in the city. So the few Shanti Sainiks who were scattered in the city functioned individually and tried to intervene, risking their lives in trying to save marooned people. Two days after the riots broke out, Shanti Sainiks started pouring into Ahmedabad from various parts of Gujarat. They tried to work in a planned way.

Relief and rehabilitation posed arduous problems. Shanti Sainiks went round the city, visiting one riot-affected area after another. They got acquainted with the problems and tried to find out ways of restoring normalcy. They went to the 'camps' organized by Government and also to places where non-official individuals and agencies had organized relief work.

Shanti Sainiks found that by far the majority of the people affected were poor slum dwellers. Some landowners and pro-prietors of houses did not want these poor sufferers to return to their original dwellings, in order to extract higher house-rents from newcomers. They found that there was no feeling of repentance for their misdeeds among the majority community. In fact, many of them rejoiced on having had a chance to teach the minority a good lesson. Shanti Sainiks saw that the younger generation in each community had become more hostile towards the other. The older generation, especially leaders among the old, was in a state of helplessness. Political leaders seemed to view everything with the coming elections in mind. Each party was laying the blame on all the others. The representatives of the State and Central governments, representing two different parties, also seemed to be at loggerheads with each other, trying to prove that the other had created a mess.

It was in this chaotic condition that the Shanti Sena started functioning in an organized way. At the call of Shanti Sena, batches of students from several Gandhian Ashrams in Gujarat joined hands to work for peace. These batches went to the riot-affected areas as volunteer-squads, removing debris and cleaning up the localities. They stayed in the riot-affected areas along with their professors. They called on the people in the neighbourhood, held discussions with them on the need to restore goodwill and followship. The volunteers worked from five to six hours a day, cleaning the debris.

Another batch of Shanti Sainiks concentrated on the re-habilitation programme. They went from house to house, trying to persuade the people to invite the riot-affected people to return and settle in their midst again. This was a difficult job in the beginning. But once the tide turned, it no longer remained difficult. Leaders of the Hindu community were persuaded to visit the camps of the displaced persons and invite them back home. Public functions were organized for their return. Local leaders vouchsafed for their security. Gradually the Muslims started to return. Such functions were organized in seven or eight localities.

For the other victims new houses had to be built. Government set up a special machinery for relief and rehabilitation. Officers were appointed to look after relief and rehabilitation. Shanti Sainiks worked hand in hand with these officers in dealing with the problems: the victims were to be persuaded to go and stay in the newly built houses; contractors were to be goaded to work more efficiently and more honestly; ministers and senior officers were to be persuaded to be more liberal in giving aid.

With the advent of winter Shanti Sena started collecting and distributing blankets for the victims. It was a measure not only of relief but of public education. Every donor in Ahmedabad had to be convinced about the need of communal harmony before he gave his eleven rupees for a blanket. Although the association of merchants in Ahmedabad was not in a mood to donate money for relief work, many members of their association were personally persuaded by Shanti Sainiks to contribute blankets. Some mill owners produced in their factories blankets according to our specifications.

Distribution of blankets was not an easy job. Ahmedabad had many pavement-dwellers. They would easily pass off as refugees and lay a claim on the blankets distributed by Shanti Sena. There were some among the riot-victims who would deprive their fellow victims of their rightful blanket in order to secure one more for their own family. There had to be some scrutiny prior to distribution. Shanti Sainiks went from camp to camp, making a survey of every family. It was only after every member of the family had been counted that 'slips' were issued for blankets. The office of Shanti Sena was crowded with refugees with slips for blankets.

One of the most difficult tasks of Shanti Sena was the rehabilitation of women. Estimates varied as to the number of women widowed during the riots. The government had announced a grant of 1,000 rupees for each woman who lost her husband during the riots. Though the problem of widowed women was on the lips of every social worker, few actually did anything for them. The backwardness of Muslim women and the dearth of women volunteers among Muslims was the chief reason for this neglect.

But Shanti Sena could mobilize women workers from all communities. Unfortunately, this aroused jealousy among some relief organizations. They tried to see that Shanti Sena did not succeed. Day after day, Shanti Sainiks had to hunt for and locate a house to keep the widows in a transit camp. Each time a house was selected for this purpose, there were telephone calls from some sources which managed to persuade the owners of the house not to let it to Shanti Sena.

Finally, Shanti Sena was able to form a committee of women for this purpose, get a house on rent, collect over a hundred widows and claim the money for them and see them settled. This was, perhaps, the greatest single act of pity in the relief activity.

A word must also be said about politics in the relief activity. The part that party-politics played in the relief activities was shocking. The party workers seemed to be more concerned about undoing the work of the other parties rather than achieving something positive on behalf of their own parties. Being a non-party organization, Shanti Sena had the consolation of enjoying lip sympathy from all parties!

Besides the relief and rehabilitation programme, the important need of the day was to work for the psychological rehabilitation of Hindus. The riots had perturbed the minds of the people and surcharged them with hatred. Shanti Sena strove to change this atmosphere into one of goodwill and mutual trust. House to house contacts, group discussions and street corner meetings were organized to educate the people on this issue.

A special activity of Shanti Sena was the publication of a bi-weekly pamphlet. It was called *Insan*, meaning a human being. The *Insan* tried to answer all the questions asked of Shanti Sainiks. It became a popular periodical. Many newspapers in Gujarat reprinted articles from *Insan* regularly. Some individuals got more copies printed and distributed them in their localities. College students volunteered to distribute copies of *Insan* in the town. Some of the boys who volunteered thus were among those who had participated in the violent activities. In a way they took up a penance for their misdeeds by giving their time for the distribution of these pamphlets.

At various places in the city, writing on wall-boards was started under the title of 'Ektane Panthe' — out the way to harmony [the road to create unity] Some young volunteers took upon themselves the responsibility to write messages of human brotherhood on these boards.

Thanks to the effort and inspiration of Shanti Sena, Id, a Muslim festival, celebrations were held in which people of all communities joined. Similarly, on 24 December which was Khan Abdul Gaffar Khan's birthday, 'Insani Biradari Day' was observed as the day for human fellowship.

One of the long term programmes of Shanti Sena was the economic rehabilitation of hawkers and petty traders who had lost the wherewithals for their profession. Shanti Sena arranged with a local bank to give them small loans and guaranteed repayment of the loans. Shanti Sena in Ahmedabad had earmarked some money for this purpose, fearing that not much of the money, loaned by the bank, may be repaid by the riot victims. But their experience belied the fear. Each month the hawkers and traders came to the office of Shanti Sena to repay their debt in instalments. This encouraged Shanti Sena to begin a programme of giving employment to more people. This programme, however, had to be limited to a few people owing to dearth of funds.

Another interesting programme of education was that of week-end camps on the communal problem for young men and women. It was organized in different localities. We began with camps for our volunteers first, but extended our activities to the local people. Some of the camps were for mixed participants, while the others were either predominantly Hindu or predominantly Muslim camps. The 'living together' techniques[1] of Shanti Sena training had its own healing effect on minds that were geared with hatred and anger.

Meeting the intellectuals and the student community in clubs, colleges and hostels was part of the educative programme of Shanti Sena.

Visits by Jayaprakash Narayan, Khan Abdul Gaffar Khan and other leaders helped considerably in easing the tensions.

The formal activities of Shanti Sena were concluded in Ahmedabad after four months of work, on 30 January. A week before that, a large-scale house-to-house contact programme was organized during which Shanti Sena was able to enlist the services of a thousand volunteers who were willing to give time for peace activities. This was an indication of the change of attitude among the people of Ahmedabad. But it must, however, be admitted that Shanti Sainiks in Ahmedabad were not able to mobilize the services of these 1,000 volunteers for some regular peace activity. Finding some follow-up programmes is still a problem that Shanti Sena has not been able to solve satisfactorily.

On 30 January, six large processions were organized in the larger part of the city. All the processions assembled at a central place and turned into a public meeting to observe the death anniversary of Gandhi as a Peace Day. The processionists shouted: 'We may be Hindus, we may be Muslims, but above all, we are human beings.' That was a new ray of hope in Ahmedabad after those dreadful days. It was a heartening sight to see thousands of Muslim women join the processions.

1969 was the year of Gandhi's birth centenary. Communal riots

in Ahmedabad, a place where Gandhi had worked for over twenty
years, was a blot on the Gandhi Centenary celebrations. Shanti
Sena, in its own humble way, tried, to rinse away that stain.
Ahmedabad tried to offer penance for its misdeeds by this act of
amity on Gandhi's death anniversary.

IN THE RIOT TORN
TOWN OF BHIVANDI

Till recently, the citizens of Bhivandi were proud of its record of
unbroken communal harmony, both before and after independence, despite its mixed population. 'We used to take tea
from each other's cup', they said, 'and celebrated each other's
festivals. Even when Bombay had violent communal riots for weeks
together, our town, situated at a distance of about 50 kilometres,
enjoyed perfect fellowship'.

What were the factors that altered this picture so drastically,
changing the town into a devastated desert of all human feelings?

It had been the accumulated result of the past few years; when a
number of socio-economic and political changes combined to
dehumanize the town. For one thing, the population of the town
shot up by almost 200 per cent within the last decade, bringing with
it a new population of industrial workers and similar other
'immigrants', who could not possibly share the spirit of fellowship
that the old community enjoyed. This was coupled with strong
economic competition between communities and classes. During
the last couple of years some communal tension was also felt, but
actual outburst of violence was avoided by several efforts of
conscious 'peace making', including the formation of a citizens'
peace committee, which, though well known for its frank-speaking
in the initial stages, was gradually waning in its influence until it
was revived again, somewhat sceptically and distrustfully,
immediately before the recent riots. There were complaints of
communal elements on both sides preaching hatred and violence.
The younger generation on each side was getting more and
more polarized. The RSS [a Hindu body], the Tamire Millat [a
Muslim body] and the Shiva Sena along with some local counter-
parts were said to be more active in these activities. Provocative
speeches both by Muslim and Hindu leaders were said to be

increasingly aggressive during recent months. 'Avenge Ahmedabad' and 'Don't trust the Muslims' seem to have been the chief slogans of the rival leadership.

The immediate reasons of the riot are better known than the hidden ones. The 'divide and rule' policy of the British had succeeded in creating two contradictory images of Shivaji among the Hindus, and the Muslims. To the Maharastrian Hindus Shivaji represented the spirit of noble nationalism; to the Muslims, a majority of whom have immigrated from Western Uttar Pradesh within the last century, his name was more associated with the Shiva Sena than anything else. The peace committee very carefully planned the celebration of Shivaji's birthday, but the very fact of careful planning suggests the knowledge of the impending danger on both the sides. The route of the procession was decided and altered. The actual slogans to be allowed during the procession were agreed upon and it was on the non-adherance to these 'rules' that the actual trouble broke out. A group of young men was arrested for shouting provocative slogans, but was soon released after the young men apologized. But when the procession entered the Muslim Machhi Market area, pro-Hindu provocative slogans were raised again. Soon after that, there was stone-throwing on the procession, presumably by the Muslims, which resulted in the dispersal of the procession. When some of the people returned home, they saw their houses in flames. The political meetings, the political procession, and the slogan shoutings seemed to be deliberate, and the stone-throwing and the arson was so perfectly timed that it leaves little doubt in one's mind that the whole affair was pre-planned. A major part of the damage was done on the night of 7 May.

When a batch of Shanti Sainiks arrived from Bombay, they witnessed a sight that reminded them of the mythological story of Lankadahan. It was a matter of some satisfaction to see a batch of about fifteen Shanti Sainiks assembled spontaneously at Bhivandi from various parts of Maharashtra on the ninth. No orders were issued to them to go to Bhivandi. They had all gathered there voluntarily, presuming that it was their duty to be present where there is violation of peace.

The first technical problem that the Shanti Sainiks faced was that of the curfew order. They could not move about the town without obtaining the necessary passes. They had to wait for a day before obtaining the passes. On an average about twenty-five Shanti Sainiks worked in Bhivandi for ten days, five among whom were women volunteers. Most of the Shanti Sainiks had come from Bombay and other parts of Maharashtra.

The Shanti Sainiks were among those very few who walked about the streets of Bhivandi in every section of the town. The camp of the Shanti Sena was in the compound of Shri Hafiz Kuddus, a factory owner of Bhivandi, who had given shelter to about five hundred Muslim refugees, besides giving accommodation to the Shanti Sena. In the surcharged atmosphere of communal distrust the fact that the Shanti Sainiks, a majority of whom were Hindus, were staying in a Muslim gentleman's compound, in the vicinity of five hundred Muslim refugees and many more Muslims living nearby, was itself a phenomenon that people in Bhivandi were surprised to hear. 'Do your women volunteers also stay there?' the Hindus asked. 'Where else could they stay?' was our answer. In fact it was our experience that the women volunteers were sometimes more courageous than the men volunteers.

What the Shanti Sainiks saw during their first visits around the town was something like the pictures they had seen of war-torn cities. Furlongs and furlongs of streets were literally strewn with broken glasses of window panes and sodawater bottles, used freely on the previous nights. Dozens of houses were still smouldering on the fourth and fifth days after the riots. The smoke continued for about a fortnight in some of the burnt houses. Some of the slum areas were completely razed to the ground by fire. The debris of powerloom factories were lying exposed like the intestines of dead animals wrenched by vultures. A huge pile of decomposed dead bodies was lying stinking in the compound of the government hospital. Over one-third of the population had become 'refugees' in their own town. Rows and rows of Telugu 'immigrant' labourers were waiting day and night for some truck to pass by in order to give them a lift to places where, they hoped, they could have better shelter.

But this was only the outside appearance. Although this scene was dreadful enough, what the Shanti Sainiks could perceive in the minds of the people was even more abominable. The first thing that struck them was the fear on both sides. Rumours spread like wild fire thriving on the psychology of fear. Sometimes, the Shanti Sainiks would see hundreds of people rushing out with lathis, iron bars, soda-water bottles and acid bulbs, just because somebody had come crying from the adjoining street where people of the other community lived. Once at about 1.45 a.m. a group of women and children came running and shrieking, complaining that they had seen hordes of people armed with lethal weapons coming in the direction of the refugee camp with an evident view to attack it. 'Look, one of the women actually had her forehead cut with a spade,' complained another person weeping. The Special Reserve Police were alerted and some of them came running, loading their guns. 'Let us go and see the place from which the hordes are said to be approaching' said two women volunteers of the Shanti Sena and immediately started towards that direction. They were accompanied by a couple of men volunteers only to return after a few minutes finding no sign of any horde anywhere. In the meanwhile, it was found that the woman who had her forehead cut, had it, not from the spade of the attackers, but from a fall while rushing in alarm towards the camp. The whole idea of attack by an armed horde was found to be completely imaginary, born out of fear.

Apart from fear — prejudice, distrust and wrath seemed to have totally possessed the minds of the people. The minds of the younger generation on both sides were evidently more polarized, and they expressed their feelings in a more uncontrolled way. Only among the older generation there were a few exceptions who were ashamed to see all that had happened in their town, but who were feeling helpless about the situation. Both the sides were unanimous in their opinion that the riots were not merely accidental, but preconceived and preplanned. Of course, both the sides laid the blame on the other community for all that had happened.

One of the first things that the Shanti Sainiks did was to go from house to house and listen to what people had to say about the ugly incident. Some of us went to see the leaders of both communities, while the rest made house to house contacts.

This was accompanied by some service activity immediately needed in the town. The first thing that came to the minds of the Shanti Sainiks was the disposal of the decomposed dead bodies, which were making the whole atmsophere unbearable with their stink. But the District Collector, Shri Kapoor, suggested that he would be satisfied if we could give him information about the dead bodies lying within or outside the municipal limits. 'While you will need transport for the disposal of the dead bodies, we may be able to do the job more easily with the trucks at our disposal,' said Shri Kapoor. 'But giving information about dead bodies lying in remote areas, where you alone can go, is something our administration cannot do.' This was not to please the Shanti Sainiks. It was a statement of facts. For while the people hesitated in giving information to the police or the CRP (central reserve police), fearing that they might be involved in some legal procedures, they could inform the Shanti Sainiks without any such apprehensions. One of the difficult service activities taken up by the Shanti Sena was the cleaning of municipal gutters. The functioning of the Municipality had almost come to a standstill for a few days. Almost all the gutters of the town were overflowing, owing to the obstructions caused by the scraps of broken buildings and the dead bodies of animals etc. Even for a person like me, who is used to cleaning gutters and latrines, it was difficult to bear the stink of the Bhivandi gutters. But I was delighted to notice that this work was taken up in all earnestness by the Shanti Sena volunteers, some of whom were completely strangers to such activities. When the Shanti Sainiks started cleaning and scavenging, the closed doors of nearby houses opened slowly and men, women and children offered their co-operation. Although strictly speaking, these people were not supposed to come out of their houses, because of the curfew order, the guards standing by were persuaded to waive that order temporarily, in order to allow these people to help. Over 300 people came out to help, and even when the Shanti Sena went ahead, they continued the work, sprinkling water on the road and giving the last finishing touches. The scavenging team had a mixed experience in some of the Hindu 'addas' of the town. The roads there were comparatively cleaner, as people living there had already done some cleaning beforehand. While some young men volunteered to join us in our sanitation activities, others started moving by our sides announcing their views such as: 'Oh, the Shanti Sena. It's a Gandhi Sena and it was Gandhi who brought doom to our nation.' While those young men who had joined scavenging tried to argue with these misinformed youths, enquiring what harm these Shanti Sainiks had done to them—after all, they were only cleaning their gutters—the Shanti Sainiks chose to continue the work silently. While the Shanti Sena was cleaning the gutter in a Muslim area, some young Muslims who had joined the group of Shanti Sainiks in the cleaning had accompanied them to the Hindu area. One of them was recognized by the Hindu young men who protested against his being in their locality. The Shanti Sainiks did not want to irritate the Hindus, but at the same time they did not want to insult the Muslim who had joined them voluntarily. They, therefore, told the crowds that the Muslim boys would return with the Shanti Sainiks as soon as the work was finished there. Luckily for the Shanti Sainiks, there was not much time left before the work came to an end and this saved the situation.

A batch of Shanti Sainiks had taken up the work of distributing rations to those rendered homeless. Another batch took up the work of giving medical aid in the refugee camps. Four doctors from Bombay had offered their help to the Shanti Sena.

Yet another activity of the Shanti Sena was to write slogans on public places, slogans that would help promote harmony. Within a day or two, almost all public places of Bhivandi were covered with neatly painted slogans of 'Mazhab Nahin Sikhata Aapasmen Bair Rakhana', or 'Hindu Ho Ya Musalman, Sabse Pahle Hai Insan'. ('Religion does not teach animosity' and 'we may be Hindus and we may be Muslims but first of all we are human beings.') Of course, there was some resistance, even to these wall writings, but it was insignificant.

Almost every day, the Shanti Sainiks had to spend sleepless nights, trying to reduce the feeling of fear from the people. During the days some of the Shanti Sainiks went to nearby villages to see how the mentality of the villagers worked. The Shanti Sainiks who went there were painfully surprised to find that systematic rumour mongering was done by some miscreants. It has been the unfortunate observation of this writer that there is a regular pattern in the rumour mongering at the time of several communal riots. The Shanti Sainiks did indeed try to expose the lie by telling the villagers what they knew as facts after moving about in every part of Bhivandi town, but their efforts were not sufficient to dispel the mischief. They felt that the machinery of the government should have been much more effective in fighting rumours.

The team that met the leadership in Bhivandi found that the best way of restoring normalcy was to create an opportunity for leaders of both the communities to meet and have a frank discussion. The confidence in the former peace committee was lost and the new committee set up for relief activity was not considered to be the right platform for a meeting like this. There was no other forum where Hindus and Muslims of Bhivandi could meet. But the Shanti Sena had an idea regarding this which was generally welcomed. It suggested that names of leading personalities of one community should be invited from members of the other community. We were able to collect the names of about ten persons from each community after some initial difficulties. One of the decisions of this meeting was that each person present would take the responsibility to maintain peace in one's own street, when the curfew order would be relaxed the next day.

Relaxation of the curfew order marked happy scenes of inter-community meeting on the streets of Bhivandi. Long queues of Hindus and Muslims touching each other's shoulders were witnessed waiting for their turn for the purchase of day-to-day requirements. The relaxation order, initially meant to be for three hours in the morning was extended for another couple of hours. This fact itself restored a lot of confidence.

The dark clouds of these riots too were not without their silver linings. Negatively speaking, one of the good things about the riots was that no complaint was heard about assault on women from any side. Positively, there were several incidents of Hindus and Muslims saving each others lives, sometimes risking their own. The action of the District Collector, Shri Kapoor, after the riots was exemplary. He had himself sustained injuries facing crowds boldly. Day and night you could see Shri Kapoor walking in the streets of Bhivandi or visiting the villages, knowing no fatigue. Although his heart was full of agony seeing the devastation of Bhivandi; he would not budge an inch from what he considered to be the principle of secularism regarding the adoption of a policy in relief activities. He flatly refused any relief articles to be distributed on communal basis. 'I know of only one community, the distressed; and the whole of it shall share whatever relief articles arrive from outside the town.' Remembering the fate of unofficial relief activity in Ahmedabad, dividing itself into rival groups of communal and of party interests, I admired the strength of Shri Kapoor in adhering to such a strict policy. (For further thoughts on communal riots see Appendix III [of Desai, 1972]).

REFERENCE

Desai, Narayan, 1972. Towards a Non-Violent Revolution. Rajghat, Varanasi, India: Sarva Seva Sangh Prakashan.

NOTE

1. See [Chapter 5 of Desai, 1972].

6

FRIENDLY PRESENCE*

LYLE TATUM

This report is an attempt to set down for the record and for study the operation of the Quaker Team at the Plenary Conference of the Revolutionary Peoples Constitutional Convention, hereafter called the Conference, held in Philadelphia, 4–7 September 1970. The Team attempted to play a third-party role in the interest of peacekeeping in a potentially explosive community situation.

The Conference was national in scope and was initiated by the Black Panthers. Friends recognized that a large Conference sponsored by the Black Panthers was apt to be a tension-producing event. A few Friends started meeting together on their own to brainstorm ideas for the use of nonviolent techniques to ease tension or intervene nonviolently in crisis situations arising at the Conference.

At about the same time, a Philadelphia police-officer was killed by Black militants in an unprovoked incident. Using possible Black Panther relationships (still unproved as this is written) as an excuse, Philadelphia police raided Black Panther headquarters in various parts of the city resulting in gunfire and police injuries. A number of Panthers were jailed. Tensions mounted.

THE PLAN

The ad hoc group of Friends — hereafter called the Quaker Team or just the Team, although that term did not come into use until later in the project — were concerned about finding a creative approach to easing tensions. The Team included a number of Philadelphia Yearly Meeting Peace Committee staff and committee members. The Peace Committee office began servicing the group. Just before the Conference, the Emergency Committee of Representatives Meeting approved the Quaker Team Project as an official

*A Quaker Peacekeeping Project. Philadelphia: Friends Peace Committee, 1970 (Duplicated).

Philadelphia Yearly Meeting Action.

Although a number of organizations other than Panthers were participating in the Conference and a number of community groups in addition to the police were hostile to the Conference, the Panthers and the police were seen as antagonists whose interaction might produce violence at the Conference. The Team decided to get as many people as possible at the Conference to serve in a third-party role. In event of a crisis, Team members would at least observe intently in order to help build a record in court or the press or elsewhere as to exactly what happened. At the maximum it was expected that Members might intervene with their bodies in a crisis.

A number of organizations were represented at weekly meetings where support for the Conference was planned and accomplishments for support, largely in housing and feeding an expected 5,000 attenders, were cleared. These were a combination of some peace-oriented groups and some left-oriented political action groups, in addition to Panthers and others who were more active in the Conference itself. The Team started sending observers to this group. It was thought that this might be a place to discuss possible Quaker Team activities but the judgement of those attending for the Team was otherwise on the spot, so the project was never discussed within that setting.

The project was discussed with individual Panther leaders in an attempt at least to be certain that the project was to be tolerated by the Panthers, if not welcomed, at the Conference. In the final confusion of Panthers going to jail as result of police raids, no official clearance by the Panthers was ever given the Team, but the conversations seeking clearance indicated that the Panthers would at least not object to the Team.

In planning for the project, there was a great deal of discussion about just what the Team would be doing in the field. Should they be identified? If identified did they need to have some visible excuse for being present? Was a badge saying 'Observer' sufficient? It was decided that a visible service for Conference attenders would not violate the concept of the third-party role. It was decided to give out information, primarily on getting around Philadelphia, and drinking water as services in addition to observing the unfolding of events.

Consensus was never reached on method, purpose and degree of identification of Team members. Individual judgement ruled in the field, and identification varied from bright red umpire vests to armbands, both of which were provided by the project. A few Team members went without public identification, other than name badges all were asked to wear. Red and black Quaker relief stars which were supposed to identify members of the unnamed body serving as an executive committee saw little use. Each participant was expected to have an identifying letter from the Yearly Meeting. It was thought this might prove helpful in case of questions by police or perhaps others. No need developed for these letters.

Identical letters were sent to the Mayor of Philadelphia, with a carbon copy to the Police Commissioner, and to the Black Panthers, reporting that the Friends Peace Committee (the Yearly Meeting had not yet approved the project) was concerned about the confrontation between the police and the Panthers and the resulting violence and that it was planned to have about 100 Friends observing at the Conference. 'At a minimum we would hope to be in a position to give the public objective reports on the activities on all the parties in and about the Conference.' Neither letter was acknowledged by the recipients.

Philadelphia Yearly Meeting issued a press release on its letterhead the day before the Conference opened. This was a single page, spelling out the third-party role a bit more than the letter to the police and Panthers. One radio station and one TV station interviewed the co-ordinator as a result of the press release. There were no news stories previous to reports on the Conference in action. In these stories, the Quaker Team received brief mention.

On 1 September, the Peace Committee mailed a recruitment flyer to selected persons asking for help on 4, 5, and 6 September 1970. Recruitment was also done by telephone. Those participating were asked to attend briefing sessions on either the afternoon or evening of the fourth. The flyer pointed out that 'We are specifically NOT asking everyone or the young or untrained or hotheaded, etc. . . . Frankly this could be a *difficult, even dangerous assignment.* Everyone is at his own risk. It is also an opportunity.'

The flyer asked for 100 Friends, a number brashly given to the police and Panthers as the number of participants expected. Everyone's fingers were crossed about the 100 Friends showing up—with no notice—to volunteer time over a three-day weekend. The morale of the project received a big boost when about 200

Friends showed up. The group included a large number of Friends who were active in their own Monthly Meeting and the Yearly Meeting. More than half the Team members were over forty years of age.

THE ACTION

The action started with a briefing session Friday afternoon and evening. These sessions were planned by the nonviolent training staff of the Peace Committee. These sessions were called briefing rather than training because the time was too short for real training. Nevertheless, some techniques were used which would have been part of a training session. Most of the time was spent on factual briefing, discussion about the Conference, the role of the Team, tactics for some possible violent situations, and some suggested 'rules of thumb' in action situations.

Yearly Meeting headquarters at 4th and Arch Streets was made available for the Conference participants to sleep, and kitchen privileges were also given. This was an action apart from the Quaker Team concept but became interwoven with the Team activity as the Team also used the Arch Street Meeting House and assigned Team members to help and observe at 4th and Arch. Although it had been suggested to the Conference that 200 was a maximum number for sleeping at Arch Street, there were 250 inside and 125 on the lawn Saturday night. Fortunately, the weather stayed good.

Quaker actions around the Conference but unrelated to the Quaker Team which are not evaluated or outlined further in this report include facilities at Germantown Friends School and Friends Neighborhood Guild for sleeping, 1515 Cherry Street, used for Conference workshops Saturday afternoon, and the posting of bail by the Yearly Meeting for a Panther leader just before the Conference started.

Participants received a mimeographed map of the 49-block area [about a square kilometre] in which most of the Conference actually would take place. This was also, of course, the area with the highest potential for crisis. Within the area were: McGonigle Hall, The Temple University building which was the main centre of activity all day Saturday; Messiah College, field headquarters for the

Quaker Team; the Panther Medical Centre, originally seen as a secondary Quaker Team field headquarters; the Church of the Advocate, Conference headquarters, and the District Police station. The map showed the location and gave the numbers of thirty-six pay telephones in the area, where the Team members could phone in communications. Phone numbers were also listed for the Arch Street Meeting House, Messiah College and the Peace Committee office which served as the nominal headquarters for the Team.

Leadership of the Team activities was built around key points on the map. George Willoughby directed duty assignments for participants and related work at Messiah College. Charles Walker was stationed at McGonigle Hall and served as field director. George Hardin shared with Chris Moore responsibilities for the Peace Committee office, where telephones were managed for twenty-four hours per day, as they were at Messiah and Arch Street. Lyle Tatum served as co-ordinator and chaired the twice daily 'executive committee' meetings responsible for policy. Ross Flanagan, who played a leading role in instigating the project, and Chris Meyer served as roving field observers and trouble shooters. All of the above named were members of the executive committee. Executive committee meetings were unannounced and at irregular times so that few of the Team members attended.

Duty assignments for Team members were divided into tables, patrols, stations and transportation. There were two tables outside of McGonigle Hall and one on a part-time basis at the Church of the Advocate. The table at the church was managed whenever large groups of Conference participants were there, perhaps half of the time. The church was Conference headquarters for registration, and some meetings were held there. There were always at least three Team members on duty at each table. Water and SEPTA [public transportation] travel maps were at each table. Aspirin tablets, salt tablets, and bandaids were also available, although major first aid was being handled by another group. Each table had a sign saying 'Aid and Info.' Most Team members at the tables wore red vests. The services at the tables were used extensively by the Conference participants. The tables were the only visible evidence of the Team at the Conference.

The patrols were Team members assigned in pairs to be about the business of observing. Some of them had cameras and tape recorders, although these were seldom used. Some were highly visible and some unmarked. Some attended Conference sessions and some were always walking through the city streets around the area. The number of patrols at any one time varied according to the number of Team members available. Patrols reported back to Charles Walker at a Team table at McGonigle Hall.

The stations included Messiah College, Arch Street Meeting House, Peace Committee office and the Panther-operated Mark Clark Medical Center. Team members were on duty twenty-four hours per day at all four places. The Medical Center had been expected to be an important field operation point, but there was no telephone there, and efforts to get one installed were unsuccessful. The Panthers had reported that they had a doctor for the Center, but none showed up. With no telephone and no doctor, the Center was relatively inactive, although there were some first-aid referrals.

Messiah College, strategically located in the centre of things and with a staff joining wholeheartedly into the mission of the Team, became the nerve centre of the entire operation. Assignments were recorded and distributed, needs voiced and met, space for rest provided, pickup meals set up, executive committee meetings held there, etc.

The Arch Street Meeting House was a secondary field station outside of the main geographic area of Conference activities but important because of the large number of Conference participants staying there. Workshops were also held there, and tables were set up by some Conference groups for literature distribution. Team members assisted building staff, answered the telephones, gave out information, policed the no-smoking rule, etc.

The Peace Committee office was listed as headquarters on the press release and was responding to press inquiries before the Conference started. With three telephone lines and being outside the area of Conference activity, it held a high potential for usefulness in case of serious community violence around the Conference. In practice, it was largely a place where new recruits to the Team could call for information. It also was somewhat of a clearing house for transportation needs.

The transportation team had two or three cars with drivers available at all times. They moved personnel or supplies to and between the various stations, stood by for emergency needs and provided additional ambulance services for medical teams on the spot.

The estimate of 5,000 attenders made in advance by the Panthers was probably fairly accurate, although as always, the numbers game by police, newspapers, Conference participants, etc. brought varying estimates, this time from 3,000 to 10,000. There were obviously a good many more than the 4,500 seats available in McGonigle Hall, causing some congestion and minor difficulties there.

The crowd, perhaps seventy per cent Black and thirty per cent White, came in a peaceable mood. The Panthers obviously wanted a peaceful Conference and kept tight security procedures, including searching all attenders each time they entered McGonigle Hall for Plenary sessions. Even fingernail files were held to be reclaimed on leaving the Hall.

The police were also eager to avoid a confrontation following a great deal of public criticism by weighty citizens frequently not heard from for such causes. We learned later that orders had gone out to police on patrol not to stop anybody for anything, in spite of the fact that the day before the Conference weapons were found by police in an out-of-state car carrying presumed Conference participants. No uniformed police were on duty anywhere about the Conference area, except for two traffic officers in front of McGonigle Hall on Broad Street. Team patrols had noticed carloads of police in plain clothes parked throughout the area, and a number of police were held in readiness outside the area, but no need for police and no confrontation developed.

The nearest occasion to a serious disorder arose out of the fact that only 4,500 people could be accommodated in the auditorium, leaving at least another 1,500 on the outside. When those on the outside realized they could not get in, they became rather angry with the guards inside the door. On one occasion when someone opened the door from inside, those nearest in the crowd grabbed the door and tried to force it open. It was at this time or soon thereafter that the Panthers announced that Huey Newton would speak at the Church of the Advocate after the meeting. He in fact did not speak, but the situation was defused. Had the situation escalated the police might well have used tear gas. This was one of the contingencies for which the Team had done some preparation and had developed hand signals.

EVALUATION

Following the weekend, those who played a key role in leadership with the Team met to attempt to evaluate the project. All Team participants received a note of thanks from the co-ordinator and a request to send in reports of interesting events at the Conference as well as comments in evaluation of the Team activity.

One newspaper reported that the Panthers kept very good order at the Conference with the unsolicited aid of the Quakers. It is doubtful, however, that the Team deserves any credit for the Conference going peacefully or the police keeping off the scene. On the other hand, the Team deserves some credit for effort in this department and was no doubt a minor influence, among many, which set the peaceful context within which the Conference was finally implemented.

There is no question but that the project was a tremendously successful operation as an educational endeavour for those Members of the Society of Friends and like-minded people who participated as Team members. Typical was the participant's evaluation stating, 'As a personal experience, the weekend was an unqualified success. I wouldn't have missed it for anything.'

The fears which produced the Quaker Team never became actualities. There was no confrontation between Panthers and police, so the Team concept remained really untested. As one Team member stated, '. . . no one had a chance at the Purple Heart, thank God.'

The project did demythologize the Panthers for the Team and made them people rather than symbols. There was an openness and interchange across cultural lines for which there are too few opportunities. Many Conference participants did receive Team services with gratitude.

One Team member wrote, 'It had a profound influence on all of us who took part, I am sure, particularly those who had not previously been really involved with either Blacks or longhairs. To be in a situation in a *helping* relationship with a commitment to reconciling and impartial concern opens one to the need of each individual with whom one comes into contact and tends to remove judgmental attitudes.'

Some Friends raised questions about seeming to be of service to a violent group. One participant answered this by writing, 'Friends might note that we never let the non-pacifism of Indians keep us from acting as their paleface allies, though of course we did not supply them with arms. Black people historically, and for the most part today, react to the violence committed against them by the status quo by turning it inward in violence upon themselves (drink, drugs, apathy, alienation) or upon one another (the ghetto crime rate). At this convention we saw black people, and white students who have increasing reason for feeling they suffer the black condition, who are determined to respond to the violence done to them by being violent back at the initial perpetrators of violence. This does not excuse violence, but it is a far healthier response than America has hitherto known, and any criticisms of their real or alleged violence should be made cautiously in full appreciation of this point.'

The biggest shortcoming in the project was clearly communication. This was true both of communication within the Team and Communication with those participating in the Conference and the community people living in the Conference area.

Communication within the Team was largely by periodic checks between roving executive committee members and through the executive committee meetings. Good telephone facilities were established and used well. Arm signals, which some Team members never heard about and others questioned their validity, were devised for communication to nearby Team members across a crowd in the midst of crisis. Walkie-talkies were explored in advance, but a knowledgeable informant questioned their usefulness in a city setting among builidngs. This possibility probably deserved further exploration. Communication between the teams and the main field outpost was also frayed at times. Internal communication is a crucial problem needing serious study.

No attempt was made at general communication with the public immediately around us. There was a little effort at reaching a broader public through the news media. In retrospect, in spite of the magnitude of literature already being passed out at the Conference, the Team probably should have explained itself and made a pitch for nonviolence via a flyer. This would have told our story and further distinguished our third-party role as being distinct from either Panthers or police.

Most of the Team felt that the services offered were a useful adjunct to the project, but others felt that the services tended to identify us with the Conference. After all, we weren't serving water to the police. There are tactical questions here deserving study.

The problem of type of or degree of identification (high visibility versus low visibility) of Team members was not resolved, but left to each to do as seemed right. Some felt the red vests to represent exhibitionism. On the other hand, it's clear a small name badge doesn't mean much if you're moving in from outside to the midst of a violent crisis. Here again, study is needed in advance of the next such project.

A number of Friends in evaluating the project raised questions about the military type of command established. Participatory democracy ruled at the briefing sessions and preliminary planning meetings. It was made clear, however, that, in action on the field, decisions were to be made by a designated few or perhaps even by a single individual given authority. Is there a more Quakerly way of decision-making in the midst of crisis?

In overall evaluation the conclusion is that, considering the time limitations and our lack of experience, the project was valid in its assumptions and intent and reasonably well executed.

NEXT STEPS

It is an interesting footnote to this report that as a result of the Team activity, the Black Educators Forum asked the Peace Committee to supply observers at the recent teachers' strike in Philadelphia. The request for obervers was met.

The response to requests for evaluation of this project brought forth some opinion that Friends should develop some structure for meeting peacekeeping needs such as a 'peace brigade', an organized, trained and on-going group prepared to serve nonviolently in potential or actual situations of community crisis. In a fragmented way, some of this has been done through the Yearly Meeting Friendly Presence concept and by Peace Committee nonviolent training. The Peace Committee will take responsibility for exploring the possible broadening of these beginnings into a more useful tool for expressing Friends' concerns for nonviolent peacekeeping.

7

KENT STATE, 4 MAY 1971:
NONVIOLENCE THIS TIME*

A. PAUL HARE

A year after violence swept the Kent State University campus, students, faculty, and administrators assembled on the commons at noon for a memorial service for the four students who had been killed. Following the official services a 'May Day Coalition' called for an unauthorized rally near the ROTC building to protest a university ban on outside speakers and House Bill 1219 passed earlier in the year by the Ohio state legislature to limit campus protest. Halfway through the coalition programme the campus Yippies urged the crowd to sit in at the ROTC building. The sit-in continued overnight. The university president and key members of the administration locked themselves in the administration building. Town police in full riot gear were on hand. Plainclothes police with walkie-talkies kept constant surveillance. The protest could have drawn a violent reaction. But violence was averted, and the sit-in turned into a teach-in. Unlike the previous year, many students and faculty had been trained in methods of nonviolent action and third-party intervention. They were constantly and unobtrusively on hand and at work. For a close view of the action, let us follow the events as they unfolded, beginning with the noon rally. My memory of events has been supplemented by listening to tapes on which I recorded part of the action, and by reading articles in the *Kent Stater* and other newspapers.

NOON MEMORIAL RALLY

Dean Kahler, a student speaking from a wheelchair as a result of gunfire wounds the year before, sets the tone for the solemn service

*Paper presented at meetings of American Sociological Association, New York, August 1973. Research supported by NIMH Grant No. 5 RO1 MH17421-03 SP.

at noon. There are more than 6,000 students and others on the commons when the Victory Bell tolls seven times, four for the students killed by the Ohio National Guardsmen at Kent, two for the students killed at Jackson State College in Mississippi, and one for 'all the victims of war, hatred, and repression'. Kahler says that people should not be afraid to get busted. 'Remember four of us died. We should all go out and work for peace.' He notes that the TV cameras do not add to the beauty of the campus. Another speaker says: 'We must rededicate ourselves.' A student reads a poem about flowers.

During the rally third-party marshals, trained in nonviolent techniques, are moving about. Only the two co-ordinators of the group wear their armbands. The others carry them and will only put them on in an emergency. Thus they maintain a 'low profile'. Some faculty observers can also be seen wearing blue armbands.

Now a speaker representing the May Day Coalition takes the mike to announce a rally near the ROTC [military training] building at 1.00 p.m. He renews their pledge for nonviolence. He asks 'all of you to come with us to struggle for peace, for freedom, and human justice'. Next Jan Way, student co-ordinator of the Life Center (a student organization committed to nonviolent activity), speaks, reminding the students that 'last year four of our brothers and sisters were murdered on this campus'. Finally Rev Jesse Jackson gives the major address, ending by leading the crowd in a chant that 'I am somebody. I may be poor. I may be in jail. But I am somebody.' The crowd disperses. About 2,000 persons walk to the front of the campus where the unauthorized rally is scheduled to begin.

THE UNAUTHORIZED RALLY

A small platform, microphone, and loud speaker have been set up on the grass about 100 yards from the ROTC building. A student opens the rally by calling attention to the ban on outside speakers. 'They are closing this campus down. We want to open this campus. One way to do it is to break the ban on outside speakers.' He introduces Tim Butz, former student and Vietnam veteran, who was helping to organize the demonstrations in Washington, DC, which are going on at the same time with various government offices as targets. Tim describes the actions in Washington, urging the audience to 'turn the death machine into a life machine'. A student gives more details of the actions in Washington, DC. She says that today it would be great if we could get together and sit around the ROTC building. There could be singing and dancing. Now Jan Way observes that 'this is one of the most beautiful sights I have seen'. She introduces George Lakey, a Quaker activist from Philadelphia, who is a featured 'unauthorized' speaker.

Lakey gives a fairly long speech about democracy. He notes that the present situation in the United States does not fit the ideal. 'The power of the ballot has pretty much had it'. (Near the end of his speech the crowd is becoming restless.) Lakey urges the audience to gather in small communities for struggle. (Parts of his speech are drowned out by applause and laughter as the Yippie-led rally begins in front of the ROTC building.)

After Lakey, a student with a rubber mask of Nixon's face takes the mike to give an imitation of President Nixon. He stretches out his arms, making the 'V' sign with his fingers. 'I have taken a stand on the bussing issue. I stand in the front of the bus and you stand in the back of the bus. These demonstrations will have no effect on my policy, but they might scare the shit out of me.'

More students speak. One student was 'shot in the back while overrunning the guard from 196 yards away'. He gives an emotional speech: 'The bell is tolling all the time for those who are killed every day. . . . End fascism and racism now. . . . The only way to be alive is to do something so that others can be alive too.'

Now Barbara is introduced to sing some movement songs. But the crowd is already turning its attention to the ROTC building. A speaker with a bullhorn can be heard: 'They have closed the building.' There is confusion. Some members of the May Day Coalition want to 'bring the stuff and go over there' to join the ROTC sit-in. Others want to continue the rally until all the scheduled speakers have been heard and then join the sit-in group. The microphone is left open and the small platform cleared as the May Day Coalition leaders helplessly wonder what to do. (Charles Walker, veteran rally organizer, has noted that a 'loose mike' at a rally is a most unfortunate event since anyone can take over the rally.) Now as the rally leaders confer among themselves, singing is heard over the 'loose' mike. A woman (an undergraduate and third-party marshal, we discover later) has stepped to the mike and is singing a sweet plaintive song. Members of the crowd turn towards her and some begin to move back in her direction. At the end of her song she says softly: 'You know there is something I have always wanted to do. Oh well, what the hell.' She lets her coat slide from her shoulders to the platform. She begins to unbutton her blouse. The crowd, largely male, wheels and moves suddenly back towards the platform. It appears that the woman is going to strip. But before any more of her intentions can come to light, someone from the crowd has led her from the platform. He counsels her that she may get in trouble if she continues in this vein. However, her task is complete; the attention of the crowd has been recaptured. The regular singer sings and Mark Lane, an attorney associated with the movement, burns his visitor's pass. After his speech the 'unauthorized' rally is concluded and the crowd is free to turn its attention to the sit-in at the ROTC building. (During the last part of the speech, faculty marshals and third-party marshals discuss the possible forms which the sit-in may take and ways of dealing with the crowd.)

AVERTING THE BUST

Earlier while the rally called by the May Day Coalition was in progress, football players and veterans appeared as counter-demonstrators. Police vans were drawn up in back of the ROTC building. There was fear of open conflict and a police bust. Tom Baker, co-ordinator for the student marshals, describes some of the moves on the part of students and faculty which averted both sources of conflict:

> After the sit-in began there was a group of football players and a group of vets. We [the student marshals, both men and women] tried to get ourselves between them. We had some hassle and people told us to sit down. The people who were nearest the vets sat down. The people who were nearest the jocks [players] moved off. Since I was nearest them I moved off. So that the vets were isolated and out in the open. So they left. Then the jocks left. Then we [marshals] drifted around to all the doorways to make sure things were all right.
>
> When there was word that there might be a bust we circulated around and told those sitting-in what it might be. Then I went up with a

member of the faculty to the administration building. We saw President White and urged him not to allow the bust. Then some other faculty came in. We came back to the ROTC building, then returned and reasserted ourselves. We got the police buses moved away from the building. There was a communications van and a van full of police in riot gear. We got them moved. Everybody was really cool. There was a counter rally, which was confusing [i.e., the Yippies in front of the ROTC building], but that was handled when some of our people went over there.

[He now describes the incident at the loose mike.] . . . Then one of the girls, one of our marshals, between the two rallies said 'help me' and started taking off her clothes. Someone got her attention in the confusion.

THE ROTC SIT-IN

Now another student, speaking through a bullhorn, instructs the crowd in front of the ROTC building. He suggests that civil disobedience is an individual decision. He explains that students will be arrested and will be suspended under Ohio law (House Bill 1219) for one year. 'I think it is about time we did test 1219. It is obviously unconstitutional. You are tried for the same crime twice.' He describes two men who were forbidden to meet together and put in jail when they did. 'I think it's about time that we all just sat down and let them know that we are going to be "disruptive" in the words of House Bill 1219. That there is not going to be such a thing as stopping free speech . . . free assembly . . . and our duty to dissent. . . . So I think we should all go over to the doors now. We should stay there until five o'clock and maybe longer. We are going to be back out here tomorrow, and we are going to talk about free speech on the commons, cause we are going to have a little bit of that too. So if everybody moves over to the door, we will move the whole show there. Bring anything you've got. Bring your poetry. Bring your music. Bring yourselves.'

As the afternoon wears on, the student marshals begin to plan for an extended period of service. Paul Kriese, a graduate student and co-ordinator of the student marshals, speaks to a small group of marshals:

'People want to go home. They do not want to stay here all night. Why don't we get together sometime this evening, the marshals who are here. Many of the marshals were up most of last night [during a candle-light vigil at the places where the four students were killed].'

Tom Baker says that he will go around to see how many marshals are on hand and see what they want to do. Half of them might stay all night and the other half could go home. 'I will stay here,' says Tom, 'because they might try something at night.' Paul says he will sleep on campus to be on call.

In the background the PA system announces: 'There will be no arrests tonight.' The crowd cheers. The announcement continues: 'The building does not open until eight o'clock tomorrow morning.'

At this point Tom Baker tells me that he took an armband away from a student marshal earlier in the day. The student seemed to be acting in a way that would incite trouble. (Here we see Tom enforcing the rules of conduct for marshals.)

A trustee of the university comes to the mike. He tells the group that he is here 'only to serve you and this university'. He asks for open communication. He says that he will not necessarily agree with the students or they with him.

A questioner:

> Most of the kids out here are protesting two things. They are protesting 1219, The House Bill passed by the Ohio legislature, which they feel is unconstitutional, and they are protesting the presence of ROTC on this campus. . . . When the ROTC people try to come into this building tomorow we will stop them visibly by putting our bodies in front of them. . . . We have discussed this issue for three years. We have petitioned. We have marched. Last year the building was burned down. This whole year the issue was discussed in hearings by the university. More than half the people there that testified wanted ROTC off the campus. Faculty Senate supported ROTC, said that it should stay on campus, and, if anything, brought in modifications that made it more attractive. And these people [sitting-in] including myself, do not believe that the status of ROTC on this campus has been changed at all. There are still people coming here in ROTC who are going to carry out the policies of a sick nation. We want ROTC off the campus for good. What are the Board of Trustees going to do about this? When are they going to say something that appeals to us?

Answer by trustee:

> The ROTC is a volunteer group with a proud tradition. . . . Your trustees have had a 100 per cent interest in keeping this university open. . . . I think we share the same concerns. I want to point out clearly that

I am not speaking for the trustees as such, but just as an individual.
. . . Should ROTC be continued on the university campus, should it be
modified, or should it be removed from the campus. These are
questions that we are considering. Whether you prostrate your bodies
here tomorrow will not affect my thinking, it will be the same, and I am
sure that the trustees' thinking will be the same. . . . You can be assured
that I will voice this opinion in trustee meetings. [It is not clear which
opinion will be voiced.]

During the afternoon the 'leadership' of the sit-in changed several
times. One of the first to take over was a Yippie leader, Jerry Persky,
who was very good at dramatizing the issues. But he was reluctant
to go on to the next phase, that of going to jail. He abdicated his
position on the grounds that there were not enough people sitting
in. 'I want to go to jail with a lot of people, man, a lot of brothers
and sisters. I don't want to go to jail with thirty people. I want more
people, 150 people . . .' (Jerry leaves the demonstration.)

There is considerable confusion as the group sitting-in breaks
into a number of small discussions. From time to time someone takes
the loudspeaker to make an announcement. The students show
solidarity by clapping in unison and chanting.

As evening approaches and the demonstrators settle in for the
night, Clyde Hayes, a graduate student and temporary leader of the
protest, Tom Baker, and I move from entry to entry to give the
students some on-the-spot training in nonviolent action. We start at
the side and back doors where there are fewer demonstrators, then
after developing our training routine, we use the same approach
with the group of about fifty persons at the front door of the
ROTC. In each case we first ask the students if they are planning to
block the entrance in the morning when people come to work or for
classes. They say yes. We ask how they plan to do it. Usually there
are several different suggestions. Some might want to lock arms,
some lie down, or use other techniques. We ask the group to 'get it
together' by choosing one technique. We then suggest a role-play in
which they take up their positions blocking the door and the three
of us pretend to be persons trying to enter the building. When they
are ready we walk over them or try to push them aside. After a
minute or so we stop and hold a critique. Were they able to block
the entrance? Did they try to talk to the people climbing over? Did
they break their nonviolent discipline? Next we ask if they plan to
get arrested. As before, we ask them to take the position they would

use when the police approach. We play police, dragging them in turn to an imaginary bus. Again the questions. How did it work? What would they do differently? We saw this training as an extension of our roles as third-party marshals. The students had agreed to sit-in nonviolently but had not had any special training in nonviolence. The week before, at a sit-in at the Selective Service building in Washington, DC, two protesters had made a grab at an employee who was trying to walk over them to enter the building. This act of aggression, which lasted no more than thirty seconds, appeared on the front page of several newspapers while twenty-four hours of nonviolent sit-in by the same group went unrecorded. (Of course, training in nonviolence does not rule out the possibility that someone will break under the tension of the moment or that a provocateur will initiate a violent incident.)

THE NEXT DAY

By the next morning there are few students left at the sit-in. Only four remain at one of the back doors of the ROTC building, while perhaps fifty cluster at the front. We ask a student at the back door why she is still there. 'I've sat by this door all night long,' she says. 'I've grown attached to it.' Another student observes that 'Twelve hours ago we were 110 people, now we are seven.'

Throughout the year at Kent the administration has been concerned about the presence of 'outside agitators'. During the weeks immediately after 4 May 1970, visitors to campus were required to have a pass. At this sit-in there are at least two non-students who are passing through. One identifies himself as from Berkeley, California, a switchboard operator. He has been to the demonstrations in Washington, DC, and is now on his way home. He says he did not have a pass but was told he would be given one. Then he had been told that the administration had decided not to give out any more passes. 'I am involved in peace demonstrations all over,' he says. 'I don't see too well where you fit . . .' replies a faculty member; 'I think you found the wrong rally.'

A student takes the mike to read a statement explaining the sit-in:

Seventy-five people sitting here are engaging in civil disobedience in protest against the genocidal policies of the US government and the maintenance of the war machine on the Kent campus where men are trained to carry out that genocide. We also sit to defy House Bill 1219, a bill we feel is unconstitutional and repressive. We reaffirm our belief in nonviolent direct action and above all peace. We sit in solidarity with our brothers and sisters in Washington, DC, and dedicate our actions of 4 May as a memorial to our four slain brothers and sisters. [Applause]

Someone calls out: 'Two more people.' There are shouts and cheers as two more persons join the sit-in.

By this time a third leader has become prominent in the sit-in. Jim Minard is a former student. He discusses the possibility of turning the sit-in into a teach-in by having students go into classrooms to talk about the ROTC and other issues. Several faculty members have assured Jim that their classes will be open. Raj Basi, Director of the newly formed Center for Peaceful Change, agrees to help with the organizational problems. Jim tells the students who are sitting-in that this is a real opportunity and that he is willing to try. He tells them that faculty members have worked hard during the night to negotiate this agreement with the administration. 'Somebody told me that we can go talk to the Board of Trustees,' he continues, 'so I am going to talk to them'. Students question the effectiveness of this move. Jim persists with his plan to have a dialogue with the administration to see if they can start a programme of teach-ins.

Jim, several faculty, and student marshals go up to the administration building to discuss the plan with Bernie Hall, the Provost. Jim explains the plan with the help of clarifying statements by some of the faculty. 'That's a wonderful idea,' says Hall. 'You go ahead and do it.' There is some confusion as Jim says that last night a board member (Mr Dix) had said that the ideas could be presented at a board meeting. Hall responds that the meeting in progress in another room is not a board meeting. Raj Basi and Jim try to explain that they would like something in writing to show the students who are sitting-in to verify the fact that they have permission to speak in classrooms. 'Now are you saying to me that if I say yes, you may go ahead and do that, that Mr Persky and all of his people will go home?' queries Hall. 'They may stay,' replies Jim, 'but they probably will stay to work on the idea.' 'They can't stay,' says Hall emphatically. 'This is the answer to that. They cannot stay. They are violating a variety of laws. They are keeping the people who legitimately have a right to be in that building from going into that building without having fear on their minds. So you go back and tell Mr Persky . . .' (I break in to say, 'He's not there, Bernie; Persky isn't there; that's not an issue.' This interchange illustrates the fact that the provost does not realize that the Yippie leader, Persky, has stepped down from his leadership position some hours before over the issue of the number of people sitting-in. Leadership has changed hands several times since then, with Jim being the most recent leader to come forward.) 'I discussed this with them,' continues Jim, 'and I told them that if I came back with this assurance in writing, that we had a chance to get into the university and talk to people about our ideas, sensibly, that we consider our effort down there a success.' A faculty member clarifies the request. 'What he wants is a written statement from you that would say that it is permissible for outsiders to talk to classes with the permission of the faculty member of that particular class.' 'It's still going to be very difficult for a professor of physics . . .' argues Hall. Others object, 'No, no.' Hall continues to make the point that anyone can go into the classroom with the professor's permission. By this time Jim seems to feel that Hall is reluctant to give a written statement. 'You mean you prefer us to remain down there,' queries Jim. 'Is that your position?' 'No, that's not the point at all,' responds Hall. 'I'm saying that where a professor feels it is relevant to his subject, he may certainly allow you to come into his classroom. As he can do that right now. He doesn't need my permission, but I am willing to put it in writing if you would like.' 'That's what they're asking,' someone adds. Others comment. 'I think that the professor has to, in his own mind, decide that it's relevant to his work,' continues Hall. 'He is paid by the state and by the university to teach a certain area, such as physics or math. Now if he thinks that this is relevant to his subject, they can go ahead and do it.' Several faculty try to interpret the request again. 'May I ask you this,' interjects Hall, 'are you a student?' 'No sir,' replies Jim. 'You are not a student,' reflects Hall. 'I was.' Hall notes, 'I am very interested. Were you there after 11 pm?' Jim: 'Yes, I was.' Hall: 'I'm glad to know that.' (Hall is showing his concern about the possible presence of outside agitators. In this case the outside agitator has been able to formulate a more creative solution to the sit-in than any of the inside agitators who preceded him in the leadership of the sit-in.) The discussion continues. Hall is told by several people that the students have voted to abide by the agreement if they can have something in writing. Hall continues to hedge, saying that he is not the Board of Trustees. Hall goes off to find out where Mr Dix is so that the students can talk to him. A reporter has recorded Hall's statement on the tape recorder. The students and faculty negotiators discuss the possibility of playing the tape to the group sitting in as a substitute for a written statement. A faculty member tries to interpret Hall's remarks to Jim. Basi volunteers the services of the Center for Peaceful Change to help. Several agree that it would be best to have a written statement. As an alternative, it is suggested that Hall go down to the rally and make a personal statement if he would prefer not to put it in writing. Now while waiting for Hall to return, Jim and some of the others decide to return to the sit-in to advise the students there of the progress of the negotiations.

Again in front of the ROTC building Jim takes the microphone: 'Bernie Hall has said that we could have done this a long time ago. What we are getting now is a written statement to the effect that we can do it now, from him and from Mr Dix. That means that we can go to faculty members and try and sell them on the idea. I have already had some faculty members tell me that they would be willing to let us in the classroom. That's not all of the 200 or 300 faculty, but it is a start. We also have the facilities of the Center for Peaceful Change. . . . I am willing to work on this. I am willing to accept their statements . . . that we can continue to come on this campus, student or no, go into the classrooms and talk about antiwar activities, economic boycotts, educating the people as to why we think we should have these things. . . . I am willing to do that. . . . By the way, he asked me if I was a student. I said no. He said were you here after 11 o'clock last night. I said yes. He said that's very interesting. (Laughter) He said I like to know those kinds of things. If he uses this kind of thing to try to keep me from doing this, they've got some big trouble on their hands. Because they've given us a chance to communicate. They've given us a chance. . . . Maybe this is the way we can get rid of the military establishment on campus. But if they stop us they are in big trouble. . . .'

A faculty member says he wants to clarify something . . . says he has been quoted as committing the faculty to letting anyone in their classrooms. He says that the faculty code of ethics says that faculty members may invite into their classrooms any invited guests whom they wish. . . . He continues to say that he could not explicitly speak for the faculty. He answers questions.

A student speaks. 'We've done something, folks. We've got somebody on the bargaining table. We are doing something. We weren't out here just for the hell of it. I don't know about you, but I'm going to go home, and I'm going to take a nap, and I'm going to get ready to do something again, working for everything that we've won. And I just want to thank you all, just for me, for coming out here and expressing yourself and putting up with all the [hassle] and the cold and taking the risks that you did, that we all took. Finally we've come out with something on top; Kent is the leader. We are going to show the world.' (Derisive shouts, indicating that not everyone agrees with this uplifting message.)

Jim is back at the mike. The word is passed that Mr Dix is back on campus. 'I got to go see Mr Dix,' announces Jim as he goes off to the administration building again. 'See you later.' After consultation with faculty, Jim goes on to announce a meeting at the Life Center at 10.00 a.m. to put the programme together. Also, 'those who are interested in staying here and showing your disgust for 1219, I suggest you do that.' A student announces that 'for starters' she will take down a list of everyone who wants to go to a classroom to speak. People begin the task of organizing the next steps and moving the group away from the ROTC.

A little later a shout goes up: 'People are trying to walk in.' Some confusion, then: 'You can walk in, but you are going to have to walk over us.' Shouts as some people try to go into the ROTC building. A marshal who has been sitting with the group in front of the door says this is the time to do something constructive.

Jim returns with a statement signed by Provost Hall. Basically it is a signed written affirmation of university policy. 'What is important is that we talked, and they listened, and they agreed with the basic concept of the idea,' Jim tells the group. 'They said that they would like us to do this and try it, for a change.' Jim reads:

'President White and I, as Provost, wish to affirm that according to the faculty code of ethics and university policy, where pertinent to the course an instructor may invite persons to appear before his class. Signed Bernard Hall, Vice President and Provost.'

Jim continues: 'That is a simple affirmation of university policy. What is important is that we told them that we are going to use this on a large scale. . . . We will go into classes to talk about the war machine. . . .' Jim then reads 'Section three [of the relevant portion of the code of ethics]' to the students. 'This is our plan of action,' Jim continues; '. . . we want to talk to these faculty members . . . to take a day out of their classes and go in there and hit those apathetic students with the facts and figures. . . . about the war machine. . . . We have the backing of faculty members and we have the full use of the facilities of the Life Center. . . . If you want to get ROTC off campus, if you want to have another referendum, you have to educate the rest of the students on this campus as to why it shouldn't be here; then they will vote against it. In the same process we must educate the rest of the faculty . . . and they will vote against it. When they vote against it, ROTC will come down. . . . This is a starting point. The doors are opening a little bit. . . . For the first time that I know of they were willing to take one of our suggestions and let us go with it. . . . This to me is the only viable alternative we have. . . . As far as this building is concerned, it is a hollow shell for them now too because we closed it without any violence. [Applause] At the same time we opened up some doors in the university administration where we can start digging in and getting the power that the students should have to them, and showing them how they can use it. So that's what I'm going to do and some people are going to help me. It is going to take a lot of work.'

The discussion continues about the provision for going in the classroom since some students are not clear. Others wonder what good it will do. 'You say we have opened doors,' says a voice from the crowd, 'but how soon are those doors going to close after we leave here?' 'It's a start,' say others. The students continue the argument in loud voices. Jerry Persky is back in the act, complaining that nothing will be done. (Apparently his forte is a rally. He seems only to be able to think of actions which can take place during a rally, such as having the members of the Board of Trustees come down to talk to them.)

By early afternoon the sit-in group has dispersed. During the next few days Jim and the others who are interested in more organized activity turn to the task of gathering information to be presented in classes. This method of opinion change is less controversial and more in line with the normal activity of the university.

A NOTE ON GROUP DEVELOPMENT

We have seen that third-parties played an invaluable role in bringing administrators and student sit-in leaders together to work out a creative solution to the problem presented by student concern over the presence of ROTC on campus and House Bill 1219. Since the members of the administration had chosen to lock themselves into the administration building and rely on radio and other indirect means of communicating with the students, we find that key administrators, such as the Provost, did not have current information on the sit-in leadership or the mood of the demonstrators which would facilitate creative solutions. Thus third-parties had to bring information to the administration as well as serve as negotiators. Since the students in turn were not familiar with university policy, the third-parties had continually to amplify and interpret statements made by the administration.

It is interesting that the sit-in went through three changes of leadership. The first leader, Jerry Persky, the Yippie, was a specialist in defining the situation and in motivating the participants. The second leader, Clyde Hayes, a graduate student, specialized in providing the necessary skills through training in nonviolent methods so that the students might achieve their goal effectively. The third leader, Jim Minard the former student, specialized in integrating the interests of the students and the administration. He helped define the roles that each side would play and negotiated the contract which would govern their interaction. It is quite possible that a fourth leader would need to emerge for the final stage, that of actually carrying out the teach-in over a period of time. This final phase in the typical cycle of group development calls for organizational skills and a leadership style which the leaders in the first three phases may not possess. Thus, in this sit-in as in all groups, leaders and members must be able to meet the four functional needs of (1) *defining the situation,* (2) *gathering resources and providing skills,* (3) *defining roles and developing morale,* and (4) *co-ordinating the group work,* if the group is to survive (Hare, 1973).

REFERENCES

Hare, A. Paul, 1973. 'Theories of group development and categories for interaction analysis'. Small Group Behavior 4 (3, August): 259-304.

8

REPORT FROM WOUNDED KNEE*

JAMES L. SCHRAG

On 28 February the tiny village of Wounded Knee began attracting international attention when it was taken over by 200–300 American Indians, members of the recently-formed militant American Indian Movement (AIM). They stated they would hold the town until three specific demands had been met, and for the first two days of the occupation they held ten hostages. These were then released, but most were Indians who chose to stay in Wounded Knee anyhow.

AIM's three demands are: (1) A Congressional Committee investigation of the Bureau of Indian Affairs (BIA), the Federal Government body controlling the reservations, (2) a high-level Senate investigation of the 371 US Government treaties with the Indians which the Government has broken, and (3) the suspension of the constitution of the local reservation, so the Indians can design a form of government more in keeping with their own traditions. (One uniform constitution was imposed on all Indian reservations in 1934 by a white lawyer in the BIA. It called for an elected 'tribal council' with a tribal 'president', a structure alien to the practices of many Indian tribes. Contrary to common belief, the Sioux never even had chiefs as we think of them: the all-powerful chief was an invention of nineteenth century US government officials who wanted someone convenient to negotiate with.)

At the time of writing, AIM has held Wounded Knee for forty-three days, beset alternately by blinding snowstorms, floods and unwanted white sightseers, and the stranglehold of encircling Federal troops. These troops have maintained a tight siege since 12

*Reprinted by permission from *Peace News*, 27 April 1973, pp. 4–5.

March. AIM's negotiation of its own demands with Federal officials has proceeded irregularly throughout March.

What are the wellsprings of such militancy? And considering that this is not an isolated incident, what is happening to the American Indian? The following paragraphs are an attempt to give some context to the Wounded Knee campaign.

Of the 843,000 Indians in the US, more than half live on or near Federally-run reservations. On these reservations, average family income is less than $1,000 per year (less than one-third of the White average); life expectancy is about forty-five years, compared with an average of seventy-two years for Whites; and White ranchers or industries control most of the usable land. Through the tribal councils, Indian 'Uncle Tomahawks' serve their own interests and those of white business: the reservations today are being strip-mined, polluted by power plants and other factories, and robbed of scarce water by collusion between BIA officials, tribal presidents, and white corporate officials. The majority of Indians on the reservations are not even told of these deals with their lands, much less consulted, and they get in return drought, air pollution, and shrinking work and living space. The reservations thus constitute a perfect example of vest-pocket imperialism, complete with a native puppet regime to provide legitimate access for the exploiting power.

In July 1970, President Nixon raised Indians' hopes all over the country by outlining and starting to implement a plan returning to the Indians much more control of their own lives and resources, partly by restructuring the BIA along lines of service rather than control. This programme was implemented just enough to really excite many Indians with the prospect of a better future when the anti-Indian powers (Congressional representatives from states where strong business interests wanted to retain control over Indian land; old-line White bureaucrats in the BIA; and various Uncle Tomahawks) united to defeat progressive legislation before Congress, and cripple the reorganization of the BIA. At this point the Nixon administration seemed to lose interest; and Indians everywhere were outraged — once again AIM exploded into national prominence at about the same time that the Nixon administration's proposals gave their last gasp.

AIM is perhaps best known for being the most militant of the coalition of Indian action groups that organized the Trail of

Broken Treaties campaign last fall. This brought several hundred Indians to Washington, DC, to present Indian grievances to the Federal Government. Through an incredible series of blunders, the government provoked the exasperated Indians into forcibly taking over the BIA building. They held it for almost a week, and turned it into a fortress when threatened with forced expulsion. A settlement was reached, and they left peacefully, taking with them thousands of pages of files documenting government and corporate exploitation of Indians.

An additional cause of Indian anger is the long-standing racism with which they are treated by Whites; it was an instance of this which helped bring about the occupation of Wounded Knee.

This January, a young Sioux man was stabbed to death in Custer, South Dakota, not far from Wounded Knee, and a white gas station attendant was charged with the minimal possible legal charge, involuntary manslaughter, carrying a maximum sentence of ten years in prison. The dead Indian's mother protested at the leniency with which the accused killer was being treated, and consequently she was arrested on a charge carrying a maximum sentence of thirty years in prison. Within a few weeks, AIM activists came to Custer and burned down the courthouse.

At the same time, full-blooded Indian elders on the Pine Ridge reservation (where Wounded Knee is located) had tried but failed to impeach the mixed-blood president of the tribal council on charges of nepotism and misuse of funds. They then invited the AIM militants in the area to the reservation, and two nights later, on 28 February, Wounded Knee was taken over. The press has generally failed to mention that AIM was invited to the Pine Ridge reservation by the combined action of three traditional and thoroughly legitimate organizations of full-blooded Sioux, representing significant numbers of Indians on the reservation. AIM people were not unwanted outside agitators.

The occupation and the siege by Federal forces were in their seventh day when the incident occurred which riveted on Wounded Knee the attention and action of peace and social justice groups throughout the country. On Wednesday, 7 March, the Federal Government issued an ultimatum for the Indians to be out of Wounded Knee by nightfall the next day—or else. Some twenty people left, and 200 determined Indians dug themselves deeper in the South Dakota hills to await a military attack. This readiness for death bore a partial resemblance to the most serious stages of some nonviolent campaigns: although the Indians were armed with many light rifles and pistols and a few automatic weapons, arrayed against them was the Vietnam-tested arsenal of the US Army, including so much heavy armour on the scene that the Federal forces could quite likely have destroyed the Indians without suffering a single casualty. At least the AIM leadership, if not all the occupiers, must have known this. So at the most serious level of confrontation they stood prepared to die for their beliefs and grievances with the knowledge that probably none of 'the enemy' would pay the same price.

The Philadelphia Life Centre, a nonviolent training and action community, held an urgent session that Wednesday evening to decide on a response to the crisis. Three actions were taken the following morning. Bill Moyer, an organizer with much experience in the civil rights campaigns of the 60s, flew to Wounded Knee to work with the third-party interposition teams already being established by the National Council of Churches (NCC). John Adams, a crisis-intervention worker for the NCC, had gained some trust from both the Federal officials and the Indians, and was working around the clock to prevent a massacre.

In Philadelphia, Phyllis and Dick Taylor and others moved into the local office of one of the state's US Senators, and patiently but firmly convinced the assistant there to get Senator Schweiker, in Washington, to pressure the Justice Department to negotiate, not attack. At the same time, others organiz~d telephone networks of people to call Washington with that same message. The nation-wide deluge of messages grew. Later reports indicated that for two days many Federal Government offices did little work other than Wounded Knee.

By that Thursday afternoon came word that the government had withdrawn its deadline. John Adams had drawn up an agreement which both sides accepted as a basis for final negotiation. Part of the agreement called for NCC observer teams to be stationed between the Federal forces and the Indians, and Bill Moyer put out a call that night for experienced nonviolent activists to come to Wounded Knee to do that. The observers acted as peace-keeping teams, recording all they saw, and discouraging both Federal forces and Indians from making incident-provoking sorties into the 'de-militarized zone' separating them. The observer cars were stationed in this zone.

That Friday night, Scott Beadenkopf, Julie Latané, and I set off on the thirty-three-hour, 1,800 mile drive from Philadelphia to Wounded Knee, and other movement activitists in other states did the same. When our car arrived at Wounded Knee Sunday morning, observer teams had been on duty until Saturday afternoon, at which time the Federal forces abruptly dismantled their roadblocks and left the scene, leaving a few carloads of FBI observers.

Saturday and Sunday were days of celebration at Wounded Knee, with much dancing and music, but by Sunday afternoon the mood was becoming more serious: the Indians declared Wounded Knee to be an independent nation (contrary to the government understanding that they would leave Wounded Knee when the roadblocks were withdrawn), and an Indian patrol wounded an FBI agent. By nightfall it seemed clear that we should set up observer teams again.

That evening I joined two other volunteers in a car on one of the back roads into Wounded Knee. There were no Federal agents around, so our major work on our seventeen-hour shift was noting the times when a few cars drove the road, and keeping the AIM guards from being uneasy about the strange carload of Whites just beyond their checkpoint. They changed shift four times while we were on duty, so every few hours we would wander down a very dark road to get acquainted with the new crew. Sunday night was peaceful, but by Monday afternoon the Federal government threw up the siege again, complete with observation helicopters, a dozen or more armoured personnel carriers, and hundreds of nervous, angry US marshals. Monday night was tense, and some government officials told us privately that our presence at that time may have been very important in preventing an invasion.

Later in the week we were forced to withdraw, for Indian-government relations had deteriorated so much that the government would not permit us to send replacement teams through their lines, although we were quite willing to do so. From Saturday until Tuesday we lived in the basement of a church near Wounded Knee and kept our observation teams ready to go at a moment's notice. Although we weren't called upon, John Adams felt that his position as third-party negotiator was immensely strengthened by our readiness to implement immediately our part of any agreement that might emerge.

Nonetheless, idle time was not a problem of our life in the basement. We learned from local Indians more about their culture and history, and about reservation life. We fed and sheltered Indian derelicts, of whom there were many, both young and old. We ran training sessions on third-party observation for our group (about thirty people). These included role plays designed to sharpen powers of observation, and quick decision exercises, including such problems as: you are an observer on a road into Wounded Knee and you see someone sneaking through tall grass towards the village. What do you do? Or: you are an observer on a road into Wounded Knee and you see an armoured personnel carrier come rolling down the road towards the village. What do you do? These exercises prepared us for the full range of incidents we might encounter, helped us further clarify our role, and reduced apprehension by making the unknown knowable. We handled our group organization and our readiness for outside tasks with a democratic group process which was an exciting achievement under the intense pressures of the situation, and something quite new to some members of our nationally-gathered team. The observation teams were never used again, because no agreement was reached which called for their presence.

Since that Saturday, the situation at Wounded Knee has been basically a stalemate, with occasional skirmishes, the wounding of one Indian and one marshal, and the exchange of many thousands of rounds of gunfire.

Now that we are home again, there has been opportunity and some cause for reflection on the implications of nonviolent activists' involvement in the Wounded Knee campaign. Pacifist involvement there began as an attempt to prevent the US Government from 'solving' a problem in vest-pocket imperialism by mass murder. The original plan was to interpose our bodies between the government and its intended victims, consulting with no one. This might well have proved to be logistically impossible, and turned out to be unnecessary. The negotiated interposition which we carried out was more effective, and all of us, as pacifists, were glad to do it.

Several factors led us to see the Indians as other than a guerrilla army. First, as noted earlier, their arms were so light and limited that they would have been useless in the face of an all-out army attack. For most practical purposes, except killing cattle for food, they were symbolic only. By policy, the guns were not used for harassment, sabotage, or murder.

Second, in a part of the country where rifles and shotguns used for hunting deer, rabbits, etc., are a common sight, guns acquire a normality. The Indians' level of armament was barely unusual for western South Dakota. The machine guns and M-16s of the Federal forces were far more intimidating. However, AIM policy was not successful in preventing a carload of hot-heads from wounding an FBI agent on Sunday, 11 March. Many of us felt some concern about working closely with a group in which this kind of undisciplined action could occur.

Some of us also had misgivings about apparent AIM willingness to use the observer teams for their own purposes, regardless of risk to team members. AIM clearly won a victory when Federal forces were withdrawn on Saturday, 10 March, but rather than leaving as per the agreement (as I understood it), they declared their independence, escalated their demands, and an FBI agent was shot. AIM was quite glad that we re-established our observation posts at the time. Did we then become a nonviolent defence force for Wounded Knee?

Earlier in the week, when the leadership of the Federal forces was belligerent, and no negotiation was in progress, our interposition was clearly an act of humanitarian concern. But if AIM had gone through two or more rounds of negotiating and then breaking agreements to escalate their demands, relying on our presence to prevent invastion, our function would have become much more confused. Already some Federal officials and conservative Indians on the tribal council had begun to accuse us of 'needlessly' prolonging the situation; since we were doing that, we clearly weren't a 'neutral third party'!

The AIM leadership may be more interested in exploring nonviolent strategies for future campaigns because they witnessed and acknowledged some of the power of nonviolence at Wounded Knee. At present, they are already under pressure from other Indian activist leaders to make more use of the strong Indian tradition of nonviolent action. Thus Hank Adams, Director of the Survival of American Indians Association, wrote in a communique to the occupiers of Wounded Knee, 'If you may recall the battlecry and spiritual communion that came forth from among the strongest voices of Indian history, "It's a good day to die," or, "It's a good day for dying," remember also that the strongest of those voices also adjudged that "Had there been any other way, we would have taken it."' (*Win* magazine, 5 May.)

The conditions for a successful violent campaign, even by AIM's definitions, will be very difficult to set up. Wounded Knee may prove to be unique. For example, AIM has been remarkably free of the informers and provocateurs which have seriously damaged such groups as the Black Panthers and the Vietnam Veterans against the War. It seems unlikely that this immunity will continue as the government comes to see AIM as somewhat threatening.

American pacifist groups agree strongly with Indian grievances and will be quite willing to work with the various Indian groups on direct action campaigns. The many implications of Wounded Knee, e.g. 'negotiated interposition', will still require much in the way of unravelling.

PART III

Partisan transnational cases

9

THE SAHARA PROTEST TEAM*

APRIL CARTER

The French Government announced in the summer of 1959 that the first French Atom Bomb would be exploded in the Sahara desert. Many African countries protested about the danger from nuclear fall-out. Africans were also angry at this further manifestation of French colonialism, which made Algeria the testing ground for the symbol of French national prestige. Jules Moch defended the proposed test at the United Nations. In France the new Gaullist regime discouraged open dissent, and few people even wished to oppose the French Bomb. So French technicians went ahead with building the atom town near the test site at Reggan, and the French authorities — who claimed that the area was deserted — made plans to send the people living round the local oases to 'camps de regroupement'.

In a last minute challenge to the French authorities, an international team left Accra, capital of Ghana, in December with the aim of travelling 2,100 miles to the test site. The team represented African opposition to the Bomb — eleven members were Ghanaians — and included peace movement representatives from Britain and the United States. There was one French woman in the team at this stage. Spokesman for the team was the Reverend Michael Scott, then widely known for his work at the United Nations for the people of South West Africa. The departure of the team was the culmination of six months' prior negotiation and planning between Accra, New York, and London; journeys to France; deputations to African Embassies in London; and debate about the politics, route, personnel and financing of the team.

The aims of the protest were to arouse the conscience of the French people and the people of other nuclear powers; to stimulate further active opposition in Africa; and to halt the bomb tests — or

*This paper, not previously published, was written in 1972.

at least to embarrass the French Government. Achieving these aims meant the team must make a serious effort to reach the test site. Three possible routes were considered. The first possibility was to start from Morocco, follow the clearly defined route to Reggan, and use the oases and official staging posts along the way. But French military passes were needed to use this route. French paratroops also patrolled the zone between Reggan and the Moroccan border, and often shot unauthorized travellers on sight. The other possible approaches lay from the south through French West Africa, starting from either Nigeria or Ghana. This journey was three times as long as the route from Morocco, and the last part involved crossing the bleak and stony Tanezrouft desert. But the likelihood of eluding the French authorities for much of the way was greater, and the risks if detected less. (For further details on the route, see Appendix I.)

The decisive reasons for choosing to start from Ghana were, however, political. An early memorandum written in London summarized the reasons for preferring Ghana to Morocco: '(1) We have contacts there who have promised us support; (2) We think the Ghana Government is less liable to pressure from the French to hand the team over, or to deport them; (3) In Morocco we are more likely to become involved with the FLN, which from the point of view of the European and American organizations, and especially the French, would be a great mistake.'[1]

Independent Ghana was also better able to give support than Nigeria, which in 1959 could only make representations about the French tests through the British Government. The Prime Minister of the Nigerian Federation wrote in reply to a request for help for the Sahara team: 'With the achievement of independence next year, the Federal Government will be free to take necessary steps by itself and in co-operation with others, to bring direct pressure to bear in the matter.'

There were also positive reasons why Ghana provided a hospitable base for the team. Anti-French feeling in Ghana was high because of the ruthless conduct of the war against the FLN in Algeria, and because of recent French treatment of Guinea. When Guinea chose complete independence, instead of membership of the French Community in Africa, the French had stripped the country of all technical and administrative equipment, down to the typewriters and light bulbs. Hostility to France added to popular anger about the Sahara test. But there were other elements in Ghanaian foreign policy which encouraged a more comprehensive dislike of nuclear strategies, and which blended with the protest team's avowed opposition to *all* nuclear bombs and tests. Ghana had become independent in 1957 and was committed to support principles which were the antithesis of the imperialism and militarism associated with the colonial powers. Nkrumah had also avoided taking sides in the Cold War and stood for nonalignment along the lines enunciated at the Bandung Conference in 1955.

In addition the fact that Ghana's campaign for independence had been based on Nkrumah's strategy of 'positive action' meant that the protest group's commitment to nonviolence could be identified with the idea of positive action.[2] It was not therefore necessary to defend nonviolence against advocacy of violence. Because Ghana's expressed ideals of disarmament and nonviolence were in harmony with the fundamental principles of the team's policy, they were able to avoid compromising these principles, despite the need to adjust to the political circumstances inside Ghana, and the attitudes of the Government there.

A further advantage was the fact that there was a Ghanaian Campaign for Nuclear Disarmament set up at the end of August 1959. The Ghana CND included representatives of the main organizations in the country and was in fact an unofficial government body. But its status and ostensible independence made it an ideal body to sponsor the protest team in a way politically acceptable to both the team and the Ghana Government. Ghana CND decided to co-operate in the Sahara direct action plan at the end of August. An important personal link between Ghana CND and the British and American organizations promoting the team was Bill Sutherland, a black American previously active in peace and civil rights campaigns. He was at that stage personal assistant to the Ghanaian Finance Minister, Mr K. A. Gbedemah.

Bill Sutherland also helped to persuade the initially reluctant Committee for Nonviolent Action in New York to support the venture. CNVA had promoted a number of civil disobedience actions against American military policy, including the 1958 voyage of the Golden Rule into the Pacific nuclear testing area at Eniwetok. They sent two of their most experienced members to Ghana: Bayard Rustin, veteran of many civil rights and peace campaigns, and A. J. Muste, then in his seventies, the leading figure in the American movement for radical nonviolent action. Both played a crucial role in the political negotiations preceding the final departure of the team.

The organization which launched the Sahara team, the London-based Direct Action Committee Against Nuclear War, already had close links with CNVA. The DAC itself had originated with an attempt by a British Quaker to enter the British H-Bomb testing zone in 1957. The Committee had gone on to organize the first Aldermaston March in 1958 and demonstrations at Thor missile bases. The DAC sent out their twenty-five-year-old chairman, Michael Randle, to Ghana to initiate practical preparations for the team. Once the British and American team members were in Accra the Committees in London and New York ceased to play an active role. Ghana CND raised the funds to equip the expedition, and the team members made the political decisions.

BUILD-UP IN GHANA

When the two British team members arrived at Accra airport early on 9 October, they received in Michael Randle's words: 'an almost royal welcome'. The Chairman of Ghana CND, E. C. Quaye, was there to greet them, along with other notables from the ruling Convention Peoples Party. A Daimler plus chauffeur and public relations person were put at their disposal.

In the afternoon the two British volunteers attended the final session of the All African Peoples Conference Steering Committee, and were introduced to Dr Nkrumah's parliamentary secretary. The Steering Committee passed a resolution urging all governments to stop testing nuclear weapons and to dismantle their stocks of bombs. The Committee also expressed support for 'Africans and humanists' protesting against the French tests.

Michael Randle and his colleague — twenty-nine-year-old artist Francis Hoyland — continued to receive VIP treatment. They were driven to observe some Urban District Elections, and were entertained to a lavish dinner by the Regional Commissioner. Michael Randle conveyed his first impressions in a letter to London:

> Ghana radio has been making regular broadcasts about our activities, even to announcing our schedule for the next day. We have become unofficial ambassadors for radical Britain and if absolutely nothing else

came out of our visit, the fact that we shall have brought home to people here that there are many in Britain who are concerned about the French tests and nuclear weapons in general could be of historic importance . . . there is a real disappointment here that Britain has made no official protest.

Ghana CND met to hear the plans for the protest team, and agreed to arrange meetings and film shows. Among the meetings subsequently organized was one at the University College of Legon, where 300 students came to listen to the volunteers. In Kumasi, the second largest city in Ghana, men and women, many with babies strapped to their backs, crowded into the small Council Chambers there. While in Kumasi the team met the Asentehene, the traditional leader of the Ashanti people, and later that day spoke with the paramount chief at Kibi, some eighty miles from Accra. Two days later this chief called an emergency meeting of the Council of Chiefs specially to hear the team. Sunday 18 October was observed in churches throughout Ghana as a day of prayer for nuclear disarmament. The timing had been arranged to coincide with the launching of the team. There was a mass meeting in Accra nine days later.

Bayard Rustin arrived in Accra on 20 October. His arresting personality and political skills enabled him to persuade the Ghana Government to move beyond official gestures — despite their royal welcome the British volunteers were feeling somewhat trapped — and to give genuine backing to the team. He began working too on promoting opposition to the Sahara tests throught Africa. The Secretary General of the Ghana Trades Union Congress invited Rustin and Randle to address a plenary session of the All African Trade Union Federation that met in Accra on 7-9 November and passed a resolution in support of the team. The team members were also able to talk privately with a number of African leaders in Accra for this conference, including Tom Mboya and Oginga Odinga. Two weeks later the Secretary General of Ghana TUC — who was also First Secretary of the Federation — called on all African workers, especially those in the French Community, to demonstrate against the French tests.

As a result of publicity about the Sahara protest plan Ntsu Mokhehle, President of the Basutoland National Congress Party, flew to Accra to join the team. He represented 150 volunteers from his own country, who for practical reasons could not take part. A

Nigerian student, Hilary Arinze, also volunteered and was accepted.

The French volunteer, twenty-seven-year-old Esther Peter, flew in a day after Rustin. She had given up her job in the translation section of the Council of Europe to join the team. Earlier she had been active in the World Citizen movement. Because no French disarmament organization could be persuaded to support such an unorthodox venture, Esther Peter was during the preparatory stages the only French team member. But the day the team left Accra they were joined at Kumasi by a French pacifist, Pierre Martin, who had just completed a work camp mission for UNESCO there. Martin, who was also on a tour for the Service Civile Internationale, had in the past spent over a year in the Sahara working with the first French oil research teams, and still had contacts in the area. He also had a record of active resistance to French military policies.

The most sensational arrival was that of Michael Scott on 17 November. A cable to the London pacifist weekly, *Peace News,* reported:

> Scott receives tumultous welcome. Government and Opposition supporters unite in backing Sahara Protest. Cheering crowds carried Rev Michael Scott shoulder high into the waiting room when he arrived by plane from the United States . . . At a press conference the following day Rev Scott told reporters of the deliberations that had been going on at the United Nations in New York. In spite of the pressures that had been brought to bear on her, however, France remained adamant . . . Since his arrival the Sahara protest has become a national issue and is headline news in press and radio.

After Scott's arrival final plans were made for the journey. Ghana CND appealed for funds over the radio and at a public rally, and, with the £4,500 raised, the team bought two landrovers and a Bedford truck. The whole team (then numbering nineteen volunteers) planned to drive the 1,000 miles to the Algerian border, if they were able to cross the French-controlled territories of Upper Volta and the French Sudan. Beyond the Algerian border the real desert began, and the military zone near Reggan was also likely to be heavily patrolled by French troops. So only ten members would attempt the last stage of the journey taking with them enough supplies to get to Reggan.

A Quaker couple in Ghana who had made the journey across the Sahara the year before, advised that:

To demonstrate the sincerity and the seriousness of your purpose to the French authorities, even though your hopes of reaching the desert are small, you should start with an even better equipped expedition than is required for this journey normally, as you do not wish to become a charge on the state for saving your lives or to lay yourselves open to justifiable ridicule.

The team aimed to follow this advice.

If the ten volunteers reached the test site they planned to try to persuade French technicians to stop co-operating with the preparations for the test, and to remain in the area as a deterrent to the bomb being dropped. The rest of the team in the Sudan would hope to keep in touch and to send news back to Ghana. In addition they would seek to act as a focus for promoting opposition to the test within French West Africa. In September the Premier of the French Sudan, Modibo Keita, had broken away from the united front presented by the French Community in supporting the test, and had made a statement condemning it. This was significant for the team since they would need help in Sudan in obtaining advice about the best routes and in acquiring a local guide. If it proved necessary to send a rescue party into the desert, this would also have to start from the Sudan.

But the first problem was to get past the French authorities at the Upper Volta border. Since the team had publicized their plans, and had officially applied for visas to enter French West Africa — which were refused — the likelihood of their being stopped was high. The team agreed that: 'Under no circumstances would we attempt to drive our vehicles on past a manned barrier as this might easily cause danger to other people or lead to a situation of panic where soldiers or police were confronting vehicles rather than individuals . . .'

THE FIRST ATTEMPT

The team set out at dawn from Accra on 6 December, and at their first stop at Kumasi were joined by Pierre Martin. The next day they drove to Tamale, where there was a rally in their honour, and twenty-five young men volunteered to join on the spot. In the afternoon they reached Bolgatanga at the junction of two roads leading to Upper Volta. Two members of the team, together with

A. J. Muste who was acting as co-ordinator, conferred with several district commissioners in the area about conditions on the Upper Volta side of the border. As a result it was decided that the team should cross from the village of Bawku on 9 December, whilst volunteers would distribute team leaflets around the other Ghanaian border village of Navrongo.

Michael Randle cabled on 9 December:

> Today 9. a.m. Chief in ceremonial robes, village elders, drummers and musicians and whole town turned out for meeting. Ntsu Mokhehle, President of Basutoland Congress Party, in speech: 'We go unarmed. We say to French do not weep for us but for yourselves and your children . . . Team now at 21 members . . . Latest members Pierre Martin and Hannah Kojo, Womens Federation, and one of the most prominent and important women's leaders in Ghana. Crossing border this afternoon. District Commissioner to lead people of Bawku to border.

As the border itself was not clearly marked, the team encountered the first French control post at Bittou, sixteen miles inside Upper Volta. Despite earlier rumours that the Upper Volta people might be unfriendly, the team was cheered during their journey through Volta territory.

At Bittou the team were stopped by three white French officers, who told them that instructions from Paris forbade the team to proceed. The officers were polite and offered the team food and drink, which were refused. Michael Scott made plain that they were not prepared to leave. The officers said they had no orders to arrest the team, and would have to go to Ouagadougou fifty miles away to get fresh instructions. They asked the team not to give out leaflets or talk politics to the Africans in the area. The team agreed not to do so before the officers returned from Ouagadougou at noon the next day.

When the officers did return, they said they had not been able to contact the authorities in Paris, but asked for the keys of all vehicles, which the team refused. Muste reported the subsequent developments in an article for *Liberation* (January 1960):

> From this point on tension built up. The Africans in the vicinity were plainly friendly to the Team, eagerly sought leaflets (which had a message in four languages: Arabic, Hausa, French and English), and listened to talks. Even some of the African police showed interest. The

local chief built a hut to shelter the team from the heat. The local butcher brought meat.

The response of the French officers to this infiltration of the anti-test propaganda into the native population was to tighten the control. By the end of the third day at the Bittou barrier there were a hundred police and soldiers on hand, armed with revolvers, rifles and machine guns.Not only did they suround the team on all sides, confining them to a space of only fifty yards in diameter, but they also kept the Africans so far away that propaganda by talk or leaflet distribution was shut off.

After five days of mounting frustration the team made a strategic withdrawal to Bolgatanga to rethink their position. They had found themselves unable to move forward either by vheicle or by foot, and they also felt in an ambiguous position in their relations with the French officers. Furthermore, the period of waiting had created a number of internal difficulties in the team—many of whom had no previous experience of direct action.

During this period a certain amount of hostility developed among some African volunteers towards the Western team members. One source of tension was the way decisions were made within the team. Although final decisions were made after discussion among all members, a policy planning committee was responsible for putting alternative proposals to the meeting. The members of this steering committee were: the two Americans, Rustin and Sutherland; two British, Scott and Randle; and two Africans—Mokhehle from Basutoland and Frimpong-Manso from Ghana. Since there were twelve Ghanaians on the team then, they felt under-represented. Pierre Martin reported that there were mutterings among the Ghanaians about European and American domination.

A second source of resentment was the role played by Esther Peter in acting as interpreter with the French officers. The Ghanaians, already very hostile to the French for political reasons, were disposed to be distrustful towards individual French people even on the team. When Esther Peter talked at length with the French officers, and sometimes went away with them, some of the Ghanaians became convinced she was betraying the team and was acting as a French spy in their midst. The suspicion that she was a spy travelled back to Accra, and later she was asked to leave the country. Interestingly this suspicion never extended to Pierre Martin—perhaps because he did not play a dominant role, and was particularly aware of the Ghanaian attitudes.

The team were joined at Bolgatanga by A. J. Muste. It was decided there that only seven people should make the second attempt to enter Upper Volta. Three other Ghanaian volunteers were to base themselves on Navrongo to keep contact with the team, and to give all travellers into Upper Volta leaflets to be distributed there. The rest of the team returned to Accra to promote activity against the test there, or went home. Rustin was needed in the United States to work on a civil rights campaign, and Mokhehle had to contest an election in Basutoland.

The decision to split up the volunteers created a more united and flexible group for further attempts to enter French West Africa. It also enabled team members to extend the scope of their political activity. Hilary Arinze returned to Nigeria where he was energetic in seeking support for the team; and Esther Peter was able to play a particularly important and necessary role in Paris in publicizing and interpreting the venture there. But the decision to engage volunteers in other political work was also a guise for dropping some members from the team, and a number of the Ghanaians who found they had little real work to do in Accra became very resentful that they were no longer regarded as being part of the protest team.

THE SECOND ATTEMPT

The members of the seven-person team were Michael Scott, Michael Randle, Bill Sutherland, and four Ghanaians: Benjamin N. Akita, a book-keeper; R. Orleans-Lindsay, a science teacher; K. Frimpong-Manso, a private businessman; K. M. Arkhurst, a driver. They crossed the Upper Volta border on 17 December, penetrated eleven miles inside French territory, and were stopped at the military post of Po.

In accordance with decisions reached after the experience of Bittou, the team this time adopted a less co-operative course with the French officials. They applied for permission to pass through several times each day, and sat down in front of the barrier after being refused. They waited two weeks at the barrier and gave out leaflets despite threats of arrest. The leaflets were confiscated from those who accepted them. At one point a large group of Moslems on their way to Ouagadougou dismounted in the forecourt of the customs place, and chanted prayers for the success of the Protest Team's mission.

On Christmas Eve Michael Randle and a Ghanaian team member found two people in the nearby town of Paga to make recordings of the text of the leaflet in two local languages. The recordings also announced that the Northern House of Chiefs was calling for a day of prayer on 1 January. The team started using the loudspeakers on Boxing Day. Randle's log book notes:

> The recordings . . . sounded as clear as if someone had been speaking into the microphone. People gathered round and seemed most interested, and in the evening one of the Moslem guards, Kodji, said that the African guards agreed that they were 'bonnes paroles'. The commandant came and told us that loudspeaking without a permit was forbidden in Volta, even for commercial firms, and threatened to confiscate equipment, prevent us from going back to Ghana for supplies etc. and stop us from using the well for water.
>
> We broadcast again on morning of 27 December. The threats were repeated. At 3 p.m. we broadcast again. This time the French officer in charge, M. Charriere, mounted the landrover and removed both loudspeakers. We gave a note to an English group passing through to deliver to our Pressman in Paga.

The group started dawn-to-dusk vigils on 29 December, in shifts of two at a time. On 1 January the whole group kept a vigil and fasted to coincide with the day of prayer by the Northern House of Chiefs. During the morning they were visited by an African deputy from Po, who asked the team detailed questions, and indicated that though the Upper Volta Government was sympathetic they had to play things cool because of their negotiations with the French.

The French officers had agreed to transmit a message to the President of the Upper Volta Parliament, asking for transit. But eventually the team were told that the matter was not under the jurisdiction of Upper Volta, but of Paris. The team decided therefore on further action. Michael Randle sent the following report on 8 January:

> Four set off at 6. a.m. on Sunday, 3 January, on foot for Ouagadougou . . . Mile past barrier surrounded by guards with rifles and bren guns. Told under arrest. Scott searched and keys of our vehicles seized. Vehicles impounded and team driven ninety miles under armed escort in police van from Po to Leo. Held all day, then taken back to Tumu in Ghana.

Team now in Bolgatanga, north Ghana . . . Another attempt imminent, form under consideration, although team heard news of action travelled to Ouagadougou, Niamey and Gao on fringe of Sahara. Learnt this from lorry drivers passing through.

SUPPORTING ACTIONS

While the seven-man team was at Po, Pierre Martin picketed the French Embassy in Accra for five days and then on Christmas Eve started a seven-day fast. The fast was in protest against the refusal of the French authorities to let the team through Upper Volta on their way to Reggan. It ended with a meeting addressed by Finance Minister Gebedemah, Mayor of Accra Quaye, and Minister of State N. A. Welbeck, and with a short religious service. Nkrumah sent a message of thanks. Pierre Martin received sympathetic letters from many parts of Africa and Europe. A Czech factory worker sent a cutting from *Rude Pravo* with a photograph of Martin in front of the Embassy. Letters of support arrived from France, and a number of French Embassy staff expressed their agreement with him. Citizens of Upper Volta living in Ghana joined in the demonstration in front of the Embassy, and sent a letter to the Upper Volta President asking him to grant the team visas.

The Nigerian volunteer, Hilary Arinze, also began a three-day fast on 4 January, outside the French Consulate in Lagos, to demand that the team should be allowed to continue. Arinze told the West African Pilot that the fast was also designed to protest on behalf of the people in Upper Volta, who could not speak for themselves because of their colonial subjection.

In London the Youth Campaign for Nuclear Disarmament picketed the French Embassy over Christmas to protest against the Sahara Bomb, and focussed on the efforts of the team. CNVA started daily lunch hour pickets outside the Fifth Avenue French Government Tourist Office in New York after the team were stopped at Bittou. Sympathisers in Hamburg had begun picketing the French Consulate each evening the day the team left Accra.

THIRD ATTEMPT

Before the third attempt to enter French territory, the Chairman of

Ghana CND, E. C. Quaye, made formal representation to the French authorities, demanding the return of the team's impounded vehicles. The demand was referred to Ouagadougou.

London and New York urged another attempt, and suggested starting from Nigeria. Randle cabled back on 12 January: 'Nigerian expedition impossible now, funds very low . . . funds and volunteers would have to be found in Nigeria itself and would take many weeks, even if same public response as in Ghana which is most unlikely.'

However, money was scraped together to buy another landrover and other necessary equipment for the third entry, and the team set out again on 17 January. Randle wrote to London: 'It is just possible we may get through this time, at least to Ouagadougou. Using Western road through Tumu which would normally avoid checkpoints. Quite likely that French have now closed this gap.'

The team slipped across the border on foot, and hitched lifts with friendly lorry drivers as far as Tenkodogo, about sixty-six miles north of the frontier. There they were noticed by Upper Volta police, and were detained by the French authorities, who searched them, confiscated their radio and binoculars, and then put them on a lorry and sent them back into Ghana.

At this point the team all returned to Accra. Randle cabled on 25 January:

All possible routes in Upper Volta now under close twenty-four hour guard. Team and Ghana Council estimate further confrontations on Volta border ineffective following eight weeks spent there already.

Michael Scott leaving Accra by air for Tunis today, to represent Ghana CND and Protest Team at All African Peoples Conference. Will appeal for Africa Day of Protest and will investigate possibility of new attempt from Morocco or other sympathetic state, by plane if possible.

Meanwhile Bill Sutherland to contact Nigerian personalities to investigate possible action from there. Nevertheless very possible further direct action will prove impossible.

Pierre Martin expelled from Trusteeship territory of Togoland. Informs us that borders police know names of all team members and are alerted to prevent our entry. Officals at Air France showed Pierre special instructions by security police Contonou not to accept him on their air lines going to Togo or Dahomey.

A fortnight later Pierre Martin learned through a friend at Air France that if he stopped off at Abidjan (Ivory Coast) on his way to

Dakar in Senegal he might be arrested there. Further evidence of the French authorities' concern was given in a letter from Michael Randle dated 4 February:

> We are still waiting for Michael Scott . . . If we could mount this plane expedition it would really shake the French. Not that they are not shaken now! Every day we get more and more evidence of it. Today a Quaker couple here asked permission to cross French territory on their way to Kenya and there was a great deal of discussion to the effect that they mustn't be allowed to stop here, or take such and such a road . . . the Embassy people are in fact completely jittery.

The team was still a focus for some expressions of opposition to the French test. Hilary Arinze had announced to the press in Enugu in January that 300 Nigerians had offered to take part in the next attempt to enter French territory. The Iraqi Federation of Democratic Youth cabled to Accra from Baghdad at the end of January saying forty-three people from Iraq had volunteered to join the team.

IN FRANCE

In Paris Esther Peter had been working to break through the barrier of silence about the team in the French press. Muste noted that at the time of the first confrontation in Bittou a French Government representative told reporters that he had 'no knowledge' of anti-bomb protesters being 'arrested' at the border. The absence of any French organizational backing for the team, and the fact that only two French nationals were involved reduced the news value of the team. (See Appendix 2 on the background of attempts to gain support for the team in France.) In addition the French press was very nervous of printing any material which indicated opposition to the test. However, Esther Peter did get *Le Monde* to print a long letter about the team in its issue of 2 January. She reported to London that *France Observateur* and *Le Canard Enchaîné* had carried stories. So did the Communist *Libération*. *Témoinage Chrétien* were persuaded to go as far as to print a map of the Sahara to show that Reggan was the last of a chain of oases. (The French Government had withdrawn all maps of the Sahara and Esther Peter found one by chance with the help of a French ethologist, who had been trying since the previous summer to publicize the fact that the test area was not uninhabited desert.)[3]

Esther Peter also contacted about a dozen French peace groups and formed an ad hoc committee for nonviolent direct action to demonstrate outside a nuclear centre near Paris. She began as well to organize parades in Paris against the French test. She wrote to London on 5 February:

'Am sending out tonight letters asking for participants in public demonstrations in Paris. It will be difficult. People are only getting over the Algerian shock and very reluctant to speak against anything De Gaulle wishes to do.'

General agitation about the bomb test mounted in the weeks just preceding the expected date of the explosion. There were officially supported mass demonstrations in Tunis on 25 January and in Tripoli, Libya, on 31 January. In Rabat, Morocco, about 2,000 demonstrators gathered outside the French Embassy despite a Government ban on the demonstration. While in Paris 500 African students from French Community countries were arrested on 11 February, when they gathered to present a petition against the test to Premier Debre.

At dawn on 13 February the French Bomb was exploded at Reggan. There were immediate protests by President Nasser of Egypt and the Arab League Council. The Moroccan Cabinet met to discuss measures against France and the Istiqlal Party called for the breaking off of diplomatic relations. Ghana froze the assets of French firms in retaliation, and Julius Nyerere of Tanganyika congratulated Ghana on her action. However, the French Community states, including Sudan, refrained from overt protest, and Ivory Coast and Chad went so far as to congratulate France on the test.

The team had been frustrated in their last minute hope of flying into the test area. Instead, team members still in Ghana diverted their energies to calling a special All African Conference to co-ordinate action against further French tests. The idea was put to Nkrumah by Michael Scott, and the Ghana Government took the initiative in calling the Conference, which was held in Accra from 7-10 April 1960.

THE ACCRA CONFERENCE

The Conference itself was immediately caught up in inter-African politics. Although Nkrumah's speech and some of the final resolutions reflected the ideas and aims of the American and British team members, their real influence was rapidly declining.

Nkrumah had broadened the conference agenda to cover the 'balkanisation' of Africa, and the two priorities in the African liberation struggle: Algeria and South Africa. The Conference was attended by representatives of all the nine independent African states and of many countries still awaiting independence. The FLN supported the Conference despite the emphasis on nonviolence in the original invitation, and fears that after their victory at Tunis in January in getting endorsement of their proposals for an African Brigade to fight in Algeria, they would either ignore the Conference or try to remove the emphasis on nonviolence. The main gap in participation was the absence of most French community leaders.

The Conference brought out some of the difficulties of getting joint African action. Tom Mboya made a powerful speech in which he pleaded: 'Let it not be said that all we can do is embark on expensive conferences and talk, and then go back home to await the next conference.' The Conference passed resolutions for action on South Africa, and endorsed again the proposal for an African Brigade to fight in Algeria. Ghanaian volunteers paraded outside the Conference Centre. Simultaneously, however, the Conference passed a resolution to set up training centres in nonviolent positive action to launch demonstrations against the French tests, and train participants in liberation struggles.

But no practical organizational or financial provisions were made to implement this resolution. So in effect any Centre would be sponsored by the Ghana Government, or not at all. An initiative by Ghana alone would, in view of the rivalries between leaders of different states, be distrusted. The Centre might be treated as a prestige symbol in inter-African power struggles.

A more serious danger, however, was that the Centre would never be set up at all. After the Accra Conference Nkrumah, who was no doubt aware of this danger, asked Scott, Sutherland, and Randle for suggestions. Nkrumah said he was willing to find funds to cover the running costs for the first year, and offered use of a school at Winneba, thirty miles from Accra. The General Secretary of the Convention Peoples' Party was to have final responsibility for choosing staff and a board of governors. It was agreed that Winneba would be a suitable site. But no further progress was made for three months. Nkrumah and other Ministers attended a Commonwealth Prime Ministers' Conference, and then in June a Conference of the Heads of Independent African States. Events in the Congo had become the centre of attention by July 1960. A proposal to send a Positive Action reconnaisance team into the Congo, and perhaps to bring volunteers from the Congo back to the Centre, was not accepted by the President. But in July Nkrumah announced publicly that a CPP training school to be called the Kwame Nkrumah Institute would be set up at Winneba. It would have two sections: one dealing with the training of Party and Trade Union members; the other for training in Positive Action.

By this stage the protest team members still in Ghana viewed their possible role in the Centre with considerable doubts. They had three main worries. First, they felt that the leading members on the staff of the Institute should be African, not outsiders. It was not clear, however, that there were any candidates available who combined commitment to nonviolence with sufficient experience and personal standing to steer the Centre through the intrigues of Ghana politics.

Secondly they became increasingly concerned that a Centre under the direct control of the Ghana Government would either have to abandon its commitment to individual civil rights, and to other beliefs associated with nonviolence (for example a general concern to decentralize power), or else sooner or later come into direct conflict with the Government. This dilemma was becoming acute by the end of August 1960, after the introduction of press censorship, the issuing of preventive detention orders against leading members of the opposition United Party, and the police harrassment of the Chairman of the United Party in a by-election in Accra.[4]

Thirdly they were concerned whether the Centre could maintain any kind of commitment to nonviolence. It was likely to be closely associated with the Bureau of African Affairs, set up in September 1959 under the Minister of the Interior after the death of Nkrumah's special adviser on African Affairs, George Padmore. Several members of the Bureau's board were bitterly opposed to nonviolence, and might try to divert the Centre to specifically violent action related to Algeria or South Africa. Nor was there any guarantee that the Board elected for the Winneba Centre would necessarily be concerned to stress or maintain a commitment to nonviolent action.

The immediate aim of the Centre had been to organize massive demonstrations against the French tests, and this idea had been incorporated in Nkrumah's opening speech to the Accra Conference. Nevertheless a few weeks later Ghana unfroze French assets, and Nkrumah gave the impression that he did not expect further French tests in the Sahara. But in September the news that France was planning a new series of nuclear tests caused a stir in Ghana and led to immediate protests.

Reports suggested that the first underground test was scheduled to take place in the Hoggar mountains—the site was about 350 miles from the nearest point on the Niger-Algeria border. Randle and Sutherland proposed that a team should attempt to reach the site through French-controlled Niger. They also suggested co-ordinated protests in African capitals, and a charter flight of Africans to Paris to stage a demonstration there. They urged the need to put the Centre into operation immediately to promote these plans. Despite their reservations about the Centre they felt it was worth pursuing attempts to organize direct action against the French tests.

Nothing came of these proposals. So Michael Randle flew back to England in October to take over the secretaryship of the newly formed Committee of 100 for mass civil disobedience against nuclear policies. He had been in Ghana a year. Michael Scott, who had already returned to Britain, was a co-sponsor of the Committee of 100. The Sahara Protest Team had, after more than fifteen months of planning and activity, finally come to an end.

POLITICAL EFFECTS OF THE PROTEST TEAM

The impact of the Sahara Protest Team varied considerably. There was almost no response to the venture in France, and even peace groups were reluctant to express support. The lack of internal support and the lack of publicity in the French press clearly constituted a major failure—even if it could be ascribed in part to the wider political situation in France.

There was virtually no publicity in the United States about the Team either. Muste commented on the absence of coverage in the American press despite reports filed by Reuters and other correspondents in Ghana. The British press, both national and local, did carry news items from the time the first volunteers flew to Ghana until the end of the third attempt to enter Upper Volta. But the team was never treated as a major news story.

On the other hand the team did have major impact in Ghana, and served as a focus for opposition in other parts of Africa. Bayard Rustin commented at the time that the Sahara team was the most significant pacifist project he had been associated with:

> In the past most of our projects have been moral protests in an atmosphere where there was no possibility of political accommodation. This project was in an atmosphere where most of Africa was already aroused and was waiting for a project round which it could rally. It had profound political implications in that it tied together the whole question of militarism and political freedom in a way that people could understand and respond to. [*Peace News*, 1 January 1960.]

Within Africa the team's main political failure was the absence of any organized support from the countries of French West Africa. Rustin explained to *Peace News* (1 January 1960) that:

> The chief reason for this is that a good deal of French West Africa is coming up for independence. The leaders in these areas, such as the Mali Federation, were in fact in Paris at the time negotiating for independence and for economic ties with France, and it was too much to expect them to defy France at that point.

The team's attempts to enter Upper Volta were nevertheless revealing. Muste reported that a Ghanaian official in Washington had said to him that the team's exposure of the illusory character of the 'self government' granted by the French to Africans was one of the most significant achievements of the project. (Interestingly the President of Upper Volta contacted Esther Peter when in Paris, and spoke to her about the nuclear test before meeting De Gaulle — though this did not prevent him from being the first African head of state to congratulate France on the nuclear explosion.)

There was some individual opposition to the French test in Community countries. A Youth Conference held in the French Sudan in August had propsed that demonstrations should be held against the tests throughout West Africa. The team may also have helped slightly to crystallize opposition. The government of the Ivory Coast cancelled grants to all its students opposing government policy in January 1960, following action by students in Paris calling for the protest team to be allowed to proceed, and for the abandonment of the Atom test. The Niger Government warned its officials in January that anyone opposing Government policy would be sacked immediately. But popular opposition never became significant.

More puzzling than the actions of French Community governments was the attitude of Guinea. President Sekou Toure publicly opposed the French test when it was first announced. But his attitude appeared to change during 1959. Muste observed in *Liberation* (New York):

> It had been assumed that Guinea and its leader Sekou Toure would give substantial support to the Sahara Team. Early in December, however, a number of African papers quoted Toure as saying in Morocco that personally he was neither for nor against the test, but that Africa was against it. Toure made no effort to deny this report.

Muste speculated that the reason might have been Guinea's dependence on Soviet economic aid. He noted that the team had received indications that Communists in Africa had little sympathy for the protest team, and suggested that Moscow was not interested in making an issue of the French Bomb, which might be seen as a divisive issue in NATO and irrelevant to the overall balance of nuclear power.

An additional factor was the very complicated relationship between Ghana and Guinea. The team made soundings to discover whether it might be possible to start from Guinea, and met with a courteous but cautious response from the Embassy in Accra. When Bill Sutherland and Esther Peter flew to Guinea they were not able to meet Sekou Toure. They had an interview with the Vice President, but received no concrete offers of assistance.

However after the Bomb test the Political Bureau of the Guinean Democratic Party, the supreme governing body in Guinea, did issue an official condemnation, stating that the French Bomb was 'an intolerable threat to the African peoples struggling for independence'.

In Ghana the team could claim not only to have focussed

opposition to the tests, but to have influenced the tone of public pronouncements about it, and to have spread both nonviolent ideas and methods. Rustin noted in his *Peace News* interview of 1 January 1960:

> Another interesting thing about it is that when we arrived (in Ghana) there was fantastic anti-French feeling concerning everything, but when we left they had responded to our view that we have nothing against France and the French people as such, but we are opposed to the testing of weapons wherever they are . . . The moral contribution which we gave came because we were able to operate from their political assumptions, bringing in our own point of view.

Muste estimated that in the opinion of many Ghanaians the idealism and the enthusiasm of the struggle for independence had been revived among supporters of Nkrumah's Convention People's party:

> Moreover, an immense propaganda job for the idea of nonviolence has been done among the masses and a considerable amount of intensive training in nonviolent philosophy and strategy has been given the twenty or so volunteers who were able to attend training sessions regularly. (*Liberation* January 1960.)

Ghanaian leaders and newspapers began to emphasize nonviolence. Nkrumah's message to Pierre Martin at the end of his fast said that this sacrifice would 'go down in history as one of the first of such nonviolent acts against imperialist aggression on the people of our continent'. The *Daily Graphic* reported on 25 January: 'About 600 students . . . staged a non-violent and peaceful demonstration in front of the French Embassy in Accra in protest against the test.' The *Ghana Times* carried a story on 1 February that: 'The vanguard activists of the Convention Peoples' Party carried out a "non-violent" demonstration in front of the French Embassy . . .' The style of action demonstrated by the team was also imitated. For example a fifty-year-old Ghanaian chief, the Omanhene of Nkoranza, undertook a week's fast in protest against the tests a month after Martin's fast.

LESSONS FROM THE SAHARA PROTEST

The relative success of the protest team in getting across their aims and ideas contrasts with their failure to launch a training centre in nonviolence. The difficulties involved in promoting the Centre suggest that the enthusiasm generated for nonviolence and disarmament was temporary and superficial. However the team could scarcely expect to exercise any profound influence on Ghanaian culture or politics, and the nature of the problems confronting the Centre have been outlined.

It may be more instructive to ask why the difficulties which beset the founding of the Centre did not sabotage the protest team. The answer lies partly in the fact that the protest team was a short-term action with limited aims. The team's goal of opposition to the French tests coincided with the policy aims of the Ghana Government. Secondly the protest team was an independent initiative which had already got under way and defined its own methods and objectives when the first volunteers reached Accra. And once the team left Accra it had complete discretion in planning its tactics. Therefore, the role of the Ghana Government was restricted. Indeed, although the team was dependent on the co-operation of the Government, each had a mutual interest in not becoming too closely identified. For the team, any government backing was to some extent compromising. The Government did not wish the team to be interpreted as an officially backed 'invasion', or to be committed to an embarrassing support of their own nations should they get into trouble in French-controlled territory. While there is bound to be some ambiguity in governmental support of nonviolent direct action, agreement on immediate aims and mutual interests may make co-operation acceptable to both sides.

On the other hand there is an inherent incompatibility between the idea of a permanent training centre for nonviolent action and government control. The Centre also dependend, for both financial and political reasons, entirely on governmental initiative, so the team members were unable to take independent action.

It could be argued, too, that when the team moved away from the realm of direct action, where it did have the initiative, to the realm of conference politics and of bidding for long term official support, it was likely to lose out to the rivalries governing that level of political activity. The team could no longer inject their own moral and political concepts into the situation. While the element of daring and simplicity which is appropriate to direct action is quite inappropriate to conventional political manoeuvring.

There was, however, a useful balance between the direct-action protest and more orthodox propaganda and political activity. The team did considerable educational work in Ghana about the effects of nuclear bombs. Michael Scott was personally presented at the United Nations during the November General Assembly debate on the French tests, and had circulated a memorandum on the proposed protest team. Indian Foreign Minister Krishna Menon quoted during the UN debate an article from the British *Observer* on the nature of the Sahara testing area — an article printed through the efforts of the Direct Action Committee. Michael Scott flew to Ghana to join the Team after a majority at the UN General Assembly had backed a resolution calling on the French to refrain from nuclear testing.

The Sahara Team and Ghana CND both engaged in exchange with the British governments about the dangers arising from the February atomic test at Reggan. The French Embassy distributed an official publication claiming that the tests would have no harmful effects. In their reply Ghana CND and the Team contested the scientific validity of the French claim that Ghana could not be affected by the fallout because of the direction of the winds.

When British Prime Minister Harold Macmillan stated at a press conference in Ghana that the Sahara test would not harm the people of Ghana, Ghana CND immediately reproached Macmillan for encouraging the French to test the bomb on African soil, and urged Macmillan not to repeat his statement in other parts of Africa. Michael Randle said for the team that he was ashamed as a British citizen that a British Prime Minister should make such an untrue statement. Ghana papers gave prominence to this refutation of Macmillan, illustrating Michael Randle's early comment that he had become an ambassador for radical Britain. Two days later Macmillan in a speech to the Nigerian Parliament declared his opposition to nuclear tests in Africa and anywhere else in the world. The chairman of Ghana CND immediately cabled thanks for this statement, and suggested that Macmillan should use his influence to restrain the French.

APPENDIX I: DEBATE ABOUT
THE ROUTE

If the primary emphasis of the team had been on reaching the test site, they could have entered Algeria clandestinely from Morocco. They would still have had to traverse the military zone undetected, which would mean avoiding the official route and finding a local guide, and would have been extremely hazardous. Politically the team would have suffered the disadvantage of not being able to mobilize public support in advance. Moreover, such tactics would require the greatest secrecy, and would therefore have conflicted with the principles of nonviolence and openness espoused by both the American and British Committees at that time.

In deciding to leave from Ghana with maximum publicity, the team chose a more symbolic role, and an open and immediate confrontation with the French. However, very careful consideration was given to making the team desert-worthy, and to the best mode of transport. Early discussion weighed the respective merits of landrovers or camels for crossing the desert. Bill Sutherland wrote on 12 September:

> I have just returned from Friends meeting where I talked to a man who has done a lot of camel riding in the Libyan desert. My other 'Sahara experts' have been very much against camels because they say they are one man animals, they may very well die on you, the chances of getting a sympathetic, experienced and trusted cameleer are much less than getting a mechanic of the same type, etc. The man from the Friends was attracted to the camel idea and thought it was less dangerous than one landrover trying the journey. On the other hand, you would have one camel per individual plus five or six for supplies and the speed would have to be that of the slowest camel, i.e. about $2\frac{1}{2}$ miles per hour. After reflection, he too thought a caravan of motor vehicles more sensible.

The distance between Ghana and the real desert in Algeria, and the fact that all the volunteers were used to cars but not camels, were decisive arguments in favour of landrovers.

Debate about a possible entry from Morocco did not end when the first team members flew to Ghana. The idea was raised again after a meeting in London in October with the Moroccan chargé d'affaires, who indicated that the Moroccan Government was prepared to give all practical assistance to any protest team trying to enter Reggan. A letter from DAC to CNVA set out the issues:

> Our Committee discussed the theoretical and practical difficulties involved in trying to send: (a) the original team via Morocco for a second attempt; (b) a second team via Morocco . . .

> At our meeting the dangers and difficulties of getting involved in the Algerian war situation were stressed — since it would be both tragic and stupid to get blown up by a landmine or shot up by mistake. There was also some discussion about the Moroccan military bases; if the USAF Bombers are based there Morocco cannot claim to be outside the Cold War as Ghana can, and therefore has less basis for protesting against the French tests . . . though there are mitigating factors, since I understand the bases were first allowed there by the French, not the Moroccans, and there is some agitation in Morocco to get rid of them.

> The pros are as follows: there is an obvious advantage in having two protest entries from two different parts of Africa. It would involve both North and West Africa in the protest against the tests; it would add to the dramatic impact of the project . . . It would also demonstrate the seriousness of our intention to try to reach the actual test area.

The team then in Ghana had misgivings about a Moroccan attempt. They argued that the volunteers could be intercepted as spies. They were also concerned about possible political repercussions in Ghana, where the Government had to some extent adopted the protest team as a part of its national campaign against the French tests. It was also difficult to find funds and suitable personnel for negotiations in Morocco. The idea was therefore abandoned until January 1960, when Michael Scott flew there for exploratory talks.

APPENDIX II: ATTEMPTS TO
GAIN ORGANIZATIONAL SUPPORT
IN FRANCE

The obstacles to gaining French organizational support for the Sahara team emerged in the course of negotiations between the Direct Action Committee in London and various individuals and groups in France. The first problem was the repressive nature of De Gaulle's regime in 1959. An American writer living in France, who personally sympathized with the plan for a protest team, advised the DAC that they would probably only get support from individuals. 'The situation here is very tricky, believe me. No organization or publication is willing to stick its neck out, justifiably afraid of having it lopped off.' He pointed out that the anti-governmental nature of the proposed Sahara team would discourage French organizations from officially supporting it.

A second difficulty sprang from the weakness of the anti-bomb movement in France. The official nuclear disarmament body, the Fedération Francaise Contre L'Armement Atomique, was founded only in April 1959. A public meeting was held in May. In November it launched a National Appeal calling on the Government to renounce the test, and to respond favourably to a proposal by the International Red Cross aimed at prohibiting nuclear weapons under international law. The Federation was hampered by the fact that left wing activists tended to regard the Algerian war as their central concern, and by apathy among broader sections of the public.

Action against the French Bomb was also hindered by awareness of the strength of French nationalism. A letter from a French sympathizer to the DAC commented: 'Too much money, too many interests, too great an amount of prestige are involved. Many Frenchmen think that if the English have their bombs, France must have its own.'

She also thought the Sahara protest would be counter-productive, since the French would view it as foreign intervention in a French concern. The French opponents of the Bomb would then be treated as traitors and agents of a foreign power.

One of the Presidents of the Federation (Pastor Trocmé) emphasized in a very hostile letter to the DAC that demonstrations should not antagonize French opinion, and should therefore be 'genuinely French, organized by the French, with the approval of French popular good sense'. The same letter commented adversely on plans for a picket of the French Embassy in London and for a Trafalgar Square rally: 'The French will take it for an anti-French demonstration organized for political purposes. The tension between Great Britain and France is pretty high today. A protest action . . . must be done in France nowhere else.'

The writer was also unhappy about DAC's co-operation in London with an African Committee with declared anti-colonialist aims.

Finally, in negotiations with French anti-war bodies, the standard objections to nonviolent direct action were raised: it was too dangerous; it was impractical; and it would alienate rather than influence public opinion. The proposal to try to cross the desert to Reggan was obviously open to the first two objections. The practical difficulties of the plan were stressed when Michael Randle met French peace-movement representatives in Paris on 15 September. This meeting decided against giving any support to the protest team, though a member of the meeting who had first-hand experience of the Sahara said privately afterwards that he thought the practical obstacles had been exaggerated.

In November the London office made renewed attempts to get some kind of French backing for the Team. A DAC letter to an individual supporter commented: 'The project has gained considerable support in Ghana and indeed throughout Africa. The situation is therefore very different from that two months ago . . .'

DAC suggested that the Federation might therefore reconsider its attitude. Alternatively perhaps a temporary committee could be set up to sponsor Esther Peter.

The reply came back that the Federation, though more sympathetic than before, was not able or willing to give active backing. Nor would it be feasible to create a sufficiently representative ad hoc committee. The only body likely to give real material and moral support was the Mouvement de la Paix, the French branch of the World Peace Council. DAC regretfully decided that this sponsorship would cast doubt on the non-aligned status of the project, since the Mouvement would certainly be seen as a pro-Moscow body.

Esther Peter on her return to Paris regarded it as a distinct advance when Professor Kastler, one of the Presidents of the Federation, was persuaded to write to the Government protesting that the team had been stopped by the French authorities. But she had to proceed independently in organizing demonstrations against the test.

APPENDIX III: CHRONOLOGY
OF EVENTS

June 1959: The Direct Action Committee (DAC) in London decides to launch the Sahara protest team and sends out preliminary letters.

July: Bill Sutherland in Ghana reports after consultation with George Padmore (who died soon after) that support in Ghana likely.

August: Michael Randle makes preliminary trip to France to try to canvass support.

28 August: Direct Action Committee and Committee of African Organizations (CAO) hold picket outside French Embassy in London.

30 August: DAC and CAO hold rally in Trafalgar Square where the protest team is publicly announced.

15 September: Michael Randle attends meeting of French anti-war groups who decide not to support the team.

17 September: The Committee for Nonviolent Action (CNVA) meeting in New York decide they can only give 'moral support' to the team.

6 October: CNVA hold another Committee meeting with Bill Sutherland and Michael Scott present, and decide that a significant start has been made in the Sahara project, and that CNVA will give financial and publicity support. CNVA also decide to send Bayard Rustin to Ghana for six to eight weeks.

9 October: British volunteers Michael Randle and Francis Hoyland arrive in Accra.

13 October: Ghana CND meets to hear plans for team and arranges a series of public meetings.

14 October: Bayard Rustin arrives in London for discussion.

18 October: Churches throughout Ghana observe day of prayer for nuclear disarmament.

20 October: Bayard Rustin arrives in Accra. Esther Peter passes through London for press conference.

21 October: Esther Peter reaches Accra.

27 October: Mass meeting in Accra.

7–9 November: All African Trades Union Federation meeting in Accra expresses support for team.

17 November: Michael Scott arrives in Accra.

18 November: Ghana CND appeals over radio for funds for team.

19 November: A fund-raising rally is held in Accra.

24 November: A. J. Muste joins team in Accra to act as co-ordinator;

2 December: Cable from Basutoland says Ntsu Mokhehle flying to Accra.

6 December: Nineteen-person team leaves Accra at dawn; Pierre Martin joins at Kumasi.

7-8 December: Team travel to Bolgatanga, joined by Hannah Kojo, confer about best route into Upper Volta.

9 December: Team cross from border village of Bawku after meeting in their honour; French stop them at Bittou.

13 December: Team withdraw from Bittou to Bolgatanga.

17 December: Seven-person team crosses Volta border again at Navrongo and halted at Po.

24 December-1 January: Pierre Martin fasts outside French Embassy.

3 January 1960: Team expelled from Upper Volta after trying to proceed on foot.

17 January: Seven-man team make third attempt and hitch-hike to Tenkodogo in Upper Volta; expelled the same day.

25 January: Michael Scott flies to Tunis to represent team and Ghana CND at All African Peoples Conference and negotiate possible attempt from Morocco.

25 January: Pierre Martin expelled from Trusteeship territory of Togoland by French.

13 February: French explode A-Bomb at Reggan.

7-10 April: Accra Conference.

NOTES

1. Sources used for this account are the Direct Action Committee files in London, which contain most of the memoranda and correspondence relating to the project; *Peace News, Liberation,* cuttings from the Ghanaian press between October 1959 and February 1960, and miscellaneous press reports. I am grateful to Michael Randle for advice on aspects of the project in Ghana, and to Esther Peter-Davis for an account of her work in Paris early in 1960. As Secretary of the Direct Action Committee at the time I have also drawn on my personal recollections of the project.

2. Nkrumah reprinted in April 1960 a leaflet written ten years earlier under the title 'What I Mean by Positive Action'. In this leaflet Nkrumah referred to India's liberation through 'moral pressure'. He defined the tactics of positive action as political agitation, press and educational campaigns, and as a last resort strikes, boycotts, and nonco-operation 'based on the principles of absolute nonviolence'. He also stressed the need for openness and fair play in dealings with the British Government, the need for democratic endorsement of the leadership's policies, and the importance of mobilizing the masses through the power of suffering for a just cause, quoting C. V. H. Rao's book on *The Civil Disobedience Movement in India*.

3. Mademoiselle Odette du Puigaudeau, a geologist who had lived five years in North Africa, had been trying since early in the summer of 1959 to get French papers to print an article which stressed that the claim made by the French Government that the area surrounding the test site was barren and uninhabited desert was untrue. According to an American writer living in France, who had tried to help Mlle Puigaudeau place her article: 'all the French publications except the *Tribune des Nations* (a specialized journal with a small distribution) were afraid of publishing the piece, although they acknowledged its importance. This went for *France-Observateur* and *Express*, both so nervous in light of past confiscations of issues that the subject of the article struck them as far too dangerous.'

4. The Ghana Government had begun to embark on a repressive course by November 1959, when nine members of the opposition United Party were detained. In January 1960 the United Party published a Blue Paper alleging intimdation in elections and growing repression. The situation deteriorated rapidly in August. A Bill introducing press censorship was pushed through Parliament in one day on 23 August. The next day preventive detention orders were issued against thirteen people, mostly United Party leaders. On 25 August the Chairman of the United Party withdrew from the by-election in Accra because of police harassment, and because three of his campaign managers had been jailed the day before. An executive instrument ordered on 3 September that no issue of the *Ashanti Pioneer* (the only daily opposition paper) could be published without prior censorship of all its contents.

10

NONVIOLENCE IN EASTERN AFRICA 1962–4: THE WORLD PEACE BRIGADE AND ZAMBIAN INDEPENDENCE*

CHARLES C. WALKER

The World Peace Brigade was founded in Beirut, Lebanon, on 1 January 1962, following an international conference called to prepare for its formation. The founding statement said that it intended to

> organize, train and keep available a Brigade for nonviolent action in situations of potential or actual conflict, internal and international . . . (and) against all war and preparations for war, and the continuing development of weapons of mass destruction . . .

> revolutionize the concept of revolution itself by infusing into the methods of resisting injustice the qualities which insure the preservation of human life and dignity . . .

> join with people in their nonviolent struggle for self-determination and social reconstruction . . . ['Statements of Principles and Aims' by the World Peace Brigade for Nonviolent Action, 1 January 1962, Beirut, Lebanon.]

The organization was a natural outgrowth of internationalizing the forces of nonviolence. Multinational projects had been carried out, among them the Sahara Protest in 1959 against French nuclear tests in Africa, and the San Francisco-to-Moscow March beginning in 1960 opposing all nuclear testing. Gandhians in India were sometimes critical of Western movements for concentrating on resistance and protest, and for not developing a more

---

*Originally prepared as A Preparatory Paper for Workshop 5, International Conference of Peace Researchers and Peace Activists At Noordwijkerhout, The Netherlands—July 1975.
The first draft of this paper was prepared as an assignment for the Cyprus Resettlement Project and a study of unarmed peacekeeping. Later the WPB papers became available.

comprehensive and integrated 'constructive programme'.

The plan to form such an organization had been adopted at the triennial conference of the War Resisters International held in India in 1961. The four major components would be the Gandhian movement, segments of the peace movement particularly in Europe and USA, groups engaged in nonviolent struggles for social justice in local or regional campaigns, and movements for national independence and reconstruction.

Sponsors of the conference included notables from six continents, such as Martin Buber of Israel, Bertrand Russell of England, Martin Niemoller of West Germany, Leo Infeld of Poland, Vinoba Bhave of India, Martin Luther King of USA. Two were to become heads of state: Julius Nyerere, Prime Minister of Tanganyika and now President of Tanzania; and Kenneth Kaunda, leader of the United Independence Party of Northern Rhodesia (UNIP), and now president of Zambia.[1]

As early as 1906, Gandhi in South Africa had broached the idea of a 'nonviolent army'. In 1922 he first organized a corps of 'volunteers for peace'. He had invited some of his most trusted colleagues to a meeting to form a Shanti Sena (Peace Brigade) to deal with problems in an independent India. He was assassinated before it could be held. Vinoba Bhave revived the idea in 1957 in the context of the land-gift mission (Bhoodan). (See Desai, 1972, chapter 14.) The idea had been suggested elsewhere, for example by Maude Royden in the 1930s, but was never carried out successfully. More recently it was formally suggested to the United Nations, and followed up informally, so far to no avail.[2]

Two themes characterized the intent of the organizers: (1) protest, resistance, nonviolent revolution; and (2) a constructive prógramme, the nonviolent transformation of society in the interests of freedom, justice and peace. At times the WPB might be partisan and join one side of a struggle, at other times it might serve as mediator or in some third-party capacity. What was needed, said Abbé Pierre of France, was not automatic partisans of governments or ideologies, but nonviolent defenders of the human race.

Elected co-chairpeople were Michael Scott, A. J. Muste and Jayaprakash Narayan. Scott is a legendary figure in Africa, known in particular for his dedicated work in the United Nations for African causes. Muste was a US radical pacifist known internationally for his political and intellectual leadership in a variety of movements. Narayan is a Gandhian whose prestige among the Indian masses sometimes rivalled that of Nehru.[3]

One region where the WPB hoped to work was Africa south of the Sahara. Immediately after the conference, Siddharaj Dhadda, an Indian delegate and later secretary of the Asian Council, travelled in eastern Africa to describe the WPB and offer its services, perhaps to establish a training and action centre in Dar es Salaam as a base for work in Africa.

ADDIS ABABA MEETING
OF INDEPENDENCE GROUPS

The organizational pace of WPB work in Africa might have been slower, involving numerous negotiations, but for a timely development. Meeting in Addis Ababa on 2-10 February were about thirty groups in the Pan-African Freedom Movements of East and Central Africa (later 'Southern' was added and the acronym became PAFMECSA). This was its fourth annual conference.

When Bill Sutherland arrived at that meeting, and Bayard Rustin a little later, they were greeted cordially by many who knew them from past associations and projects. Both had played major roles at the WPB conference. Sutherland had been secretary to the finance minister of Ghana when he served as government liaison to the Sahara Project. Rustin, a major US civil rights leader, had also participated in that project, and had worked on several assignments in western Africa at the request of Nnamdi Azikewe, Prime Minister of Nigeria and the Cameroons, and Kwame Nkrumah, President of Ghana. Despite the suspicions of some, a WPB team of observers was agreed to: Sutherland, Rustin, Dhadda, and Michael Scott.[4]

Michael Scott had been a participant in a dramatic example of indigenous, mass nonviolent civil disobedience, led by Chief Gomani of the Angoni people in Nyasaland, opposing the imposition of the Central African Federation. ('African episode', London Africa Bureau.)

The conferees at Addis Ababa were aroused by a formidable set of problems, among them postponement of independence, an increase in terrorism, and economic consolidation of European interests. Nonviolence was vigorously debated. Defeats and setbacks in South Africa were recounted, victories by violence described and promised. On the other hand, representatives such as Kenneth Kaunda presented a strong case for militant nonviolent action at that stage in political development and in the light of forces operating in the region. A resolution specifically commending nonviolence was narrowly defeated. Kenneth Kaunda was nevertheless elected chairperson of PAFMECA, and support was pledged to his campaign for independence.

CRISIS IN NORTHERN RHODESIA

Northern Rhodesia was one of three countries which the British had incorporated into the Central African Federation; the others were Southern Rhodesia and Nyasaland. UNIP had been agitating for independence with considerable effect, and Federation Prime Minister Sir Roy Welensky felt survival of this political unit was threatened. In 1961 the British Colonial Office had announced plans for a new constitution, one failing because of White opposition, the other because of bitter African resistance. Welensky said in February 1962 that he was determined to maintain the status quo and implied he would do so by whatever means necessary.

The Federation appeared to many Africans as a way to slow down the coming of independence, and to maintain White settler control Also at stake was the continued exploitation of the vast mineral wealth in areas stretching across the middle of the continent. Wielding major influence in the Federation were European and American interests which were part of the interlocking directorate of operating companies in the region.[5] Welensky had publicly supported the Katanga secession, and was friendly to the South African regime — a touchstone issue among independence groups.

Kaunda and UNIP proposed that if the Welensky forces remained adamant, and major disruptions appeared to block the scheduled election in Northern Rhodesia, then a general strike would be called. Co-ordinately, an international Freedom March would be mobilized, to cross from Tanganyika into Northern Rhodesia. Numbering in the thousands, it would be composed primarily of Africans but would be joined by supporters from many countries outside that continent. The march had been broached by WPB personnel, and the WPB was expected to organize the international contingent.[6]

Britain was feeling the pressure, and Colonial Secretary Reginald Maudling tried to find a formula. British officials reproved Nyerere for opposing the Federation, American officials warned Rustin about meddling as an outsider.

Welensky disdained the language of diplomacy and said, 'The vicious influence of African nationalism has turned their bone marrow to jelly' and he declared flatly, 'The Federation is mine' and that he would 'go whole hog' implying armed force.[7]

Kaunda ordered food stocks prepared for the general strike. Beginning plans for the Freedom March were known to Federation authorities. Welensky stationed troops along the border between Northern Rhodesia and Tanganyika and numerous harassments were reported. (A few years later a former police officer in Northern Rhodesia who became a *Standard* reporter in Dar es Salaam told Bill Sutherland of the considerable preparations to deal with the marchers and the government's concern that the combination of the march and the general strike would be difficult to cope with. The plan: let the marchers cross the border into a desolate area and then seal them off.[8])

Some black African leaders echoed the speeches at Addis Ababa and pressed for violent solutions. Offers came to them for training in guerrilla tactics. On the other hand, if the independence struggle could succeed by nonviolent action, and establish a progressive society not based on racism, this could have a profound effect not only on other independence movements but on the whole of southern Africa.

AFRICA FREEDOM ACTION

To pursue nonviolent initiatives, and support the strike and march, a working committee was established called Africa Freedom Action (AFA). It was comprised of three representatives from each of four groups: UNIP, TANU (Tanganyika African National Union, leading party in that country), PAFMECA, and the World Peace Brigade. It was pledged to nonviolent action and took action by consensus.

The rationale for the march was formulated in more precise terms:

1. It would be a significant act of international solidarity with those determined to achieve their independence.

2. It might serve in some measure as a deterrent to the violence that was foreshadowed in incidents along the Northern Rhodesia-Tanganyika border, violence that might well intensify in face of thousands 'invading' from the north.

3. Marchers could help preserve a nonviolent discipline in Northern Rhodesian political rallies; not a few of these had ended up in violent incidents, and UNIP charged that provocateurs were responsible.

4. Marchers could help rebuild villages and areas destroyed in violent incidents.

Beyond this were other possibilities for action in the region, to be mentioned later in this report. One was a proposal by Michael Scott about Southwest Africa (Namibia).

Kaunda representing UNIP, and Rashid Kawawa, Vice-President of TANU, after consulting with Nyerere, issued a statement which included the following:

> In the light of the grave struggle for freedom in Africa, we welcome and encourage the generous support offered by the World Peace Brigade in response to our appeal for co-operation from men of goodwill throughout the world.
>
> We are particularly heartened that a group whose members have engaged in positive action in so many countries should add their experience to our own long efforts to achieve freedom in Africa through nonviolent resistance and a direct economic struggle . . . In particular we are convinced that such action applied now in Northern Rhodesia may yet prove to be the key to the liberation of Central and Southern Africa.
>
> The active support and co-operation of freedom loving peoples everywhere is urgently needed if Africa is to move as quickly as she should toward true freedom; on the other hand, our struggle for African freedom is not for Africa nor for ourselves alone. It is part of humanity's struggle for a just and peaceful world.[9]

WPB alliance with Africa Freedom Action was criticized from two sides. On the one hand, some militant Africans felt that an alliance with the WPB would impose restraints upon their freedom of action, and saw nonviolence only as a matter of immediate tactics. On the other hand, some pacifists critized the coalition because they feared the fate of a nonviolent project if it was put into the hands of those whose commitment to nonviolence might weaken or change quickly.

The project moved ahead because (1) The Freedom March was a potent idea that required WPB help at the international level, (2) WPB leaders on the spot took the view that mass movements are working alliances of many forces, and (3) It was clear that a nonviolent *strategy* would prevail for a time even as the crisis intensified.[10] These judgements were quickly vindicated. Seldom in the life of Africa Freedom Action were the debates and discussions about nonviolence as the strategic option; rather they were about implementation, or on other questions of politics or organization.[11]

BRIGADE MOBILIZES

WPB set as its initial goal getting teams of three people from ten countries each, to provide the core of the organizing effort. One of the three, it was hoped, would be a well-known personality. The AFA had urged this because the march was seen as a confrontation that guaranteed worldwide news coverage by the participation of an international contingent. Rustin drew up extensive and detailed plans for a dramatic event that could not be brushed aside by the press or the authorities.

A few volunteers were sent immediately, among them Quaker Philip Seed, a social worker; John Papworth, who had completed an extensive tour of Africa eighteen months earlier — both were from England. Another was Niels Mathiesen, WRI secretary in Oslo for several years. Rustin, Scott, and Sutherland pledged to go. Jayaprakash Narayan and his wife Prabhavati would lead a substantial Indian delegation. Responses also came from West Germany, Italy, France, and Canada.

Bringing in these volunteers immediately was a way to show seriousness about the action, generate intermediate publicity, and to demonstrate the capacity of WPB to mobilize volunteers.

The march route was checked out, in Tanganyika by TANU and in Northern Rhodesia by Anton (Ax) Nelson, who reported that the 500-mile route in Northern Rhodesia was feasible despite the problems posed by some desolate areas in the north. (It was 640 miles from Dar to NR border via Mbeya; John Papworth prepared a detailed route plan.)

In addition to the international aspect, the WPB was asked to draw up plans for training 'second echelon leaders' in the philosophy, strategy, and tactics of nonviolent action. Such trained cadres would be assigned a major role in the march, to cope with the many problems that could arise in such a venture involving many thousands from different countries, crossing a border without permission.

The fast pace of these new developments posed a dilemma. It put the WPB in business at once, in the midst of a struggle with far-reaching implications. Serious theoretical questions about power and nation-state politics had to be dealt with, organizational decisions made with little advance consultation at a time when precedents were being set and morale tested. Improvisation in the field is always necessary but groups differ on how much, and tend to react strongly when they disapprove a decision. The dilemma was posed: relevance (as some perceived it) vs. adequate participation in decision-making at the start of the organization's development. The peremptory needs of the Africa project also gave impetus to organizing efforts in the other regions—Europe, North America, Asia—despite the rumbling of disagreement on politics, organization, and to some extent philosophy. A difficult problem to cope with was leadership style, which varied so much between movements and cultures.[12]

PAFMECA RESPONDS

While the WPB concentrated on non-African participation, Africa Freedom Action decided that the overwhelming majority of marchers would be Africans, and most of these from the immediate region. (The WPB had adopted such a policy at its founding.)

To the constituent freedom groups in PAFMECA, from the Congo to Zanzibar, Secretary General Mbiyu Koinange sent a letter which included this remarkable statement:

> . . . Although this support from overseas is very encouraging, it is up to us, particularly those in PAFMECA, to be the first to respond to the call from our brothers in Zambia. We therefore call upon all our members to select three representatives, including one outstanding personality, to stand by ready for positive action which may involve civil disobedience such as crossing frontiers without official permission.

> Each representative must be so dedicated to the freedom and unity of Africa that he accepts without question the following risks: being shot at and wounded or killed, being beaten, being arrested, being brought to trial and imprisoned for a long time, or being held in jail for a long period without trial.

Thus the African militants—in this organized expression of their work—far from diminishing the nonviolent character of the march, underlined it in unmistakable terms. The many thousands who attended rallies in Kenya and Tanganyika indicated the potential that could be mobilized. (See under 'Rallies', below.)

THE 'ELECTION'

The combination and accumulation of pressures made it apparent that a new situation was in the making. Kaunda had testified before the UN Committee on Colonialism, in New York. The various British proposals for a new constitution foundered. Publicity and knowledge of plans for the strike and march had some effect, according to reports reaching AFA from the region and elsewhere.

In a sudden move, Sir Roy Welensky handed in his resignation to the Governor-General on 8 March. Under the British parliamentary system, this dissolved the Federal Assembly and set the stage for new elections on 27 April. But it was to be held on the same old basis of discrimination against African voters. With a population of about 2.5 million Africans, Northern Rhodesia had about 5,200 Africans on the Federal voters' roll. So complete was the election boycott urged by the African nationalists that fewer than 100 of the 5,200 voted. Sir Edgar Whitehead, Prime Minister of Southern Rhodesia, said in a public speech the day before the election that it was 'a bit of a farce' because the opposition refused to put up candidates. As expected, Welensky and the United Federal Party held fifty-four seats in the Federal Assembly of fifty-nine members.

British authorities concluded that the situation could not be resolved in defiance of UNIP. New constitutional provisions were drawn up that 'won the grudging participation of all political parties', as one observer put it.[13] UNIP was divided at first on whether to participate. This uncertainty had its immediate effect on plans for the march, and its planners were asked to await further developments.

A crisis faced WPB at this point. Mobilizing for such a venture, with the forces this released in various countries and in several organizations, was a formidable task. Expectations were raised, money collected, organizational staff adjusted to help out. Michael Scott wrote:

> We cannot switch peoples' enthusiasm and activities on and off. And to bring people from Europe and America on a venture that may cost them their liberty and perhaps their lives demands a lot of effort and organization at both ends, and the people who come may have to give up their jobs in some cases and make provision for their work and families, and have budgeted for a possible spell in jail or of being physically out of action . . . (all) for an as yet unspecified date.[14]

He suggested it might be necessary to arrange for supporting action after the strike began, or organize a symbolic action at the border and then call for volunteers if and when the strike began.

It would not have been surprising if some in UNIP regarded both the strike and march as threats, to be advertised or muted as the situation seemed to require. Kenneth Kaunda nevertheless wrote to Michael Scott:

> I must say at once that I admire your courage and determination to stand up to so many things. I do know that your waiting patiently for us to move in Northern Rhodesia takes a lot of courage and energy. I do hope, however, that you will not have long to wait now before we decide one way or the other.[15]

The outcome of UNIP's decision would be a critical turning point in the struggle, there were legitimate issues to debate, and dealing with the British Colonial Office and the Federation was not a simple matter.

On the other hand, WPB had no desire to impose its own organizational problems or needs on others. It was entirely in accord with the idea of self-determination, and had offered its services to those with the prime stake in the outcome. An unintended effect of forestalling the march was ironic: its possibility had suddenly plunged the newly formed WPB into a significant political struggle, and the postponement just as quickly put a dent into its fortunes.

Kaunda repeatedly urged, even after deciding to co-operate in the elections, that the march idea be held in readiness. Who knows, he said, whether things will work out as promised? Will agents provocateur stir things up so badly that the election will be held off? Will Welensky come up with some new gimmick? So the march was neither cancelled nor called for; it was held in abeyance.

This seemed to vindicate the criticism of those who had warned against putting the organization's fate in the hands of others. Scarce funds had been expended on needless travel, as one example. Sutherland and others replied that it was precisely the threat of mounting problems for the Federation and the British, including the march, that had helped to produce the new situation, that the prospect of militant and dramatic action had enabled UNIP and its allies to keep initiative and move forward, that it should be considered fortunate that suffering could be averted.[16]

TRAINING CENTRE

At Beirut a training centre, perhaps at Dar es Salaam, had been envisaged as a base for organizing in eastern Africa. The experience of organizing the Positive Action Center in Accra a few years earlier was known to some of the principals. The training concepts that prevailed at Beirut were not those that would envisage trying to turn people into pacifists. Rather, training would be designed to accord with the practical needs of the particular group or individuals who were involved. Action and training would reinforce each other, and hopefully be based in protracted campaigns or sustained efforts for development and social reconstruction.

The WPB set up a small centre pending the availability of more funds and personnel. Its four main purposes were to (1) explore the relevance of application of nonviolent action to issues at local, national and regional levels, (2) serve as a forum for various socio-economic programmes that would express African aspirations and meet needs of the people, (3) help with immediate and intermediate action, provide some skill training, promote self-help projects, and (4) assist individuals and groups engaged in freedom struggles, in particular to develop international contacts.

A hostel was set up initially with four UNIP people, Sutherland and later Suresh Ram, who had been sent by the Asian Council as a full-time staff worker. Ram was a veteran Gandhian, arrested as a student during the 'Quit India' campaign, active in the land-gift movement, sometimes a journalist and author of two books on

Vinoba Bhave. (Prime Minister Nehru sat in on one of the meetings where it was decided to send Ram to the centre.)

The work of the centre was suspended for a time when WPB people became involved in daily meetings about the march and related matters. When the march was held in abeyance, the work began again. Time was taken up in finding a suitable location for an expanded centre. In the meantime, discussions on independence issues were held, nonviolence examined in its African context, current issues explored. Typing lessons were given to eight people each morning, self-help building projects undertaken nearby, speaking engagements carried out. Political refugees stayed there occasionally, some required emergency funds in straitened circumstances. It was called the Positive Action Centre.

Africa Freedom Action was also considering action in other parts of Africa, notably Southwest Africa. Refugees from that area who came to the centre engaged in numerous discussions about action projects. PAFMECA included more than a dozen constituent groups, each with pressing problems. Work continued on aiding UNIP's election campaign, especially fund-raising.

RALLIES

Extensive meetings were held during May 1962. PAFMECA planned a huge rally at the town of Mbeya, near the Taganyika-Northern Rhodesia border. Planning for it provided the occasion for the three WPB co-chairpeople to meet, the first time since Beirut, to re-evaluate the situation in consultation with African leaders.

A meeting of the Working Committee of AFA was held. Among those on hand were Nyerere, Kaunda, Kawawa (Tanganyikan Prime Minister), Munaka (his parliamentary secretary), Koinange (general secretary of PAFMECA), Makasa (UNIP representative), Scott, Rustin, Sutherland, Ram, Jayaprakash Narayan who had just come from India, and Muste from USA. Kaunda again emphasized the need to keep the march in the picture until the election demands were fully met, to raise money for the elections, to keep up the pressure through such occasions as the Mbeya rally, and to maintain morale and discipline among the people.[17]

A rally of more than 4,000 people was held in Dar es Salaam on

10 May, with Nyerere as chairperson (an unusual size for a political rally in Dar, it was said).

A giant rally was held at Mbeya on the weekend of 12-14 May. It was called the 'PAFMECA Special Conference with Active Co-operation of UNIP and WPB'. The crowd numbered perhaps 10,000 and included 140 Zambians who crossed the border for the meeting. They braved heavy downpours of rain to hear speakers from Kenya, Zanzibar, South Africa, Southern Rhodesia, Nyasaland, Ethiopia and Uganda (PAFMECA speakers). From the Peace Brigade were Narayan, Scott, and Rustin. Nyerere, Kawawa, and Kaunda also spoke. Not all spoke for nonviolence, of course; some held that if nonviolent means could not be mobilized or applied, then they would take other measures. Nevertheless, that such a gathering could be held in such numbers, and with endorsements of varying degrees in a nonviolent enterprise aimed at affecting the history of eastern Africa and neighbouring regions — that was of no small significance. It was an enormous morale booster.

The co-chairpeople received the following letter from Mbiyu Koinange, secretary general of PAFMECA:

> The Co-ordinating Freedom Council sitting in special session at Mbeya, Tanganyika, on 14 May 1962, asked me to convey to the World Peace Brigade through you its sincere appreciation for your wholehearted efforts in cooperating unselfishly with the United National Independence Party's struggle to free Zambia from imperialism, colonialism, neo-colonialism and European domination. The World Peace Brigade did a lot in initiating the Africa Freedom Action in Dar es Salaam and as one of its sponsoring organizations has helped in focusing world attention upon the cause of freedom in Central Africa . . .[18]

Later consultations indicated that further and more detailed plans for the centre needed to be firmed up immediately, and then carried out effectively. Kaunda said he hoped the WPB could establish a powerful centre in a free Zambia which would serve the whole southern region of Africa. When asked specifically if the nonviolence represented by the Brigade was a political embarrassment, he emphatically stated the opposite.

Nyerere urged the WPB to continue, and to lay before him specific plans for a new version of the centre. He agreed that it should adhere firmly to nonviolence despite the problems that would inevitably arise. Others at various official levels endorsed these views.[19]

EDUCATING, ORGANIZING

J. P. Narayan and his wife Prabhavati spent five weeks in the area. A major part of the work was fund-raising, in particular among the Indian population. Funds were needed for the forthcoming election (he rather quickly raised £1,000) and for WPB. In his talks Narayan emphasized the co-ordinate aspects of nonviolence: *resistance* to colonialism and suppression, as well as *social reconstruction* for a new society (the Gandhian term is *sarvodaya*, the welfare of all).

A side-effect of Narayan's efforts was that Asians in Tanganyika began to take an active role in TANU, whereas heretofore they had been criticized for not playing a more active part in political struggles. Good meetings were held in Kenya; Jomo Kenyatta acted as interpreter at a large mass meeting near Nairobi. The feelings of many were expressed in this cable afterwards:

> We thank you for coming to our aid stop Your presence with the World Peace Brigade had had tremendous effects stop Your support draws our two countries closer stop The Peace March may still be necessary so Indian volunteers should be at the ready stop KAUNDA.[20]

UNITED NATIONS TESTIMONY

The UN Special Committee on Colonialism met in Dar es Salaam on 4 June to accommodate petitioners who could not go to New York. On 5 June Michael Scott, Bill Sutherland and Suresh Ram appeared as the first petitioners. Scott read a carefully drafted statement recounting the interlocking economic interests in the region, their political impact, and the need for drastic action to forestall violence and disorder in which the cause of freedom would be jeopardized further.[21]

That afternoon Narayan flew back from Nairobi to add impromptu testimony. He was questioned closely about the march and its possible consequences. (WPB learned the committee was pleased with the presentation.) For the next three days staff helped

UNIP prepare documentation about harassment, even murders, of UNIP people. These documents were later used by Africa Freedom Action in educational work.

At this point, friendly critics said that the WPB had too uncritically enlisted on the side of UNIP, and ignored the violence and harassment of critics practised on occasion by UNIP people. It appears in retrospect the charge may have had some merit. The time of a public testimony may not have been the most appropriate occasion to ventilate such criticism. Kaunda was not averse to recognizing publicly the difficulty of restraining political workers even under harassment. Indeed, he said the presence of the march idea was a restraining force in face of such problems.

THE NEW CENTRE

Nyerere approved plans for an expanded centre. A site was finally located near Kivukoni College. Freedom issues became the main focus of various kinds of work. Dar es Salaam as then the major centre in the southern part of the continent for political refugees and their organizations. WPB staff were often in touch with these groups, and contacts developed that could have been significant for future work. John Papworth often used the centre for his organizing work for UNIP in the forthcoming election.

At the request of several groups, a seminar was organized by WPB on the future of nonviolence and constructive development in Africa.[22] Eduardo Mondlane, after several discussions with Bill Sutherland, asked him to draft a programme for nonviolent action that could be used by FRELIMO, the leading resistance group in Mozambique of which Mondlane was the acknowledged leader. (It was from some of the Algerians that he had discovered the role that nonviolent action sometimes played in that struggle.) Sutherland and a colleague did draft a proposal but it was turned down by the FRELIMO executive group.

SOUTHWEST AFRICA PROJECT

From the outset of the Brigade's founding, Michael Scott, who had worked arduously for Southwest Africa on several fronts, envisaged some form of direct action project from outside, co-ordinated with internal action. In a political memorandum drafted in January 1962 (by Scott, Rustin and Michael Randle, the latter the former director of the Accra Positive Action Centre), the march idea was first advanced on the basis of this perception:

> The fate of all these territories is bound up one with the other; a victory or defeat in one area has its repercussions in all the other areas. This is particularly true of South and South-west Africa whose future may largely depend on whether Verwoerd and Welensky can succeed in establishing their stronghold or whether, on the other hand, the present Central African Federation can be broken up and South Africa isolated. Northern Rhodesia is probably the key point as it is the most vulnerable area in the Verwoerd-Welensky axis.

After analyzing the futility of a military approach, they said:

> As the white extremists concentrate their economic and military forces, it is clear that to challenge them successfully positive action campaigns have to be developed with even greater efficiency. Just as in violent campaigns strategy, tactics and discipline have to be worked out with care, leaders have to be trained and strategy studied, so in campaigns using nonviolent positive action there has to be intensive and special preparation and training.

They proposed Tanganyika as the site for a training and action centre because 'it is the nearest independent territory to the area concerned and adjoins Northern Rhodesia where the greatest chance of a breakthrough exists'. The memorandum then suggested the co-ordinated plan for the march from Tanganyika into Northern Rhodesia, and then later a further march across the Caprivi Strip 'into Southwest Africa demanding the return of the lands from which Africans have been forcibly evicted to their rightful owners and demanding that the territory be handed over to UN jurisdiction'.[23]

At the London meeting of the International Council of WPB, a detailed proposal was drafted.[24] Co-ordinated with the march would be action by national groups in their own countries, deputations to governments and the UN, demonstrations at embassies and headquarters of mining companies or other commercial interests in London, Geneva, New York and Brussels. At the initiative of some Germans in WPB, this idea emerged:

> Coinciding with the freedom march it is proposed that an

internationally sponsored programme of land reclamation should take place in an adjoining African territory where the people and government are friendly towards the UN and the efforts of African states in experimenting in forms of co-operative agricultural enterprise. One object of this would be to provide land in at present unsettled or desert areas for settlement by African people who are denied land elsewhere and wish to experiment with new methods and forms of organization, and new agricultural techniques.

(The proposal is presented in such detail here for three reasons: first, it was the focus of much discussion in AFA and the centre; second, it illustrates well the twofold emphasis of WPB, on both resistance and social organization interacting; and third, it is a valuable scenario illustrating the possible application of a non-violent political strategy—with further implications apparent —in a politically sensitive and pivotal area on the world scene.)

At the request of SWA (Southwest Africa) leaders, on occasion the North American Council organized demonstrations in New York, at embassies and elsewhere, on behalf of issues that needed more visibility and international support. Michael Scott and A. J. Muste met with U Thant at the United Nations about ways the WPB could be useful to the UN in the areas of its work in Africa. The SWA proposal remained only that, for lack of agreement among African groups, even if it could be staged from an independent Zambia.[25]

UNIP WINS ELECTION

In the October election UNIP emerged as the clearly dominant party. That ended the march idea. Inasmuch as the Southwest Africa project didn't prosper, no direct action programme appeared relevant. So the work of the WPB, the centre in particular, took on a more conventional character. Statements by African leaders and organizations were solicited for the 1963 March on Washington, and against the Vietnam War. Educational work continued, but without a dramatic project at hand money was hard to come by. Appeals from Sutherland and Ram for help yielded limited results. The WPB mounted another major project in Asia: the Delhi-Peking March in the wake of the Sino-India border clash in 1963. This absorbed the energies, funds, and work time of many in the North American Council, which had the major responsibility for aiding the Africa project.

As part of a re-assessment, a WPB delegation which included Bayard Rustin and Bill Sutherland had a long interview with Julius Nyerere. He paid tribute to WPB work, wished it could be of larger scope and impact, and in an unusual comment, expressed appreciation that some WPB people had several times expressed serious concern about dilemmas he would face if he moved in a more authoritarian direction.[26] Sutherland was asked to take a government post in Tanganyika.

FADE-OUT

The WPB as an international organization began to lose momentum in 1964. The voyage it sponsored from London to Leningrad to protest Soviet nuclear testing (late 1962) had some effect but did not put the European groups into business as happened in Africa. In the US the civil rights movement was burgeoning and absorbing the energies of nearly all the WPB people there, some of whom were key fundraisers for WPB too: Muste, Rustin, Robert Gilmore of New York Friends Group. Michael Scott did not, for a time, find it possible to use the Dar centre as an African base of operations. Requests from Dar for staff additions and replacements could not be met.

The base of the WPB did not expand significantly. It was maintained largely by radical pacifists in the US, the Shanti Sena in India, and by European groups, English in particular. As the civil rights movement turned US leaders inward to an increasing degree, the Indians were caught up in problems arising from the Sino-Indian conflict, and the WPB march there. The competition for funds was intense.

Some of its proposals erred because they tried to transpose to the international scene action methods more appropriate to a national setting. The WPB was unable to commit key people to assignments at critical times. Perhaps the main reason for the demise of Africa work was simply the fact that no action programme finally emerged, for whatever reason one may assign. Narayan believes that, in addition to these reasons, the two main reasons for WPB's problems and inability to become a viable organization were lack of funds—it underestimated the cost of international organization too—and the lack of mechanisms to consult enough at the international level.[27]

The WPB was never formally laid down. It fell into disuse, leaving an ambiguous legacy of what Theodore Olson called 'vision and failure' but perhaps invaluable experience on which to build at a more propitious time (Olson, 1964).

In recognition of what the WPB contributed to the struggle for independence of Zambia, Michael Scott and Bill Sutherland were invited to sit on the speakers stand at the 1964 independence ceremonies.

WHAT WAS GAINED?

(What follows is a personal evaluation. It is based on participation in the founding conference, service as one of its training specialists, membership in the North American Council, and participation in the Delhi-Peking March. I have interviewed most of the principals in later years. Jayaprakash Narayan in 1971, Sutherland and Scott more recently. I have examined the extensive files of the Africa project recently obtained by the Swarthmore College Peace Collection, made available by Bill Sutherland.)

1. The WPB helped, if modestly, in the unfolding events leading to Zambian independence.

2. The march idea was an antidote to the frustration and bitterness that were affecting groups in PAFMECA, as evidenced at Addis Ababa. The idea was new enough and sufficiently dramatic that it added a new dimension to some of the political dialogue.

3. By Kaunda's testimony, the march idea provided help in maintaining morale and positive movement at a critical time in Zambia.

4. By Nyerere's testimony, and from what Michael Scott learned later in London, the march combined with the threatened general strike was a factor in the British revised attitude toward the viability of the Federation, if Welensky persisted in the old ways.

5. The idea of militant nonviolence was projected in a particular context so that its potential could be better understood by thousands of Africans.

6. Jayaprakash Narayan's travels, speeches and fundraising activities produced positive effects, direct and indirect, among groups and political leaders in the region. They also led to more Asian participation in TANU (Narayan, Sutherland and Ram raised about £5000 for UNIP).

7. In later years, Kenneth Kaunda carried further his hope for a training centre in a free Zambia. He asked the American Friends Service Committee (Lyle Tatum negotiated the matter) to establish a centre in Lusaka to give specific form and direction to the general ideas of nonviolence associated with the Kaunda regime and the independence movement. Implementation was interrupted by UDI: Unilateral Declaration of Independence by Southern Rhodesia.

The fact that nonviolent actionists could work out practical strategies regarding resistance to colonialism, develop tactics applicable on a mass scale, and establish a cordial working relationship with a variety of independence groups is perhaps some indication of the potential of nonviolence, if more assidiuously pursued in its organizational and political aspects.

REFERENCES

Deming, Barbara, 1962. 'International peace brigade'. The Nation 194 (April 7), 303-6.

Desai, Narayan, 1972. Towards a Non-Violent Revolution. Rajghat, Varanasi, India: Sarva Seva Sangh Prakashan.

Olson, Theodore, 1964. 'Vision and failure'. Our Generation Against Nuclear War (June).

Wolfe, Alvin M., 1962. 'The economics of the jungle.' Liberation [New York] (January).

NOTES

1. Some other sponsors: Prof. Iwao Ayusawa of Japan, Bernhardt Jensen of Denmark, G. Nadjakov of Bulgaria, Alan Paton of South Africa, Tibor Sekelj of Yugoslavia. Few of the sponsors could attend, but it is difficult to imagine that the outcome of the conference would have been substantially different.

2. Letter from the Shanti Sena to U Thant, 1971. Letter from the International Peace Academy to UN Missions, 1971. See Nonviolence-International, a documentation service edited by Charles C. Walker, No. 1, Haverford College, USA. Available from the Gandhi Institute, Box 92, Cheyney, PA 19319, USA. Also 'The Idea of International Peace Contingents', by Charles C. Walker, Paper No. 1, Working Party on Peace Contingents,

Haverford College.

Unless otherwise stated, all items mentioned in this and subsequent notes can be found in the World Peace Brigade papers at the Swarthmore College Peace Collection, Swarthmore, PA. USA.

3. For an account of the conference, see Deming (1962). The official founding meeting was held in Beirut on 1 January. The preparatory conference was held at Brummana, a suburb, 28-31 December 1961. The founding parley is usually referred to as the Brummana Conference.

4. Some of the same people in the WPB had been involved in the Sahara Protest in 1959 — Scott, Sutherland, Muste, Rustin, Randle. See 'Sahara Action' by April Carter (included in the present volume).

5. Documented by Wolfe (1962).

6. 'Memo on Project in Africa from Policy Group D', proceedings at the Brummana Conference. 'Memornadum on Positive Action In Southern Africa' by Michael Scott, Michael Randle and Bayard Rustin, January 1962. Also 'World Peace Brigade — Africa Freedom Action Project', a reflective memorandum by Bill Sutherland, 8 January 1963.

7. *Time,* 9 March 1962, pp. 35-6.

8. Tape recording No. 1, Beverly Sterner interviewing Bill Sutherland in Dar es Salaam, 1975.

9. Quoted in 'World Peace Brigade Submission to UN Committee on Colonialism', p. 1. Dar es Salaam, 5 June 1962.

10. Interview with Bill Sutherland by the author, at Wayne, PA, 19 December 1974.

11. Tape Recording No. 2, Charles Walker interviewing Bill Sutherland, Philadelphia, PA, 19 December 1974.

12. Reflected, for example, in Minutes of Meeting No. 7 and Meeting No. 9 of the London Working Committee of WPB.

13. Lyle Tatum, American Friends Service Committee representative stationed in Salisbury. May 1962 report.

14. To Bayard Rustin, 8 April 1962.

15. From Lusaka, 2 May 1962.

16. Interview with Bill Sutherland by the author, 19 December 1974, Wayne, PA.

17. 'Report of the Chairmen', WPB, 23 May 1962. Dar es Salaam. Prepared after several meetings and interviews with African leaders.

18. On PAFMECA stationery, 19 July 1962.

19. 'Report of the Chairmen', WPB, 23 May 1962. Dar es Salaam.

20. 'Newsletter', Positive Action Centre, 30 June 1962.

21. 'World Peace Brigade Submission to UN Committee on Colonialism', eight pages. Dar es Salaam, 5 June 1962.

22. 'Proposed Seminar On Basic Problems of New African Societies', by Bill Sutherland, attached to letter to Kenneth Kaunda, 31 January 1963. Expanded in another undated memorandum.

23. 'Memorandum On Positive Action In Southern Africa' by Michael Scott, Michael Randle and Bayard Rustin. January 1962.

24. 'Africa Freedom Ride', A confidential memorandum. Pehaps during Council meetings of 30 July to 2 August in London.

25. Discussions with SWA people and others in PAFMECA reported in 'Newsletter No. 2', Africa Freedom Action Project, 1 September 1962.

26. For example, letter from Bill Sutherland to Julius Nyerere, 17 January 1963.

27. Interview with Jayaprakash Narayan by Charles Walker, New Delhi, Summer 1971.

11

CULEBRA: NONVIOLENT ACTION AND THE US NAVY*

CHARLES C. WALKER

Culebra is a tiny island, seven miles long and three at its widest, a municipality of Puerto Rico with about 725 inhabitants. Evidence suggests it was R. L. Stevenson's 'Treasure Island'. Despite its natural beauty, especially the beautiful curving beach at Flamingo Bay, life on Culebra is no idyll.

For more than thirty-five years, the US Navy has been using Culebra as a bombing and gunnery range. Nearly all the ships in the Atlantic Fleet fire at this island some time during the shipyard-to-shipyard training cycle. It meets uniquely many of the requirements for combined naval training manoeuvres, in particular such exercises as Operation Springboard involving NATO and South American ships as well.

Along with the large naval base, Roosevelt Roads, at the eastern end of Puerto Rico and the neighbouring island of Vieques, Culebra serves as 'a keystone in the Atlantic Fleet weapons range', according to a former commander of the Caribbean Sea Frontier.

Few protests were heard until the Navy intensified its pounding of the island in 1969, bombing and shelling for an average of $9\frac{1}{2}$ hours per day, Monday through Saturday, and $3\frac{1}{2}$ hours on Sunday. During 1970, the bombardment intsensified substantially beyond that. The Navy tried to get more of the island, and appeared to want all of it.

The overall effect has been a major and persistent disruption in the lives of the Culebran people. Families were relocated by fiat, and many left the island. Fishers found their nets destroyed, lobsters and other fish entrapped on the floor of the sea, and coral reefs smashed. Cattle tenders were forced into new areas, and few remain in the business. Exploding shells gone awry started fires

---

*Reprinted by permission from *Gandhi Marg*, October 1971. The last section ('Culebra — the chapel lives!', March 1976) has not previously been published.

which burned off grazing areas. Teachers complained of the disturbing noise, night and day, especially at times of intensified manoeuvres, and how it affected school children.

Culebrans remember bitterly the accidents and injuries suffered over the years: an eye or arm lost as someone picked up live ammunition and it exploded, Alberto Garcia killed in 1935 when he hammered on a grenade left on the beach. The *Armed Forces Journal* last year documented these as well as many near misses, as it effectively disputed Navy claims or versions of incidents. The Navy itself suffered casualties: nine Navy men were killed when a plane dropped its ordnance on an observation post painted the same colour as the target.

While the Culebrans complained, and occasionally filed claims, there were few to hear them. The cumulative impact was a feeling of helplessness and frustration. Their hopes were raised when their story began to attract notice and help, and when they began themselves to protest and organize. They marched and petitioned, held meetings, found Puerto Rican allies. They marched from their town hall to a navy observation post near the beach and Mayor Ramon Feliciano read a strong statement of protest. They drew upon their meagre resources to lobby in Washington. Senators Charles Goodell, Henry Jackson, and Edward Kennedy showed interest; Congressional inquiries were made and hearings held. Mayor Feliciano and others tried to involve the executive branch. A prominent Washington law firm, Covington and Burling, came into the case and began to roil the Washington waters. A court case was instituted but failed. The Navy began to feel the pressure and made a few concessions. Congressional efforts were stymied by the likes of Rep. Mendel Rivers, and from the White House came ritual letters, 'Thank you for expressing your feelings on this subject to the President'.

Direct action
The Puerto Ricans began to intervene by direct action. The Puerto Rican Independence Party, committed to 'pacific militancy' (nonviolent action) as eloquently enunciated by its thiry-one-year-old president Ruben Berrios, conducted a swim-in on Flamingo Beach. This past summer the PIP held a three-day encampment there, defying Navy guns. Starting as a relatively small project, it

swelled to more than 600 participants. They had no guarantee that the Navy would withhold fire, and indeed the Navy cancelled exercises only fifteen minutes before the firing time. The group slept on the impact area, and no Navy manoeuvres were held there during that three-day period.

On 10 June 1970, twenty Culebrans, most of them young people, stood together on the target area as the Italian ship Vittoria prepared to engage in ship-to-shore shelling practice. Navy personnel on the island pleaded with the group to leave, but the Culebrans refused to back down. Without firing, the ship returned to Roosevelt Roads.

In an October interview, Mayor Feliciano told me that he feared violence was simmering just below the surface. Culebrans were discouraged by failure or inaction on the legal and political fronts.

The Navy, at the urging of some members of Congress, had offered about thirty-five jobs to Culebrans, one category at $5,212 per year, another at $6,548. This was a lot of money for one of the lowest-income areas in the US. Some of those who accepted jobs, including guarding the beach, were not from the ranks of the unemployed, but were municipal employees who heard about it first and resigned to take the higher-salaried jobs. Instead of mollifying the Culebrans, though some were pleased, this ploy generated more antagonism. The mayor hoped to forestall ugly incidents (e.g. the guards might be attacked some night) thus providing marvellous propaganda for the Navy—'patriotic Culebrans support Navy'—and discrediting the nonviolence which had been a hallmark of their struggle so far.

In a December incident, the Navy killed thousands of fish, completely wiped out a fifty-foot area of rich coral and damaged another 200 feet, as it carried out underwater demolitions to clear the area of unexploded ammunition. Angry Culebrans cursed the demolition team; a petition was circulated; the New York Times carried a long story.

Later in the month when the Navy again started a demolition operation, Culebrans took three boats out to 'picket' the intended explosion point. After the commander ordered a team member to 'pull the pin', two of the boats retreated but three women who had brought one of the boats refused to leave. The boat was hastily towed away just before the explosion. This incident as much as any deepened the anger and resentment of the people. Some began to plan for violent retaliation.

The Chapel

Years before, after a 1941 executive order by President Franklin Roosevelt enabled the Navy to expropriate land there, homes were torn down and targets erected. Greg Walter in *Life* magazine quoted Mayor Feliciano: 'They came and told us we had forty-eight hours to get out. They cut down my house, the place where I was born—it is the second "tank" you see over there on the hillside.' Another casualty was a small Methodist chapel at Flamingo Beach.

Somewhere on Culebra was born the idea—four people claim some version of it—to rebuild the chapel, non-denominational, in the impact area in the line of Navy fire. The idea was discussed in the Rescue Culebra Committee, a group appointed in earlier days at a public meeting to plan strategy and tactics. The president is Anastacio Soto, who is also president of the fisher's association; the vice-president John Vincent, a Methodist missionary and long-time proponent of nonviolence, who had been school principal but lost his post when he became a vigorous opponent of the Navy's role.

The chapel-building idea became the focal point for an action jointly planned and carried out by three groups, aided by Culebrans: the Puerto Rican Independence Party (Partido Independentista Puertorriqueno—PIP); the Clergy Committee to Rescue Culebra (Comite .Clerigos pro-rescate de Culebra); and A Quaker Action Group (AQAG), a Philadelphia-based organization. Each of the organizations in this three-way alliance had a unique role.

The PIP had not only carried on educational activities and testified at hearings in Washington, it had also sponsored nonviolent direct action at Flamingo Beach, standing fast before the threat of Naval guns. The PIP saw the struggle not only as one to get the Navy off Culebra, but as salient in a larger struggle to resist US dominance of Puerto Rico. Therefore, it insisted, the issues should be cast in such a way as not to entrench the US military presence—'See, the Navy can be reasonable if you go about it the right way'—but rather to weaken that hold and promote Puerto Rican independence.

The clergy group's best known figure is Catholic Bishop Antulio

Parrilla Bonilla. Bishop Parrilla favours independence, led a massive anti-draft rally at Lares last spring, and has visited US draft resisters in prison. Luis Rivera, of the Evangelical Seminary in San Juan, is another activist (he once hired a small plane and dropped leaflets on a large-public meeting in San Juan).

The Quaker team had a double task: to resist the US Navy's presence on Culebra, first through helping to build the chapel, and to serve as a link between Puerto Rico and the US mainland where interest needed to be aroused and pressure developed in Washington.

The plan to build the chapel was announced on 4 January 1971, simultaneously in New York City and San Juan, in response to a call from the Rescue Culebra Committee for concerned groups to help the islanders get the Navy off Culebra. Two dates influenced the timing. January 18 had been announced as the beginning date for the Navy's combined and intensified manoeuvres, called Operation Springboard. The US 1971 contingent involved 60,000 troops, 70 ships and 180 planes. Also participating were four Latin American countries—Brazil, Venezuela, Colombia, and the Dominican Republic (Ecuador declined at the last minute)—and four NATO nations: Great Britain, Canada, West Germany and the Netherlands. Tension was rising on Culebra as the time for Operation Springboard drew near.

The other target date was 1 April, when a Department of Defence study, called for by Congress, was to be presented to President Nixon. This report was to include an evaluation of possible alternative sites for training activities. Action to escalate resistance on Culebra, and to release a new political impetus in Puerto Rico, neded to be translated into political forces that would be felt in Washington before the 1 April deadline.

The AQAG team arrived in San Juan on 4 January, and spent the week in training, orientation, and organizational discussions, much of it under the auspices of PIP. The team of eight included William Davidon, Haverford College physics professor later named a co-conspirator in the Berrigan case; Margaret DeMarco, a community organizer; Robert Swann, of the New England Committee for Nonviolent Action; Jaime Fernandez, a Chilean working in Washington, DC; Shepherd Bliss, a Methodist minister, of the Chicago area Group on Latin America; Tom Davidson, anti-draft organizer; and Dan Balderston, a student at Pendle Hill, a Quaker study centre. Ivan Gutierrez, of the Puerto Rican Peace Centre, joined the team in San Juan. Later from Washington came Phil Wheaton, a Latin American specialist, and Elizabeth Ewing, a nurse.

The Navy's 'Treaty'

Then came a surprising move by the Navy. Through Richard Copaken, who represented the Culebrans in Washington, the Navy offered what was first termed a 'peace treaty' (the phrase was later crossed out but was still visible). The treaty proposed concessions by the Navy and commitments by Puerto Ricans. The Navy said it would phase out nearly all targets except the northwest peninsula, return two-thirds of the shore line, relinquish its rights to obtain easements on some land, and refrain from firing on weekends and Sundays 'except to meet an urgent operational commitment'. It promised to search for 'feasible alternatives' for training operations. In turn the governor, the mayor and others would 'use all regulatory and legal devices available to the Commonwealth and the Municipality of Culebra to assure that no dwellings or other habitable structures are constructed in the northwest safety zone for as long as the Navy uses the northwest peninsual for naval gunfire support training'. Furthermore, these same parties would 'use their best efforts, including moral suasion, to obtain the co-operation of everyone in keeping the land and sea safety zones for the remaining targets clear of people during scheduled training operations'.

These proposals were presented at a hastily called public meeting on a Saturday night, read in English, then translated into Spanish (the available Spanish version was deemed not 'elegant' enough). No copy was left on the island afterwards. If the Culebrans couldn't agree, it was said, the Navy would deny that the proposal existed. The crowd dwindled as the meeting wore on, and the final vote was about 50–6 to accept the offer (eyewitness reports differ on the size of the pro vote).

On Sunday, the Culebrans appeared more divided and uncertain. Many were unhappy about the haste and pressure of the meeting. The situation had been festering for years and suddenly the Culebrans were offered a take-it-or-leave-it document with little chance to discuss it and no chance to study it. That night the Rescue Culebra Committee decided to ask Mayor Feliciano to call for more time before signing. On the same day the mayor, the lawyers, Senate President Hernandez Colon, and Governor Luis Ferre further discussed the proposals in San Juan. Another provision was added saying that the Puerto Rican principals wanted the Navy to 'terminate all training operations on Culebra and its neighbouring Cays within a reasonable period'.

Somewhere along the line, Mayor Feliciano was led to believe that the Navy had agreed to start leaving Culebra completely within three years. Committee members, hearing this report over the radio on Monday morning, did not ask the mayor to delay signing, believing they had 'won'. This false and damaging rumour allayed doubts that might have forestalled the signing ceremony later that day.

Secretary of the Navy, John Chafee, arrived at the diminiutive City Hall, along with Governor Luis Ferre and other dignitaries. Culebrans stood around impassively, singularly unimpressed by the presence of these 'bigshots'. To them the powerful were those who fired at their island, hurt their fishing, created oppressive noise, and threatened to take the island entirely. In his ceremonial speech, Mayor Feliciano said, 'This document has guaranteed the return of all land used by the Navy on Culebra.' Secretary Chafee picked up on this and similar phrases to point out that the Navy had pledged to look for other feasible sites, but if none was found the Navy would not be able to leave 'within a reasonable period'. This apparently shook up the Puerto Rican officials, but the lawyers smoothed things over and the signing proceeded. 'Now there will be peace and harmony', predicted Secretary Chafee, with unwarranted optimism.

As the officials hurried away in their helicopters, taking most of the press with them, Ruben Berrios denounced the agreement as providing for 'bombing by consent'. The Quaker Action team, which had arrived on Culebra for the first time about an hour before the ceremony, issued a statement saying it would 'persist in the struggle'.

The next night, the Seabees began to construct a cyclone fence across the peninsula, blocking off part of Flamingo Beach. Before this, Culebrans had free access to the entire beach when no firing operations were scheduled. Later, lawyer Copaken was to write to the Navy, 'The erection of this fence, in the manner described, was perceived by the townspeople of Culebra as a serious and gratuitous affront'.

Commander Archie Benton, who had been monitoring the Culebran situation from Roosevelt Roads, in a conversation with Susan Dinga at the beach on 19 February, gave two reasons for putting up the fence: (1) 'to prevent some innocent people from going out there and getting blown up'; (2) 'we knew this confrontation was going to come up and we definitely did want to keep him (Berrios) out . . . we wanted to have a clear demarcation line'.

On Wednesday, two days after the signing of the treaty, a Navy jet dropped a missile near Dewey, and training exercises nearby employed live ammunition, 'in violation of assurances made to Mayor Feliciano by Assistant Secretary of the Navy, Frank Sanders'. Before long, the Rescue Culebra Committee repudiated the treaty. Both sides kept complaining that the letter and the spirit of the agreement were being ignored or breached.

Preparing to build the chapel

The chapel builders proceeded with their plans. They pitched camp (the mayor had cancelled their room reservations), changed the chapel design, chose alternative building sites, and consulted with the Rescue Culebra Committee.

On the eighteenth, one week after the signing ceremony, about seventy people marched from the town plaza, singing 'La Borinquena' as two young men carried Puerto Rican flags. A two-mile hike brought them to Flamingo Beach where they found police officers waiting for them. Said Officer Octavio Cintron, 'We are here to guarantee your rights' and he then read a Navy regulation saying trespassers would be arrested for entering Navy property.

After about ten minutes of talking, six people, including Berrios and AQAG's Jaime Fernandez, climbed the gate and went around the cyclone fence into the 'impact area'. The police did not arrest them, possibly because government plans called for only federal marshals to carry out arrests. Others in the group then carried materials into the impact area to construct the chapel. A San Juan reporter wrote, 'What followed can only be described as a cross between a tug-of-war and a sandlot football game'. Marines tried to take away some two-by-fours, unavailingly, as demonstrators and Marines tugged and shoved, some demonstrators throwing football blocks to keep Marines away while more materials were carried in. Again, possibly the Marines did not press the issue, despite embarrassment, because they were not empowered to make arrests. Orders came from Big Mary, the nearby Navy observation post, to let the building go ahead. In three days the building was finished. It was open at the sides and ends, of 'elegant design' as one reporter put it. The designer was Bob Swann; he had helped rebuild churches burned in the South during civil rights campaigns. Encamped only ten yards away were the fence-building Seabees, under instructions not to talk with these unconventional chapel builders. At night they were friendly enough, and told of their misgivings about their assignment.

On Thursday the twenty-first, the shelling was scheduled to start. At 8.30 a.m. US marshals arrived with a temporary restraining order restraining the group from further interference with the Navy and ordering them from the area. A dedicatory service was held in the chapel, conducted in Spanish by AQAG team member Phil Wheaton. Berrios and Balderston also spoke. Then all left but the six who had been chosen to face arrest, while others would organize and plan further action. The 'altar', covered with flowers, was carried outside the gate, set on an up-ended suitcase, and a second dedicatory service was held.

The group repeatedly defied court orders to leave. The following night, while the group slept — and townspeople and reporters had left — the US marshals came to arrest them. They were flown to San Juan where Federal Judge Jose Toledo charged them with failing to obey his injunction, then released them on their own recognizance pending a hearing on 18 February. The group had arrived about midnight, but when they emerged from the court at about 1 a.m. they were greeted by nearly a thousand demonstrators. The six arrested were Ruben Berrios, Paqui Rodriguez, and Luis Avalo, of the PIP; Benjamin Perez, a Culebran and PIP member; Luis Rivera, of the Puerto Rico clergy group; and Dan Balderston of the AQAG team.

During these two days of legal manoeuvring about the civil disobedience on the beach, the Navy had cancelled its shelling practice on the peninsula. Reporter Bill Wingell tells what happened the following week when target practice was scheduled:

Four more demonstrators entered the target area, slipping around the Navy fence under cover of darkness, and again delayed the firing until being arrested and taken to San Juan like their predecessors. This time, however, even as the four were being driven out of the zone in a Navy truck under armed guard, three more protesters slipped by the fence (it extends into the bay but can be waded around) and took up their vigil in the target area.

One youth, Luis Alonso, twenty-three, managed to get away from his Navy guards, moving further into the two-mile-long firing zone. Two Canadian destroyers, the HMCS Ottawa and Saint Laurent, were ordered to halt their shelling while Navy search parties sought Alonso.

The delay lasted four hours. Finally, the ships started firing again, despite the fact that Alonso was still in the target area. Twenty minutes after the resumption of shelling, the youth walked out of his own accord. 'I just got tired', he told this reporter. He said he had hidden in two different trees, and although helicopters and ground parties had passed right by him, he had not been spotted. 'That's why they're losing in Vietnam', he said. (*Thursday's Drummer* (Philadelphia), 11 February 1971, p. 4).

The chapel area continued to attract this kind of harassment, and the Navy did something about it. On the night of the twenty-ninth, the chapel mysteriously fell down. The Navy said it blew down. Two Culebrans nearby heard what sounded like a jeep, then a crash, followed by laughter. Next morning, Balderston saw what appeared to be black cable marks on the wood of the front truss. This time it was largely Culebrans who came out with their tools and rebuilt the chapel (the gate was open since the restraining order had expired). They planted coconut and almond trees around it, along with seagrapes and lilies. Now it was really 'their chapel'.

Not all Culebrans though so. In Dewey a new group appeared calling itself Sons of Culebra. They marched under the banner of an American flag, demanded that 'outsiders' leave, and called for peace and tranquility.

Religious services were held at the beach on weekends. On one occasion, some women brought a cross made of flowers to be put in the chapel during services, but the gate was closed. A Culebran started through the wire, intending (another said) to ask permission to put it in the chapel. Marines grabbed him, took him from view and worked him over. This aroused the crowd; they removed the barbed wire from across the beach, went into the chapel and held a religious service, including somewhat inexplicably a stanza of 'Onward Christain Soldiers'. AQAG team members drew up leaflets to pass out to military personnel, one for Culebra, another for other areas of Puerto Rico.

The Navy's troubles mounted. The schedule for Springboard had run into rough weather. Claro Feliciano, a seventy-five-year-old farmer, had said earlier: 'The Navy is a ghost. It is everywhere — in the water, in the air, on the land, and in the earth. But we cannot speak with it. It is not in contact with this village or people.' But now the ghost had been exorcized, and in its place were real people who said and did foolish things — a Goliath who had trouble with a lot of little Davids. The myth of Navy invincibility had been punctured. Finally the Navy decided it had enough. On 8 February, a 'structural engineering team' inspected the chapel and declared it a safety hazard. The Marines tore down the chapel, piece by piece.

While this was going on, the gathering crowd became increasingly incensed. Some Culebran youths tried to rally the crowd to go in to save the chapel, despite a platoon of Marines armed with rifles. Finally, some of the crowd advanced through the open gate, unarmed, toward the chapel. The Marines tried to repel them, seized Susan Dinga, then fired tear gas grenades (the first one hit the windshield of a police car). The crowd retreated, the Marines closed the gate, and the people kept shouting at the Marines to release Susan Dinga. At this point, Culebrans threw several Molotov cocktails over the fence. When the Marines cames to the gate to release Susan Dinga, a brief scuffle prompted them to throw more tear gas into the crowd. Molotov cocktails were thrown at the small wooden guard house and it caught fire. A Culebran pulled off the gate with a small truck and chain (the gate disappeared) and others finished off the guard house.

For some time, the two groups harassed each other, Culebrans trying to tear down the cyclone fence, Marines throwing tear gas canisters and trying to repair the fence, followed by more Molotov cocktails and three Marines burned. A helicopter buzzed the crowd. Finally, about 11.30 p.m., Puerto Rican police arrived, as did the mayor — he too was teargassed. After some persuasion, the crowd gradually dispersed and after more than three hours of confrontation, the melee was over. Despite all the action, the only serious injury was a Marine's second-degree burn.

For the third time, the Navy had torn down a chapel on Culebra. They not only took the wood away but even removed the trees and flowers that had been planted. Only the fence was left. Culebrans fastened an improvised cross to the fence and under it put this sign:

'You tore down a chapel but you can't destroy the spirit that builds it ever again.'

The trial

At the 18 February trial in San Juan, the defendants were charged with contempt of court, for violating a federal injunction requiring them to stop interfering with Navy operations. Judge Jose Toledo declared the proceedings must be held in English, but the Puerto Ricans insisted on speaking in Spanish. When the judge asked whether they pleaded guilty or not guilty, they replied: 'Que viva Puerto Rico libre!' The judge directed a not guilty plea, and the government went on to show that the defendants had indeed refused to leave the chapel and the restricted zone.

Ruben Berrios spoke in Spanish for the twelve Puerto Rican defendants. He readily agreed they had 'violated the law of the Empire', but declared, 'To violate the law of the Empire is to fulfil the law of our native land.' He gave a passionate defence of civil disobedience, quoting Jose Marti, Ghandhi, and Thoreau. 'Innocence before this court would be guilt before our conscience,' he said. 'If to defend the right of our compatriots on Culebra to live in peace without being subject to Naval bombardment is to be guilty, then we are guilty. If to defend the right of Puerto Rico to its territorial integrity, and to insist upon the return to our people of all territory that the United States usurps for military bases is to be guilty, then we are guilty·. . . . Long live Puerto Rico in freedom.'

Dan Balderston read a statement in English, saying he acted because the restraining orders 'try to protect the bombing on Culebra from the accusing voice of humanity, which has seen too much killing'. He said that his great-great-grandfather refused to pay war taxes during the Civil War and the government expropriated several of his hogs. 'The Quakers have fallen with the rest of the Babylonians, but there is a remnant', he said, 'which tries to be faithful.'

Judge Toledo sentenced the defendants to three months in prison, some double sentences to run concurrently. Berrios, himself a professor of law at the University of Puerto Rico, then stepped before the bench and, speaking in Spanish, told the judge that he did not recognize the court's authority. 'Before our people we are innocent and that is our only court,' he declared. 'The repercussions of these sentences will rebound one and a thousand times against this court until Puerto Rico is free, independent and socialist. History cannot be stopped.' The judge interrupted to say this was a political speech, to which Berrios retorted, 'Your decision is political.' Applause broke out in the courtroom, and many sang 'La Borinquena' as the defendants were led out, to be taken to the state penitentiary in Rio Piedras. After the trial, numerous demonstrations were held, a daily vigil was established at the prison, and at one point 4,000 people massed in support of the prisoners.

The week after the trial, more protesters interrupted Springboard and were arrested, five from the PIP and two from the Pro-Independence Movement (MPI). On the last day of the naval Operation Springboard, a boatload of protesters, including MPI chief Juan Mari Bras, entered Flamingo Bay and some swam ashore, stopping Colombian and Dutch destroyers from bombardment for a time.

On the same day, in Washington AQAG carried a replica of the chapel from embassy to embassy of some of the nations involved in Springboard, sending deputations to talk with officials at the Canadian, British and Brazilian embassies. Earlier AQAG had first built the replica at the Pentagon, and talked with Undersecretary of the Navy, Joseph Grimes (two team members returned from Culebra were in that group).

On Culebra, an encampment has been kept at the fence near the place where the chapel had once stood (the Navy seems to be worried about it). A children's park was started there, with playground equipment (the mayor donated four telephone poles). A garden was dug and planted.

On 15 March, Culebrans celebrated the first anniversary of their march to Big Mary; there a year earlier they had delivered an ultimatum to the Navy to leave or be subject to a direct action campaign. Anastacio Soto reiterated his belief that the struggle must go on. The People's Park was dedicated to the thirteen prisoners serving time in Rio Piedras. The Clergy Committee To Rescue Culebra led religious services.

A Puerto Rican community development group, called PRISA, is planning a 'multiproject' on Culebra, in which young people can work along with Culebrans to point the way to paths of development the people want. The first two ideas are a community orchard and a motor repair shop. The American Friends Service

Committee has been asked to consider holding a work project on Culebra this summer.

The islanders do not want to get the Navy out only to be engulfed by developers who dream of converting those beautiful beaches into another San Juan. If vactioners come, they say, let them be ecology-minded families who would respect the land and the life of the people there.

Will the Navy leave?

On 31 March, Governor Luis Ferre announced, and a Pentagon press release confirmed, that the Navy would use no live ammunition in its training manoeuvres on Culebra after 1 January 1972. Furthermore, the Navy may leave entirely after June 1975 if an alternative site can be worked out.

The announcement appeared to be compromised by references to more studies, and to a poll of Culebrans, to be taken later, on whether they *really* wanted the Navy to leave. Prior to this announcement, some Navy brass had expressed fears that 'politicans' were 'giving Culebra away'. While this announcement would not allay those fears, it is too early to tell what will happen by June 1975. The two Navy-moves—the peace treaty and the new announcement—have come in response to pressure; only continued pressure, education and persuasion are likely to produce results. Some suspect that the Pentagon report may pave the way for a 'pacification' effort. Another thirty-five or so Navy jobs have been offered to the Culebrans.

An article by Drew Middleton in the *New York Times,* quoting Navy sources, suggests that the Navy is somewhat gloomy about its prospects. It still complains about 'outsiders' agitating. The Culebrans see the Navy as the outsider, until recently intent on taking over the whole island. The Navy also has compiled a long list of 'incidents' and tries to characterize recent events—especially regarding the chapel—as violent, telling of the burned Marine.

The leading practitioner of violence had been the US Navy, with its bombs and guns, with its massive technology and heedless power. This overwhelming presence has dominated the situation there for many years. When A Quaker Action Group demonstrated outside Fort Gulick in the Panama Canal Zone in 1969, it stated: 'Entrenched and prolonged injustices conspire against peace. Those who defend privilege and repress efforts to achieve justice pave the way for armed and explosive upheavals. In such situations, those who cry peace in the name of "order" are either blind or hypocritical, ignoring the seeds of disorder and violence in their exploitation and oppression.' The 8 February incidents notwithstanding, it has been effective and disciplined nonviolent action which has not only forestalled ugly outbreaks of violence, but has once more shown what power a people have when they act with courage and imagination.

The imperial mentality

In the name of defence, the Pentagon presides over an enormous and far-flung complex of land, resources, technology, and personnel. The impact of this power is massive and pervasive. Far from being merely a 'shield', it is an active, organizing force, sometimes blatantly having its way, at other times more subtly shaping the course of events, patterns of development, choice of allies, and cultural values.

The Navy has behaved crudely at times on Culebra, but this is part of the larger picture in Puerto Rico. The Pentagon has insisted it 'has' to stay in Puerto Rico, and Culebra particularly, to implement political, military and economic objectives far beyond the nation's shores: in Central and South America, in the Caribbean (the Dominican invasion was launched from Puerto Rico), in the South Atlantic Ocean, even on the Atlantic coast of Africa. The appeals of a tiny island, or those of its stronger allies in Puerto Rico, can scarcely penetrate the impervious logic of these designs.

The Quaker Action team, in its statement at the time of signing the treaty, said that among its purposes was to see first hand the effects of neocolonialism. It said further that the Culebran example could 'show other oppressed peoples—in Vieques, in barrios and ghettos elsewhere, in Vietnam and in the United States—that they can take strength and persevere against the military and colonial mentality'.

Within three months, forces little noticed outside Puerto Rico erupted with dramatic effect. It was direct action that set the stage. Pentagon script writers found that the players wouldn't recite the old lines. Instead of another chorus of 'Yankee Doodle Dandy', they had to cope with guerrilla [street] theatre. The Culebra story testifies again to what Vinoba Bhave calls 'the self-reliant power of the people'.

CULEBRA—THE CHAPEL LIVES!

The US Navy ceased all gunfire training activities on Culebra on 30 June 1975. Later in the year, all activity ceased also on the nearby Cays.

In April 1971, in the wake of increased Puerto Rican protests, American Secretary of Defense Melvin Laird announced that naval activities would be moved from Culebra by mid-1975, a policy he reaffirmed in November 1972 just before the Puerto Rican gubernatorial election. A month later, Laird reversed himself and said that shelling and air bombardment operations would continue until at least 1985!

In May 1974, Elliot Richardson, in one of his final acts as Secretary of Defence, ordered gunnery and air bombardment training on Culebra to end, and to be transferred to two uninhabited islands, Desecheo and Monito. A presidential order the following month, on 27 June, set the mid-1975 date again (*New York Times,* 25 May 1974).

This vacillating behaviour appeared to result from pressures and counter-pressures, related to internal Puerto Rican politics, Department of Defense resistance to being forced out of what is regarded as a favourable position, and the anti-US feeling the issue continued to generate in Puerto Rico.

The Chapel Rises
Word came to the island that the Navy would leave entirely by 30 September 1975 (later proved inaccurate). Political leaders scheduled a celebration, but many of those who had engaged in the nonviolent struggle felt they were being left out—deliberately. They decided—fifty-two Culebrans—to rebuild the chapel as a symbol of the peoples' resistance and their contribution to victory.

A behind-the-scenes argument developed among the authorities about whether to court another confrontation over the chapel. Political leaders in San Juan associated the chapel with the independentistas, and would never concede that the chapel contributed to resolving the issue. Wiser heads argued it was best to let matters take their course without intervention.

The Culebrans started building quietly at 10 p.m. on 28 September, at the Flamingo Beach site where the chapel had stood, before being torn down by the Navy. The original plans, drawn up by Robert Swann of Quaker Action Group, did not arrive in time. But the townspeople remembered the design—called 'elegant' by reporters—and had previously rebuilt the chapel after it had been pulled down one night in a mysterious incident. By next day it was recognizable.

Puerto Rican police arrived and took away five members of the Puerto Rican Independence Party. One of them, John Vincent, asked if they were under arrest, and was told the district attorney wanted to 'counsel' with them. Counsel turned out to be vociferous denunciation, and arrest orders had already been made out. The group was finally released without posting bail. They went back to build some more of the chapel.

In December, those arrested were taken to court. The judge appeared to be surprised at the composition of the group: Vincent (former school principal), a fisher, an employee at the laboratory. No state witness was in court to say to whom the land belonged at that time, thus weakening the state's case.

The judge asked if there were any fights, any bad language, any contentions? No, no, no. What were they doing? Building a chapel. How big? So big. Was there a cross on it, did it appear to have religious significance? Perhaps so. Judge: *Not Guilty*.

The chapel stands, still needs some finishing and waterproofing. It was erected three times—pulled down in a heap once, totally dismantled another time. Perhaps this time it will stand as a shrine of freedom.

Land Authority

A land authority was created to supervise the development and conservation of Culebra. The land is now under GSA (Government Services Administration) with sections to be turned back to Puerto Rico and supervised by the land authority. Mr Juarbe, heading it up, has shown no desire to listen to Culebrans, according to a spokesperson, but is following policies given him by San Juan authorities.

Culebran squatters are to be taken out of three areas in

particular—but to go where? Action against them may unite Culebrans and lead to another confrontation. Says John Vincent: 'The people have learned well the methods of nonviolence and civil disobedience, and if things go strongly against the grain these methods will likely be taken up again.' (Report to Charles Walker, March 1976.)

There is no unemployment on the island now, even after the Navy dismissed all its employees there (it is a serious problem in Puerto Rico generally). The population is also up to about 1,100, an increase accounted for by islanders who have returned. Culebrans have often said they want to develop the island according to their own desires and traditions, and not become another St Thomas. They had projected their own plans for development, and now the time is at hand for a new chapter in the life of Culebra.

Final note

Many forces interacted to produce this denouement: in San Juan, in Washington, in political councils, on Flamingo Beach. What remains clear is that building the chapel forced a new agenda. Old policies had to be changed or reaffirmed at increasing cost. Tiny ripples from this island ran to various parts of the world: the Caribbean, across the Atlantic, to Vietnam, to South America. One got the feeling issues were being affected that could be seen only vaguely on the surface.

However the power for change might be apportioned, the Navy might still be there but for those who faced the guns, courted harassment, sat on the beach, built the chapel, spent time in jail, endured private sorrows, and braved the wrath of overwhelming powers. What power they did have they continued to believe in—and they made a difference.

12

OPERATION OMEGA*

PEACE NEWS

[In April 1971, following an article by Roger Moody describing conditions in East Bengal (Bangladesh) after a take-over by the Pakistan army, the following note appeared in *Peace News* (16 April 1971, p. 5):

> The possibility is being explored by a small group of Londoners of sailing relief supplies into East Bengal, regardless of the consequences to the participants, whom it is hoped, would comprise an international team. The project would bear obvious similarities to nonviolent interventions of the recent past—especially the Phoenix Voyages by a Quaker Action Group in 1967-1968. Potential volunteers, physically fit and not hampered by personal ties, are asked to write (not phone please) to Roger Moody at Peace News as soon as possible. Any other queries and offers of help or advice—by letter—would be appreciated.

In June a second call for help was printed under a headline 'Operation Omega' (*Peace News,* 11 June 1971, p. 1):]

OPERATION OMEGA

OPERATION OMEGA is not a mission of relief. It is an act of interference.

On 25 MARCH Pakistan's Army invaded East Bengal whose government then declared itself the Republic of Bangla Desh. In the months since, five million Bengalis have fled from the east to India. As the world knows, their fate is terrible, and help has come too late. But the prospects for those left behind—some seventy million—are even more appalling. Their rights to succour, shelter, and self-determination have been trampled on. These people are confronted with a nightmare even more desperate than that of the refugees who have escaped.

*Reprinted by permission from *Peace News*.

SINCE THE INVASION these men, women and children have been denied almost all outside relief. And as long as Pakistan occupies Bangla Desh, it seems bound to ensure that relief goes only to those who submit to its authority.

THE ONLY REAL SOLUTION to the *cause* of this catastrophe as opposed to its *effect* is the withdrawal of the Pakistani army from Bangla Desh.

THE PAKISTAN REGIME IS BANKRUPT. IT CONTINUES ITS OCCUPATION ONLY WITH THE SUPPORT OF FOREIGN GOVERNMENTS—THROUGH ECONOMIC AID AND LOANS.

BUT, INSTEAD OF CUTTING OFF THIS AID, AND FORCING PAKISTAN TO GET OUT, THESE GOVERNMENTS—AMONG THEM BRITAIN—CONTINUE TO RESPECT ITS AUTHORITY IN BANGLA DESH.

IN ADDITION, RELIEF AGENCIES CONCERNED ABOUT THE SITUATION STILL SEEK THE CO-OPERATION OF THE REGIME IN DISTRIBUTING THEIR AID.

WE DO NOT RECOGNIZE PAKISTAN'S AUTHORITY OVER BANGLA DESH. Nor do we respect those governments that do. We are ordinary people, convinced that the world's humanitarian aid to a despairing people must not be used for its own political ends by the Pakistan regime.

OUR INTENTION is to take food and medical supplies into Bangla Desh and distribute it ourselves. WE PLAN to obtain landrovers, recruit teams that include medical workers and mechanics, and drive overland to Bangla Desh.

OMEGA ONE is the name of the first vehicle in the operation. Our hope is that several other teams will follow from Britain and more from Overseas. On a chosen date the vehicles will assemble along the Indian border. The teams will take the relief supplies to a village or distribution point within Bangla Desh. The Pakistan government will be told of the convoy's intent, and so will governments throughout the world. But no permission will be sought for it to enter Bangla Desh.

OPERATION OMEGA is a tiny, imperfect drop of help in an ocean of misery. But it is not *just* another mission of relief.

WE NEED HELP: More Landrovers, volunteers, doctors, nurses, mechanics, medical supplies, vitamins, high protein foods, and money.

WE WILL HELP other groups who want to join OPERATION OMEGA.

INITIAL SPONSORS: . . . [War Resisters' International, Community Research & Action Group, and Action Bangla Desh].

The Omega sign — Ω — is used to symbolize human unity. 'The Age of Nations is past. The task before us now, if we would not perish, is to build the earth.' (Teilhard de Chardin).

OMEGA'S FIRST CONFRONTATION

[By 17 August the first Omega team had assembled in Calcutta and passed the border into Bangladesh on their first mission (*Peace News,* 24 September 1971, pp. 2-3).]

This account the team-members give of Omega's first mission involves us more intimately than any graphic film version could. The arguments about civil disobedience, the Major's instruction to demonstrate against something else, the problems of decision-making — these are things familiar to us all.

At a time when the members of the Omega teams are very remote from us, our natural attitude might be to think about and praise their exceptional qualities. But the importance of Omega is not the glamour that may become attached to the mission or the team-members but the simple truth that these are ordinary people, some not even experienced in nonviolent action, who through their actions are making an impact on the course of events.

It does not belittle Operation Omega to say that this account clearly shows that inspiring nonviolent action is not the prerogative of charismatic heroes.

Omega 1 and 2 crossed the Indian checkpoint sixty kilometres outside Calcutta at noon on Tuesday, 17 August, passing the flagstaff flying the Bangla Desh flag, which the mukti bahini raise and guard every night while the Pakistan army make sorties against it to within fifteen yards of the Indian border. In Omega 1 were Marc Duran, Christine Pratt, Roger Moody and Dan Due; in Omega 2 were Ben Crow, Dan Grotta, Doreen Plamping and Freer Spreckley.

The road was narrow with potholes every few feet. The two vehicles entered at about 3 mph and 100 yards apart, in case the road was mined. We crawled forwards 250 yards and heard a loudspeaker. Roger said he could see a soldier ahead, behind a tree. We stopped: then went on. As the voice went on repeating the same message we stopped again, make ourselves known through our loudspeaker, and heard the words:

'Get down from your vehicles. Proceed on foot in twos. Do not step off the road.' We did so, and two more soldiers appeared, smiling and greeting us. Then a Major, all smiles, asked us who we were. Roger introduced us and all shook hands.

As the Major said he did not know who we were, Roger told him we were Operation Omega and stated our intent. The Major asked if we had passports and visas. On hearing that we had no visas, he asked why not. We said we didn't feel we needed visas to bring food to people in need. We were told to go back to India and asked why hadn't we come in through Dacca to distribute supplies through the proper channels or through the United Nations.

Walking with the Major

We replied that we had brought food from ordinary people in England and other countries to distribute directly ourselves, explaining our mission several times at intervals. The Major, contradicting his original statement, said that he had been awaiting us since 10 a.m. and that he appreciated our humanitarian mission.

He asked us to come to Jessore and leave our vehicles. We replied that we could not leave our supplies. He said we could not take our vehicles any further. When asked why, he said it was impossible. When pressed, he said that the road was impassable for military reasons.

The point was also raised that Pakistanis have to obtain visas before going to England — why had we come to Pakistan without visas. We replied that we were acting independently of our governments and were against their visa regulations. The Major also said that he had expected us to bring refugees with us.

Finally he told us that we could go to Jessore to discuss all these matters with his superiors but we must first talk to his commanding officer who was waiting for us. He agreed to let us discuss these matters privately among ourselves and then we walked back to our vehicles for a discussion. We decided to send the four members of

Omega 1 and informed the soldiers of our decision.

During the whole of this period the vehicles were clearly in sight of the Indian border post. Now the officers asked us to move our vehicles to the side of the road. We agreed and then Omega 1 left with the Major and two Captains,who were very apologetic about the long walk through paddy fields and across flooded sections of countryside.

We walked for about five minutes when we came across a length of white tape which stretched for about 100 yards at the end of which it formed a small enclosure in which were standing two old wooden chairs. When questioned about this, they said that they were expecting refugees.

After about forty-five minutes' walking across some difficult terrain and through a torrential monsoon downpour, we arrived at a building with a sign on the outside wall saying 'Reception Centre'. We were taken inside and met by a Lt-Colonel, several soldiers and two men in Western clothes. The Lt-Colonel said that he had been waiting for us since 10 a.m. and was under the impression that the English were supposed to be punctual. He was alternately angry, fanatical, racist, and even friendly.

He admitted that there was need for food but told us that our half ton of biscuits was an insult, a cloak for our underhand intentions. He asked us why we didn't sit-in at London airport against our visa law and why we didn't take our mission to Ireland. Aid should be negotiated on a government to government basis and all governments had laws which people had to obey.

We told him that when laws are not operating for the benefit of the people, it was time for individuals to disregard laws and act with individual responsibility. He said that we were anarchists and that his country had not time for such people. He said that our minds had been fixed by the propaganda of our newspapers and the BBC and that he didn't want this 'Omega business in Pakistan'.

We then returned, under escort, by a different route, arriving at the vehicles about 5 p.m. During the time that Omega 1 had been away, Omega 2 had either stayed in the road or taken shelter in the vehicles from heavy monsoon rain.

Arrested

We discussed the alternatives: (1) to send a group of us, or all go to

Jessore; (2) to stage a sit-in with the vehicles; (3) to start walking in the morning with a tin of biscuits each. There were two problems about the first: we felt that everyone should go which would mean leaving the vehicles and also that we could not accept the Pakistan Army's hospitality in Jessore. By this time it was obvious that Roger was very sick. We decided to spend the night in our vehicles and discuss further in the morning.

On being informed of our decision, the soldiers were very upset, said it was impossible for us to stay there the night, and pleaded with us to go to Jessore. We were told we were behaving like children. By around 7 p.m. we had settled down to sleep in our respective vehicles. We were all very concerned about Roger's condition.

Around 9.20 p.m. the soldiers returned and asked us to come immediately to their commanding officer. Much argument ensued and we refused to leave our vehicles and supplies voluntarily. One of the officers then arrested us. Roger stated that he would not co-operate with arrest, as did Chris and Ben. Omega 1 and 2 were then pushed back on to the road by a group of soldiers. About now Doreen asked the soldiers for a doctor for Roger.

Jessore

The officer asked those who were prepared to walk to stand on the side of the road. Roger again refused to move and the officer immediately ordered a stretcher. When the stretcher arrived, about half an hour later, Chris and Ben still refused to move while Roger was lifted out onto the stretcher and put on the road.

There was then an argument between Chris, Ben, and other team members as it was obvious that if Ben and Chris still refused to move they would be left with the vehicles. Chris and Ben eventually were persuaded that it was a bad idea for the team to be split. Further delays seemed fruitless in view of our states of mind and Roger's condition, so we decided we should all walk.

After wading through a four-foot-deep river and across some paddy fields, we got into two military vehicles and were taken to the Lt-Colonel's quarters. Marc and Ben arrived first and received a barrage of comments — 'Fucking foreigners why have you kept my soldiers up all day and night'. Then the rest of us arrived. Roger, it was said, was obviously a Hindu/Indian spy, everything that had happened was a Hindu plot. As far as possible we remained silent and only Freer argued.

A doctor attended Roger and diagnosed intestinal cholic and wanted Roger to see a specialist in the morning. He administered a pain-killing injection and suggested that Roger be admitted to hospital that night. Roger said that he did not wish to go to hospital. Doreen asked if she could be given the prescription to administer — the reply was non-committal.

The army vehicles came to take us to Jessore. On the road we saw groups of civilians with staves at maybe hundred yard intervals and checkpoints at half mile intervals. These civilians were 'local volunteers protecting the culverts in the road and their local area against miscreants from across the border'.

We arrived in Jessore about 2 a.m. and were shown into three rooms in the officers' quarters. We were offered food but refused. We were awakened for breakfast about 7.30 and all refused. We met to decide strategy. Early in this meeting Ben was called away by a Captain and told we were to prepare to meet a higher officer. We disagreed about the alternatives available and finally decided to tell the officer no more than that our intention was to distribute our relief freely. At this time Doreen had just taken Roger's temperature — 104.6. He was told that he required immediate medical attention but said that he would not go to hospital.

At 9.30 a.m. a Brigadier, the Lt-Col, and some other officers came into the room. The Brigadier said he appreciated our humanitarian gesture but that we should apply through the proper channels. We did not reply whereupon he began a short racist monologue on the theme of the cultural superiority of West Pakistanis over Indians — those 'animals who wear these dhoti things between their legs', and grovel on the ground, whereas West Pakistanis ate at tables and sat on chairs etc. How dare we English presume to dictate to him — our days of dominanace were over. Towards the end of his tirade he told us that 'this time you will be pushed back to India. If you return you will be handed over to the civil authorities for trial according to International Law.'

We were then left alone to wait for the vehicles which would take us back. We discussed briefly whether or not to resist being moved and decided against.

The journey back was physically uneventful but mentally harrowing. We saw very few people and many empty houses — on the whole trip from Jessore to Benapol, Roger counted 150 people in the fields. Some houses were burnt down, some demolished and many looked in various stages of delapidation. At least one village (probably Benapol itself) was burnt completely to the ground and uninhabited.

We returned to our vehicles without mishap, with some of us carrying Roger on a stretcher. As far as we could tell the vehicles were completely untouched. We got in and waited. Then it dawned — there had been some misunderstanding. The Captain was waiting for us to drive back to India while we were waiting to be pushed. The Captain called the Major who stormed across the paddy in high dudgeon, shouting and swearing ferociously. After cooling his temper, we arrived at a compromise. They would push us to the point where we had stopped the previous day and from there we would drive back.

The officers seemed genuinely afraid that they would be shot if they approached the Indian border any closer than this. We also agreed that several of us should walk in front of the vehicles both to make plain that they were not some Pak Army 'trojan horse' and to allay the soldiers' fears of being shot.

There were no formalities on our return. The Indian guards were friendly and interested to hear how we had fared. They asked a few questions of military interest. They offered us tea which Doreen and Freer refused because they felt the reason we had refused the hospitality of the Pak army applied equally to the Indian Army.

Then, the Barricades down, we drove on and were met by a beaming Bernard and a joyous Joyce.

[After the first mission, team members were divided in their opinions on the best strategy for further missions. Some thought that open confrontation should be continued in the orthodox Gandhian tradition, while some thought that the distribution of relief, even if it had to be done with secrecy, was the more important objective. As a result the team split into two, and both missions were attempted. An account of the action appeared in *Peace News* on Friday, 10 September 1971, p. 1, as follows.]

One Omega Mission Accomplished
Operation Omega's Number Two team completed their first aid-giving mission without incident on Monday last — crossing the

border in an area where the Pakistan Army are no longer in control, distributing enough food to last 800 people for three days and returning to Indian territory for more supplies. Omega's Number One team crossed the border at Petrapol (as before), were stopped by Pakistan Army soldiers and led away out of sight of observers. On Tuesday evening it was learned that they had been imprisoned in Jessore.

Both objectives have, therefore, to all intents and purposes been achieved. The objective of the team which crossed the guarded borderpost at Petrapol was to defy the authority of Pakistan over Bangla Desh, and imprisonment was an expected part of this political gesture. At the same time, the need to get the free distribution of food flowing inside Bangla Desh was of equal priority.

To the best of everyone's knowledge, this relief was the first to actually get distributed inside Bangla Desh from any relief organization since the Pakistan Army invasion of 25 March, apart from cyclone rehabilitation agricultural work, and certainly since the need for a massive food lift to avert Autumn starvation became paramount with the disruption of normal planting activity at the beginning of the monsoons.

The First team — Christine Pratt, Joyce Keniwell, Ben Crow and Dan Due (with Ellen Connett acting as link-member at the border) — walked into Bangla Desh at 12.24 local time last Sunday, 5 September, carrying token relief supplies. After walking for about 300 yards, they were met by two or three Pakistan soldiers. There was a brief exchange, after which the soldiers walked away, leaving them standing on the road. The team stayed there until 12.55, when three more soldiers (perhaps officers) appeared from the side of the road and spent an hour in discussion, other soldiers coming and going during this time.

At 1.55, soldiers surrounded them and walked them away along the road, and they were soon out of sight of observers at the Indian borderpost. Roger Moody surmised at the time that they had in effect been arrested, but it was still then possible that they had been told to move with the troops in order to meet the commander of the forces in the area.

Then there came an unconfirmed report, given to Omega (London) on Tuesday by the Leytonstone-based Pakistan Action Group that they had been held for questioning at Benapol on

Sunday night and that no charges had then been preferred because the Army personnel were waiting for instructions from Dacca. They may, say PAC, be moved to Kushtia and then to Dacca.

The Second Team — Freer Spreckley, Marc Duran and Gordon Slaven — moved in, with a vehicle, to Bangla Desh territory also during last Sunday. Their mission was successful. They carried out a two-day operation covering some thirty-three square miles inside East Bengal, during which time they distributed enough high-protein food for three days' sustenance for 800 people. They drove their vehicle to the water's edge and then loaded the half-ton weight of supplies onto a boat, which took them across the water to where distribution could begin.

Their main items off-loaded were: 1,000 loaves of high-protein brown bread; some biscuits; and 350 saris. They were accompanied by Bengali guides, whose presence ensured a more equitable distribution of food than would otherwise have been possible — since large numbers of hungry people rushed towards them in an effort to get 'first in the queue'.

Most of the people who received relief were refugees, trekking from East Bengal towards the Indian frontier. They had been 'on the road' for four to five days, with no food, except what little they had been able to carry with them, and with little prospect of getting enough to eat when, and if, they managed to gain entry into India's refugee camps.

What was most needed inside East Bengal, reported the team later, were clothes and starch foods. There was no rice at all inside that area of the country — probably due to flooding, and there was rice rationing in India. The Second Team are to re-enter Bangla Desh territory today (10 September) with more supplies.

Continuation
[Through 1973 *Peace News* continued to report on various Omega teams as they continued to give aid in various forms, and to help with reconciliation and long-term reconstruction projects, especially with the Bihari minority. However, by August 1973 some of the volunteers in Bangladesh had dismissed the reconstruction projects as 'long-term relief work' and argued that Omega should withdraw from these within four months, leaving them to end or continue independently of Omega. Instead, they suggested

concentrating on a campaign for a 'political solution' for the subcontinent (*Peace News,* 10 August 1973, p. 3).]

PART IV

Nonpartisan transnational cases

13

PEACE IN NAGALAND*

M. ARAM

[In December 1963 Nagaland became the sixteenth State of the Indian Union. Since 1947 there had been a direct confrontation between the Naga underground fighters and the Government of India concerning the independence of Nagaland as a territory. From 1963 the situation involved the Naga underground and the Nagaland State Government, with the third-party being the Government of India.

The anger and the fury of the underground now turned against the State Government. They assassinated Dr Imkongliba Ao, President of the Naga People's Convention, and attacked other officers of the state administration. The situation became troubled and abnormal. It was at this juncture, early 1964, that the Church leaders took the initiative and formed the Peace Mission (Aram, 1974, p. 88).

From 1964 to 1972 M. Aram represented the Gandhian Sarvodaya (Uplift of All) movement as a Peace Observer to help maintain the ceasefire agreement between the Government of India and the underground forces in Nagaland. At times the Peace Observers Team consisted only of M. Aram, Marjorie Sykes (a British citizen with long service in the Gandhian cause) and two military representatives, one from each side. The Peace Observers Team was part of a larger Peace Mission which included, among others, Jayaprakash Narayan, A Sarvodaya leader, and Michael Scott, also from Britain, who was active in the world peace movement. The following extracts from M. Aram's book describing the 'Phezhu Controversy', the 'General Elections (February, 1967)' and 'Extending the Ceasefire (October, 1967)', are representative of the work of the Team over the eight-year period.]

*Reprinted with permission from *Peace in Nagaland*, New Delhi: Arnold-Heineman Publishers, 1974. Pp. 98-103, 124-7, and 139-140.

PHEZHU CONTROVERSY

On 14 March (1966) the underground sent a communication to the Peace Mission informing that their armed personnel would be passing through Kohima on their way to Phezhu, a hillock not far from Kohima. This was the site chosen by the underground for the celebration of their Republic Day.

The next day we received a letter from the Chief Secretary, Shri U. N. Sharma, objecting to the proposed movement of underground armed men. Subsequently the Federal Secretary wrote a letter to the Peace Mission clarifying their intention. Rev Michael Scott issued a memo on the whole subject. The next day some villagers of Jotsoma wrote to the Peace Mission stating that Phezhu was a part of Jotsoma and they had given permission to underground civil officers to have their offices there.

The four members of the Observers Team, namely, Miss Marjorie Sykes, Brig Pande, Maj Aomeri and myself were extremely busy those days. We passed through some excruciating moments. Tension was building up in spite of our efforts to bring about understanding.

On 18 March the Observers visited the site of the proposed celebrations. There we met Mr A. K. Lungalang, underground Commissioner. He showed us around. Many huts were in the making. He said it was their intention to make the site the headquarters of the Pangtong, underground District Officer. They planned to accommodate Naga armed personnel in that area during the celebrations.

While we were talking, Mr Isaac Swu arrived. He informed us that the personnel of the Naga army participating in the Republic Day celebrations would not exceed 500 men — 300 armed and 200 unarmed. We asked whether it would not be possible to accommodate these personnel at some other place further away from Kohima. He seemed to favour this suggestion.

The Observers Team met the Governor, Shri Vishnu Sahay, and reported on the situation. Our suggestions were: (i) armed personnel should withdraw from the camp, (ii) a token force with arms could be allowed as a Guard of honour on 22 March and (iii) the celebrations be allowed at the present site. We informed the Governor that the Federal leaders were anxious to maintain peace.

The Governor agreed with our suggestions.

We proceeded to Chedema Peace camp and met the Ato Kilonser

and his colleagues. They indicated their willingness to withdraw the armed personnel as suggested. The next day, 19 March, Mr Isaac Swu came to see us and reported that the Naga army had already been withdrawn and messages had been sent out to prevent other units from coming. As regards the ceremonial parade, he said his government must reserve the right to decide the exact number of armed participants. He assured us, however, it would be 'a very small number'.

Again we met the Governor. Then went to Chedema. We informed the Ato Kilonser and his colleagues that the Governor was of the view that 'the exact number of armed men in the ceremonial parade was not the main point at issue'.

He would be agreeable to the demonstration on 22 March 'provided that it is clearly understood that the spirit and the intention of the ceasefire terms is that there should be no parading with arms in the vicinity of towns, villages, administrative centres'.

On the twentieth the Peace Observers Team sent in writing our proposal to the Ato Kilonser and the Peace Mission. We were hoping that the Ato Kilonser would send us an answer.

On 21 March the answer came, but it said: 'The question of parading with arms within the vicinity of villages and towns in future will be taken up at the next talks with the Prime Minister of India.'

As we knew this would not bring satisfaction to the Government, we decided to go to the Phezhu camp where we met the Ato Kilonser, Mr Kughato. Rev Scott accompanied us. Mr Kughato was just about to leave the camp on some urgent personal business and we talked while standing by his jeep.

We explained once more the exact nature of the assurance which the Governor had requested. The Ato Kilonser replied in Sema language and his assurance as translated by Mr Isaac Swu appeared adequate. Therefore Miss Marjorie Sykes wrote it down as exactly as she could. Mr Kughato had left but Mr Isaac Swu and Rev Scott read it and confirmed that it was a correct record of what Mr Kughato had actually said.

Miss Sykes made a duplicate copy and requested Mr Issac to include it in the official letter which he would be sending us. We asked whether we might convey this orally to the Governor in anticipation of the official letter. To this he agreed.

We, the four Observers, went to the Governor. After

consultations with the Cabinet he informed us that our draft was satisfactory.

The Federal letter was delivered in the evening. We were disappointed that it did not contain the phrases agreed to. We went once more to the Phezhu camp. After a long discussion, it was obvious that Mr Kughato was not in a position to modify the letter. We, therefore, returned to Kohima and delivered the Federal letter to the Governor around 1 a.m. We actually woke him up from the bed.

When we returned to the Peace Centre in the early hours of the morning we were thoroughly exhausted and sleepy. We were also dispirited since we could not bring the negotiations to a satisfactory conclusion. Minoti Behn who was waiting for us for so many hours made us eat our dinner at 1.30 a.m.

At 5.30 a.m. the telephone in the Peace Centre rang. It was unusual to get a call so early in the morning.

It was one of our friends from the Mission compound telling us that a large number of people had gathered with the intention of proceeding to Phezhu. The Government had imposed a curfew and their way was blocked. He wanted the Peace Observers urgently to proceed there and help. We got ready in a hurry.

I took the jeep out and in a few minutes Miss Sykes and I had reached the spot where a large procession of women with banners etc. was standing. There was a large contingent of armed police obstructing the path. We also saw the Deputy Commissioner, Shri S. C. Dev. He was talking to the group which was translated into Angami by an official interpreter. He told the people that there was a curfew and they could proceed only on his dead body.

It was a tense situation. Miss Sykes and I reached the processionists. Several of them were our friends. We exchanged greetings and talked a little. We quickly sized up the situation. It was necessary somehow to alter the state of confrontation and find a way out.

Miss Sykes spoke briefly to the people. She said that there was a ceasefire and both sides wanted to preserve the peace. The public who wanted peace so much should not do anything in anger which might result in the breakdown of peace. The listeners appreciated this appeal.

We walked a little to join the Deputy Commissioner and considered with him how the impasse could be resolved. We suggested that the people should be allowed to proceed a little further on the main road and then take a side road which would actually be a short-cut to Phezhu. Thus the honour of the administration would be upheld in that the public would not be using the main road all the way in contravention of the curfew order. On the other hand, the processionists also would have their intentions fulfilled.

In order to avoid any further complications Miss Sykes and I decided to divide forces. She went with the processionists while I took the jeep and drove by the main road and reached the point where the processionists would rejoin the main road.

Our solution was a compromise no doubt. Some were unhappy. But a bad crisis was tided over and tension was reduced.

Rev Lungalang, the Zeliang Church leader, came with an urgent message from Rev Michael Scott who was at the Phezhu camp. He wanted to know from the authorities whether it was their intention to open fire, and whether it was their intention to attack the Federal camp at Phezhu.

We requested Rev Lungalang to proceed to the Chief Secretary to get an immediate reply. Obviously those at Phezhu were greatly concerned over the news of the curfew ordered in Kohima town. The Republic Day programme had not yet started. They saw some army movements in the jungles above Phezhu.

We felt we should go to Phezhu ourselves to apprise them of the situation in Kohima and also to learn what was actually going on there. So we drove to Phezhu. On the way we saw some troops and armoured cars.

Rev Scott and the Federal friends were happy to see us. They were all waiting to see how things would develop. The armed parade over which so much negotiation took place was abandoned. The main function was yet to begin. We assured everyone that the crisis in Kohima was over.

Soon the function began at Phezhu. The highlight was the address of the Federal President Mr Scato Swu:

'I will do all in my power to strengthen peace between India and Nagaland. My approach to the problem which confronts us is one of humility.

'It is my firm conviction that the only practical solution to the problem of Indo-Naga relations is self-determination.'

Mr Scato referred to the forthcoming talks with the Prime

Minister at New Delhi and said, 'I very much like to believe that the Government of India will adopt a realistic attitude and not harp on the same old tune by repeating baseless slogans and propositions about the status quo of Nagaland.'

Because of the tense circumstances prevailing in Kohima and its surrounding areas many could not come to the meeting. Still there was a large gathering.

We returned to Kohima in the afternoon. The curfew was lifted by then. Normalcy was returning. We heaved a sigh of relief that the crisis had blown over.

But that was not the end. On 23 March, the next day, the Chief Secretary, Mr Sharma, wrote a letter to the Peace Observers Group requesting us 'to kindly take necessary action' to have the underground camp at Phezhu removed within seven days. 'If the camp is not removed, this Government will take such action as it considered necessary to prevent the camp continuing at this site.'

In the meanwhile there was a big uproar in the Lok Sabha at New Delhi. Mr Hem Barua had tabled a question on the Phezhu meeting. He asked Mr Dinesh Singh, Minister of State for External Affairs, 'Whether holding of such a meeting and hoisting of another flag did not amount to a rebellion on Indian soil?'

When Mr Dinesh Singh replied in the negative, there was an uproar from the Congress benches as well as Opposition benches. Two Congress members asked, 'What else is it?' Another shouted, 'It is a shame he speaks like that.' Another Congress member got up and said, 'We could not permit the Minister to answer like this.'

Mrs Indira Gandhi intervened and said, 'They asked for permission and the Governor gave them the permission to hold the meeting.' This statement provoked a storm of protest. One Congress member was heard saying, 'Impeach the Governor, if that is the case.'.

Members from different sections of the House took exception to the presence of Rev Scott in the Federal camp. Again there was a general demand that Rev Scott should be expelled from Assam.

Mr Swaran Singh agreed that the presence of Rev Scott was objectionable 'and inconsistent with the spirit of the Peace Mission'. He further said that the next round of talks with the underground Nagas will be a direct one and the Peace Mission itself 'might become progressively redundant'.

Mr Swaran Singh further appealed to the Members of the Lok

Sabha not to attach undue significance or give exaggerated importance to the meeting on 22 March.

In April and May we were exercised over the dismantling of the Phezhu camp.

The Peace Mission took charge of the camp from 1 April with the concurrence of all concerned. Caretakers were appointed and a white flag was hoisted.

Finally the structures were dismantled and the Peace Observers arranged for some money for this purpose.

Referring to the Phezhu controversy, Shri Jayaprakash Narayan said in a letter, 'It was lucky that you and Marjorie Behn were in Kohima, otherwise I am afraid the Republic Day affair might have blowed up the ceasefire.'

GENERAL ELECTIONS (FEBRUARY 1967)

The elections were held all over the country. In Nagaland there was no contest. Mr S. C. Jamir was again returned to Parliament. But there was contest in Manipur. Not only Parliamentary elections but also elections to the State Assembly. The Manipur Government utilized the services of the Peace Observers in the ceasefire-bound Naga areas.

I went on a preliminary trip to the Ukhrul region and held discussions with Mr L. Phanitphang, the underground commissioner for Ukhrul and Tengnoupal areas. (Phanitphang means one born in a festival). I suggested to him that it would be a good gesture if he could instruct all underground people not to create any violence during the election period. This would be a good thing especially since the peace talks with the Government of India were still going on and everyone was hoping for a final solution of the political problem.

Mr Phanitphang, a person of peace, readily appreciated my plea. His only point was that the Government authorities should not use force to compel villagers to vote. I said, compulsion was out of question in democratic elections. In any case, I agreed to convey his concern to the authorities at Imphal.

The authorities at Imphal had no hesitation in making it clear that no compulsion would be used in the elections. It was a privilege of the citizen to vote, to vote for this candidate or that candidate, or not vote at all. But the leaders of the Manipur Government told me that as per Government regulations, the polling stations would be guarded by armed police and the ballot boxes would be taken to the headquarters under armed protection. This I conveyed to Mr Phanitphang. He sent a circular to all concerned in his area not to resort to violence.

During those days, I had the opportunity to meet often the Chief Commissioner, Shri Baleshwar Prasad. Once I took Mr Phanitphang to him. As always, Shri Prasad was frank and forthright. He told Mr Phanitphang that he had no objection to any political movement but objected to the setting up of a parallel Government. 'Even the Indian National Congress did not set up a parallel Government,' he said.

Shri Baleshwar Prasad, now Lt Governor of Delhi, used to regale us with interesting stories about INA (Indian National Army). He was a close colleague of Netaji Subhas Chandra Bose.

The elections in Manipur were staggered in four phases. This was necessary because the polling stations were located in far-flung places and the police personnel were limited. They had to be used in rotation.

Miss Marjorie Sykes and I camped in Manipur for almost a month. We divided the area between ourselves. I took responsibility for the Ukhrul region whereas Miss Sykes was responsible for Tamenglong and Mao-Maram. We would meet at Imphal, compare notes, and go our ways to our respective regions. Those were intensive days of touring.

Once I was proceeding from Imphal to Ukhrul. On the way I heard there was a confrontation between a polling party and an underground group. As I left the main road and went some distance on a kacha road, I found a long caravan of jeeps stalled. I left my jeep and walked towards where the Chief Polling Officer was resting. He told me that they could not proceed further because they had come to learn that a good-sized underground group was not far away and had intentions to obstruct the polling party. He had already sent a WT (Wireless Transmission) message to Imphal and was awaiting instructions.

My Tangkhul colleague and I went a little further on foot. After covering two furlongs, my colleague, Mr Kapangkhui asked me to wait and said that he would go and find out. In half an hour or so he returned with an underground Captain, in uniform and fully armed. We greeted each other and had cordial discussions. I explained to him that there was a ceasefire, peace talks were going on and already it had been agreed that there should be no violence or obstruction during the elections. He readily agreed to withdraw his men from the area. He said that the polling party could proceed without let or hindrance. I was glad that the problem could be solved so easily.

A more interesting experience came a few days later. I had gone back to Imphal after a four-day tour in the interior. I was staying in the Circuit House, getting ready for another round of touring. In the afternoon, there came an urgent message from the SP (Superintendent of Police) that one polling party which was proceeding to a village on the Burma border was finding difficulty. He asked whether I could proceed immediately so that the party could reach its destination in time. I started immediately.

We reached Ukhrul town around 8.00 p.m. The SDO (Sub-Divisional Officer) had already received instructions and was waiting for us. After a quick meal, we were on the road again. Along with a guide, my Tangkhul friend Mr Kapangkhui and I left Ukhrul around 9.00 p.m. We drove and drove. Finally we reached a place called Pushing at 5.00 a.m. We met a small group of VVF boys (Village Volunteer Force) in a small camp. They were glad to see us. They prepared tea for us.

In the meanwhile I prepared urgent messages which some village friends of Pushing would take to the underground leader as well as the Chief Polling Officer. I learned that it was a long way from Pushing to Chamu, the. village on the Burma border. The total distance was twenty-two miles. The jeep could not go. One had to walk all the way, going up and down two major mountain ranges.

After an hour's rest, we started off. It was a long, long trek but it was a most charming country of breath-taking beauty. Here and there we saw small hamlets where lived people in primitive conditions. In one village we stopped. They gave us tea and spontaneously gave some cash donation to the Peace Mission. We walked and walked. The upward climb was always the more difficult.

We reached a small village in the evening. The sun was about to set. Chamu was still seven miles away. Mr Kapangkhui asked whether we should spend the night there.

Very tired as we were, our objective was still Chamu. After

refreshing ourselves we started off again. We had two torches. It was thick jungle all the way through. There was the possibility of encountering armed people. Mr Kapangkhui, who was leading the group all along, now prudently went behind. We pressed forward. There was some moonlight. Finally, when we sighted Chamu, it was around 8.00 p.m. Slowly and slowly we negotiated the last climb and dragged our bones somehow up to this border village. We found there was nobody. The whole village was deserted.

Presently, however, one or two persons showed up. Later the village chief, who had fled into the jungles, returned. We got into his house and sitting around the fireplace, had our well-earned tea.

The chief was very happy that 'the Peace Mission' had come. He told me that the underground captain and his group were not very far. They had taken position on the path to the village and were going to shoot at the polling party. But after receiving our message, they called off the ambush. The polling party had diverted their course and had gone in a different direction. The chief said that I could meet the underground captain next morning.

I tuned the transistor and it was time for nine o'clock news. The broadcaster happily said, 'General elections were held peacefully throughout the length and breadth of the country, from Kashmir to Kanyakumari, from Rajasthan to Burma border.' I was happy at the mention of the Burma border where I actually was. I was also happy that we had done a little bit to prevent violence in that far-off corner.

EXTENDING THE CEASEFIRE (OCTOBER 1967)

The extension of ceasefire period became an issue. The underground felt that they had been taking the initiative ever since the Peace Mission ceased to exist. Since the ceasefire was a matter of mutual concern, why not the other side too (i.e. the Government of India) show interest and take initiative—so they thought.

The Government of India seemed willing enough for further extension of the ceasefire. In their view, after the disbandment of the Peace Mission which used to make proposals for ceasefire extension, the Peace Observers Team was the right body to do it.

In the meanwhile, several Naga friends dropped in at the Peace Centre at Kohima and suggested that we should take initiative to propose extension. As Conveners of the Peace Observers Team,

Miss Sykes and I had made such proposals in the past. We would informally consult both sides about the possible period of extension and then propose what was likely to be agreeable to both.

We sounded the two sides informally. The Chief Secretary, Mr R. Khathing, reflecting the feeling of the Government of India, seemed to favour three months extension. We went to Chedema and talked to Mr Kughato, Mr Ramyo and others. They were friendly as always and said that they wouldn't be the first party to open fire. They did not, however, give an indication of the possible period of extension acceptable to them.

On our return from Chedema, we made a formal proposal to both sides suggesting three months extension.

On 25 October the Government of India announced their concurrence with the proposal of the Peace Observers Team. On 27 October the official announcement said, 'By a fresh order the Governor of Nagaland has extended the suspension of operations up to 31 January 1968.'

In the meanwhile, the Federal side expressed their displeasure at the Peace Observers Team having taken the initiative for ceasefire extension. The underground letter to us said that the question of ceasefire extension should be directly negotiated between the two 'contracting parties'. The main task of the Peace Observers Team was to 'uphold strict observation of the ceasefire terms'.

A reply was necessary to clarify the position of the Peace Observers Team. While the Peace Observers Team certainly appreciated the fact that the ceasefire was a matter of direct concern between the two contracting parties, it was also true that there was a great deal of public concern over the continuance of peace and the Peace Observers Team acted only in response to this concern and in keeping with past procedure. 'Peace is a vital matter and perhaps it is not inappropriate for a body like the Peace Observers Team to make suggestions for continuance of peace.'

Later I received another letter from the Federal Secretary, Mr Savizo Hozoye, saying that they had no objection to the Peace Observers Team or anyone else making suggestions for ceasefire extension. They were only pointing out that the ceasefire agreement was a matter between the two contracting parties.

Finally the Federal side announced extension for two months, i.e. till the end of 31 December, one month short of Government extension. This was the first time the ceasefire was extended by two different periods. In the past it was always a mutually agreed period.

14

YOUTH RESPONDS TO CRISIS: CURACAO*

A. PAUL HARE, FRANK CARNEY, AND FRED OVSIEW

Curacao is an island in the Caribbean Ocean. It is forty miles long and about twelves miles across at its widest. The population of about 140,000 is less than five per cent White, with a majority of the citizens having African and other non-European backgrounds.

In May of 1969 there was a crisis on the island of Curacao when rioters burned and looted part of the major city. The people of the island sought help from various sources to understand the social problems which had led to the riot and to promote a process of nonviolent social change. As one response, a group of professionals, government officials, and business people joined with some consultants from the United States to form the Antillean Institute of Social Science, a summer institute held in 1970, which would provide a means for all citizens who wished to learn more about the economic, social, and political problems.

One of the courses planned for the institute was a workshop on 'Youth and Social Change'. Since we wished to make the point that youth could play a valuable part in the process of change, we included in the American staff two people who were at the time both undergraduates at Haverford College: Frank Carney and Fred Ovsiew. Both were experienced in the theory of nonviolence and the process of change in the United States.

In the pages which follow we will first present an account of the development and the activities of the Institute, written by Paul Hare who was the Co-director. This will be followed by comments by Frank Carney and Fred Ovsiew on their role in the Institute and the questions this role raised for them as agents of change in

*Paper presented at meetings of the American Association for the Advancement of Science, Philadelphia, December 1971. Report No. 57, completed under National Institute of Mental Health Grant No. 5 R01 MH17421-03 SP.

another culture.

AN ACCOUNT OF THE ANTILLEAN
INSTITUTE OF SOCIAL SCIENCE
(BY PAUL HARE)

The first sessions of the Antillean Institute of Social Science were held on the island of Curacao, Netherlands Antilles, during June, July, and August of 1970. The Institute had been designed as an approach to nonviolent planned change as one response to the violent change which had occurred on the Island on 30 May 1969, when rioting workers burned and looted in the town of Willemstad, after which the government of the Netherlands Antilles resigned.

The riot

A full account of the riot, including an hour-by-hour summary of the events of 30 May, has been issued in Dutch by the Government Commission appointed to study the riot. There is also a paperback book, written in Papiamentu, in the form of a novel, which illustrates the emotional involvement of those who participated in the events. At the time of the Institute, over a year later, little had intervened to dim the memories of the excitement of the day. Unfortunately few visible changes in the social structure of the Island had occurred. Planned change was especially difficult because a formal local government for the Netherlands Antilles was not re-established until July 1970. However, basic governmental services were available during this period since the Islands are in fact part of the Kingdom of the Netherlands.

In September 1969, Frank McDonald summed up the situation in a paper for the Institute of Current World Affairs (McDonald, 1969). He said in part:

> A few months ago, no one would have thought that the Dutch government would be airlifting paratroopers to quell rioters in quiet, sun-soaked Curacao. But on May 30 what started as a small strike directed against Shell Oil of Curacao became an island-wide, forty-million-dollar insurrection. The immediate cause, a group of plumbers demanding higher wages from a Shell Oil Contractor (Wescar Inc.), was of course only a surfaced expression of the more serious economic

and social woes in Curacao. For behind the facade of some of the Caribbean's most glamorous duty free shops, international hotels and tourist resorts lurk numerous pockets of poverty, vast numbers of unemployed and a growing resentment of Dutch control of the island.

Requests for expert advice

Members of the business community of Curacao were accustomed to seek expert advice to solve management problems or introduce new manufacturing and marketing techniques. Many of the business people had already taken part in several management training workshops with experts, primarily from the US, who would come to the Island to conduct a course. The fact that there were about a dozen modern computers on the Island was another measure of their success in keeping abreast of current business practices. Thus when a major social problem erupted on the Island, it is not surprising to find these same people turning once more to outsiders for advice.

One group of business people from the Chamber of Commerce had read about the success of David McClelland's 'achievement motivation' training which had been developed at Harvard University. A member of McClelland's applied research institute (Sterling Institute) was invited to the Island to conduct a survey and make a proposal for action. The proposal, which was accepted and implemented, called for a series of workshops to introduce business and government leaders to achievement motivation techniques so that they in turn could conduct workshops for several hundred other community leaders. Concurrently, new organizations were to be developed to plan and implement change (Berlew and Le Clere, 1974).

Although the Sterling Institute programme and the Antillean Institute of Social Science programme were related to organizations which were independent in the United States they merged on Curacao in both intended and unintended ways. Some of the same community leaders were eventually involved in the boards and committees of each programme, the sources of funds were often the same and thus competing. Since the Sterling Institute arrived on the Island first, the Antillean institute was described, at one point, as a sub-project of the Sterling Institute programme to provide some necessary integration for the individuals involved as well as for the members of the society who sought to respond to both programmes. Since the Sterling Institute programme concentrated on weekend training workshops and long range planning while the Antillean Institute concentrated on teaching and research, the two programmes were actually complementary.

The development of the Sterling Institute programme is a story in itself. We will not attempt to give any more details here. Nor will we do any more than note that these were not the only individuals and groups interested in social change or research to visit the Island after the riot. However the activities of the Sterling Institute and the Antillean Institute played the more prominent part in the efforts towards social change during the summer of 1970.

A request to Haverford College

Concurrent with the inquiries to the Sterling Institute by the Chamber of Commerce, Victor Pinedo, Jr, a former Haverford College (Pennsylvania) student, wrote to Dr Peter Bennett, a member of the staff he had known at Haverford, to ask for the help of a research team to study the social-psychological aspects of the problems underlying the riot. Pinedo, a native of Curacao, was at that time the president of the Lions Club and the manager of a number of food and soft-drink companies.

Pinedo's letter written in June 1969, read in part:

> As a result of the riots a number of stores in the heart of the business center were burnt to the ground, 1,000 people will remain unemployed and about $50,000,000 of property was damaged. This is the first occurrence of its kind in Curacao and the reaction of the people after the riots showed that there is a great deal of wrong in the values of the population.
>
> In view of the above, the community leaders feel that there is a big psychological problem in the population. As there are no experts on this Island to point out where the problem lies and find its solution, I am writing you this letter to find out whether you know of any behaviour scientist team which could come to Curacao to make a study of the situation and advise the community as to what action they should take to remedy the problem.

Since I had had some experience doing research and working with Peace Corps in the Philippines and doing research and teaching in Africa, Pinedo's letter was passed on to me. In an exchange of letters I suggested that one week be devoted to a preliminary survey of the problems on Curacao as a basis for a proposal for research. During the first two days of the week I asked that we meet some of the people who would be important to enable us to carry out any action research proposal we might formulate. We should also meet some of the persons who would be potentially members of the research or action team. Finally we should interview a set of persons who represented a cross section of those who had been actively studying the riots or who were principally affected by them. By midweek we would stop, draw up a tentative plan, and then modify the plan and determine the possible interest in the plan during the remaining days of the week.

Stages in the development of the Antillean Institute
The planning which eventually led to the first sessions of the Antillean Institute of Social Science passed through the four stages which have been observed in successful group development in many different situations (Hare, 1973). In the first stage the basic idea of the group is established. In the second stage the resources necessary for the group task are gathered or manufactured. In the third stage the roles for the leaders and other group members are specified and attention is given to developing group morale. In the final stage the group members carry out the task which brought them together.

In the case of the Antillean Institute the activities of the first stage were concentrated in one week of November 1969 when Pinedo and I developed the basic plan. The second stage reached a high point when I returned to the Island in January 1970 with several colleagues to begin a major fund raising drive for the $60,000 we had budgeted for the Institute. The third phase was again concentrated in a week in May when we recruited staff and worked out the details of the teaching and research activities. The final phase consisted of actually holding two five-week sessions of the Antillean Institute of Social Science during the months of June, July, and August 1970.

In many respects the Antillean Institute looked like any other summer institute in social science. There were courses, research seminars, public lectures, and informal gatherings. However there were also some marked and dramatic differences and some of these at least can be traced to our efforts to be responsive to two sets of values, one set proposed by the advocates of Gandhian nonviolent direct action (cf. Hare and Blumberg, 1968) and the other derived from the radical critiques of social science (cf. Szymanski, 1970). (These values were not necessarily shared by all staff.)

Gandhi's Principles: Truth and Love

The keys to Gandhi's principles of nonviolent change are to be found in two concepts, truth (satya) and love (ahimsa). Gandhi called the power behind his approach *satyagraha* (truth force) rather than 'passive resistance' or 'nonviolent resistance' because the earlier terms did not reflect the action and initiative of his approach. The truths he sought were especially about people's relation to one another.. He began his campaigns in South Africa where the European settlers placed severe restraints on the action and development of the Indians, Bantu, and other minority peoples. He continued his campaign in India where the Indian caste system placed restrictions on all classes of Indians and where the British Empire placed restrictions on the whole nation. The main truth Gandhi sought was the sense of a wider identity which would allow groups, previously segregated by custom, to come together and work side-by-side as human beings. Truth was not simply reaching an agreement whereby the will of the majority would be accepted by the minority, but finding a new over-arching sense of identity which would provide more freedom for all.

The concept of *ahimsa* literally means 'non-injury' which in the Indian tradition means that a person should not injure another living thing. However, looked at the other way around, the concept stands for *love*. Here love means that we so value our fellow humans that we not only would not harm them but also would accept 'self suffering' should they fail to understand and seek to harm us. Love also means a warmth and closeness of interpersonal relations which gives us a sense of 'community' allowing us to 'live the revolution' now rather than postpone our involvement in life until some drastic, perhaps violent, change has brought about the ideal society. (For further discussion of Ghandhi's approach to nonviolent action cf. Dhawan, 1946; Erikson, 1969; Ghandhi, 1951; Horsburgh, 1968; Lynd, 1966; Sharp, 1970; and Sibley, 1963.)

The Radical Critique of Social Science

The radical critique of social science has developed over the past two or three years as younger social scientists have challenged the older 'establishment' social scientists in confrontations at professional meetings and in articles in the professional literature. The advocates of the radical position suggest that professional social scientists should be willing to take stands on current issues of national importance, such as the war in Vietnam, and should be willing to do research on behalf of the people they study, rather than on behalf of the government 'establishment' which usually provides the research funds (cf. Szymanski, 1970; Rapoport, 1970).

In the case of research in a developing country, the typical research process has involved someone from a developed country deciding on a research problem without consulting persons in the developing country, securing his or her own funds and staff, and conducting the research using the persons in the developing country only as subjects. The data were taken home to be analysed and published, some years later, in a journal or monograph which probably never reached the hands of the subjects who supplied the data.

Although in many cases the research process still takes this form, in others the process has evolved through a stage of participant observation, on to a stage of mutual co-operation between researchers from both countries, and finally to a stage in which the research becomes part of the process of social change rather than a preliminary step towards beginning the process. The research on Curacao took the final form. Rather than respond to a request for research by simply sending in a research team, we evolved a process by which the members of the community could look at themselves while they were learning social science theory and skills.

Planning the Institute

By the middle of the week's visit in November, Vic Pinedo and I had drafted an outline for a 'Summer Institute in Social Science'.

The plan called for an Institute to be held during June, July, and August 1970 for from 100 to 300 students who would be primarily high school graduates. Since there is no formal education beyond high school in the Netherlands Antilles, we were not competing with any local university. The curriculum was to include general social science courses as well as special courses in business and industry, Curacao studies, and education. Each of the courses or seminars was designed to meet some need which had been identified by one or more of the community leaders who had been interviewed during the first few days of the week. We expected that the local government would provide classroom and office space and the industry would donate computer time and other facilities. Our first budget was set at $60,000 which provided for a Curacaoan staff of nine or more, four senior professors from the US, and four additional specialists representing journalism, computer programming, and youth work.

The single page was stencilled and given out on the Island to members of the Lions Club and other community leaders who were asked to comment on the proposal. One copy has the letters 'CIA' on the top of the page written by Stanley Brown as part of his comment on the proposal. Brown, who was a prominent member of the 'Frente de Obrero', a political party which was formed after the riot and which identified primarily with the workers who were involved in the riot, was suggesting that we probably represented the US Central Intelligence Agency. My response was, 'Sure, Stanley, that stands for Curacao Improvement Association.'

On several occasions I had an opportunity to speak about nonviolence during the week. One was a half-hour national television programme where I was interviewed about Gandhi and his methods.

The January visit was designed to publicize the plan for the Institute as a prelude to fund raising and to recruit more teaching staff. This time I was accompanied by Professor Glickman (Political Science) and Professor McGaffey (Anthropology), both of Haverford, and Professor Bramson (Sociology) from Swarthmore College, who were expected to be senior members of the Institute staff. Dr Loescher, sociologist and retiring director of the US-South Africa Leader Exchange Programme, also accompanied us at his own expense to see if he might be able to suggest some action possibilities based on his South African experience.

Pinedo and the others had laid out a heavy schedule for us. We were met at the airport by television camera operators. Our discussions and panel presentations were covered by the local newspapers. We appeared on the national television network with some of our Curacaon colleagues. We met representatives of the national and local governments. We presented our revised plans to our new Board of Directors with representatives of both the government and private sectors (since the project had already outgrown Lions Club sponsorship). We held our final press conference and left the Island with the feeling that the project might well succeed.

During the weeks that followed, the Institute staff on Curacao sent out an appeal for funds asking local business people and government representatives to pledge $200 'scholarships' for students for the Institute. The call for contributions included a brief description of the Institute (now with its own 'Instituto Antillano di Sciencia Social' letterhead), a list of the twenty-five members of the Board of Trustees, quotations about the Institute, and a pledge form.

At the same time I sent out written appeals or phoned to about a dozen foundations in the US from a list supplied by the Development Office of Haverford College. The list included Ford, Rockefeller, Shell, Kellogg, and the US government AID branch. The letter asked for $25,000 to bring additional specialists for the Institute. No foundation responded with a grant. Various reasons were given. Some were concerned about their US tax status if the project had political implications. One foundation did not want to finance 'gringos' who might meddle in Latin American affairs.

Fortunately, some $50,000 was pledged from sources on Curacao so that we were able to go ahead with the planning by cutting out some of the special projects. As it turned out, not having US funds made us somewhat less open to charges of being agents of the CIA although this suspicion was never fully dissipated. Near the end of the project, after we had established ourselves as a going concern, we were still advised against bringing even one more American resource person to the Island. The American influence was already seen as great enough by some Antilleans and the extra person might just be the feared CIA agent.

During February, March, and April members of the Board and staff of the Institute on Curacao were very active. They prepared a questonnaire in both Papiamentu and Dutch which was sent to prospective students to determine the relative interest in a list of twenty possible courses.

We were actually considering up to twenty-five different courses at that time. Six were eventually dropped or combined. Professor

McGaffey received a grant to do research in the Congo and could not come. He was replaced by Professor Vera Green who was given the task of taking over McGaffey's courses as well as those of an Antillean sociologist who was not going to be on the Island for the whole term. This combination turned out to place an undue burden on Professor Green. Other courses were dropped because they were judged to be too controversial for one reason or another.

Also during April the Institute was formally registered as a 'Stichting' [nonprofit organization] according to Dutch law.

Final decisions about courses were made during my third visit to the Island in May. This time I was accompanied by Professor Bramson who helped work out final details and made preliminary arrangements for a research project in education. Herbert Kritzer, a computer programmer, also made the trip to begin to prepare the computer programs for the courses on research methods and the actual research we planned to do during the summer.

Near the end of this visit a concern was expressed that the Institute staff was being dominated by the American group. In response we cut down on the number of courses to be taught by Americans, told a few additional Americans who were potential staff members that we could not use them, and did not use family members of the American staff as part of the American team. (Although my daughter, Sharon Hare, an anthropologist, assisted Professor Green in the anthropological research, she was not included on the payroll.) I also offered to step down as Co-director to become the liaison with the American staff. My offer was not accepted, but the other changes were made. Since we did not hear about the final outcome of the deliberations of the Institute Board until after we had returned to the US, we left the Island the third time on an anxious note. It was possible that the 'revolution within the revolution' might bring the Institute to a halt.

It was little consolation that the revolt against the leadership typically takes place in the third phase in groups of many types (see the discussion of phases of development, above). In theory, what we see happening is that members who might have gone along with the basic definition of the Institute (*Pattern Maintenance* phase), thinking that the Institute would never be able to raise the money and survive the *Adaptation* phase, now find that they must settle any differences in the *Integration* phase as the group works out its leadership patterns and other roles, if they are to have any influence on the outcome. Once the group moves into the final *Goal-attainment* phase the major task becomes that of working toward the goal as it has been defined. Although minor revolts might be expected at the end of each phase, just before the group moves on to the next phase, the third phase revolt seems often to be the most dramatic. Rather than revolt, some persons may leave the group at each stage. Thus some drop out because they do not like the basic definition, some because they disagree with the allocation of funds, and finally some, as in this case, consider dropping out when they find they do not like the arrangements for leadership or for other member roles.

Formal specifications for the roles of the American staff were then expressed in 'Contracts for Services'. Providing the housing called for in the contract turned out to be another difficult problem. Few houses were available during the ten-plus weeks of the Institute. As a result some American staff moved several times during the summer and others were unhappy with arrangements for various periods of time. This problem provides one of the main reasons for recommending a six-week Institute in the future which would coincide with the school vacation when a number of teachers would be off the Island. Providing services of all kinds turns out to be the major hidden 'cost' (both monetary and psychological) of using foreigners as staff.

The Summer Sessions

Everyone who wanted to attend the Institute was allowed to register. There were no fees other than for books. This was in keeping with the other forms of public education on the Island which have government support. Students could choose from nineteen different courses. Acting as Dean of Students, Drs Harold Arends provided orientation for all students. In a few cases there was a shift in the teaching staff. A few popular courses such as the introduction to sociology, introduction to anthropology, leadership and group dynamics, child psychology, and youth and social change were offered twice so that the total enrollment in any one class could be kept to about thirty persons.

Each class met twice a week for one hour and twenty minutes over a five-week period. One set of classes was held Monday and Wednesday at 7.00 p.m. or at 8.40 p.m., and the other set of classes was held on Tuesday and Thursday at the same time periods. Jaap van Soest, the Institute administrator, arranged the class hours so that there would be a minimum of conflict in individual schedules since most students were taking at least two courses. The first five-week session of the Institute was held from 15 June through 17 July and the second session from 20 July through 21 August.

At the end of the first session several short summary reports were prepared for a meeting of the Board. The typical class was attended by twenty-five to thirty students. On the average about eighty per cent of those who registered for the classes attended. As expected, some persons registered but did not attend, and some dropped out as the pressure of other activities increased. Compared to other experiences with adult education on the Island, some members of the Curacaoan staff judged our attendance figures to be quite good.

The majority of the students were between twenty and thirty years of age. For education the majority held the HBS, or secondary-school degree. There is a negative correlation between age and years of education. The younger participants tended to have a higher educational level. This probably reflects a similar trend in the general population.

Of the 269 students enrolled, the largest number were taking two courses. Almost twice as many students were enrolled for the First Session only (ninety-six) as for the Second Session only (fifty-one). The typical (modal) participant was either taking two courses in each session (forty-two) or taking two courses in the first session and none in the second (fifty).

Research

The various research projects were conducted with active collaboration between American and Antillean staff. In some cases the research was conducted as a part of a seminar at the Institute, in others by a special project team or 'Task Force'. In each case it was hoped that the Antillean members would be able to continue the same project or conduct similar projects after the Institute was over. We recognized that there will be a continuing need for accurate data about the state of the society and accurate measures of the effectiveness of programmes for change.

Brief summaries of research in progress were prepared for the

July Board meeting and the August Board meeting. More detailed reports were written by some of the staff at the end of the Institute.

The major research projects were as follows:

Education — Bramson and his colleagues prepared questionnaires to be given to a sample of approximately 500 teachers and 1,500 students in the secondary schools as a major study of education and aspiration on Curacao. When completed, this study could be compared with a similar study conducted on the island of St. Croix.

Voluntary Associations — Green and her colleagues interviewed members of many of the voluntary associations on the Island. These data will be compared with similar data from Aruba to show the role that voluntary associations play in the social system. Professor Green has submitted a first report on the project in a separate paper.

Labour Force — As a demonstration of the uses of sampling and computer-based statistical techniques, Hare and a 'Task Force' of volunteers representing a cross section of the Island, drew a sample of every thirtieth person from the file of approximately 33,000 persons registered at the Government Labour Office. To this were added samples of employees from Shell, island and national governments, and other categories of workers not ordinarily carried in the government files. The data have been left in a 'data bank' at the Institute and a few copies have been distributed. In addition to providing an estimate of some of the characteristics of different segments of the labour force, the project can serve as a model for analysis when Jan Spit, head of the Government Labour Welfare Service, completes his projected total registration of all Island employees.

Computer Programs — As a special project Herbert Kritzer of the Institute staff and Paul Tevreden of the IBM World Trade Corporation adapted a set of statistical and data processing programs for use at the IBM Data Center. The programs include scoring and data screening and manipulation routines, and statistical programs for correlations, factor analysis, regression, analysis of variance, t-test, frequency distribtutions, means, standard deviations, sums, cross tabulation, and contingency analysis. Each of the programs, together with directions and sample data, is available at the IBM Center. Treveden and several other computer programmers on the Island are familiar with their use and can help prepare data for analysis. During the latter part of the summer the programs were used for the Labour Force study, the research on the Barrio of Sta. Rosa conducted by the research methods class, and for an analysis of personnel ratings by a 'Task Force' of representatives of Texas Instruments and Hendersons.

Political Analysis — During the second session Harvey Glickman interviewed a number of people on the Island to identify areas for research concerning the partial dissolution of traditional patterns of leadership and support. He has summarized his impressions in a separate paper.

Economic Development Policy—Also during the second session, Sayre Schatz collected data for his 'Report on Economic Development Policy for Curacao' which has already been submitted to the Institute. His report includes sections on the nature of the Curacaon economy, wage increases, and suggested policies for planning and foreign exchange-earning activities.

Community Activities

Brief reports on the community activities of the Institute are given in the memoranda prepared for the Board Meetings.

Several projects were related to the work of the students in the course on Youth and Social Change, taught by Ger Van Atten, Frank Carney, and Fred Ovsiew. The projects included developing a proposal for an Antillean Youth Service Corps, conducting a two-week programme to develop Barrio [district] libraries and reading programmes, and working with a group of young men who were developing the Casa Manita as a youth centre for the urban area.

Another project of the Institute which was enjoyed by members of the Institute and the community at large was the journal *Voz Di Inansiso* produced by the members of the workshop on journalism during the first session. The workshop was directed by Zelbert Moore and Norbert Hendrikse.

The project which reached the largest number of people in the Netherlands Antilles was the marathon 'teach-in' organized by Harold Arends and other members of the Antillean staff. The teach-in began at 9.00 a.m. one Saturday near the end of the second session and lasted well into the early morning hours of the next day. Some people were talking outside the Center for the Arts, where the event had been held, at three o'clock in the morning. The events of the day included a series of panel discussions on vital topics for the Netherlands Antilles: the Antillean identity, the state of the economic and political systems, and the values and aspirations of youth. After each panel, members of the audience could ask questions for as long as the topic held their interest. It was, in fact, an exciting example of freedom of speech — the first time that there had been an open discussion of the problems and prospects of the Netherlands Antilles since the riot of 30 May 1969. The entire programme, including one rather heated exchange near the end during which some persons left the main hall to meet in protest in the corridors, was carried live on a national radio station. At intervals, food and entertainment were offered in the lounge. In all it was a memorable occasion. Through it our 'students' revealed the fact that they had learned their lessons and were able to discuss the social problems they faced from new perspectives and with a new openness to the views of others.

Plans for the Future

By the end of the second session we were already looking ahead to the possibility that the Institute might be held again the following year. A plan was submitted to the Board which called for a smaller budget for a single six-week session during the school vacation. More emphasis would be placed on the Antillean staff. Ideally a small central staff would be able to continue some of the activities of the Institute throughout the year. Since a successful weekend 'Institute' had been held on Aruba in July there were plans for a similar Institute to be held on Aruba the following year. Each of the Island Institutes might be combined in an overall Antillean Institute. Finally I suggested some guidelines for planned change based on a functional analysis of social systems.

As it turned out, the Institute was not held the following summer. Although the government remained unsettled for some time, buildings in the centre of the city were gradually being rebuilt and Curacao gave the appearance of returning to normal. With the major crisis over, there was no longer the same motivation to seek creative solutions to problems of change.

OBSERVATIONS BY FRANK CARNEY

One of the greatest problems I had working on Curacao was getting over the role I had anticipated for myself. I had anticipated working with people who had recently rioted to show their frustration about their social situation and were ready to do things to solve some of their problems. This was a great mistake. The people in the course, which was set up as a vehicle to organize work units, were not interested in working. There were a few difficulties that arose from our side that could have augmented the difficulties. One was that we didn't speak Dutch or Papiamentu (their most frequently used languages). This made communicating a little difficult. The second was that we were viewed as American imperialists. The difficult part was that I agreed with them. In light of these problems, we decided to set up the course so that the Curacaoans would dominate the sessions. This caused complete confusion. A few intellectual leftists took advantage of the situation to make our 'American' presence more difficult. But unfortunately even their zeal was short-lived. In the end we abandoned the hope of inspiring working groups and decided to lead talks about Gandhi, Fanon, and Marx, etc, hoping at least to give the class a different perspective on society.

We were able to have some effect on at least two existing groups. One was a group that was trying to set up what would be the equivalent of a neighbourhood recreation centre. Our presence alone seemed to be the incentive for them to work harder. They were very 'establishment'-oriented. They seemed to be trying to impress us with their ability to organize. The other group was interested in reviving knowledge of the island's folklore traditions. They were very interested in what similar black groups in the United States were doing, so I was able to draw parallels with black activity on Curacao and the United States for them. An interesting end to one conversation was that black people in the United States should emigrate.

The difficulty that I had with redefining my anticipated role was that I lacked the skills the people needed, so I kept looking for a group that could use the skills I could offer.

OBSERVATIONS BY FRED OVSIEW

I have three points to make about what I learned in Curacao. It is our learning that I must emphasize, for a number of reasons: we have had little feedback from Curacao, and it would in any case be hard to evaluate our impact on them; and the change in us is most germane for this panel. But I must say right off that there are hard questions to be asked about the legitimacy of our going to Curacao, earning large salaries, complaining about the lack of air conditioners, and then concerning ourselves with our learning.

This leads me to the first dimension that I want to discuss. I learned to ask, who's in it for what? Each of us Americans was on a different trip. The youth workers, I think, had fantasies of leading a revolution of third-world people; another member of the team forthrightly was there to do research, and if the locals didn't work the way he wanted, he would take his data and go home (as he made quite explicit). And we were all there to take a vacation in the Caribbean and have an unusual learning experience. For anyone on Curacao to evaluate our work intelligently, we would have had to expose our own hidden agendas. Perhaps more important, if we had wanted to avoid a haunting sense of frustration and failure, we would have had to be honest with ourselves about what we were all about. When we couldn't pinpoint these anxieties, perhaps we had a clue to unadmitted goals.

But we didn't own up, I believe, to all of our hidden agendas. And thereby we kept ourselves from being confronted by our clients, or for that matter by ourselves or each other.

A second important dimension that I clarified for myself in Curacao involves support and estrangement. We were, after all, working in an alien culture. At times we all longed for more familiar surroundings, for at least the ease of communication that would come with speaking the same language. How did we handle the anxieties that developed in this situation?

I believe that we used a number of defences. Most important, we stuck together. Like the Jews in Exodus, when confronted with a painful and ambiguous situation with no certainties, we returned to the Golden Calf that we knew. On weekends we went swimming—with each other. We enjoyed talking with each other about Americana. Some of the Americans brought their families and made a home away from home.

We used other defences. We idealized the people we were working with, who became for some of us gallant representatives of an assaulted culture; or alternatively some of us didn't work with them at all but chose to use Curacaoans as research material and assistants. We planned grand plans that seem in retrospect, at least to me, to be out of reach for and irrelevant to Curacao.

I feel some anger about our using these defences, because I think they made us come on more patronizing and less available. But, on the other hand, they helped us function. We all felt limits as to how far we could extend ourselves, and it wouldn't have been productive to venture too far and collapse. This, in any case, is a common phenomenon. One reason for the retreat of the young left of the past few years into mountain communes is that people were burned out after years of struggle without support, in a foreign land called America. I am saying that this is a dimension that has to be considered in every effort at social change. And it is not simply a drawback, that people engaged in making change have limitations. The lesson, it seems to me, is that we are human too, and our creative learning involves building a situation not so threatening that we must insulate ourselves from growth.

I would make one more observation. A great deal of what we were able to do depended on our entry-point into the society. We had been invited initially through the Lions Club. Our first contacts were with important people in the business community; we had quick access to the key people in government and education as well. This worked both ways. Our access to resources that were unavailable to people who had lived their whole lives on Curacao worked to the advantage of poor people on a couple of occasions. On the other hand, our credibility with some of the radicals was impaired. But on the whole they were very open to us, and were willing to accept us for what we actually did. What was more destructive was that quick access works both ways. We were not just identified with the people who invited us, but were objectively most available and indebted to them. Naturally enough, the easiest people for us to listen to were the wealthy and educated: the people who spoke the best English had our ear. So when we were searching for a project, it was convenient to do some labour studies with the support and assistance of the personnel managers of the large (foreign) corporations. But the question must be asked of this, as of the whole project, whose interests were served?

REFERENCES

Berlew, David E. and William E. LeClere, 1974. 'Social intervention in Curacao: A case study.' Journal of Applied Behavioral Science 10 (1): 29-52.

Dhawan, Gopi Nath, 1946. The Political Philosophy of Mahatma Gandhi. Ahmedabad, India: Navajivan Publishing House.

Erikson, Erik H., 1969. Gandhi's Truth: On the Origins of Militant Non-violence. New York: Norton.

Gandhi, M. K., 1951. Nonviolent Resistance. Ahmedabad, India: Nava-Jivan Publishing House. (Also published in 1961, New York: Schocken Books.)

Hare, A. Paul, 1973. 'Theories of group development and categories for interaction analysis'. Small Group Behavior 4 (3 August): 259-304.

Hare, A. Paul and Herbert H. Blumberg, 1968. Nonviolent Direct Action: American Cases: Social-Psychological Analyses. Washington and Cleveland: Corpus Books.

Horsburgh, H. J. N., 1968. Nonviolence and Aggression: A Study of Ghandi's Moral Equivalent of War. London: Oxford University Press.

Lynd, Staughton, 1966. Nonviolence in America: A Documentary History. Indianapolis, Ind.: Bobbs-Merrill.

McDonald, Frank, 1969. 'Insurrection in the Dutch Antilles.' Letter for Institute of Current World Affairs, dated 1 September.

Rapoport, Robert W., 1970. 'Three dilemmas in action research: With special references to the Tavistock experience.' Human Relations 23: 499-513.

Sharp, Gene, 1970. Exploring Nonviolent Alternatives. Boston: Porter Sargent Publishers.

Sibley, Mulford (ed.), 1963. The Quiet Battle. Boston: Beacon Press.

Szymanski, Albert, 1970. 'Toward a radical sociology'. Sociological Inquiry 40 (1): 3-13.

15

CYPRUS—CONFLICT AND ITS RESOLUTION

A. PAUL HARE AND ELLEN WILKINSON

The action on Cyprus carried out by the Cyprus Resettlement Project was *nonpartisan* and *transnational*. An account of the project (Hare, 1974) has been supplemented by an informal memo by Ellen Wilkinson (1974). Because of the invasion of Cyprus by the Turkish army in 1974 the project was forced to an abrupt halt.

A front page story in the *Cyprus Mail* about 'Further aid to displaced Turks' on 12 December 1973 announced the fact that the Government of Cyprus would repair houses of Turkish Cypriots who had left their homes and villages ten years before during the 'time of troubles'. The next day the paper quoted Mr Osorio-Tafall, the United Nations Special Representative on Cyprus, as saying that this step by the Government 'would contribute to more understanding and would create better conditions for furtherance of a solution' to the Cyprus problem. In press releases both the Greek and Turkish sides noted the contribtuion of the Cyprus Resettlement Project in helping to facilitate the process of resettlement.

The Cyprus Resettlement Project has involved about twenty-five volunteers who are committed to work for peace and social change without violence. Their backgrounds represent several related traditions. Some are followers of Gandhi and have worked with the Shanti Sena (Peace Brigade) in the villages and cities of India and some are Quakers. Both of these groups draw on experiences with refugees and conflict resolution in many parts of the world. Other members of the project are social scientists or have other relevant skills. Volunteers have come from India, the United Kingdom, the United States, and South Africa.

The first team of five persons arrived in Cyprus in August 1972 to seek ways in which a group committed to nonviolence might work in conjunction with the mandate of the United Nations to help restore peaceful conditions to Cyprus.[1] Their concern for establishing 'nonmilitary peace contingents' grew out of proposals to the United Nations by Vinoba Bhave and the Shanti Sena in India and members of the International Peace Academy. After considering the possibility of working in areas such as health, education, or welfare, the team chose to work on the problem of resettlement of displaced persons as a humanitarian problem, at the suggestion of Mr Osorio-Tafall.

In March 1973 Mr Denktas, Vice President (representing the Turkish Cypriot leadership) and Mr Veniamin, Director General of the Ministry of Foreign Affairs (representing the government administration) endorsed a proposal that a 'working party' be formed with members of the Cyprus Resettlement Project acting as a third party to try to find a way to begin the resettlement process. Following this, a team of five persons came to Cyprus for the month of July and negotiated an agreement to begin the work in four villages.

Allowing time for the Turkish leadership to interview villagers to determine who wished to return, a team of about twenty volunteers arrived in November 1973 to continue the work through January 1974. This was the period of the most extensive work of the project. There were teams of three or four volunteers living in the villages of Dhiorios, Peristerona, Nisou, and Pano Lefkara. Each team collected information related to resettlement from the villages in its area, and tried to find ways to increase involvement of the villagers in the resettlement process. Some members of the project helped with negotiations between the Ministry of Foreign Affairs and the Turkish Cypriot Leadership.

During the month of January the Turkish side completed the survey of villagers who wished to return to four villages and the Government engineers surveyed the homes to determine the cost of reconstruction. The Project arranged the first meeting between the two sides to discuss in detail some of the next steps in resettlement. A representative of the United Nations was also present since the United Nations had agreed to resume its former third-party role in relation to resettlement when members of the Cyprus Resettlement Project were not present on the island.

The most recent team, again of five persons, arrived in the middle of April 1974 to review the progress of resettlement and to decide whether or not any further service by the Project seemed desirable. They found that a new political development had brought the Intercommunal Talks to a halt and that the Government had not yet voted the money to begin the reconstruction in the four villages. However it appeared that the political situation might be 'clarified' by the end of May, allowing the work to proceed. As an interim project to assure some movement towards resettlement and as a sign of the goodwill of citizens on both sides the volunteers proposed that a four-week work camp be held in one of the villages, beginning in the second week of July. At the end of April, Ellen Wilkinson stayed behind to help organize the work camp.

As a final phase of the Cyprus Resettlement Project the April 1974 team also proposed that after the Government had completed building the first set of houses four volunteers return to Cyprus for a period of six months. The volunteers would live in one or two of the villages and be concerned with all of the villages to which Turkish families were returning. Where necessary, volunteers would act as third-parties on any issues arising from the resettlement and help with plans for the continuation of the resettlement process. The Government approved both the plans for the work camp and for the final phase of the project.

After leaving the island in July Ellen Wilkinson reported that during the week before the military *coup d'etat* and subsequent Turkish invasion of Cyprus a small group of Turkish and Greek Cypriot students were working together in the village of Peristerona rebuilding six houses of Turkish Cypriots who had left their homes in 1963 during the island's intercommunal troubles. The fourteen students lived, worked, and relaxed together, not an extraordinary story except on Cyprus where this rarely happens as the youth of the two communities have been effectively separated for eleven years. The *coup* brought a halt to the work in Peristerona and like all other business on the island, the project stopped completely when Turkey invaded Cyprus on 20 July.

Ellen Wilkinson describes some of the details of the work camp as follows:

When Paul Hare, three other CRP members, and I returned to Cyprus in April to check on the progress of our work, we found that nothing could be done until money was passed by the Government to begin the reconstruction. As an interim project a work camp was suggested. The Turkish side agreed to the participation of their youth in a mixed project. We considered it to be one way to achieve our previous goals of resettlement and contact between the communities on a private, non-political level. It was the latter area which came to be the workcamp's most important aspect as Cypriots not only arranged the details of the camp but began visualizing how the experience might be expanded or adapted in the future.

To undertake the project we needed the approval of the officials and leaders from both communities. To this extent we were depending on political support.

The officials on the Greek side seemed to have trusted us as neutral and reliable workers. If they felt that as a whole the workcamp was innocuous, at least one of them felt strongly that any association between Cypriot youth would be valuable and should be encouraged.

The Turkish side's interest came from the hope that houses would actually be completed. They also saw the scheme as a way to find money in the future from sources outside the island and thus not have to depend on the Greek Cypriots if large, governmental funds were never allocated.

While waiting for verbal support from our political sources, we went to representatives of various private business and social groups for an idea of the kind of interest we could expect if we were to undertake the project. Several people from the private sector responded favourably, and eventually representatives of both communities gave us verbal approval. Paul Hare and the other CRP members left Cyprus, as they had planned, in the first days of May. I stayed to organize the workcamp with the one guideline that I should find what assistance I could by the end of May and proceed only if our support looked adequate at that time. This was primarily a Turkish concern as they wanted to guard against the work turning into a show of intercommunal harmony accomplishing nothing substantive. Neither side wanted any publicity about the camp for we would have no control over its coverage by the press.

We chose the second week in July as a target starting date. This gave me just over two months to organize the camp. I had to find assurances of monetary support before proceeding, yet many of the organizational details, such as recruiting the students, had to be begun by mid-May. To compound the problems the site of the workcamp was changed in late May because a large construction project was about to begin in the village we had originally chosen. Peristerona, the second workcamp site we chose, was in many ways a better site but the switch meant a time-consuming duplication of work as we had already chosen the houses to be repaired and had listed the materials we would have needed.

By the end of May enough support had been promised to make our randomly-chosen goal of 5,000 Cypriot pounds, about $15,000, seem realizable. There was, however, no formal review of the project and no one asked to see any exact figures. I was frequently in touch, however, with the people who were concerned with the job — primarily the District Officer and a man from the Turkish side's social services.

Dan Sipe, an American not previously involved with the CRP, arrived on Cyprus on 2 June to help co-ordinate the project. By 8 July, when the workcamp began, we had arranged a technical committee to plan for the supplies and oversee the construction, had found students from technical schools and various youth organizations, and we had raised approximately $1,300 in cash and over $3,000 worth of supplies and equipment from private individuals, clubs, and companies. In addition, we received $6,000 from the Cyprus government which would go directly to building costs and would have been enough to finish any work not completed during the camp. We also put $1,500 of our CRP grant directly into the workcamp fund.

We would not have been able to find such support had we remained alone, approaching individuals as two Americans with another do-good project for the residents of Cyprus. During the first month I made contact with as many clubs and business organizations as possible. Interested members from these groups plus people from social and technical agencies formed a loose committee to raise money and oversee construction details. Most of these volunteers were found through people who had come to know one or more members of the CRP when the group was on Cyprus in the winter. As groups lent their support their individual members were contacted easily and not necessarily by us.

When Dan Sipe arrived, he took over many of the technical and all the financial matters. He also organized the details of the co-ordinating work so that our Cypriot helpers each had a reasonable amount of responsibility and so that our own job stayed as much in the background as possible.

The Cypriots who helped did so for varied reasons. Some felt that the project was cosmetic in its fundamental nature but also felt they must participate to appear to maintain the hope that eventually the communities could live in concord. We two were the first to admit that it would not be through scattered projects such as the workcamp that a situation of trust and mutual confidence between the two sides would be created. The workcamp's appeal was first, that it could be seen as a symbol of these possibilities, and secondly, that it touched a feeling in many of the older generation that their children's separation was sowing the seeds for future hatred and strife.

The camp itself started on schedule on 8 July, with all the confusion of last-minute details one might expect but can't anticipate. We were using dishware borrowed from the Ministry of Education, beds and bedding from the United Nations, and tables and chairs from a Turkish boarding home. We hired a cook from the village, used the two village schools for sleeping, and were addressed the first night by the head of the village who spoke out in favour of better relations between the two communities. We would have held a party for our supporters and the villagers the night of 15 July if there hadn't been a *coup d'etat*.

We could have reasonably expected three more weeks of 'gratifying social interaction' but the fact that the students could get along perfectly well socially might now be judged against the fact that their communities can not get along politically. Though the workcamp was totally different in nature and backing than the early CRP work, they both, in the end, failed because of political reasons.

As a project, the two-and-one-half months preparation for the workcamp was beneficial in that it:

1. gave Cypriots a means of making a small step towards reconciliation and in a way that they could, in the future, initiate their own follow-up work.

2. provided a way to bring to a large number of private citizens details on a political matter, in this case resettlement. For example, some members of the clubs we contacted were also active in politics and did not have up to date information on the resettlement issue.

3. raised some peoples' interest in the possible usefulness of international groups such as the CRP. If given the chance, several of our contacts would have liked to do similar work in other

countries.

The material benefits of the workcamp, the number of houses to be built (six) and the number of students to be involved (forty in all), were insignificant. The fact that so many Cypriots helped, wanting to see it work and eventually lead to something more substantial, was what can be counted as the workcamp's success.

The workcamp did not end quickly on the day of the coup. During the first two days of the coup I was stranded in Nicosia under curfew and without a car. On Wednesday, 17 July, I returned to Peristerona to find six of the students and the foreman, a Greek Cypriot hired with the government's grant money, still working on the houses. Three students had been in Nicosia and returned to their families the first day of the *coup*. The others had left by private means to their homes in neighbouring villages. Dan Sipe had left Cyprus for America two hours before the *coup* broke out.

After finding transportation home for the remaining students I set about reorganizing the workcamp. I probably would have ended the project at that point if the foreman and one of the most technically qualified students, both Greek Cypriots, had not urged me to continue. They laid the plans for a scaled down but feasible continuation and I looked for and received local governmental approval and promises for the continued delivery of materials. We would have resumed work on Monday 22 July.

The Turkish invasion of Saturday 20 July, again brought a halt to our plans. The Turks of Peristerona were confined, by their Greek neighbours, in the village mosque, perhaps ten yards from the house the students had nearly finished. One of the boys who had helped on the project was among the eighty or so Turks in the mosque. The student who had helped re-organize the work stayed in the village though he was one of the few Greek Cypriots of his age who did not carry a gun.

I was allowed to visit the mosque whenever I wished. In the village, I was given hospitality by various Greek Cypriot families in Peristerona, many of whom showed concern over their neighbours in the mosque. The Turks who were being held saw me as a possible guarantor of their well-being and the Greeks perhaps viewed me as someone who would tell the outside world how they treated the Turks. Under the conditions, I felt the Greek Cypriots made every effort to respect the lives and properties of the Turks. This was especially due to the vigilance of several older Greeks who knew the village Turks well.

I stayed in Peristerona for about a week until all the Turks, except the fighting age males, were released from the mosque. At that particular time most people on the island felt a peace agreement would be forthcoming and, indeed, a ceasefire was soon put into effect. I left the remaining workcamp funds with the person who had been the main organizer of the camp, a Greek Cypriot from Nicosia. The money was to be used to finish one of the houses, provide a donation to the village, and any remaining funds be given to island relief agencies.

I do not know what has become of the villagers. As of 16 September, Peristerona was still in Greek hands. It seems to me, however, that the security of the Turkish Cypriots held in Peristerona depended a good deal upon the relations which had been built over years of living and working alongside their Greek neighbours.

The fact that the Greek villagers made every effort to accommodate the Turks and protect their lives and property from outsiders was an indication to me that the security which the Turkish Cypriots have so long been seeking did not finally lie in the hands of the politicians or armies. The goals and ideals behind the Cyprus Resettlement Project affirm the principle, that security comes from good neighbours more than from good politics or armies.[2]

Termination of Project

No one from the CRP visited Cyprus from September 1974 when Ellen Wilkinson left until April 1975 when I returned to the island. The project was formally terminated after I spent two weeks on Cyprus to see if there was any further way in which the Cyprus Resettlement Project could be of service. I was advised both by Mr Veniamin (who was then the Minister of Interior) and Mr Denktas (who had become President of the Turkish Federated State of Cyprus) that the situation was so dramatically changed that our previous project of building houses for Turkish displaced persons was no longer applicable. In addition the informal communication channel which we had provided was now served by the United Nations High Commissioner for Refugees, the International Committee of the Red Cross, and other organizations. Any further work in reconciliation at the village level awaited a political settlement. A 'Termination of Mission' Report was prepared and distributed to both sides, to the United Nations Representative on Cyprus, and to other organizations which had been involved in the project.

REFERENCES

Doob, Leonard W., 1974. 'A Cyprus workshop: An exercise in intervention methology'. Journal of Social Psychology 94 (December): 161-78.

Hare, A. Paul, 1974. 'Cyprus—Conflict and its resolution'. Inaugural Lecture, New Series No. 25, University of Cape Town.

Wilkinson, Ellen, 1974. 'A report on the summer workcamp in Peristerona'. Cyprus Resettlement Project.

NOTES

1. The first team included Narayan Desai, secretary of the Shanti Sena, Lyle Tatum, the Peace Secretary of the American Friends Service Committee, Charles Walker, a peace activist, Julie Latané, a social psychologist, and Paul Hare. When President Makarios learned that Narayan Desai was in Cyprus, he asked that a meeting be arranged, where he told Narayan Desai that Gandhi had been one of the major influences on his life. Thus our nonviolent approach was clear to the Greek side from the beginning.

2. For an account of another project on Cyprus also halted by the *coup* and invasion see Doob (1974).

PART V

Analysis and Application

16

THEORIES OF PROCESS AND CHANGE

HERBERT H. BLUMBERG

There are a number of analytic viewpoints which might loosely be called theories that are helpful in understanding the different case studies.

FUNCTIONAL CATEGORIES

Functional (AGIL) analysis is outlined in the cases concerned with Kent State and Curacao, and elsewhere in papers on group decision by consensus (Hare, 1973) and persuasive interaction (Hare et al., 1972). Even if they were of no other use, the four functional areas could serve as a mnemonic device for the reader, a checklist for each case study to see whether any important area has been left out of consideration — and to evaluate special difficulties and successes in solving problems in each area: resources and information (*A*daptive), the action itself and the force which impels it (*G*oal-attainment), interpersonal matters (*I*ntergrative), and basic values (*L*atent pattern maintenance). In a kind of infinite regress, each of the four areas can be subdivided into four AGIL subareas and also can be dealt with at four system levels (cultural, social system, personality, and organism). Existing material — e.g. Jackson (1969) — could often be re-analysed in terms of functional theory.

Just to give a few examples of the relevance of the four areas: most of the chapters mention resources (A) — the question of how to support the various actions. As regarding resources — most difficult of all are the transnational cases, where it can be quite difficult to find the transportation and money to bring together and support a team from many parts of the world, especially if the project *focus* is on supplies (e.g. bringing food to avert famine). Information, also within the Adaptive sector, varies from internal communication to external publicity. King (1961: 67-71) talks about the mass-attended weekly 'pep talk' which, in addition to affirming the values of nonviolent action, maintaining solidarity, and keeping the bus boycott going, also provided everyone with current information. In many of the actions, including the Gandhian ones, stress is laid on giving out leaflets (and making use of other communications media) so that people will understand what the group are trying to do. Freire (1972) and Illich (1973a, 1973b) both talk about information as such: the fact that education cannot be limited to skill learning but must include dialogue and be related to what people themselves find of value. In all of the nonpartisan cases, the third-parties themselves served as communications media. When groups are in conflict, communications often break down and rumours are pervasive. So one role of third-parties is to provide good information to all groups and also to serve as links between groups who will not talk directly with one another but will talk with trusted, impartial third-parties.

Third-parties also serve as personal (I) and action (G) links. In the process of cleaning up streets after riots, as described in Desai's accounts, members of the Shanti Sena would find that other people would slowly come out of their houses and join in, thereby showing solidarity with the group and also joining in their activity. Similarly, the leaflets and pep talks mentioned above serve not only to provide information but also to invite solidarity and action. In many of the cases cited, the basic values (L)—which 'control' all of the other aspects of the activity—have, at least in principle, to do with a force toward peace and love, and against oppression. In general, the question of conflict itself falls mostly within the Goal-attainment area, as it has to do with the interplay of forces directed toward carrying out activity.

CONFLICT THEORY

We are concerned here with one particular version of conflict theory—anyone generally interested in theories of human conflict and the nature of aggression is referred to a readable text by Scherer et al. (1975).

Many of the dimensions mentioned in Coser's treatment of conflict theory (Coser, 1968) are salient in the literature on conflict resolution. One is that conflict is an ordinary characteristic of life:

social interaction is not static but is in a dynamic equilibrium. People and groups are making decisions all of the time, most decisions being nearly automatic, some of them requiring thought, and a very few of them characterized by perplexing dilemmas. The case studies in the present set of readings represent the tail of the distribution—decisions related to people's and society's knottiest problems as it were. Although all of the case studies have both realistic aspects (multiple claims for the same scarce values or goods) and emotional ones, they do vary in emphasis from the Culebra example, where both the US Navy and the Culebrans wanted control over the same *piece of land*, to the Friendly Presence case, where the main potential difficulty stemmed from the potentially mutually hostile *attitudes* of the police and the Panthers.

Coser points out that conflict is likely to have less impact on the social structure itself in pluralistic societies, where the same people will be on the same side of one issue and opposite sides of another. In contrast, in the example which King talks about, there were probably a wide variety of issues that could have split the society on a single axis—i.e. a cleavage along racial lines—and it was probably only because of the continual *affirmation* of the common humanity of both sides, drawing in this case on Christian and Ghandian values, that a nonviolent solution-oriented manner prevailed.

EXCHANGE THEORY

The main point of exchange theory (described by Sid Waldman, 1972) is simply to suggest that people often make 'exchanges' with each other to the benefit of both parties. Such exchanges are not limited to commodities—e.g. one party has a surplus of food and gives some to another party in trade for cloth—but also can include a variety of abstractions such as information and sentiments.

Exchange theory can be viewed as being 'two dynamic steps removed' from stimulus-response learning theory. The main point of learning theory is that behaviour which is rewarding tends to be repeated. The primal image is of a Skinner box with a rat in it, where the rat learns to press a lever because pressing the lever sometimes causes food to be dropped into the cage. (The strength of the learning depends on how hungry the rat is, the timing of the operations, and the regularity with which the food appears). One certainly does not have to approve of the imposition of behavioural controls to agree in principle that organisms do tend to do what is rewarding — especially, if 'reward' is defined broadly so as to include emotional and altruistic phenomena. Decision theory is one step removed from learning theory in stressing that we are confronted with what could metaphorically be described as: not one, but numerous levers, each connected to different kinds and amounts of rewards. That is, one often needs to decide among alternatives, and the action chosen will be the one viewed as most rewarding. According to this decision-making paradigm people act as if they (a) estimate the likelihood that different actions will lead to different outcomes, (b) tally up the positive and negative rewards of each outcome (depending on immediate needs and values), and (c) choose the most rewarding of the various actions that seem possible. Finally, exchange theory is a step removed from decision theory in that the metaphorical levers are not all wired to food-dropping machines and paths through the woods, but some are connected directly or indirectly to other levers operated by other people. So that a dynamic system exists whereby one person's actions influence other people's actions, and moreover each person can take *anticipated* reactions into account when deciding on any act. An important implication of this paradigm is that people will, by intent or otherwise, carry out mutually rewarding exchanges whenever, for example, two parties both have things that are more rewarding to the other party than to themselves.

Waldman's application is partly impressionistic but nonetheless insightful. He suggests that the resolution of conflict (and of numerous miniconflicts along the way) depends on an exchange of some sort — an exchange which might have been unacceptable or unavailable at earlier stages of the conflict. In the partisan cases, the actions typically ended with some kind of agreement, for instance that a direct action campaign would be halted in exchange for the realization of certain objectives (such as the end of segregated seating on buses). Some of the possible reasons why agreement might not be reached straightaway but is obtainable later are as follows: a change in the relative distribution or visibility of the power and/or resources of the different sides, an incidental realization of objectives (such as publicity for one's cause), a change in values, or the realization of common values as a result of communication/mediation between parties. In the nonpartisan cases, the third-parties act as catalysts, facilitating agreement or joint effort between parties that were previously relatively unable to carry out mutual exchanges. Similarly, 'education' as described by Freire (1972) and Illich 1973a) 'enables' people to enter into dialogue with one another and with their oppressors.

Although four main analytical approaches to nonviolent liberation are represented by functional theory, conflict theory, exchange theory, and several problem-solving orientations (which are considered at the end of this section on analyses), several other viewpoints could also be regarded as theoretical analyses.

OTHER VIEWPOINTS

Militant nonviolent action. Barbara Deming (1968) suggests that the same principles which Fanon describes (in suggesting that freedom can be achieved by violent opposition to oppression) can also bring to light the value of militant nonviolent action. According to Deming, the main advantage of nonviolent action is that it permits people to remain much more in control of the campaigns they carry out. The experience gained in such action is directly applicable to an ongoing future. The main suggested rule is that one must not injure the antagonist. Although—even in a nonviolent struggle that is won—one might expect to endure more injuries than do the antagonists, one nonetheless is harmed less than would have been the case if one had fought violently.

'Vengeance is not the point; change is.' If a confrontation is nonviolent, there is said to be less risk that desperate, resentful oppressors will go on resisting *even 'when it is no longer in their own interest'*. Every effort is made to keep communications open between different sides:

> We had experience of this often on the Quebec to Guantanamo walk while we were in the South. There were any number of times when, at the edge of a town, we would find ourselves confronted by police who would inform us that we weren't going to be allowed to walk through. We had a constitutional right to walk through, and a few people in the group were always in favour of simply saying, 'Try to stop us!' or saying nothing at all—and marching forward. What we actually did, always, was to stop the walk for an hour or two, drive into town and discuss the

matter with the chief of police. We would talk very quietly and always show courtesy, and respect for proper authority (for example, where traffic control was concerned), but in the course of the talk we would let it become clear that . . . a lot of trouble [would be saved] by letting us walk through; we knew what our rights were and had been to jail before for them and weren't afraid of going again. Time and again, after a certain amount of bluster on the chief's part, we would be allowed to walk. A few people in the group were always dissatisfied with this way. For it felt like deferring to the authorities. If we had simply marched forward, of course, feeling very bold, we would not have made our way through the town — we would have made our way right into jail, the authorities doing with us what they liked. The action that felt less bold won us our way. [Deming, 1968:19]

Deming feels that where recruitment among the oppressed is difficult, this is not because violence is missing but because *assertive* action is lacking.

Gandhi/Guevara. Olson's (1970) analysis does not represent simply a broad theory of social change but rather a careful account of major similarities and some differences between the approaches of Gandhi and Guevara. Several parallels are described, among them: (a) the need to broadcast the truth about injustice, (b) seeing all opponents as potential allies, (c) always maintaining initiative and perseverance, (d) individual and group discipline, but only among people who freely choose to recognize it, and (e) a realization that these recommendations do not constitute a *programme* but rather are *principles* to be adapted to particular situations. According to Olson, the chief differences between Gandhi and Guevara do not reduce to a matter of 'democracy vs. dictatorship', but rather have to do with how one's force is deployed: in the Guevarist model, the preservation of an armed force (typically clandestine and mobile) is crucial, whereas the Gandhian model 'relies on massive displays of unarmed offensive action' carried out by people who are from the population at large and who act openly, with 'deliberately accepted vulnerability'.

Social change. (Various approaches — truth and love, planned social change, group dynamics, organizational training, and functional theory — are set forth, below, in Hare's chapter on 'Applying the third-party approach'. cf. Hare, 1970.)

Analytic/quantitative. Chaterjee and Bhattacharjee (1971) provide an example of an analytic/quantitative approach. They quantified a table (that had been compiled by Gene Sharp) of nine types of nonviolent action (e.g. moral resistance; selective nonviolence) and the extent to which each type has various characteristics (e.g. 'otherworldly': love toward opponents). Then they subjected the table to various statistical manipulations (hierarchical syndrome analysis and factor analysis). Within this frame of reference, the most important factor which distinguishes among different kinds of nonviolence appears to be: extent of an absolutist moral-ethical commitment to nonviolence. Among other dimensions — all independent of one another — seem to be: specific-v -general use of nonviolence, degree of active striving, and tactical expediency-strategy use of nonviolence.

For instance, a high degree of active striving (the third factor) is closely identified with Ghandhian *satyagraha*-type nonviolence (described in detail in the first chapter of this volume). In different times and places, this degree of striving might or might not be associated with moral commitment, action in a broad variety of contexts, and/or tactical expedience.

Whether these dimensions will correspond to the AGIL functional categories (described at the beginning of this chapter) and/or to dimensions of interpersonal behaviour (see Hare et al., 1972) remains to be seen. Work such as this might help us to analyse, or at least to describe, our own feelings and actions toward particular situations and possibly enable us to modify our approach.

PROBLEM SOLVING

Finally, liberation can be viewed as a kind of resolution of problems of oppression, and one can examine the literature on problem-solving to gain some insights as to how such resolution can be achieved. In Hare's (1976, chapter 15) review of the literature on group productivity, perhaps the main finding is that productivity *is* in part predictable on the basis of group characteristics. Although a number of studies are cited, they seem to reduce to ability to overcome difficulties in the four functional areas, as already described. A variety of training procedures, such as roleplaying, have been developed for groups carrying out nonviolent direct action (Blumberg et al., 1974); although truly experimental evaluation of these procedures remains to be carried out they do have face validity as means for increasing both social solidarity and task productivity. Indeed, some form of 'on-the-job training' is urged in most of the case studies that we have been considering. Since Hare deals with a variety of interlocking findings, it may be that the best use of his material could be made if a group first carried out *some* training (and/or action) and then examined his analyses, one point at a time, to see which bits might prove helpfully suggestive in the circumstance.

Several generalizations are as follows: Where there are crucial differences between a 'field' situation and a 'laboratory training' setting, it may be that field productivity is best predicted by the effectiveness of the social organization appearing in the laboratory, rather than by the productivity. Unless individual goals are commensurate with group objectives, productivity might be achieved only at the expense of members' satisfaction. A few other hints: a subgroup working on a particular problem should be as small as is practical. Communications should be open, close rather than distant, and involve 'feedback from receiver to sender'. Effective leadership is important (but how it is achieved is not yet quite clear).

One way in which certain laboratory results might be applied to social action could be to attempt to compose teams on the basis of compatible characteristics, so that—for example—people preferring warm, close relationships are not on the same team with others who prefer greater social distance. (Most of the case studies did not specify whether project members preferred warmth or relative distance.) However, in liberation groups, that should be setting an example of how people can live together, it would appear to be an absurd expedient for people to be segregated according to temperament, and it might be better at least to begin by allowing time and perhaps training for the resolution of interpersonal difficulties. Individuals can probably learn to tune themselves to the closeness appropriate to particular situations.

Is there any model to describe how the direct-action and third-party teams actually go about their business, solving problems that come up along the way, in a manner that is consistent with the teams' values? One method, 'group decisions by consensus', is covered in a paper that describes how members of a particular religious denomination, the Society of Friends, dealt with demands made by a group of militant black people (Hare, 1973).

Consensus is distinguished from unanimity and majority. 'Majority rule' is a kind of expedient whereby a decision can be implemented even though some people, a minority, disagree with it. At the other extreme, if there happens to be unanimity, then there is no contest — everyone has the same position, and obviously that position is taken by the group. In contrast with both of these possibilities, consensus ideally requires that some plan be found that meets everybody's needs even though these needs are not unanimous.

> On routine affairs little or no discussion may be necessary, and the clerk may assume that silence gives consent. In such matters the clerk may prepare his minute before the meeting begins, but it must in any case be read and approved in the course of the meeting. On matters which require it, time should be allowed for members to deliberate and to express themselves fully. A variety of opinions may be voiced until someone arises and states an opinion which meets with general approval. This agreement is signified by the utterance of such expressions as 'I agree', 'I approve', . . . If a few are still unconvinced they may nevertheless remain silent or withdraw their objections in order that this item of business may be completed, but if they remain strongly convinced of the validity of their opinion and state that they are not able to withdraw the objection, the clerk generally feels unable to make a minute. . . . Chronic objectors must be dealt with considerately, even though their opinions may carry little weight.
>
> If a strong difference of opinion exists on a matter on which a decision cannot be postponed the subject may be referred to a small special committee of the meeting. Often an urgent appeal by the clerk or by some other Friend to obstructive persons will cause them to withdraw their objections. It must be remembered, however, that minorities are sometimes right. When a serious state of disunity exists and feelings become aroused, the clerk or some other Friend may ask that the meeting sit for a time in silence in the spirit of worship. The effect of this quiet waiting is often powerful in creating unity. . . . To succeed fully the members should be bound together by friendship, affection and sympathetic understanding. [Brinton, quoted by Hare, 1973:75-6].

It would be helpful if the description could be supplemented by laboratory experiments in which decision by consensus is compared with alternative problem-solving procedures (e.g. parliamentary procedure), but, in the absence of such experimental contrasts, at least a model of the consensus method is offered for inspection. Another question is how to apply the method to large-scale complex movements. If a group have expanded to a large geographical area, one practice is for local groups to send representatives to regional conferences and workshops, which in turn join in national and international gatherings. Here, too, more experimental work is needed.

The final problem-solving paradigm to be considered here is 'game theory', where one specifies numerical properties which might capture the essence of people bargaining to reach agreement on some particular matter. One can actually stage a real game in which players take turns, making offers which are either accepted or rejected; or one can examine, in the abstract, the results of various assumptions—by developing mathematical models of a process and/or simulating a large number of trials, possibly using a computer. The issue is not one of whether people behave quantifiably and rationally, but whether specific quantifiable properties help us to understand at least some facets of, in this case, social action. An analogy can be drawn with a town plan, where the map does not capture the excitement of the people or the beauty of the buildings, but does provide a useful guide. Although it is difficult to find material on relevant aspects of Game theory that is comprehensible to non-specialists (but see Morgenstern, 1968), four topics are especially worthy of comment: (a) strategies including minimax, (b) coalitions, (c) bargaining, and (d) zero-sum games and Prisoner's Dilemma. Integration among these areas is still largely lacking (see Patchen, 1970).

A minimax solution is simply one where the *max*imum potential loss is *mini*mized. Imagine that you and some others are trying to decide on which of ten places to go for a retreat to plan community action or even for a holiday week-end. Each place has its own range of costs and benefits in terms of money, travel time, being with people you might know there, meeting your general values for countryside instead of city (or whatever your values might be). And for each location you do not know exactly what the week-end would be like, but you can imagine the *best* and the *worst* possible likely weekends you might have in each particular place. To do this, one needs to take into account various unpredictable circumstances such as whether it will rain or whether financial support for the retreat will come through on time. Now, if you take all ten of the worst possibilities and go to the place corresponding to the 'best' of these, that would be a minimax solution. It is a bit like taking a safe bet in gambling or investing, so that the worst that can happen will not be too bad. Unfortunately, such a choice might also mean that the *best* that can happen would not be too good. You could wind up spending your week-end retreat on a nearby beach, where it does not cost too much to get there, the actual carrying out of the trip would be easy, and you already might know some people in the area and what to expect. But on the other hand, you could be pretty sure that it would not be an *outstanding* week-end, such as you might have if you took the risk of going to a more distant place, that was more expensive to get to, and where you might meet new people who hold exciting new values.

The point, in terms of our examples of liberation without violence, is that the various teams of people were *not* taking safe, minimax solutions, but were carrying out their actions with certain safeguards that hopefully rendered the worst outcomes possible but unlikely. The minimum possible immediate risk might often be associated with maintaining the status quo: continuing to pay the salt tax, not voicing objections to the navy's target practice, not trying to change the educational system. In the nonpartisan cases, the least risk is obviously in standing somewhere *other* than between a crowd of demonstrators on the one side of you, and a group of police with clubs on the other side of you. However, in choosing a relatively risky alternative, the ways in which people have kept down the likelihood of an especially bad outcome have to do with trying not to be too great a threat: being open about one's plans, keeping communication channels available, showing at least some empathy and solidarity for all people on all sides, and—in the cases that we have been looking at—avoiding physical violence.

As the number of parties increases, some of them—if experimental findings are any guide—will find it advantageous to pool their power and/or resources to varying extents to form *coalitions* or subgroups. In general, *coalitions* occur when two or more people (or groups or nations) decide to pool their resources to achieve a scarce goal when, otherwise, *another* person or group would have enough resources/power to achieve the goal. Because people with very large resources may claim an especially large share of the goal (depending on the goal), coalitions may tend to be comprised of people who collectively have (a little more than) *just enough* resources to achieve the goal (Stryker, 1972). The teams in the case readings do join with other groups having common goals, but the question comes up as to how different the to-be-joined-with group can be without sacrificing a group's own goals/principles. This question seems to be resolved pragmatically.

Some aspects of *bargaining* are described by Waldman and in the comments (see above) on his chapter on exchange analysis and also in the literature on group processes (Hare, 1976).

To investigage the more inclusive cases where people confront one another, a number of studies of *bargaining* in general have involved players in negotiating a 'sale' while using rather elaborate profit tables for sellers and for buyers. Such studies could be viewed as bearing limited analogy to, not only cases of real bargaining, but also general instances of people reaching agreement with one another. One typical bargaining strategy which players have been found to employ is: to explore successively lower levels of own profit until a mutually satisfactory agreement is reached (Kelley & Schenitzki, 1972). Happily, such agreement is likely to realize the 'maximum joint profit' even if only one player follows this strategy and even if both players are ignorant of each other's profits.

A person's adaptation level, or level of aspiration, is determined in part by the level of reward the person has come to expect. Players with high levels of aspiration wind up with larger profits and if both players have high levels of aspiration then, not surprisingly, 'the bargainers have a great deal of conflict and a low rate of agreement (Kelley & Schenitzki, 1972:330). Results may differ for different numbers of bargainers, and some of the individuals in a group who are bargaining with one another may work together or form coalitions.

The important point to reiterate is that one typical strategy is for people to explore successive lower levels of profit to see which alternative at each level is most acceptable. As long as there is some communication—hence the value of the third-party nonpartisan services—and as long as either party (e.g. the nonviolent partisan team) follows the strategy of exploring successive lower levels of own profit, a maximum joint outcome typically occurs even when the sides do not know one another's 'payoff matrices'.

Pruitt (1972) has analysed bargaining and various other methods for resolving differences of interest. At one point he cites several approaches to 'integrative bargaining': '(a) state one's position in terms of a problem to be solved rather than a solution to be accepted by the adversary; (b) retain one's flexibility by not becoming committed to a fixed position; (c) make every effort to understand the adversary's viewpoint; and (d) present to the adversary an accurate picture of one's own needs and motives so that' the adversary can think up options that satisfy the needs of both parties (summarized by Pruitt, 1972, from suggestions by Walton and McKersie). Although these tactics may 'subvert the aim of eliciting concessions', they foster 'the development of new options that better satisfy the needs of both bargainers'.

Third-party judges might possibly facilitate conflict resolution by giving suitable advice to bargainers (Erickson et al., 1974), but it is not yet generally clear as to what kind of advice is best for different circumstances.

Zero-sum games are those in which one party's gains are directly felt as another party's losses (see the discussion of Prisoner's Dilemma — Brown, 1965; McClintock, 1972). Many real-life situations — generally including those described in the case studies — are *not* 'zero-sum games' and the challenge is to find solutions in which everyone gains.

REFERENCES

Blumberg, H. H., A. P. Hare, C. Fuller, C. Walker, and H. Kritzer, 1974. 'Evaluation of training for nonviolent direct action'. Mental Health and Society 1: 364-75.

Brown, Roger, 1965. Social Psychology. London: Collier-Macmillan.

Chatterjee, Bishwa and Shyam S. Bhattacharjee, 1971. 'Meanings of non-violence: types or dimensions?' Journal of Peace Research 2: 155-61.

Coser, Lewis A., 1968. 'Conflict. III. Social aspects'. Pp. 232-6 in David L. Sills (ed.), International Encyclopedia of the Social Sciences. Volume 3. New York: Macmillan and Free Press.

Deming, Barbara, 1968. 'On revolution and equilibrium'. Liberation [New York] (February): 10-21.

Erickson, Bonnie, John G. Holmes, Robert Frey, Laurens Walker and John Thibaut, 1974. 'Functions of a third party in the resolution of conflict: the role of a judge in pretrial conferences'. Journal of Personality and Social Psychology 30: 293-306.

Freire, Paulo, 1972. Pedagogy of the Oppressed. Harmondsworth, Middlesex: Penguin.

Hare, A. Paul, 1970. 'Instituting peaceful change at Kent State: moving toward life's center by grasping truth and realizing love'. Nonviolent Action Research Project (Haverford College), Report No. 11.

——, 1973. 'Group decision by consensus: reaching unity in the Society of Friends'. Sociological Inquiry 43:75-84.

——, 1976. Handbook of Small Group Research. Revised Edition. New York: Free Press.

Hare, A. Paul, Herbert M. Kritzer and Herbert H. Blumberg, 1972. 'Functional analysis of persuasive interaction in a roleplaying experiment'. Nonviolent Action Research Project (Haverford College), Report No. 45.

Illich, Ivan D., 1973a. Deschooling Society. Harmondsworth, Middlesex: Penguin.

——, 1973b. Tools for Conviviality. London: Calder and Boyars.

Jackson, Edward Robert, 1969. 'Toward the nonviolent resolution of racial conflict'. Dissertation Abstracts International 29:4067-A.

Kelley, Harold H. and Dietmar P. Schenitzki, 1972. 'Bargaining'. Pp. 298-337 in Charles Graham McClintock (ed.), Experimental Social Psychology. New York: Holt, Rinehart and Winston.

King, Martin Luther, Jr, 1961. Stride toward Freedom. New York: Ballantine.

McClintock, Charles G., 1972. 'Game behavior and social motivation in interpersonal settings'. Pp. 271-97 in Charles Graham McClintock (ed.), Experimental Social Psychology. New York: Holt, Rinehart and Winston.

Morgenstern, Oskar, 1968. 'Game theory: theoretical aspects'. Pp. 62-9 in David L. Sills (ed.), International Encyclopedia of the Social Sciences. Volume 6. New York: Macmillan and Free Press.

Olson, Theodore, 1970. 'Forcing social change: Gandhi and Guevara'. Nonviolent Action Research Project (Haverford College), Report No. 10.

Patchen, M., 1970. 'Models of cooperation and conflict: a critical review'. Journal of Conflict Resolution 14: 389-407.

Pruitt, Dean G., 1972. 'Methods for resolving differences of interest: a theoretical analysis'. Journal of Social Issues 28(1): 133-54.

Scherer, Klaus R., Ronald P. Abeles and Claude S. Fischer, 1975. Human Aggression and Conflict: Interdisciplinary Perspectives. Englewood Cliffs, New Jersey: Prentice Hall.

Stryker, Sheldon, 1972. 'Coalition behavior'. Pp. 338-80 in Charles Graham McClintock (ed.), Experimental Social Psychology. New York: Holt, Rinehart and Winston.

Waldman, Sidney R., 1972. Foundations of Political Action: An Exchange Theory of Politics. Boston: Little, Brown.

17

APPLYING THE THIRD-PARTY APPROACH*

A. PAUL HARE

Current texts in social change remind us that the process of social change is continuous, takes many forms, and may be planned or unplanned (cf. Etzioni and Etzioni, 1964; LaPiere, 1965; Moore, 1963).

Bennis, working in the tradition of group dynamics, has identified eight species of change (Bennis, 1962). He has grouped these species according to three major variables. Along the vertical axis of the paradigm he shows two variables: mutual goal setting and deliberateness of change. Along the horizontal axis the power distribution among the parties is shown: 0.5/0.5 indicating a fairly equal distribution of power and 1/0 indicating a one-sided situation.

In brief the eight species of change are as follows:

1. *Planned change* — mutual goal setting initiated by one or both parties, an equal power ratio.

2. *Indoctrination* — mutual, deliberate goal setting but with an unequal power ratio, as in many schools, prisons, mental hospitals, and other total institutions.

3. *Coercive change* — examples are thought control and brain-washing.

4. *Technocratic change* — relies solely on collecting and interpreting data, where the 'engineer' assumes that the problem is due to lack of knowledge.

5. *Interactional change* — example: good friends who help each other, without selfconsciousness or any definite change-agent-client relationship.

6. *Socialization* — example: parent-child relationship.

7. *Emulative change* — example: formal organizations where

*The chapter is based in part on selections from 'Third party role in ethnic conflict', Social Dynamics, 1975, 1 (1 June), 81-107. Copyright © 1975, University of Cape Town.

there is a clear cut superior-subordinate relationship and the subordinate identifies with the 'power figures'.

8. *Natural change* — change brought about with no apparent deliberateness and no apparent goal setting on the part of those involved. Example: unanticipated consequences of earthquakes, floods, etc.

Following Bennis' paradigm, each of the cases of nonviolent action described here is an example of planned change. The closest fit with the model is with the Antillean Institute of Social Science since all sectors of the community were given the opportunity to suggest topics for seminars and subjects for research. However, Fred Ovsiew, one of the US staff members who worked with youth groups, has argued that we found it easier to associate with the upperclass English-speaking members of the business community who raised most of the money for the institute than the lower class Papiamentu-speaking labourers whose plight led to the riot.

Cyprus clearly involved making arrangements for mutual goal-setting between Greeks and Turks for the resettlement of displaced persons. But it was also clear that the Greeks held more political and military power up to the time of the arrival of the Turkish military forces.

Actually Bennis does not consider the role of the third-party. If the two sides to the conflict were equal, then a third-party might not be necessary. However in each of these cases, including Curacao, there was an unequal distribution of economic, political, and military power. It was part of the task of the nonviolent third-party, acting either as partisans or nonpartisans, to provide channels for mutual goal setting on a more equal basis. In the partisan actions a first step would be to help bring the grievances of the relatively powerless to the attention of the relatively powerful.

Chin (1962) compares a 'model for changing' in the group dynamics tradition with two other models for change. The first of these models, the 'System model', is a version of Bennis' 'indoctrinational change'. The second model, the 'Developmental model', would seem to coincide with Bennis' 'Technocratic change'. The major advantage of Chin's paradigm is that it spells out some of the principal variables in the process of change.

The system-model approach assumes that social systems tend towards equilibrium but some stress may induce the process of change. The goal of the change agent is to reduce tension and bring the system back to equilibrium. Chin reveals his anti-system model bias by assuming that the goal of adjustment is set by 'vested interests' who are presumably management. While it may be true that more attempts at planned change have been made to date on behalf of management or government, there is nothing in systems theory which says who will make the change.

Chin is reflecting a running controversy between the 'systems (or functional) theorists' (cf. Parsons, 1964) and the 'conflict theorists' (cf. Dahrendorf, 1964). Thus, the developmental model, which assumes that change is in the 'nature of organisms' and is outside rational control, does not require that an 'external diagnoser and actor' come in to solve the problem. Even if Chin's first two models have something of a 'straw man' quality, they at least highlight the 'ideal' qualities of his third 'model for changing' which calls for rational, controlled, and collaborative improvement in the 'here and now'. The nonviolent-third-party approach has most in common with this model for change.

Writing in 1965, Schein and Bennis provide a comprehensive review of the theory and practice of laboratory training as it is used to promote personal and organizational change. It is evident from their presentation that the change agent in the group-dynamics tradition was accustomed to entering a social organization on behalf of the management. They summarize the aims of change agents as:

1. to effect a change in values so that human factors and feelings come to be considered as legitimate, and

2. to assist in developing skills among managers in order to increase interpersonal competence (Schein and Bennis, 1965: 208).

Later in the text they underline this point: 'In undertaking any planned social change, legitimacy for the change must be gained through obtaining the support of the key people' (Schein and Bennis, 1965: 229).

After obtaining the support of key people the laboratory training is often conducted at a training centre at some distance from the organization whose staff is being trained. On this 'cultural island' new behaviours are learned to be applied in the 'back home' situation. This approach was being introduced on Cyprus in the last few months before the arrival of the Turkish army. Leonard Doob, a psychologist who had used the workshop approach with conflicts in East Africa and Ireland, had completed all of the organizational steps for a workshop with selected leaders from the Greek and Turkish communities to be held in Italy. The outbreak of hostilities in July, 1974 forced a cancellation of the plans. (See Doob, 1970; Doob, 1971; Doob and Foltz, 1973.)

Here we can see two differences in the approach of the Gandhian and the group-dynamic agent of change. First, Gandhians would not rely entirely on the support of management before beginning a programme of change in an organization. Although they would seek the management's co-operation and enter into negotiation with them (as Gandhi did at the mills at Ahmedabad), they would also press their case for change in spite of management's objections if they believed that 'truth' required some direct action. Second, the Gandhians would probably prefer to conduct training on location in the form of 'on the job' training.

ORGANIZATIONAL TRAINING

The work of Schmuck *et al.* on organizational training comes closer to a design which could be useful in a third-party approach than the earlier versions of T-group training (Schmuck, Runkel, and Langmeyer, 1971; Langmeyer, Schmuck, and Runkel, 1971). They have designed their method to change the social system rather than the participants in the system. Although they also use the T-group, it is not the major resource.

So far most of their work has been done in secondary schools. The important features of these schools are that they are made up of basic units (classrooms, departments, committees, etc.), they are goal-directed (in general they aim to prepare young people for productive adulthood in a complex, industrialized society), they are always changing, and they have within them a 'variety pool' (many resources that are not being used). Included in the 'variety pool' are patterns of behaviour which might ordinarily be thought of as 'deviant'. In one school, a common deviant behaviour may be 'goofing off' or talking cynically about others. In another, it might be bootlegging topics or teaching methods not prescribed in the official manuals. In a third, it may be teachers meeting out of school to plot ways of obtaining more power over policy. In any of these cases, such events present evidence that organizational training could be useful in directing deviant behaviour towards useful goals. Deviant behaviour can usually be treated as a richness of resource rather than a danger about to get beyond control.

Schmuck *et al.* suggest three stages for effective organizational change:

1. Improving communications skills—especially as they relate to problem-solving.

2. Changing norms—especially interpersonal openness and helpfulness.

3. Structural change—building new functions, roles, procedures, or policies.

In their paper on 'Technology for organizational training in schools', Langmeyer, Schmuck, and Runkel (1971) outline many of the techniques used in their organizational training. These techniques include a variety of individual and groups tasks. One of these is a procedure to improve problem-solving which they have used repeatedly in organizational training with schools. This sytem is essentially the one used by nonviolent actors for effective problem-solving.

The sequence is as follows:

1. What is the ideal state? (specify behaviours, attitudes, knowledge, etc.)

2. What, to date, has been done to move us closer to the ideal state?

3. What is the present state? To where have we got ourselves?

4. If the present state is not desirable: (*a*) what forces are restraining us from moving? (*b*) what plans or solutions seem appropriate? (*c*) what other things do we have to know about before making a plan or proposing a solution?

5. Set up a summary chart of proposed activities and order them.

6. Commit individuals and the group to some plan of action. Who will do what and what should the outcome be?

AGENTS OF CHANGE IN DEVELOPING AREAS

The experience of persons who have worked for the Agency for International Development (AID) or other US agencies overseas can provide a useful contrast with the group-dynamic approach which was developed primarily by US nationals working within their own country. In their book on *Introducing Social Change*, Arensberg and Niehoff note that 'change must be accepted voluntarily by the host people' for 'customs and beliefs constitute the culture of each group of people and understanding this culture can spell the difference between success and failure in introducing new ideas and methods' (1964: 3-4). Further, Arensberg and Niehoff caution that 'knowing the elite alone will not be enough' (1964: 7). In the Gandhian tradition one begins by serving the people. Only through service does one earn the right to represent the people in negotiations on their behalf.

In this book on *Modernization: Protest and Change*, Eisenstadt, a professor at The Hebrew University in Jerusalem, draws on observations from many parts of the world (1966). He finds that youth movements are essentially 'dreams of a new life' (1966: 27). However, youth face reactionary parents and successful revolutionaries who do not want them to change society (1966: 30).

Eisenstadt describes three major themes of social protests:

1. Seeking principles of social order and justice acceptable to broader strata of society.

2. Seeking new common symbols of personal and collective identity.

3. Seeking to obtain full expression of human and cultural creativity, overcoming alienation in relation to work, the social settings, and other people (1966: 32-4).

All three of these themes can be found in the Gandhian approach.

The passing of a traditional society does not guarantee that a new, viable, modern society capable of continuous growth will develop (1966: 146). Some initiative must be taken by innovative groups. Three major variables affect the pattern that modernization will take:

1. The modernizing orientation of different elites.

2. The relations between these innovating groups and the broader strata and the institutional settings within which they operate.

3. The temporal sequence of modernization (1966: 147)

Eisenstadt's summary serves to remind us that the nonviolent third-parties are not the only innovating groups at work in any situation. Their success will depend on the willingness of the established elites to co-operate with them.

THIRD-PARTY FUNCTIONS IN
CONFLICT SITUATIONS

The functions of persons who enter conflict situations as explicit 'third-parties' are similar to those of the 'agents of change'. Experience has been recorded for a variety of social system levels: laboratory experiments (Johnson and Tullar, 1972), college campuses (Mann and Iscoe, 1971), social and government agencies (Walton, 1968, 1969; Shaw, Fischer, and Kelley, 1973), and international crises (Young, 1967, 1972).

Representative of this experience is an article by Fisher (1972) on 'Third party consultation: A method for the study and resolution of conflict'. He suggests that the general goal of the behavioural scientist who intervenes in a conflict is to change a hostile win-lose orientation of the two parties into a collaborative problem-solving orientation. He describes the ideal third-party role as faciliative, noncoercive, diagnostic, nondirective, and nonevaluative. The functions of the third-party include: inducing and maintaining mutual positive motivation between the two parties, improving communication, diagnosing the conflict, and regulating the interaction

Hopefully, the third-party approach represented in the case studies included here approximate Fisher's ideal type. To the extent that they do there is nothing 'new' in the general outlines of the approach we have used here. The distinguishing characteristics are probably to be found in the strength of the commitment to nonviolent solutions and in the emphasis on the total system. However, up to this point other approaches have been compared with the nonviolent approach without giving much detail of the nonviolent method. We now turn to this analysis, primarily from the perspective of functional theory.

THE NONVIOLENT APPROACH

The nonviolent approach as it is summarized by Erikson in his book *Gandhi's Truth* (1969) is based on two principles: the search for truth (*satya*) and the realization of love (*ahmisa*, noninjury or more generally love). Gandhi and his followers in India today search for truths about people which are not so much what they are today but what they can become when they treat each other as humanly as possible. The Gandhians believe that human life is more precious than any cause. Thus any process of change which wishes to affirm life cannot take life as a means to that end.

The Quakers also place a primary value on human life because to them each human being is part of the divine. They say: 'There is that of God (truth) in every man.' Like the Gandhians they reach decisions through a process of consensus rather than by voting. That is, all members of the group must agree before an action is taken in the name of the group. No minority is asked to submit to the will of a majority. No individuals are coerced to change their attitudes on an issue.

In the terminology of game theory the Gandhians and the Quakers will only play 'non-zero-sum' games (Morgenstern, 1968). The typical 'game' that people play is a 'zero-sum' game. One side wins (say plus one) only if the other side loses (minus one). The sum is zero. The gains on one side are equally balanced by the losses on the other. In the 'non-zero-sum' game both sides can win. A group continues to work on a problem or discuss an issue until all present can see some gain in the proposed course of action. As long as anyone feels that he or she has something to lose the group continues to search for a broader goal that will incorporate the goals of each member (see Hare, 1973a).

Another important aspect of the approach as it was applied in Cyprus was a consistency in method at all social levels. Within the project the same approach was used within the team itself, at the village level, the district level, and the national level. This could be contrasted with the members of the United Nations forces who also played a third-party role. Within the United Nations forces a direct military command was used for decision making. Third-party interventions at the village level were carried out by military police, at the district level by Force Economic Officers, and at the national level by Mr Osorio-Tafall and Mr Miles the chief political officer. Thus on the UN side different personnel with different backgrounds and training are used at each level. If problems require action at more than one level the information must be transmitted to a different group. Within the Cyprus Resettlement Project the same volunteers could be talking to villagers, district officers, and members of the national government on both the Greek and Turkish sides during the course of one day. This continuity provided a personal understanding of the problems and concerns of people at each level which would have been difficult to transmit in formal or informal reports. Although the collection of statistics about various aspects of resettlement was a necessary part of the process of finding the 'non-zero-sum' solution it was often the direct knowledge of how persons at all levels would react to proposed solutions that made it possible to reach consensus in such a short time.

A FUNCTIONAL THEORY OF GROUPS, SOCIETIES, AND SOCIAL CHANGE

Although a number of different theoretical perspectives might be used to identify the salient aspects of the nonviolent action teams, of the societies of which they work, and of the process of social change, the theory which I know best and have found most useful is 'functional' theory, which is represented principally by the work of Parsons (Parsons *et al.*, 1961: 30–71). Three illustrations of the application of the theory will be given here: first the four basic functional categories, next a theory of group development and social change, and finally the cybernetic hierarchy of control as it applies to issues of conformity to norms and attitude change.

Functional theory suggests that all groups, whether small face-to-face groups or whole societies must meet four basic needs if they are to survive. The basic needs are: (L) the members must share some common identity and have some commitment to the values of the groups, (A) they must have or be able to generate the skills and resources necessary to reach the group goal, (I) they must have rules which allow them to co-ordinate their activity and enough feeling of solidarity to stay together to complete the task, and finally (G) they must be able to exercise enough control over their membership to be effective in reaching their common goal. In Parsons' terms the 'L' function provides for 'latent pattern maintenance and tension management'. That is, the overall pattern of values of the group must be maintained even when the group is latent (i.e. when the members are not actually together). Also tension which arises in any area, especially from success or failure with the group's task, must be handled since it will affect the group's basic conception of itself. The 'A' function provides for 'Adaptation' to the outer environment of the group by generating resources. The 'I' or 'Integrative' function defines the formal and informal relationships between members. The 'G' or 'Goal attainment' function provides for the actual day-to-day work of the group. In a large society these four categories are represented by the familial and religious substructures (L), the economic substructure (A), the legal substructure (I), and the political substructure (G). (See Figure 1.)

FIGURE 1

FUNCTIONAL PROBLEMS AND THE SUBSTRUCTURES AT THE
SOCIAL SYSTEM LEVEL

Adaptation (A)	Goal-Attainment (G)
Economic	Political
Familial and Religious	Legal
Latent pattern maintenance and tension management (L)	Integration (I)

FIGURE 2

FOUR SUBSYSTEMS OF THE TOTAL ACTION SYSTEM
CLASSIFIED BY FUNCTIONAL SECTOR

Adaptation (A)	Goal-Attainment (G)
Organismic level	Personality level
Cultural level	Social system level
Latent pattern maintenance and tension management (L)	Integration (I)

A review of the literature on group development in small laboratory, training, therapy, and classroom groups suggest that groups usually develop through five stages in the order L-A-I-G with a terminal stage of L (Hare, 1973b). In a learning group such as a classroom group, the phases seem to be as follows: the work of the group requires that the purpose of the group be defined (L), that new skills be acquired (A), that the group be reorganized so that the members can try out the new skills without being too dependent on the leader (I), and that the group's members work at the task (G). Finally, there is a terminal phase in which the group returns to 'L' to redefine the relationships between the members and the group as the group is disbanded. The amount of time the group spends in each phase is determined by the activity of the leader (direction or nondirection) and by the skills and emotional strengths of the members. Presumably the leader is 'ready' for each stage at the outset, having been through the stages before. However, members come to the group with different degrees of problem-solving skills or preferences for different emotional modalities (for example, a preference for fight-flight, pairing, or dependency; Bion, 1961). Subgroups tend to form on the basis of these skills or emotional modalities. If the subgroup with the appropriate skills and emotional state for each stage of group development is large enough, it can carry the whole group through that phase (Bennis and Shepard, 1956; Mann, 1967). If not enough members of the group are ready for a particular stage, more intervention by the leader may be necessary. Some groups never progress beyond the early stages. These same stages of development are evident in the social change which occurs in larger social systems and in forms of collective behaviour such as mass movements or riots (Smelser, 1963).

The 'cybernetic hierarchy of control' is a concept which can be applied to both physical and social systems. The basic idea is that a unit containing information will be able to control a unit containing raw energy. Thus a thermostat which processes information will control a furnace which produces heat or a computer will control the sequence of activities on an industrial production line. In the case of groups the highly generalized normative elements of the system generally guide and control the more specific aspects of action. Thus the area of pattern maintenance (L) controls the intergrative area (I), which in turn provides more control than the goal-attainment area (G). The adaptive area (A) ranks lowest in its influence on other parts of the system.

Up to this point the four functional areas have been considered as they would appear in small groups or in whole societies. Each of these groups is in turn part of the *social system level* of the total system of human action. There are four major system levels which fit into the same fourfold paradigm which has been identified. (See Figure 2.)

The four system levels are cultural, social, personality, and organismic. They are also related to each other in the cybernetic hierarchy of control. That is, in the total action system, the values represented by the culture are more controlling than the norms of the social system, which are in turn more controlling than the personality of the individual. Finally personality characteristics account for more of the variability in social interaction than the biological traits and processes of the physical organism.

The concept of the cybernetic hierarchy of control as it is applied to the four functional categories is useful in understanding the effects of various types of pressure which are brought to bear on individuals in an attempt by others to attain conformity to group norms. An attempt to urge conformity by offering money or by giving facts can be seen as a pressure in the *adaptive* area. An attempt to coerce opinion change through leadership or majority opinion is a pressure in the *goal-attainment* area. A pressure which urges conformity for the sake of friendship or because some positive or negative reference group holds a given attitude uses the *integrative* area. When one urges conformity on the basis of common values and stresses commitment to issues the *pattern-maintenance* area is used. (See Figure 3.)

An attitude based on a presentation of facts or on payment of money would be the easiest to change since a new set of facts or a new payment would alter the opinion. An opinion based on the coercion of a leader or a group majority would be harder to change since the individual would not be free until moving to another group. An opinion based on the attitudes of a references group (say the family or a group of friends) would be even more difficult to change since the individual can conform to the norms of a group felt as important even if the group is not physically present. Finally opinions based on values which an individual has internalized are the most difficult to change since they represent part of an individual's self-conception. The opinions cannot be changed without changing the individual's self-conception. Groups which make decisions by voting tend to exert pressure through facts and majority opinon while those using consensus tend to emphasize reference groups and values. This is another reason why decisions made by consensus are more compelling for group members.

FIGURE 3

CATEGORIZING PRESSURES TO CONFORM IN TERMS OF AGIL

Category	Behaviour Characteristics of Person	
	Urging Conformity	Responding to Pressure to Conform
Adaptation (A)	Gives information as if facts will speak for themselves.	Asks for information or gives information on issues.
Goal-attainment (G)	Attempts to be coercive by personally bringing weight to bear on subject, or by citing majority opinion, or opinion of someone who might be expected to have power over subject.	Shows concern for majority opinion. Makes clear that she or he is (or is not) a free agent in making decisions.
Integration (I)	Urges conformity for sake of friendship. Actor indicates he or she will be very pleased with subjects if they conform. Cites positive value of belonging to a group of people who have conformed.	Shows concern for personal feelings of actor. Cites a reference group which would support his or her opinion.
Pattern-maintenance (L)	Urges conformity on basis of common value (i.e. you are a good citizen); stresses commitment to issue.	Affirms or denies common value system.

Code: 5, 6, or 7 when act is in interest of conformity (7 = High).
Code: 3, 2, or 1 when act is in interest of nonconformity (1 = Low).
Code: 4 when act seems neutral.

SOME APPLICATIONS OF FUNCTIONAL ANALYSIS

Since the third-party approach was most clearly developed in the Cyprus case, we will use this material for an application of each aspect of the functional perspective. These examples will be followed by others drawn from Culebra, Curacao, India, and Zambia. In Cyprus on some occasions I used functional analysis quite consciously to diagnose a problem faced by the group of volunteers either within a group or in relationship to Cypriot society. However most problems were solved on a day-to-day and indeed hour-to-hour basis without explicit reference to any theory. As actors in the situation we tried to make our best judgements at the time, all things being considered. An observer of our group would have been able to note more examples as the action unfolded. Looking back over our activity we can identify situations to which we can apply the three major hypotheses: that social interaction can be divided into four functional categories, that groups develop through a sequence of phases, and that the power of factors influencing decisions follows the cybernetic hierarchy of control.

First we can use the AGIL categories to sort out the values held by the members of our team. As third parties we were not 'value free'. We would not have endorsed social change in any direction by any means. The value on which we placed the greatest stress was the use of *nonviolent* methods of conflict resolution. Our other basic values were perhaps more evident in our actions than in our pro-clamations, since we had not come to Cyprus to bring about a particular kind of society, but rather to help the Greeks and Turks reach common goals. Still one could identify values in each of the four functional areas which were shared by most of the members of the teams. (We should note that there was variation, even on the issue of nonviolence. However, we would expect a group of this kind continually to examine the basic values of its members as it attempts to find solutions to social problems in the light of these shared values.) Examples of the ideas about the ideal society which were represented in our approach are:

A—Economic—There should be an equal distribution of resources.
G—Political—The society should provide for maximum autonomy and self control.

I—Legal/Social class—The society should minimize social distinctions and maximize integration and belonging.

L—Religious—There should be a supreme value placed on human life, with minimal religious differences (we are all human beings).

The phases in group development are most easily seen in the development of the whole project. First, even in developing the idea of the project there were four phases which could be considered as sub-phases of 'L' or defining the basic meaning. The original idea for peace contingents came from the Gandhians and the Peace Academy (L_1). To test the idea for Cyprus we needed to raise 'seed money' to finance the first visit (L_a). With the seed money we were able to assemble a team and decide on our roles (L_i). Then on Cyprus we were able to select a particular focus for the work (L_g). Once the Greeks and Turks had agreed on our proposal we again had to raise money (A) and assemble and train a team (I) to act as third parties in reaching the first agreement (G). This cycle was repeated in the development of the work camp idea. Termination brought the final phase of 'L' when we once again had to sort out 'the meaning of all this' for volunteers, for Cyprus, and for the future of transnational efforts at conflict resolution.

Our conscious use of the cybernetic hierarchy of control in making decisions is evident within the teams, where we use consensus rather than voting. Our emphasis on values rather than on economic gain is also evident in our approach to the Greek and Turkish sides. We help them find 'non-zero-sum' solutions which are based on humanitarian motives rather than those which are primarily concerned with redistribution of resources or of political power. Recall that Mr Osorio-Tafall of the United Nations had suggested that we help with the return of displaced persons because it could be seen as a 'humanitarian problem'. Thus our task was made easier than if we had been asked to help with the whole 'Cyprus problem' which requires a political solution.

We believe that the same nonviolent third-party process can be used with problems which are basically political. The Gandhians have experience in India in developing the 'Gramdan' or village government movement for formerly landless people (the 'untouchables') who now own land communally and manage their own village affairs for the first time in history. In 1974 some Gandhians, including Narayan Desai, the head of Shanti Sena, and other people who had served with the Cyprus project were asked to take over as an interim government in some states in India. Members of the state governments had resigned in the face of charges of corruption and the Gandhians made the 'political' decisions until new governments could be formed.

From time to time members of the Greek or Turkish sides made remarks which indicated that they understood and appreciated our approach. After we had negotiated the agreement to hold a work camp a representative of the Ministry of Foreign Affairs told us that the Government found it easy to approve of the project because, after all, we were doing it 'for Cyprus'.

CULEBRA

In the account of the action on Culebra we see the Quakers moving back to 'square one', the 'L' stage, when they arrived in Puerto Rico. They had already defined the meaning of their protests in Press releases which were issued jointly in New York and San Juan just before they flew from New York. Their preference was to define the action at the value level (peace) and at the social level (friendship), but the Puerto Rican Independence Party (PIP) insisted on defining the action as political.

The Quakers were persuaded by the Puerto Rican Independence Party (PIP) to spend a week in training, orientation, and organizational discussions. The PIP was hoping to win seats in a forthcoming election in Puerto Rico. The leader of the party, Ruben Berrios, pointed out that whatever the outcome of the protest against the Navy, some political party would claim the credit or place the blame, so that the Quaker group could not expect to be 'non-partisan' in this respect. The Quakers were already clear that they were acting for the Culebrans and against the US Navy. Since the Quaker religion is traditionally pacifist, the anti-military action was consistent with their basic beliefs.

The Quakers' second set-back was on arrival in Culebra. Plywood and other building materials for the 'chapel' had been purchased in San Juan and brought over by boat. Since the Quakers thought that the protest would be stopped by police long before any building could be begun in the target area, they had purchased material for a small eight by ten foot cabin which would be primarily symbolic of a larger chapel, serving about the same purpose as a large poster or banner. However when the local members of the Save Culebra Committee saw the plans for the 'chapel' they were disappointed. They had expected something more appropriate. The Quaker who had designed the building then stayed up most of the night working out a new design with the available material. He was able to devise a rather elegant structure approximately twenty by thirty feet which was mainly roof, with sides open to the sun and air. Since no arrests were made until several days after the protesters had entered the target area, this version of the chapel was actually constructed and served as a chapel for several religious services representing different denominations.

The Quakers were prepared to build a *symbolic* chapel, but the Culebrans saw this was a *real* event and they wanted a *real* chapel. In this case the Culebrans were proposing the more effective action. From our observations of nonviolent protests in the US during the 1960s we had concluded that the most effective actions were those which involved real events (such as building a chapel) which also had symbolic meaning. Other examples would include the Omega team taking medical supplies into East Pakistan in 1971 or Gandhi's salt march in 1930. These types of acts, in contrast to vigils, marches, and guerrilla [street] theatre, go beyond a statement of a problem to demonstrate the kind of activity envisioned for when the 'new society' is formed.

A third incident in Culebra also illustrates a problem in the basic pattern maintenance area (L), that of obtaining sufficient commitment from the participants to carry them through the action. In this case the commitment displayed by the women who risked their lives when the Navy was about to demolish more of the reef and fish was all that was required. The commitment to be willing to risk one's life for the cause is also usually sought by those who advocate violent solutions to conflict. A crucial difference is that the nonviolent actor values human life above a cause.

CURACAO

On Curacao the stages in group development are evident in the series of one-week visits during which the plans were developed for the Antillean Institute of Social Science. First the L stage when the idea was proposed, next the A stage of fundraising, then the I stage which included recruiting staff, and clarifying roles, especially that of the leadership. The final G stage was the actual summer institute.

For a finer grain analysis we can identify four phases within each stage. Thus for the first stage of L we have the phases of:

L_1 = Vic Pinedo proposes action research
L_a = Funds are raised for the fact-finding visit
L_i = Vic and I find a small group of Curacaoans who are interested in the idea of the Institute
L_g = The broad outlines of the Institute are developed
In a similar way the fundraising venture takes an idea, some 'seed' money for brochures and other publicity materials, a fundraising team, and the work of fundraising. The same fourfold process continues through the Integrative and Goal-attainment stages.

At each stage in development some individuals may drop out. This happened on Curacao. Those who are not satisfied with the final formulation of the basic idea drop out at the L stage; and those who feel that there is not enough money or other resources, at the A stage. By the time the group reaches the I stage the members are committed and see that resources are available. If they find that they do not like the leadership structure or role distribution more are inclined to try to change the structure rather than drop out. Thus the 'revolution within the revolution' is likely to occur at this stage. Once the group passes the I stage there is nothing left to do but carry out the task. Success or failure in the task will lead to a redefinition of the purpose of the group, thus bringing the group back to L, until they finally disband and pass through L for the last time.

On Curacao and also in the World Peace Brigade example we see groups going through this final stage, with the phases in reverse order. The work of maintaining the organization stops (L_g), the leaders give up their roles (L_i), the funds and other supplies are redistributed (L_a), and finally the group dies (L_1), or sometimes slowly fades away.

To be effective as an agent of change in social systems a third-party needs to be aware of the interconnections between aspects of the system. The teach-in sponsored by the Institute illustrates this point with discussions and debates on the Antillean identity (L), the economic system (A), the aspirations of youth for a redefinition of their role (I), and the political system (G).

INDIA

The Shanti Sena also take a total social system approach. Their work includes not only riot control (I) as described in this paper, but also protest (L), promoting home industries (Kadi) (A), and helping landless peasants organize co-operative village governments (Gramdan) (G). In this case all four aspects of AGIL could be considered as the work (G) of the Shanti Sena. Their own internal problems of L, A, and I are often centred in a small community (ashram) or training centre (kendra) where the Shanti Sainiks live together.

Of particular note is the method the Shanti Sainiks use to deal with rumours which can provide provocative definitions of a situation (L). To counter the rumours the Shanti Sainiks continually collect facts, work in the streets to show others that the situation is not out of hand and that extreme violence is not necessary to restore order, and issue a daily bulletin. Rumours are most devastating when the basic identity of a people is at stake. Thus rumours of atrocities (or actual events) are especially powerful since they suggest that the opposite side places no value on the persons or the identities of those who are being attacked.

NORTHERN RHODESIA

The activities of the World Peace Brigade in Northern Rhodesia illustrate the problems of forming a coalition between nonviolent and violent revolutionary forces. The nonviolent actors have to find a way to endorse the goals of the liberation movements without endorsing their methods. In this case there was general agreement in the *strategy* of nonviolence for the duration of the Peace March, so that the work could go forward.

The proposal for a general strike, while not offering violence to individuals, nevertheless could be very disruptive for the social system controlled by the opposing side. This makes the point that the nonviolent actors are 'unviolent' rather than 'non assertive'. However, the threat of possible violence if the nonviolent strategy failed, which was used by leaders of some of the groups included in the coalition, plays no part in the orthodox nonviolent approach. On the other hand, decision making by consensus, used in this case, is consistent with the nonviolent approach whereas a system of majority rule would not be.

We note the continuing stress on training and on the development of a training centre. Training is important, even for those with long experience in nonviolence, so that they may have an opportunity to anticipate the situations they will face. This is often done through role-playing hostile incidents so that a nonviolent response can be practised (Oppenheimer and Lakey, 1964).

Some of the difficulties in maintaining a transnational team at a distance from their homes, with funds in short supply, are also illustrated in this case. Even though the training centre in Dar es Salaam was small it played a major role. It may be surprising that a few people acted as third-parties can make a difference in an action on this scale. This was also true on Cyprus, with all of the resources of the United Nations available, where one might have thought that a small group could add little. Yet for all the 3,000 men in the United Nations force, only seven were involved in work with communities and only two in political negotiations.

EIGHT STEPS FOR RESOLVING NATIONAL OR INTERNATIONAL CONFLICTS

While we are waiting for the evidence to be assembled on which a last judgement can be made, we can summarize our experience thus far by proposing eight steps to follow for resolving national or international conflicts by nonviolent means. These steps are, of course, only the chapter headings of the book that would be needed to begin to give the details necessary for action.

1. Decide how to respond to a need for aid in the resolution of a conflict between groups. (In the small world of today there are no 'outsiders'.)

2. Prepare background papers from information publicly available in newspapers, from interest groups and from official statements of the parties involved.

3. Make a visit to the area with a team of from two to five persons representing a cross section of the skills and viewpoints which will be used in the solution of the problem.

4. Select a point of entry into the social system. Try to find a humanitarian problem for your first task.

5. Raise money to support an exploratory team who can live and

work in the area for a month or more. Try to combine with local people when possible.

6. Write papers showing your understanding of the viewpoint of each party in the conflict. After it is clear that they understand that you understand each viewpoint, secure agreement that you will be welcomed as a third-party.

7. Raise new money, recruit a new team, and return to help solve the problem.

8. When the time is right, disengage.

Or in even shorter form, if you wish to solve conflicts without violence, use the best theories available, combined with valid facts, so that a multi-disciplinary team can make a day-by-day application of principles with sensitivity and understanding.

REFERENCES

Arensberg, Conrad M. and Arthur H. Niehoff, 1964. Introducing Social Change. Chicago: Aldine.

Bennis, Warren G., 1962. 'A topology of change processes'. Pp. 154-6 in W. G. Bennis, K. D. Benne, and R. Chin (eds.), The Planning of Change. New York; Holt, Rinehart, and Winston.

Bennis, Warren G. and H. A. Shepard, 1956. 'A theory of group development'. Human Relations 9: 415-37.

Bion, W. R., 1961. Experiences in Groups: and other Papers. New York: Basic Books

Carter, April, 1972. 'Sahara Action'. Report of the Non-violent Action Research Project, Haverford College, October. (Also printed in the present volume).

Chin, Robert, 1962. 'The utility of system models and developmental models for practitioners'. Pp. 201-14 in W. G. Bennis, K. D. Benne, and R. Chin (eds.), The Planning of Change, New York: Holt, Rinehart, and Winston.

Dahrendorf, Ralf, 1964. 'Toward a theory of social conflict'. Pp. 98-111 in Amitai Etzioni and Eva Etzioni (eds.), Social Change. New York: Basic Books.

Doob, Leonard W. (ed.), 1970. Resolving Conflict in Africa: The Fermeda Workshop. New Haven, CT: Yale University Press.

Doob, Leonard W., 1971. 'The impact on the Fermeda workshop on the conflicts in the Horn of Africa'. International Journal of Group

Tensions 1 (1): 91–101.

Doob, Leonard W. and William J. Foltz, 1973. 'The Belfast Workshop: An application of group techniques to a destructive conflict'. Journal of Conflict Resolution 17:489–512.

Eisenstadt, S. N., 1966. Modernization: Protest and Change. Englewood Cliffs NJ: Prentice-Hall.

Erikson, Erik H., 1969. Gandhi's Truth: On the Origins of Militant Non-violence. New York: Norton.

Etzioni, Amitai and Eva Etzioni (eds.), 1964. Social Change: Sources, Patterns, and Consequences. New York: Basic Books.

Fisher, Ronald J., 1972. 'Third party consultation: A method for the study and resolution of conflict'. Journal of Conflict Resolution 16:67–94.

Hare, A. Paul, 1973a. 'Group decision by consensus: Reaching unity in the Society of Friends'. Sociological Inquiry 43(1):75–84.

— —, 1973b. 'Theories of group development and categories for interaction analysis'. Small Group Behavior 4(3):259–304.

Johnson, Douglas F. and William L. Tullar, 1972. 'Style of third party intervention, face-saving and bargaining behavior'. Journal of Experimental Social Psychology 8:319–30.

Langmeyer, Daniel, Richard Schmuck, and Philip Runkel, 1971. 'Technology for organizational training in schools'. Sociological Inquiry 41(2):193–204.

LaPiere, Richard T., 1965. Social Change. New York: McGraw-Hill.

Mann, Richard D., 1967. Interpersonal Styles and Group Development. New York: Wiley.

Mann, Philip A. and Ira Iscoe, 1971. 'Mass behavior and community organization: Reflections on a peaceful demonstration'. American Psychologist 26:108–13.

Moore, Wilbert E., 1963. Social Change. Englewood Cliffs, NJ: Prentice-Hall.

Morgenstern, O., 1968. 'Game theory: 1: Theoretical aspects'. Vol. 6, pp. 63–8 in D. L. Sills (ed.), International Encyclopédia of the Social Sciences. New York: Macmillan and Free Press.

Oppenheimer, Martin and George Lakey, 1964. A Manual for Direct Action. Chicago: Quadrangle.

Parsons, Talcott, 1964. 'A functional theory of change'. Pp. 83–97 in Amitai Etzioni and Eva Etzioni (eds.), Social Change. New York: Basic Books.

Parsons, Talcott et al., 1961. Theories of Society. New York: Free Press.

Schein, Edgar H. and Warren G. Bennis (eds.), 1965. Personal and Organizational Change Through Group Methods: The Laboratory Approach. New York: Wiley.

Schmuck, Richard, Philip Runkel, and Daniel Langmeyer, 1971. 'Theory to guide organizational training in schools'. Sociological Inquiry 41(2):183–91.

Shaw, Jerry I., Claude S. Fischer, and Harold H. Kelley, 1973. 'Decision-making by third parties in settling disputes'. Journal of Applied Social Psychology 3(3):197–218.

Smelser, Neil J., 1963. Theory of Collective Behavior. New York: Free Press.

Walton, Richard E., 1968. 'Interpersonal confrontation and basic third party functions: A case study'. Journal of Applied Behavioral Science 4:327–44.

— —, 1969. Interpersonal Peacemaking: Confrontations and Third-Party Consultation. Reading, MA: Addison-Wesley.

Young, Oran R., 1967. The Intermediaries: Third Parties in International Crises. Princeton, NJ: Princeton University Press.

— —, 1972. 'Intermediaries: additional thoughts on third parties'. Journal of Conflict Resolution 16(1):51–65.

BIBLIOGRAPHIC GUIDE

HERBERT H. BLUMBERG

Readers are advised to consult the general index to this book as well as consulting the present bibliographic guide.

For the most part, this list includes a selection of books and pamphlets, published between 1966 and 1976, dealing with nonviolent liberating action and relevant background informa-tion—particularly in a third-party context. Emphasis is given to recent works, to anthologies and sourcebooks, and to materials which emphasize ways for people to participate.

For a longer version of the present guide, see *Nonviolent Liberation; a bibliography* (Brighton: Smoothie Publications [P.O. Box 450, BN1 8GR, UK], 1977). The longer version—intended for researchers in the field—contains about 1700 items and a description of sources for future updating of the list. Reprinted in an appendix to the longer version are the index from *Nonviolent Action* and the bibliography from *Nonviolent Direct Action* (see the next paragraph). Both the longer and shorter versions of this guide consist mainly of English-language materials, many of which were initially found by searching the *British National Bibliography*, (American) *Subject Guide to Books in Print*, and books and pamphlets noted in *Peace News* (8 Elm Avenue, Nottingham) or *WIN* (503 Atlantic Ave., Fifth Floor, Brooklyn, NY 11217). Annotations that are quoted—e.g. from reviews in *Peace News* or *WIN* or *News from Neasden*—are shown within quotation marks.

Mostly excluded from the present shorter version of this guide are works already included either in *Nonviolent Action* (a selected bibliography by April Carter, David Hoggett, and Adam Roberts. London: Housmans, 1970) or the annotated bibliography in *Non-violent Direct Action; American Cases, Social-psychological Analyses* (A. Paul Hare and Herbert H. Blumberg, editors. Washington, DC: Corpus Books, 1968).

Similarly, books which have been described elsewhere in the present volume are generally not listed below. Readers are therefore advised to consult the general index under the same headings as are used in the present guide. Also, the index contains cross-references among the headings.

In the main listings of the present guide, each item is displayed only under the heading that seemed most relevant. A question mark after a year does not necessarily mean that the work itself bears no date. In some cases, place of publication is shown as the current (1976) location of the publisher, which is not necessarily the same as that imprinted on the particular book. For some items, if the primary location is not British, then a British imprint (if any) might be shown in brackets after the primary location. For some entries, bibliographic details were checked only indirectly (against bibliographic sources such as the *National Union Catalog*).

The headings used in the present guide are as follows:

Key sources
Alternative life styles; communes; land reform
Black liberation (mainly American works)
Civil liberties, general civil rights, human rights
Civilian nonviolent defence
Community — action and organizing
Community — miscellaneous
Co-operative movements, etc.
Disarmament and arms control
Ecology action; alternative technology
Education; children's rights
Feminism; antisexism
Gay liberation
Health and mental health
Housing
International conflict resolution
International co-operation and peaceful change
International organization and peacekeeping
Media — alternative/community
Mediation and conflict resolution; labour/management
Minorities; prejudice; social problems
Miscellaneous

Nonviolence — general
Peace action, pacifism, conscientious objectors, and related information
Penal reform
Poverty action
Problem-solving, conflict resolution, conflict theories
Protest, civil disobedience, and revolutionary action — general
Protest examples and background — against American involvement in the Vietnamese war
Protest examples and background — Chavez/United Farm Workers/American farm labour
Protest examples and background — Gandhian/Indian
Protest examples and background — Martin Luther King
Protest examples and background — other specific places
Radical perspectives; anarchism
Research — social and peace
Social action
Social change
Social service
Songs and poetry, etc.
Student/youth activism
Volunteers

KEY SOURCES

(Agitprop red . . .), 1976. 'Agitprop red pages.' Time Out, No. 319 (April 23–9): 3–14. (Annotated and indexed directory of nearly 500 London (and other English) political and community groups.)

(Alternative England . . .), 1975. Alternative England and Wales. London: Nicholas Saunders (65 Edith Grove, SW10). (A model compendium. Some of the topics covered are housing, food, work, law, help, information services, publishers/bookshops/publications, mystical groups and topics, drugs, sex, crafts, community action and projects, ecology, children, husbandry, technology, political groups, women, transport, gay groups, legal frameworks. Geographical and general indexes.)

(Alternative Free . . .)????, Alternative Free Press Directory. NY: Alternative Press Syndicate. (APS has arranged for commercial microfiliming of most of the 200 member papers.)

(Alternative News . . .), Alternative News Service, 97 Drummond St., Carlton 3053, Australia. (Issued fortnightly. Also publish Education/Malayan/black/women's news services.)

(Alternatives in . . .), 1976. Alternatives in print 77–8; a catalog of social change publications. 5th Ed. San Francisco, CA: Glide. (Books, and also pamphlets, films, and tapes; all arranged by publisher — mainly approximately 900 organizations and small presses. Subject index — also includes list of distributors and directories.)

Atherton, Alexine L. (ed.), 1976. International organizations; a guide to information sources. Detroit, MI: Gale.

Blumberg, Herbert H., Karen Eigenbrot, and Janvier Hamell (eds.), 1973. Periodicals concerned with nonviolence and social change — with organization, geographic, and subject indexes. Haverford, PA: Nonviolent Action Research Project (Haverford College) (Monograph No. 21). (International list of about 5,000 periodicals and organizations. Entries include title, address, source of information, subject codes, current status, and — for many of the periodical entries — an annotation especially prepared by the editors of the given periodical. The subject index includes roughly the same topics as the present bibliography. Can be consulted in various libraries, among them the British Library Reference Division (British Museum), British Library of Political and Economic Science, and Haverford College.)

Brand, Stewart (ed.), 1974. The whole earth epilog. Baltimore (and Harmondsworth, UK): Penguin. (Encyclopedic coverage of 'access to tools', in the broadest sense, and where to obtain and read about them. Also, *Updated last whole earth catalog*. NY: Random, 1974.)

Central Committee of Correspondence, 1976. Mailing list of movement organizations. Philadelphia (3414 Spring Gardens St.): CCC. (About 5,000 groups/publications/bookshops, mainly American, for peace, human rights, and/or radical social change. Arranged geographically. Free to prisoners. $2; $5 on gummed labels. Revised annually.

Combat non-violent. (Bp 26, 71800 La Clayette, France.) (French periodical devoted to news about nonviolent action.)

(Encyclopedia of . . .), 1975. Encyclopedia of associations. 9th Ed., Vol. 1. Detroit: Gale Research Co. (About 100 relevant items are included under the headings civil liberties, civil rights, and peace.)

Haimes, Norma (compiler and editor), 1974. Helping others; a guide to selected social service agencies and occupations. NY: John Day. (In addition to the private and public American agencies which are described and indexed, there is an annotated bibliography of over 100 items including further directories, guides, etc.)

Harris, Norene, 1975. The integration of American Schools; problems, experiences, solutions. London: Allyn & Bacon.

Harvard Law School Library, 1965-7. Catalog of international law and relations. 20 Vol. Dobbs Ferry, NY: Oceana.

Housmans Bookshop, 1976. World peace diary. London: Housmans (5 Caledonian Rd., N1). (Includes an international list of about 500 organizations and their addresses and periodical publications. Carefully revised each year. Also available from Housmans are lists of publications on the following topics: alternatives, anarchism, conflict studies, ecology, Gandhian, gay liberation, Housmans publications, new books, pacifism and nonviolence, poetry, War Resisters' International publications, and women's liberation.)

Hyatt, John, 1972. Pacifism; a selected bibliography. London: Housmans. (See entry, below, in the section on 'Pacifism, . . .'. Some of the Resources listed in the bibliography are: General Reading List (Institute for the Study of Nonviolence, PO Box 1001, Palo Alto, CA 94302, USA), Creative approaches to social change; select bibliography on history of the American Peace Movement (Pendle Hill, Wallingford, PA: USA). Campaign booklists (FOR, 9 Coombe Rd., New Malden, Surrey). AFSC Peace Literature Catalog (160 North 15th St., Philadelphia). Literature List (NE CNVA: RFDI, Box 197-B, Voluntown, CT). Libraries with special collections: UK (Bradford University; Friends House, London; International Confederation for Disarmament and Peace and Peace Pledge Union, both at 6 Endsleigh St., London WC1) and USA (Swarthmore College; Haverford College; Lennberg Center for the Study of Violence, Brandeis University, Waltham, MA; Wisconsin State Historical Association, 816 State St., Madison, W1; World Without War Council, 175 5th Ave., NY 10010).)

(Index to . . .), ????. Index to CPL Exchange Bibliographies. Monticello, IL (PO Box 229, 61856): Council of Planning Librarians.

(International Cooperation . . .), 1976. International Cooperation Directory. Northridge. CA 91324: International Cooperation Council (ICC) (17819 Roscoe Blvd.). (Listings include about 200 organizations devoted on fostering unity and peace.'

Liberation News Service, 1976. Publications and organizations on the Liberation News Service subscription list. NY: LNS (160 Claremont Ave., 10027). (Corrected to March, 1976, issued yearly. About 400 entries including name of periodical, address, and subject code (high school, Native American, printshop, women, news service, organization, radio, etc.).)

Marx Memorial Library, 1972-5. Catalogue. London: Marx Memorial Library. (Issued in parts.)

Miller, Albert J., 1972. Confrontation, conflict and dissent; a bibliography of a decade of controversy, 1960-70. Metuchen, NJ: Scarecrow.

Moody, Roger (ed.), 1973. 'Directory of concerned, organizations'. Peace News (5 January): 7. (International list based on directories 'of groups concerned with tribal rights'.)

Noyce, John (ed.), in press. Directory of British alternative periodicals 1965-74. Brighton, Sussex: Harvester Press.

Oaks, Priscilla S., 1975. Minority studies; an annotated bibliography. Boston, MA: G. K. Hall.

(Peace Research . . .), 1964ff. Peace Research Abstracts Journal. Oakville, Ontario (119 Thomas St.): Canadian Peace Research Institute. (Each issue contains 750 abstracts or summaries of articles, books, pamphlets, reports, etc. on questions related to peace and war. Monthly, with an annual subject and author index.)

Pickus, Robert, and Robert Woito, 1974. To end war; an introduction to the ideas, organizations, and current books. New Ed. NY: Seabury. ('A series of bibliographies and lists of organizations sandwiched between right-liberal politics and punctuated by jabs at the left.' Some of the topics covered in the essays and detailed annotated bibliographies are: causes of war, disarmament, world community, international organizations, international relations, ethical/religious/philosophical considerations in ending war, conscientious objection, nonviolent social change, peace movements, peace research, context and resources for action.)

Sharp, Gene, 1975. The politics of nonviolent action. Boston: Porter Sargent. ('Compendium of information. . . . basic reference work . . . on all aspects of nonviolence—theory, . . . practice, and . . . history.' Also, bibliography of about 500 references.)

Spahn, Theodore J., et al., 1972. From radical left to extreme right; a bibliography of protest, controversy, advocacy, or dissent, with dispassionate content-summaries to guide librarians and other educators. Vol. 2. 2nd Ed. Metuchen, NJ: Scarecrow.

Spiers, John, 1974. The underground and alternative press in Britain; a bibliographical guide with historical notes. Brighton: Harvester. (One value of this list—in contrast with more comprehensive alternatives—is that indexed material is available on microfilm/microfiche.

Additional packages are to be produced on 'The Left in Britain'.)

Stanford, Barbara (ed.), 1976. Peacemaking; a guide to conflict resolution for individuals, groups, nations. NY: Bantam. (Includes articles by Cesar Chavez, Martin Luther King, Jr., Gene Sharp, Theodore Lentz, George Lakey, etc.)

Stanford University. Hoover Institution on War, Revolution and Peace. 1969. Catalog . . . Boston, MA: G. K. Hall. (Catalogues of the Arabic, Chinese, Japanese, Turkish and Persian, and Western Language Serials and Newspaper collections. About 25 Vols.)

Suffet, Stephen, 1974. 'A guide to the new new left'. WIN 10 (8) (7 March): 12-13.

(UAPS/Europe's list . . .), 1976. (UAPS/Europe's list of 'alternative' papers/organizations.) Margate, Kent (22 Dane Rd.): UAPS/Europe. (Lists about 300 serials from more than 35 countries.)

United Nations. UNESCO . . . Social Science Clearing House. Reports and Papers in the Social Sciences. (No. 28), 1973. International repertory of institutions for peace and conflict research. NY: UNIPUB. (The following kinds of organizations are listed: peace research organizations (international and national), institutions at present engaged in peace research, and institutions promoting or supporting peace research. Descriptions are detailed.)

US Library of Congress — General Reference and Bibliography Division, 1968. Guide to bibliographic tools for research in foreign affairs. 2nd Ed. Westport, CT: Greenwood. (Originally, 1958.)

War Resisters League, ????. (Literature list.) NY (339 Lafayette St., 10012): WRL.

Wilcox, Laird M. (compiler), 1970. Guide to the American left. Kansas City, MO (PO box 1832, 64141): US Directory Service. Among approximately 2500 entries are 1400 American organizations, 800 American periodicals, 150 Canadian organizations, and 100 periodicals and organizations from other countries.)

ALTERNATIVE LIFE STYLES; COMMUNES; LAND REFORM

Chianese, Robert L. (ed.), 1971. Peaceable kingdoms; an anthology of utopian writings. NY: Harcourt Brace.

Dreifus, Claudia, 1971. Radical lifestyles. NY: Lancer. ('Profiles of six colourful Americans whose dynamic alternatives to middle-class culture may guide you to liberation.')

Fairfield, Richard, 1972a. Communes Europe. San Francisco: Alternatives Foundation.

——, 1972b. Communes Japan. San Francisco: Alternatives Foundation.

——, 1972c. Communes USA; a personal tour. Baltimore: Penguin.

——, 1972d. Utopia USA, San Francisco: Alternatives Foundation. (Anthology.)

Fitzgerald, George, 1971. Communes; their goals, hopes, problems. Paramus, NJ: Paulist/Newman.

Goldstein, Lee, 1974. Communes, law and common sense; a legal manual for communities. Boston: Beacon.

Gordon, Michael (ed.), 1972. Nuclear family in crisis; the search for an alternative. NY: Harper.

Gorman, Clem, 1971. Making communes; survey/manual. Bottisham, Cambridgeshire: Whole Earth Tools.

——, 1975. People together. St Albans: Paladin. ('A guide to communal living.')

Hedgepeth, William, 1970. The alternative; communal life in new America. NY (and London): Collier.

Guinness, Os, 1973. The dust of death; a critique of the establishment and the counter culture—and a proposal for a third way. London: Inter-varsity. (Christian radicalism.)

Hill, Arthur M., 1972. Making do; basic things for simple living. NY: Ballantine.

International Independence Institute, 1972. The community land trust; a guide to a new model for land tenure in America. Cambridge, MA: Center for Community Economic Development.

Kanter, Rosabeth Moss, 1972. Commitment and community; communes and utopias in sociological perspective. Cambridge, MA: Harvard Univ. Press (and London: Oxford Univ.).

Kanter, Rosabeth Moss (ed.), 1973. Communes; creating and managing the collective life. NY (and London): Harper.

Kromer, Helen (ed.), 1972. Communes and communitarians in America. NY: Grossman (and London: Jackdaw).

Lamperti, John, 1976. 'Defending Denmark's free city nonviolently'. WIN 12 (no. 11, April 1): 4–7. (Christiana, in Copenhagen.)

Loomis, Mildred (ed.), 1965. Go ahead and live. NY: Philosophical Library. (Introduction to the life-styles of the new back-to-the-land movement.)

Machan, Tibor R. (ed.), 1974. The libertarian alternative; essays in social and political philosophy. Chicago: Nelson Hall.

Melville, Keith, 1972. Communes in the counter culture; origins, theories, styles of life. NY: Morrow.

Morgan, Griscom (ed.), 1971. The intentional community handbook. NY: Comm. Serv.

Musgrove, Frank, 1974. Ecstacy and holiness; counter culture and the open society, London: Methuen.

Prasad, Devi, 1972?, Gramdan; the land revolution in India. London: War Resisters' International. (Pamphlet. About Vinoba Bhave's campaign.)

Rigby, Andrew, 1974a. Alternative realities; a study of communes and their members. London: Routledge.

——, 1974b. Communes in Britain. London: Routledge. (Five examples.)

Roberts, Ron E., 1971. New communes; coming together in America. Englewood Cliffs, NJ: Prentice-Hall.

Roszak, Theodore, 1970. The making of a counter culture; reflections on the technocratic society and its youthful opposition. London: Faber.

Stephen and the Farm, 1974. Hey Beatnik! This is the farm book. Summertown, TN: Book Publishing Co.

Sundancer, Elaine, 1973. Celery wine. Yellow Springs, OH: Community Publications Cooperative. ('On the commune/drop-out/homesteading scene'.)

True Light Beaver Commune of Woodstock, 1972. [Eat, Fast,] Feast; a tribal cookbook. Garden City, NY: Doubleday. ('Solid guide to good alternative living.')

Veysey, Laurence, 1973. The communal experience; anarchist and mystical counter-cultures in America. NY (and London): Harper.

Ward, Colin, 1974. Utopia. Harmondsworth: Penguin. (Accounts, dreams, photographs, diagrams. Some of the indexed recurrent themes are community, conflict, maps, resources.)

Wizansky, Richard (ed.), 1973. Home comfort; stories and scenes of life on Total Loss Farm. NY: Saturday Review Press. ('Life on' an 'agricultural commune'. A 'moving, honest, beautiful, graceful, talented, and maybe — even — helpful' volume.)

Wright, Barry, and Chris Worsley, 1975. Alternative Scotland; a passport to Scotland. London: Wildwood House. (Thorough.)

BLACK LIBERATION
(MAINLY AMERICAN WORKS)

Allen, Robert L., 1970. A guide to black power in America; an historical analysis. London: Gollancz.

Barbour, Floyd B. (ed.), 1969. Black power revolt. NY: Collier.

Blaustein, Albert P., and Zangrando, Robert L. (eds.), 1970. Civil rights and the black American; a documentary history. NY: Washington Square. (1619 to 1968.)

Brooks, Thomas R., 1974. Walls come tumbling down; a history of the civil rights movement 1940-70. Englewood Cliffs, NJ (and London): Prentice-Hall. (Best general history of the civil rights movement.)

Coleman, James S., 1971. Resources for social change; race in the United States. NY (and Chichester, Sussex): Wiley.

Commager, Henry Steele, 1972. The struggle for racial equality; a documentary record. Gloucester, MA: Peter Smith.

Deming, Barbara, 1970. Prison Notes. Boston: Beacon. (A month in a Georgia jail with 30 civil rights protesters.)

Fager, Charles E., 1974. Selma 1965; the town where the South was changed. NY: Scribner's.

Farmer, James, 1972. The making of black revolutionaries; a personal account. NY: Macmillan.

Freedman, Jill, 1971. Old news; Resurrection City. NY: Grossman.

Grant, Jerome (ed.), 1972. Black protest; history, documents and analyses; 1619 to the present. Greenwich, CT: Fawcett World.

King, Martin Luther, Jr. (See sub-head under PROTEST EXAMPLES . . .)

Mabee, Carleton, 1970. Black freedom; the nonviolent abolitionists from 1830 through the civil war. NY: Macmillan.

Meier, August, and Elliott Rudwick, 1973. CORE; a study in the civil rights movement; 1942-68. NY: Oxford Univ. Press.

Meier, August, Elliott Rudwick, and Francis L. Broderick (eds.), 1971. Black protest thought in the twentieth century. 2nd Ed. Indianapolis, IN: Bobbs-Merrill. (Comprehensive.)

Wynn, Daniel W., 1974. The black protest movement. NY: Philosophical Library.

CIVIL LIBERTIES, GENERAL CIVIL RIGHTS, HUMAN RIGHTS

Berger, Nan, 1974. Rights; a handbook for people under age. Harmondsworth: Penguin.

Burke, Joan M., 1974. Civil rights; a current guide to the people, organizations & events. 2nd Ed. NY: Bowker.

Christiano, David (ed.), 1975. Human rights organizations & periodicals directory. San Francisco: Meiklejohn Civil Liberties Institute.

Coote, Anna (ed.) and Lawrence Grant (Legal ed.), 1973. Civil liberty; the NCCL guide. 2nd Ed. Harmondsworth: Penguin.

Cox, Barry, 1975. Civil liberties in Britain. Harmondsworth: Penguin.

Eide, Asbjorn, and August Schou (eds.), 1968. International protection of human rights; proceedings of the seventh Nobel Symposium, Oslo, September 25-7, 1967. NY (and Chichester, Sussex): Inter-science.

Jackman, Robert W., 1975. Politics and social equality; a comparative analysis. NY (and London): Wiley. (Careful quantitative investigation of 'variations in the inequality of within-nation distributions of material goods', access to health care, etc.)

Liebknecht, Karl, ????. Libertarian anthology. NY: Gordon Press.

Macdonald, John, 1969. Bill of rights. London: Liberal Research Department. (A proposed British bill of rights; text and justification.)

Pious, Richard M., 1973. Civil rights and liberties in the 1970's. NY: Random.

Robertson, A. H., 1970. The international protection of human rights. Nottingham: Univ. of Nottingham.

Van Dyke, Vernon, 1970. Human rights, the United States, and world community. NY (and London): Oxford Univ. Press.

War Resisters' International, 1968. Human rights; a handbook. Enfield, Mddx.: WRI. (Pamphlet.)

Wicklund, Robert A., 1974. Freedom and reactance. NY (and London): Wiley. Experiments on 'reactions to infringements on freedom'.)

CIVILIAN NONVIOLENT DEFENCE

AFSC working party, 1967. In place of war; inquiry into nonviolent national defense. NY: Grossman. ('Feasibility of mobilizing nonviolent power for national defense.')

Boserup, Anders, and Andrew Mack, 1974. War without weapons; nonviolence in national defence. London: Frances Pinter.

Kritzer, Herbert, 1974? 'Nonviolent national defense: concepts and implications'. (In) Peace Research Reviews 5.

Roberts, Adam (ed.), 1969. Civilian resistance as a national defence; nonviolent action against aggression. New Ed. Harmondsworth: Penguin. (Systematic anthology 'with discussion by experts' on techniques 'such as strikes, civil disobedience and unarmed defiance'.)

——, 1972. Total defense and civil resistance. Stockholm: Research Institute of Swedish National Defense ('Problems of conceptualizing and implementing nonviolent defense strategies.')

Sharp, Gene, 1968? The political equivalent of war—civilian defense. NY: Carnegie Endowment for International Peace. ('A means of conflict which does not violate' the 'principle of nonviolence'.)

COMMUNITY — ACTION AND ORGANIZING

Adeney, Martin, 1971. Community action; four examples. London: Runnymede Trust. (Pamphlet. English neighbourhood examples: equal opportunity, social services, education, community control.)

Altshuler, Alan A., 1970. Community control: the Black demand for participation in large American cities. NY: Pegasus.

Ball, Collin, and Mog Ball, 1973. Education for a change; community action and the school. Harmondsworth: Penguin.

Barr, Alan, 1972. Student community action. London: Bedford Square Press. (Describes and analyzes a selection of activities in Britain.)

Bayton, James A., 1971. Tension in the cities; three programs for survival. London: Ward Lock Educational. (American local government programmes.)

Cahn, Edgar S., and Barry A. Passett (eds.), 1971. Citizen participation: effecting community change. NY: Praeger.

Cot, Fred M., et al. (eds.), 1974. Community-action, planning, development; a casebook. Itaska, IL: Peacock.

Golany, Gideon (ed.), 1975. Strategy for new community development in the United States. Stroudsburg, PA: Dowden.

Greifer, Julian L. (ed.), 1974. Community action for social change; a casebook of current projects. NY (and London): Praeger.

Grosser, Charles F., 1973. New directions in community organization; from enabling to advocacy. NY (and London): Praeger.

Hawley, Willis D., and James H. Svara, 1972. The study of community power; a bibliographic review. Santa Barbara, CA (and Oxford, England): ABC- Clio. (Abstracts of about 400 items.)

Holman, Robert, 1972. Power for the powerless; the role of community action. London: British Council of Churches, Community and Race Relations Unit.

Huenfeld, John, 1974. The community activist's handbook; a guide to organizing, financing and publicizing community campaigns. Boston, MA: Beacon.

Jones, W. Ron (ed.), 1971. Finding community; a guide to community research and action. Palo Alto, CA: James Freel (Page-Ficklin).

Kramer, Ralph M., and Harry Specht (eds.), 1975. Readings in community organization practice. 2nd Ed. Englewood Cliffs, NJ (and London): Prentice-Hall. (Comprehensive; recommended.)

Levine, Felice J., 1970. Community resource orientation among low-income groups. Chicago, IL: American Bar Foundation.

Marris, Peter, and Martin Rein, 1973. Dilemmas of social reform; poverty and community action in the United States. 2nd Ed. Chicago, IL: Aldine.

Marshall, Sol H., 1975. Public relations basics for community organizations. 5th Rev. Ed. Hollywood, CA: Creative Book Co.

Morris, David, and Karl Hess, 1975. Neighborhood Power. Boston: Beacon. ('How local community involvement is restoring immediacy to government.')

Noyland, John, 1974? Handbook of community festivals. London (7

Leonard St, EC2): Young Volunteer Force Foundation.

O. M. Collective, 1971. The organizer's manual. NY: Bantam. ('Practical suggestions for grass roots organizing.')

Olson, Theodore, and Lynne Shivers (eds.), 1970. Training for non-violent action. London: Friends Peace and International Relations Committee and War Resisters' International. (Pamphlet. Comprehensive introduction.)

Perlman, Robert, and Arnold Gurin, 1972. Community organization and social planning. NY (and Chichester, Sussex): Wiley.

Poston, Richard W., 1976. Action now! A Citizen's guide to better communities. Carbondale, IL: Southern Illinois Univ. Press.

Rothman, Jack, 1974. Planning and organizing for social change; action principles from social science research. NY (and London): Columbia Univ. Press. (Compendium of generalizations—their limitations, implications for action, and degree of support in empirical literature—on various matters, some of which are the practitioner—change agent, organizational framework, community setting, citizen participation (voluntary associations, social and political movements), social change processes. Bibliographies.)

Rowe, Andrew, 1975. Democracy renewed; the community council in practice. London: Sheldon press. (Potential functions and organization, in Britain, for community councils.)

Source Collective, 1971. (Source catalog. Vol. 1): Communications. Chicago: Swallow.

——, 1972. (Vol. 2:) Communities/housing. Chicago: Swallow.

——, 1974. (Source Catalog 3): Organizing for health care. Boston: Beacon.

Strauss, Bert, and Mary E. Stowe, 1974. How to get things changed; a handbook for tackling community problems. NY: Doubleday.

Thomas, David N., 1975. Organising for social change; a study in the theory and practice of Community work. (Britain.) Mystic, CT: Verry.

Turner, John E. (ed.), 1968. Neighborhood organization for community action. NY: National Association Social Workers.

Warren, Ronald L., 1965. Studying your community. NY (and London): Free Press/Collier-Macmillan.

Yates, Douglas, 1973. Neighborhood democracy; the politics and impacts of decentralization. Lexington, MA (and London): D. C. Heath.

Zimmerman, Joseph F., 1972. The federated city; community control in large cities. NY: St Martin's Press.

COMMUNITY — MISCELLANEOUS

Bell, Colin, and Howard Newby (eds.), 1974. The sociology of community; a selection of readings. London: Cass.

Bell, Gwen, Edwina Randall, and Judith E. R. Roeder (eds.), 1973. Urban environments and human behavior; an annotated bibliography. Stroudsburg, PA: Dowden (Golany).

Bender, M. P., 1976. Community psychology. London: Methuen.

Clinard, Marshall B., 1966, Slums and community development; experiments in self-help. NY (and London): Free Press/Collier Macmillan. (Examples from various countries.)

Goodlad, Sinclair (ed.), 1975. Education and social action; community service and the curriculum in higher education. London: Allen & Unwin.

Hornstein, Harvey A., Barbara Benedict Bunker, W. Warner Burke, Marion Gindes, and Roy J. Lewick, 1971. Social intervention; a behavioral science approach. NY (and London): Free Press/Collier Macmillan.

McGee, R., 1974. Crisis intervention in the community. Baltimore, MD: Univ. Park Press.

CO-OPERATIVE MOVEMENTS, ETC.

Ames, J. W., 1971. Without boundaries; co-operative Sweden today — and tomorrow. Manchester, Lancashire: Co-operative Union.

Bray, Jeremy, and Nicholas Falk, 1974. Towards a worker managed economy. London: Fabian Society. (Pamphlet.)

Clegg, Ian, 1971. Workers' self-management in Algeria. London: Allen Lane.

Coates, Ken, and Tony Topham, 1974. The new unionism; the case for workers' control. Harmondsworth: Penguin. (Also includes a selected bibliography.)

Derrick, P., and J. F. Phipps (eds.), 1969. Co-ownership, co-operation and control. Harlow, Essex: Longmans.

Great Atlantic and Pacific School Conspiracy, 1972. Doing your own school; a practical guide to starting and operating a community school. Boston: Beacon.

Hough, Eleanor M., 1966. Co-operative movement in India. 5th Ed. London: Oxford Univ. Press. (Describes and evaluates agricultural, economic and other co-operation.)

Hubley, John, 1973. Gramdan lives! an account of a summer spent with Gramdan — the non-violent land revolution in India. Edinburgh: World Development Movement.

Kriyananda, Swami, 1972. Cooperative communities; how to start them and why. New Ed. Nevada City, CA: Ananda.

Linton, Erica, 1971. Gramdan; revolution by persuasion. London:

Friends Peace and International Relations Committee. (Pamphlet.)

Roberts, Ernie, 1971. The Industrial Relations Act! The U.C.S. struggle! Unemployment! The solution is workers' control. Nottingham: Bertrand Russell Peace Foundation. (Pamphlet.)

Tabb, Jay Yanai, and Amire Goldfarb, 1970. Workers' participation in management; expectations and experience. Oxford, England: Pergamon.

Vanek, Jaroslav, 1971. The participatory economy; an evolutionary hypothesis and a strategy for development. Ithaca, NY (and London): Cornell Univ. Press.

Viteles, Harry, 1970. A history of the co-operative movement in Israel; a source book in 7 volumes. London: Valentine, Mitchell.

DISARMAMENT AND ARMS CONTROL

(Arms control . . .), 1973. Arms control; readings from Scientific American. San Francisco: Freeman.

Barnet, Richard J., and Richard A. Falk (eds.), 1965. Security in disarmament. Princeton, NJ: Princeton Univ. Press. (Covers inspection, verification, organization, responses to violations, limitations, peaceful change, resolving international conflict; selected bibliography.)

Benoit, Emile, and Kenneth E. Boulding (eds.), 1963. Disarmament and the economy. NY (and London): Harper.

Bertram, Christoph, 1972. Mutual force reductions in Europe; the political aspects. London: International Institute for Strategic Studies.

Graubard, Stephen (ed.), 1975. Arms, defense policy and arms control. Cambridge, MA: Daedalus.

Saaty, Thomas L., 1968. Mathematical models of arms control and disarmament; application of mathematical structures in politics. NY (and London): Wiley.

Scoville, Herbert, et. al., 1972. The arms race; steps toward restraint. NY: Carnegie Endowment (Taplinger).

Stockholm International Peace Research Institute, 1975a. Disarmament or destruction? Stockholm: SIPRI. (Pamphlet. Serves as a clear introduction.)

——, 1975b. World armaments and disarmaments; SIPRI yearbook. Cambridge, MA: MIT Press.

ECOLOGY ACTION; ALSO, ALTERNATIVE TECHNOLOGY

Arango, Jorge, 1970. The urbanization of the earth. Boston: Beacon.

('How sound modular land-use planning can make development and renewal possible while maintaining community structure.')

Artin, Tom, 1973. Earth talk; independent voices on the environment. NY: Grossman. ('. . . of extreme importance to anyone concerned with nonviolent social change. . . . Dai Dong . . . conference explored the major elements that have brought this planet . . . to its present . . . militarism, economic injustice, environmental fractures, nationalism, etc.)

Barlow, K. E., 1971. The discipline of peace. 2nd Ed. London: C. Knight.

Barr, John (ed.). 1971. The environmental handbook; action guide for the UK. London: Ballantine/Friends of the Earth/Pan.

Bayliss, Sylvia, et al. (eds.), 1970. Career opportunities; community services and related specialists. NY: Doubleday.

Beves, Louis R., and Harry R. Targ, 1974. Reordering the planet; constructing alternative world futures. Boston: Allyn & Bacon.

Bock, Alan, 1971. Ecology action guide. Plainview, NY: Nash.

Boyle, Godfrey, Peter Harper, and the editors of Undercurrents (eds.), 1976. Radical technology. London: Wildwood House.

Brown, Peter, 1974. 'Resources'. WIN 10 (no. 23, 27 June): 17. (On environmental action.)

Chesterman, John, Mike Martin, John May, Maggie Murphy-Ferris, Nadine Moggs Secton, Lee Torrey, Jon Trux, and Joy Watt, 1974. An index of possibilities: energy and power. London: Clanose/Wildwood. (Universe, earth, world, body, mind, god, and fundamentals.)

Civic Trust, 1972. An environmental directory; national and regional organisations concerned with amenity and the environment. Rev. Ed. London: Civic Trust.

Clarke, Robin (ed.), 1975. Notes for the future; an alternative history of the past decade, London: Thames and Hudson.

Dickson, David, 1974. Alternative technology and the politics of technical change. London: Fontana.

Dunn, Ted (ed.), 1975. Foundations of peace and freedom; the ecology of a peaceful world. Swansea: Christopher Davies.

The Editors of The Ecologist (Goldsmith, Edward, et al.), 1972. Blueprint for survival. Harmondsworth: Penguin.

Falk, Richard A., 1972. This endangered planet: prospects and proposals for human survival. NY: Vintage.

——, 1975. A study of future worlds. Amsterdam: North-Holland (and NY: Free Press).

Fanning, Odom, 1975. Man and his environment; citizen action. NY (and London): Harper.

Forstner, Lorne J., and John H. Todd (eds.), 1975? Readings on the ecological revolution. Lexington, MA: Heath.

Fromm, Erich, 1970. The revolution of hope; towards a humanized technology. London: Colophon/Harper.

Herring, Horace (ed.), 1975. Alternative technology series. Brighton: Smoothie (Volume 1 includes introduction, small developing countries, worker self-management, and unconventional energy sources. Among other items in the series is a *Guide to Environmental Resources*. Also, *Bibliography of Recycling* by Graham Tubb.)

Holliman, Jonathon, 1971. Consumers' guide to the protection of the environment. London: Pan.

——, 1972. Environment, resources and man; an annotated list. London: National Book League.

Johnson, Stanley, 1972. The green revolution. NY: Harper.

Kimber, Richard, and J. J. Richardson, 1974. Campaigning for the environment. London: Routledge.

Lang, Jon, Charles Burnette, Walter Moleski, and David Vachon (eds.), 1974. Designing for human behavior; architecture and the behavioral sciences. Stroudsburg, PA: Dowden (Golany).

Little, Charles E., and John G. Mitchell (eds.), 1971. Space for survival; blocking the bulldozer in urban America. NY: Pocket Books.

Nobile, Philip, and John Deedy (compilers), 1973? The complete ecology fact book. Garden City, NY: Anchor/Doubleday.

Papanek, Victor, 1972. Design for the real world. NY: Pantheon. ('Useful ideas for alternative technology.')

Schumacher, E. F., 1973. Small is beautiful. London: Blond and Briggs. ('On the necessity of decentralization and an economic system on a human scale.')

Slater, R. Giuseppi, 1970. The earth belongs to the people. San Francisco: People's Press.

Sprout, Harold, and Margaret Sprout, 1971. Toward a politics of the planet earth. NY (and London): Van Nostrand.

United Nations Conference on the Human Environment/Friends of the Earth, 1972. The Stockholm Conference; only one earth; an introduction to the politics of survival. London: Earth Island.

Ward, Barbara, and Rene Dubos, 1972. Only one earth; the care and maintenance of a small planet. Harmondsworth: Penguin.

EDUCATION AND CHILDREN'S RIGHTS

(Action education . . .), 1973. Action education kit. London: National Union of Students. ('. . . wealth of short essays describing . . . exciting experiments . . . , particularly in terms of making education relevant to community action and social change.')

Blaze, Wayne, Bill Hertzberg, Roy Krantz, and Al Lehrke, 1974. Guide to alternative colleges and universities. Boston: Beacon.

Brown, Cynthia, 1975. Literacy in 30 hours. London (14 Talacre Rd., NW5): Writers and Readers. (Pamphlet. 'Shows . . . how revolutionary literacy is achieved.')

Buckman, Peter (ed.), 1973. Education without schools. London: Condor/Souvenir.

Carnoy, Martin, 1974. Education as cultural imperialism. NY: McKay.

Carr-Hill, Roy, and Olav Magnussen, 1973. Indicators of performance of educational systems. Paris: Organisation for Economic Co-operation and Development (and London: HMSO).

Coates, Gary J. (ed.), 1974. Alternative learning environments. Stroudsburg, PA: Dwoden (Golany).

Community Relations Commission, 1972. Education for a multi-cultural society; a bibliography for teachers. London: CRC. (Pamphlet.)

Council for Environmental Education 1972? DELTA— a directory of environmental literature and teaching aids. London: Council for Environmental Education. ('Comprehensive guide including . . . books, films, slides, posters, study kits, games, etc.')

Curle, Adam, 1973. Education for liberation. London: Tavistock Publications. (Some of the contents include present difficulties and future possibilities; teaching nonviolent techniques of change.)

Fantini, Mario, and Marilyn Gittell, 1973. Decentralization; achieving reform. NY: Praeger.

Farber, Jerry, 1970. The student as nigger; essays and stories. NY: Pocket Books. ('Radical non-violent direct action applied to high schools and colleges.')

Freire, Paulo, 1976. Education, the practice of freedom. London: Writers and Readers. (Previously published as Education for critical consciousness..)

Graubard, Allen, 1973. Free the children; radical reform and the free school movement. NY: Pantheon.

Hemmings, Ray, 1972. Fifty years of freedom; a study of the development of the ideas of A. S. Neill. London: Allen and Unwin.

Holt, John, 1973. Freedom and beyond. Harmondsworth: Penguin (and NY: Dutton).

Illich, Ivan, 1974. After deschooling, what? London: Writers' and Readers'. (Pamphlet. Originally in Alan Gartner (ed.), After Deschooling, What? NY: Harper.)

Lister, Ian (ed.), 1974. Deschooling; a reader. London: Cambridge Univ. Press.

Reimer, Everett, 1971. School is dead; an essay on alternatives in education. Harmondsworth: Penguin.

Richmond, W. Kenneth, 1973. The free school. London: Methuen.

Schrank, Jeffrey, 1974. The seed catalog; a guide to teaching/learning materials. Boston: Beacon.

Spring, Joel, 1975. A primer of libertarian education. NY: Free Life.

Taylor, L. C., 1972. Resources for learning. 2nd Ed. Harmondsworth: Penguin.

Vaughan, Mark (ed.), 1972. Rights of children; report of the first National Conference on children's rights, . . . London: National Council for Civil Liberties.

Verma, G. K., and Christopher Bagley (eds.), 1976? Race and education across cultures. London: Heinemann. (' . . . scholarly bases for the development of equality and justice in education.')

(Zephyros deschool . . .), 1974? Zephyros deschool primers no. 1-12. San Francisco, CA (1201 Stanyan St.): Zephros Educational Exchange, ('high quality non-traditional' 'curriculum material appropriate for early childhood through graduate level classes.')

FEMINISM; ALSO, ANTI-SEXISM

Adams, Carol, and Rae Laurikietis, 1976. The gender trap; a closer look at sex roles. London: Virago/Quartet. (Three volumes. Book I: Education and work.)

Adelstein, Michael, and Jean G. Pival (eds.), 1972. Women's liberation. NY: St Martin. (Textbook.)

Ahlum, Carol, and Jacqueline M. Fralley, 1976? High school feminist studies. Old Westbury, NY: Feminist Press.

Allen, Sandra (ed.), 1974. Conditions of illusion; papers from the women's movement. Leeds: Feminist Books. (Britain, since 1970.)

Altbach, Edith Hoshino (ed.), 1971. From feminism to liberation. Cambridge, MA: Schenkman.

Andreas, Carol, 1971. Sex and caste in America. Englewood Cliffs, NJ (and Hemel Hempstead, Hertfordshire): Prentice-Hall.

Anticaglia, Elizabeth, 1972. A housewife's guide to women's liberation. Chicago: Nelson-Hall.

Arnold, Roxane, and Olive Chandler (eds.), 1974. Feminine singular; triumphs and tribulations of the single woman; an anthology. London: Femina Books.

Atkinson, Ti-Grace, 1974. Amazon Odyssey. NY: Links. ('The first collection of writings by the political pioneer of the women's movement.')

Boston Women's Health Book Collective, 1971. Our bodies ourselves; a book by and for women. NY: Simon and Schuster. ('Best book available on women and health.')

Brownmiller, Susan, 1975. Against our will; men, women and rape. NY: Simon and Schuster. ('Combines a scholar's meticulousness with a journalist's willingness to generalize . . .')

Chesler, Phyllis, 1972. Women and madness. NY: Avon.

Clemens, Lois G., 1975. Women liberated. New Canaan, CT: Keats.

Comer, Lee, 1974. Wedlocked women. Leeds: Feminist Books. ('What it's really like to be married.')

Cooke, Joanne, et. al. (eds.), 1973. The new women; a motive anthology of women's liberation. NY: Fawcett World.

Coote, Anna, and Tess Gill, 1974. Women's rights; a practical guide. Harmondsworth: Penguin.

Coussins, Jean, 1976. The equality report; one year of . . . The Equal Pay Act, The Sex Discrimination Act; The Equal Opportunities Commission. London: NCCL.

Dahlström, Edmund (ed.), 1971. The changing roles of men and women. Boston: Beacon. ('How sex equality has helped liberate men as well as women in Scandinavia.')

Deckard, Barbara Sinclair, 1975. The women's movement; political, socioeconomic and psychological issues. NY (and London): Harper.

Dworkin, Andrea, 1974. Woman hating. NY: Dutton.

Edry, Carol F., and Ginnie Goulet (eds.), 1973. This is the women's yellow pages; original sourcebook for women. Boston, MA: Women's Collective.

Epstein, Cynthia Fuchs, and William J. Goode (eds.), 1971. The other half; roads to women's equality. Englewood Cliffs, NJ (and Hemel Hempstead, Hertfordshire): Prentice-Hall.

Faulder, Carolyn, Christine Jackson, and Mary Lewis, 1976. The women's directory. London: Virago/Quartet. (Comprehensive British guide.)

Flexner, Eleanor, 1975. Century of struggle; the woman's rights movement in the United States. Rev. Ed. Cambridge, MA (and London): Belknap. (Careful, well-documented.)

Frankfort, Ellen, 1973. Vaginal politics. NY: Bantam.

Frazier, Nancy, and Myra Sadker, 1973. Sexism in school and society. NY (and London): Harper.

Freeman, Jo, 1975. The politics of women's liberation; a case study of an emerging social movement and its relations to the policy process. NY: McKay.

Fritz, Leah, 1975. Thinking like a woman. Brooklyn, NY: WIN Books (and Free Life Editions). ('Essays . . . cover the radical anti-war movement, the struggle for community control of N.Y.C. schools, and the growth of the women's movement . . .')

Greer, Germaine, 1971. The female eunuch. London: Paladin.

Harrison, Cynthia Ellen, 1975. Women's movement media; a source guide. NY (and London): Bowker.

Heilbrun, Carolyn G., 1973. Toward a recognition of androgyny. NY: Knopf. ('. . . the movement away from sexual polarization.')

Hewitt, Patricia, 1975. Rights for women. London: National Council for Civil Liberties. (Guide to the Sex Discrimination and Equal Pay Acts.)

Jones, Ian, 1974. 'An introduction to men against sexism.' Peace News 1979 (September 20): 11.

Jongeward, Dorothy, Dru Scott, et. al., 1973. Affirmative action for women; a practical guide. Reading, MA (and London): Addison-Wesley.

Komisar, Lucy, 1971. The new feminism. NY (and London): F. Watts.

Krichmar, Albert, 1972. The women's rights movement in the United States 1848–1970; a bibliography and sourcebook. Metuchen NJ: Scarecrow. (Classified annotations of about 6,000 items!)

Librarians for Social Change Collective (Compiler), 1975. Sexual politics; and basic reading list. London (1 Elgin Ave., W9): Release Publications. (Pamphlet. Source for a number of entries on the present feminist and gay liberation lists.)

Lynn, Mary C. (ed.), 1975. Women's liberation in the twentieth century. NY (and London): Wiley.

Millett, Kate, 1972. Sexual politics. London: Abacus.

Moffat, Mary Jane, and Charlotte Painter (eds.), 1974. Revelations; diaries of women. NY: Random House.

Morgan, Robin (ed.), 1973. Sisterhood is powerful; an anthology of writings from the women's liberation movement. NY: Vintage.

National Council for Civil Liberties, 1974. A model bill to prevent discrimination on grounds of sex, together with an explanatory memorandum. London: NCCL.

Negrin, Su, 1972. Begin at start; some thoughts on personal liberation and world change. Albion, CA: Times Change.

The New York Radical Feminists, 1974. Rape; the first sourcebook for women. Bergenfield, NJ: New American Library.

Peterson, Deena (ed.), 1975. A practical guide to the women's movement. NY: Women's Action Alliance. ('Descriptive listings . . . of over 200 women's groups. . . . 500 books and periodicals.')

Pleck, Joseph H., and Jack Sawyer (eds.), 1974. Men and masculinity. WIN 10 (13, April 11): 27–9. (Classified bibliography of about 150 items.)

Pleck, Joseph H., and Jack Sawyer (eds.), 1974. Men and masculinity. Englewood Cliffs, NJ: Prentice-Hall.

Rennie, Susan, and Kirsten Grimstad (eds.), 1975. The new woman's survival sourcebook. NY: Knopf.

Rooke, Patrick John, 1972. Women's rights. London: Wayland. (Brief and readable; 1772-1972.)

Rosenberg, Marie Barovic, and Len V. Bergstrom (eds.), 1975. Women and society; a critical review of the literature with a selected annotated bibliography. Beverly Hills, CA: Sage.

Rossi, Alice (ed.), 1974. The feminist papers; from Adams to de Beauvoir. London: Bantam.

Rowbotham, Sheila, 1973a. Hidden from history; 300 years of women's oppression and the fight against it. London: Pluto.

— —, 1973b. Woman's consciousness, man's world. Harmondsworth: Penguin. ('the social and economic conditions which have given rise to the recent emergence of the women's movement.' 'Links women's liberation to a socialist revolution.')

— —, 1973c. Women, resistance and revolution; a history of women and revolution in the modern world. Harmondsworth: Penguin. ('. . . the most important overall synthesis since . . . de Beauvoir . . .')

— —, 1973d. Women's liberation and revolution; a bibliography. 2nd Ed. Bristol, England: Falling Wall Press.

Scott, Hilda, 1974. Does socialism liberate women? experiences from Eastern Europe. Boston: Beacon.

Smedley, Agnes, 1973. Daugher of earth. Old Westbury, NY: Feminist Press. (And London: Virago.)

Spacks, Patricia Meyer, 1975. The female imagination. NY: Knopf.

Tanner, Leslie B. (ed.), 1970. Voices from women's liberation. NY: Signet. (Historical and contemporary.)

Wandor, Michelene (ed.), 1972. The body politic; writings from the women's liberation movement in Britain, 1969-1972. London: Stage 1.

Wilson, Eva (ed.), 1975. The woman's handbook. London: New English Library.

(Women's legal . . .), 1975. Women's legal handbook series on state government affirmative action programs today. 18 Vols. Butler, IN: Ford Associates.

(Women's struggle . . .), 1970. Women's struggle for social and political equality in the United States. 6 Vols. Cincinnati, OH: Collectors Editions.

GAY LIBERATION

Altman, Dennis, 1974. Homosexual oppression and liberation. Rev. Ed. London: Allen Lane. ('One of the basic texts.')

Birkby, Phillis, et al., (eds.), 1973. Amazon expedition; a lesbian-feminist anthology. Albion, CA: Times Change.

Gay Information, 1973. Psychiatry and the homosexual; a brief analysis of oppression. London: Gay Information. (Pamphlet.)

Gay Liberation Front, 1971. The gay liberation front manifesto. London: GLF. (Pamphlet.)

Humphreys, Laud, 1972. Out of the closets; a sociology of sexual liberation. NY: Prentice-Hall.

Jay, Karla, and Allen Young (eds.), 1972. Out of the closets; voices of gay liberation. NY: Douglas/Links. ('America and Britain'— 'life before liberation, the liberation process and gay activism'.)

Librarians for Social Change Collective (see FEMINISM list, above).

Martin, Del., 1972. Lesbian—woman. Toronto (and London): Bantam.

Milligan, Don, 1973. The politics of homosexuality. London: Pluto.

Richmond, Len, and Garry Noguera (eds.), 1973. The gay liberation book. San Francisco: Ramparts.

Righton, Peter, 1973. Counselling homosexuals; a study of personal needs and public attitudes. London: Bedford Square.

Tripp, C. A., 1975. The homosexual matrix. NY: McGraw-Hill ('. . . important theoretical work on homosexuality (male).')

Weinberg, George, 1973. Society and the healthy homosexual. NY: Anchor.

Weinberg, Martin, and Alan Bell (eds.), 1972. Homosexuality; an annotated bibliography. NY: Harper. ('Will need to be updated . . .')

HEALTH AND MENTAL HEALTH

Delworth, Ursula, et. al. (eds.), 1972. Crisis center hotline; a guidebook to beginning and operating. Springfield, IL: C. C. Thomas.

Fairweather, George, David H. Sanders, and Louis G. Tornatzky, 1974. Creating change in mental health organizations. Elmsford, NY (and Oxford, UK): Pergamon. (Report of a five-year national experiment.' 'The results are summarized as a list of principles for creating social change.')

Holleb, Gordon P., and Walter H. Abrams, 1975. Alternatives in community mental health. Boston: Beacon.

Illich, Ivan D. 1975. Medical nemesis; the expropriation of health. London: Calder.

Robertson, Leon S., John Kosa, Margaret C. Heagarty, Robert J. Haggerty, and Joel J. Alpert. 1974. Changing the medical care system; a controlled experiment in comprehensive care. NY (and London): Praeger. (Study done in Boston, MA).

Rossi, Jean J., and William J. Filstead, 1973. The therapeutic community; a source book. NY: Behavioral Publications.

Schulberg, Herbert C., Alan Sheldon, and Frank Baker (eds.), 1970.

Program evaluation in the health fields; a strategy of change in community action and community mental health programs. NY: Behavioral Publications.

Shneidman, Edwin, 1976? Program evaluation in the health fields; a strategy of change in community action and community mental health programs. Vol. 2. NY: Behavioral Publications.

Szasz, Thomas S., 1970. The manufacture of madness; a comparative study of the inquisition and the mental health movement. NY: Harper.

Wigley, Richard, and James Cook, 1975. Community health; concepts and issues. NY: Van Nostrand.

Wilson, Michael, 1975. Health is for people. London: Darton, Longman and Todd.

HOUSING

Cutting, Marion, 1974. The housing rights handbook. London: Shelter.

Saltman, Juliet Z., 1971. Open housing as a social movement; challenge, conflict and change. Lexington, MA (& London): Heath.

Shelter, 1974. Empty property; shelter's guide for carrying out a survey and using the results. London: Shelter.

Ward, Colin, 1974. Tenants take over. London: Architectural Press.

INTERNATIONAL CONFLICT RESOLUTION

Dietterich, Paul M., ????. Making a difference; a process guide for dealing with crisis issues in justice, liberation and development. NY: Friendship Press.

Doob, Leonard W. (ed.), 1970. Resolving conflict in Africa; the Fermeda workshop. New Haven, CT (and London): Yale Univ. Press. (Informal workshop on the clashes between Somali nomads and the police or soldiers.)

Stenelo, Lars-G., 1972. Mediation in international negotiations. Malmo, Sweden: Student litteratur. (Covers a variety of situations and strategies.)

Young, Oran R., 1967. Intermediaries; third parties in international crises. Princeton, NJ: Princeton Univ. Press. (Analysis and applications—particularly United Nations. Classified bibliography of about 225 items.)

Zawodny, J.K., 1966. Man and international relations; contributions of the social sciences to the study of conflict and integration. Two Vol. San Francisco: Chandler. (Comprehensive set of readings at all levels from intrapersonal to international.)

INTERNATIONAL CO-OPERATION AND PEACEFUL CHANGE

Akindele, R. A., 1975. The organisation and promotion of world peace; a study of universal-regional relationships. Toronto: Univ. of Toronto Press.

Bar-Yaacov, Nissim, 1974. The handling of international disputes by means of inquiry. London: Oxford Univ. Press.

Boasson, Charles, and Max Nurock (eds.), 1973. The changing international community; some problems of its laws, structures; and peace research and the Middle East conflict. Hague, Netherlands: Mouton. (Also covers peaceful coexistence, world pluralism, normative controls on international violence, international law and organization, Swiss neutrality, Commission on Human Rights, UNESCO tensions project, and the UN declaration on human rights.)

Buchan, Alastair, 1974. Change without war; the shifting structure of world power. London: Chatto and Windus.

Clark, Grenville, and Louis B. Sohn (eds.), ????. Introduction to world peace through world law. NY: Seabury.

Cobb, Roger W., and Charles Elder, 1970. International community; a regional and global study. NY (and London): Holt. (Theory and empirical study regarding integration among nations.)

Davis, Morris (ed.), 1975. Civil wars and the politics of international relief. NY (and London): Praeger. (Careful impressionistic description and evaluation, including Burundi, Bangladesh, Dominican Republic and Biafra.)

Davison, W. Phillips, 1974. Mass communication and conflict resolution; the role of the information media in the advancement of international understanding. NY (and London): Praeger.

Donelan, Michael D., 1971. Peaceful settlement of international disputes; report of a conference at Ditchley Park, 8-11 January 1971. Oxford: Ditchley Foundation. (Pamphlet.)

Held, Virginia, Sidney Morgenbesser, and Thomas Nagel, 1974. Philosophy, morality, and international affairs. NY (and London): Oxford Univ. Press.

Kohr, Leopold, 1973. Development without aid. Llandybie: C. Davies. ('. . . readable book on social economics . . . His advice for "developing" countries is that they break down into small autonomous areas, break off most trade relations, refuse all offers of aid, and go it alone through the hard work and co-operation of their own people.')

Marwell, Gerald, and David R. Schmitt, 1975. Cooperation; an experimental analysis. NY (and London): Academic Press.

Mendlovitz, Saul H. (ed.), 1975. On the creation of a just world order.

Tompkins, E. Berkeley (ed.), 1971. Peaceful change in modern society.

Stanford, CA: Hoover Institution Press.

Wagar, W. Warren, 1971. Building the city of man; outlines of a world civilization. NY: Grossman.

INTERNATIONAL ORGANIZATION AND PEACEKEEPING

Boyd, James M., 1971. United Nations peacekeeping operations; a military and political appraisal. NY (and London): Praeger.

Cot, Jeanne Pierre, 1972. International conciliation. London: Europa.

Cox, Arthur M., 1967. Prospects for peacekeeping. Washington, DC: Brookings.

Falk, Richard A., and Saul H. Mendlovitz (eds.), 1966. The strategy of world order. 4 Vols. NY: World Law Fund. (Includes Vol. 1, Towards a theory of war prevention. Vol. 2, International law. Vol. 3, The United Nations. Vol. 4, Disarmament and economic development.)

Gould, Wesley L., and Michael Barkun, 1972. Social science literature; a bibliography for international law. Princeton, NJ: Princeton Univ. Press.

Grieves, Forest L., 1969. Supernationalism and international adjudication. Urbana (and London): Univ. of Illinois Press.

Haas, Michael, 1973. International organization; an interdisciplinary bibliography. New Ed. Stanford, CA: Hoover Inst. Press.

Hamzeh, Fuad S., 1967. International conciliation. Amsterdam, Netherlands: Djambatan. (History, modes, and examples.)

Higgins, Rosalyn, 1969-70. United Nations peacekeeping, 1946-1967; documents and commentary. Vol. 1: The Middle East. Vol. 2: Asia. London Oxford Univ. Press.

Higgins, Rosalyn, and Michael Harbottle, 1972. United Nations peacekeeping; past lessons and future prospects. London: David Davies Memorial Institute of International Studies.

International Peace Research Association, 1966ff. Proceedings. Vol 1: Inaugural proceedings. Vol. 2: 2nd Conference: Pt. 1, Studies in conflict; Pt. 2, Poverty, development and peace. Vol. 3, Cooperation in Europe. Vol. 4: 3rd Conference: Pt. 1, Philosophy of peace research; Pt. 2, The international system; Pt. 3, Case studies, simulations and theories of conflict. Atlantic Highlands, NJ: Humanities Press.

Jacob, Philip E., Alexine L. Atterton, and Arthur M. Wallenstein, 1972. Dynamics of international organization. Rev. Ed. Homewood, IL: Dorsey. (Includes security, econcomic and social considerations.)

Laszlo, Ervin, 1974. A strategy for the future; the systems approach to world order. NY: Braziller. ('A plausible and comprehensive nonviolent populist strategy for drastic global reform.')

Lillich, Richard B., 1973. Humanitarian intervention and the United Nations. Charlotteville, VA: Univ. of Virginia Press.

Luard, Evan, 1970. The international regulation of frontier disputes. London: Thames and Hudson.

Meadows, Dennis, and Donella Meadows (eds.), 1973. Toward global equilibrium; collected papers. Cambridge, MA: Wright-Allen.

Nordlinger, Eric A., 1972. Conflict regulation in divided societies. Cambridge, MA: Harvard Center for International Affairs.

Paxman, John M., and George T. Boggs (eds.), 1973. The United Nations, a reassessment; sanctions, peacekeeping and humanitarian assistance. Charlotteville, VA: Univ. Press of Virginia.

Reed, Edward (ed.), 1968. Beyond coexistence; the requirements of peace. NY: Grossman.

Rikhye, Indar Jit, Michael Harbottle, and Bjorne Egge, 1974. The thin blue line; international peacekeeping and its future. New Haven (and London): Yale Univ. Press. ('. . . lessons learned from United Nations peacekeeping operations, and their applications in the training of military and civilian officials for neutral intervention in international disputes.')

(Sources of . . .), 1975. Sources of information on international organisations. London: Department of Education and Science.

Taylor, Alastair, David Cox, and J. L. Granatstein, 1968. Peacekeeping; international challenge and Canadian response. — : Canadian Institute of International Affairs. (Also, includes bibliography.)

Tewary, I. N., 1975. The peace-keeping power of the United Nations General Assembly. Mystic, CT: Verry.

Tompkins, E. Berkeley (ed.), 1972. United Nations in perspective. Stanford, CA: Hoover Institution Press.

Wainhouse, David W., 1973. International peacekeeping at the cross-roads; national support, experience and prospects. Baltimore, MD (and London): Johns Hopkins Univ. Press.

Walker, Charles C., 1969. Peacekeeping 1969. Philadelphia, PA: Friends Peace Committee. (Pamphlet.)

MEDIA—ALTERNATIVE/COMMUNITY

Biren, Andi, 1975. Basic video in community work. London (14 Talacre Rd., NW5 4PE): Inter-Action.

Concord Films Council, 1974ff. 1974 catalogue of 16 mm films for hire. Nacton, Ipswich, Suffolk: Concord. (Plus periodic supplements, including March 1976 combined supplement to the 1974 edition.) ('. . . educational and film library specialising in documentary and TV film about contemporary problems.')

Dougall, Lucy, 1970. War/peace film guide. Berkeley, CA: Inter-Council Publications. Committee (for the World Without War Council of Greater Seattle). ('. . . the best films on the subject and how to obtain them.')

Glessing, Robert J., 1971. The underground press in America. Bloomington, IN: Indiana Univ. Press.

Great Atlantic Radio Conspiracy, 1975? (Catalog.) Baltimore (2743 Maryland Avenue, 21218): GARC. ('. . . tapes for use on the radio on a variety of subjects either not dealt with, or not dealt adequately, by the established media.')

Janowitz, Morris, 1967. Community press in an urban setting; the social elements of urbanism. 2nd Ed. Chicago: Univ. of Chicago Press.

Lawrence, Robert de T., 1965. Rural mimeo newspapers; guide to the production of low-cost community papers in developing countries. NY: Unipub.

Lewis, Roger, 1972. Outlaws of America; the underground press and its context. Harmondsworth: Penguin.

Morris, Mark, 1974. 'Alternative record companies.' WIN 10 (no. 42, December 12): 4-6.

Noyce, John, 1974. Alternative publishers in Britain. Brighton: Smoothie. (Pamphlet.)

Rety, John, 1975? Community newspapers; Inter-Action Advisory Service Handbook No. 5. London: Inter-Action/Writers and Readers. ('Editing, printing, money, survival, layout and contacts; . . . getting support; . . . list of existing . . . papers.')

Rogovin, Mark, et. al., 1975. Mural manual; how to paint murals for the classroom, community center, and street corner. Boston: Beacon.

Sim, John C., 1969. Grass roots press; America's community newspapers. Ames, IW: Iowa State Univ. Press.

(Some alternative . . .), 1976. 'Some alternative libraries.' Librarians for Social Change (No. 11, Spring/Summer): 14-16.

Turner, Nigel G., 1974. Makin' it; a guide to some working alternatives. Petersham, Surrey (The Loft, The Manor House, River Lane): Paper Tiger Productions. ('. . . alternatives in manufacturing, publishing, cinema, information services, education, food growing, food co-operation, shops, and record companies.')

United States. Library of Congress, 1953ff. National Union Catalog. Motion Pictures and Film-strips. Ann Arbor, MI: Edwards (since 1963). (Issued in the same cumulative years as the author lists for books. The subject index follows the alphabetical title list of films and can be entered with the headings and co-headings that are used in the present bibliography.)

Woodsworth, A. (ed.), 1973. Alternative press in Canada; a checklist of underground, revolutionary, radical and other alternative serials from

1960. Toronto: Univ. of Toronto Press.

MEDIATION AND CONFLICT RESOLUTION; LABOUR/MANAGEMENT

Albright, W. Paul, 1973. Collective bargaining; a Canadian simulation. NY (and London): Wiley. (Simulation game for students.)

Baer, Walter E., 1975. Strikes; a study of conflict and how to resolve it. NY: American Management.

Confederation of British Industry, 1970. Disputes procedures for the avoidance and settlement of disputes arising at the place of work. London: Confederation of British Industry.

Feather, Victor, 1971. The essence of trade unionism. New Ed. London: Bodley Head.

Flanagan, Robert J., and Arnold R. Weber (eds.), 1974. Bargaining without boundaries; the multinational corporation and international labor relations. Chicago (and London): Univ. of Chicago Press.

Flanders, Allen (ed.), 1969. Collective bargaining; selected readings. Harmondsworth: Penguin.

Fleeman, R. K., and A. G. Thompson, 1970. Productivity bargaining; a practical guide. London: Butterworths.

Maggiolo, Walter A., 1971. Techniques of mediation in labor disputes. Dobbs Ferry, NY: Oceana.

Margerison, Charles, and Malcolm Leary, 1975. Managing industrial conflicts; the mediator's role. Bradford, West Yorkshire: Resource Development Associates.

Matles, James J., and James Higgins, 1974. Them and us; struggles of a rank-and-file union. Englewood Cliffs, NJ: Prentice-Hall. (United Electrical, Radio and Machine Workers of America.)

Parker, P. A. L., W. R. Hawes, and A. L. Lumb, 1971. The reform of collective bargaining at plant and company level. London: HMSO.

Prasow, Paul, and Edward Peters, 1970. Arbitration and collective bargaining; conflict resolution in labor relations. NY (and Maidenhead, Berkshire): McGraw-Hill.

(Resolving labor . . .), 1973. Resolving labor management disputes; a nine-country comparison. NY: Conference Bd.

Ross, N.S., 1969. Constructive conflict; an essay on employer-employee relations in contemporary Britain. Edinburgh: Oliver and Boyd.

Towers, B., T. G. Whittingham, and A. W. Gottschalk (eds.), 1972. Bargaining for change. London: Allen and Unwin. (On management/employee productivity bargaining.)

Trades Union Congress, 1973. A guide to the avoidance of disputes between unions and the settlement of disputes with employers. London:

TUC. (Pamphlet.)

Wedderburn, K. W., and P. L. Davies, 1969. Employment grievances and disputes procedures in Britain. Berkeley, CA (and London): Univ. of California Press.

MINORITIES; PREJUDICE; SOCIAL PROBLEMS

Allen, Robert L., and Pamela P. Allen, 1975. Reluctant reformers; racism and social reform movements in the United States. NY: Doubleday.

Kinch, John W. (ed.), 1974. Social problems in the world today. Reading, MA (and London): Addison-Wesley.

Mauss, Armand L., 1975. Social problems as social movements. Philadelphia, PA: Lippincott.

Rubington, Earl, and Martin S. Weinberg (eds.), 1971. Study of social problems; five perspectives. NY (and London): Oxford Univ. Press.

Smigel, Erwin O. (ed.), 1971. Handbook on the study of social problems. Chicago: Rand McNally. (One of the sections deals with approaches to social change.)

Weinberg, Martin S., and Earl Rubington (eds.), 1973. The solution of social problems; five perspectives. NY (and London): Oxford Univ. Press.

Whitaker, Ben (ed.), 1972. The fourth world; victims of group oppression; eight reports from the field work of the Minority Rights Group. London: Sidgwick and Jackson. (It is 'cheaper to buy the individual reports — and benefit from more up-to-date comment . . . available from MRG at 36 Craven St., London WC2.')

Wilson, Des, 1973. Minority report; a diary of protest. 1970-1973. London: Quartet. (Documentation and impressions about homelessness and about the treatment of a variety of minority groups in England and, briefly, elsewhere.)

MISCELLANEOUS

Dyal, James A., William C. Corning, and Dale M. Willows (eds.), 1975. Readings in psychology; the search for alternatives. 3rd Ed. NY: McGraw-Hill.

Newfield, Jack, 1971. Bread and roses too. NY: Dutton. (' . . . collection of articles and book reviews most of which appeared in the Village Voice and the New York Magazine between . . . 1965 and . . . 1971.')

Nhat Hanh, Thich, 1976. The miracle of being awake. Nyack, NY: Fellowship Books. (Pamphlet. '. . . ways in which people like ourselves can create spaces in which to learn the basics of meditation and find in routine activities . . . opportunities that transform the activity.')

North, Michael (ed.), 1976. Time running out? Best of Resurgence. Chalmington, Dorchester, Dorset: Prism Press. ('. . . not exactly . . . ecology or . . . decentralism or . . . the peace movement . . .')

Peck, James, 1969. Underdogs vs. upperdogs. Cantergary, NH: Greenleaf. ('Autobiography of a nonviolent direct actionist.')

Pirsig, Robert, 1974. Zen and the art of motorcycle maintenance. NY (and London): Bantam.

Wilson, E. Raymond, 1975. Uphill for peace. Richmond, IN: Friends United Press. (History of 'Friends Committee on National Legislation (FCNL). . . . practical . . . guide to lobbying.')

NONVIOLENCE — GENERAL

Bell, Inge P., 1968. CORE and the strategy of nonviolence. NY: Random.

Bernstein, Saul, 1970. Alternatives to violence. NY: Association Press.

Bondurant, Joan V., and Margaret W. Fisher (eds.), 1971. Conflict; violence and nonviolence. Chicago: Aldine/Atherton. (Some of the contents include: Bondurant's search for a theory of conflict; the American/European peace movement from 1945 to the early 1960s (Roy Finch); the new pacifism (Stephan Thernstrom); civil disobedience (Harry Prosch; Darnell Rucker); symbolic violence (Ernest Jones; Bondurant); alternatives to violence—fractionating conflict (Roger Fisher; Lawrence S. Finkelstein); techniques of nonviolent action (with 84 classified examples—Gene Sharp), and nonviolent civilian defence (Thomas C. Schelling); and Gandhian and other approaches to conflict (Margaret W. Fisher).)

Commission on Non-Violent Action, 1973. Non-violent action—a Christian appraisal; a report commissioned for the United Reformed Church. London: SCM.

Deming, Barbara, 1971. Revolution and equilibrium. NY: Grossman.

Douglass, James W., 1972. Resistance and contemplation; the way of liberation. NY: Delta. (Relevant religious philosophy and action.)

Einstein, Albert, 1968. Einstein on peace. NY: Schocken. (Edited by Otto Nathan and Heinz Norden.)

Eisenberg, A., and J. Ilardo, 1972. Argument; an alternative to violence. Englewood Cliffs, NJ: Prentice-Hall.

Horsburgh, H. J. N., 1968. Non-violence and aggression; a study of Gandhi's moral equivalent of war. London: Oxford Univ. Press.

Hyatt, John (ed.), 1972? The Indian experience of nonviolence; essays on Satyagraha and Gramdan. London: Peace Pledge Union.

(Pamphlet.)

Kumar, Satish, 1969. Non-violence or non-existence; Satish Kumar introduces the Gandhian ideology of non-violent society. London: Christian Action.

Kumar, Satish (ed.), 1969. School of non-violence; a handbook. London: Christian Action and Housmans. ('International anthology' by Vinoba Bhave and others.)

Lanza Del Vasto, 1972. Definitions of nonviolence. South Acworth, NH: Greenleaf.

Moulton, Philip P., 1971. Violence, or aggressive nonviolent resistance. Wallingford, PA: Pendle Hill.

Ng, Larry (ed.), 1968. Alternatives to violence; a stimulus to dialogue. NY: Time-Life.

Pelton, Leroy H., 1975. The psychology of non-violence. Oxford, England: Pergamon.

Regamey, Pie Raymond, 1966. Non-violence and the Christian conscience. London: Darton, Longman & Todd.

Sandperl, Ira, 1974. A little kinder. Palo Alto, CA: Science and Behavior Books. ('. . . a series of letters written in 1971. . . .' 'To learn more about love and nonviolence' 'in a more intimate sphere.')

Stiehm, Judith, 1972. Nonviolent power; active and passive resistance in America. Lexington, MA: Heath.

Trocme, Andre, 1974. Jesus and the nonviolent revolution. Scottdale, PA: Herald Press.

Unnithan, T. K. N., and Yogendra Singh, 1969. Sociology of non-violence and peace. New Delhi: Research Council for Cultural Studies. ('Empirical study of the value systems of elites,' non-elites, 'and students in India, Ceylon, and Nepal with regard to non-violence and peace.')

——, 1973. Traditions of non-violence. New Delhi (and London): Arnold Heinemann. (Religious values and social philosophies associated with Hindu, Chinese, Islam, Judaic and Christian traditions; and structural sociological treatment.)

PEACE ACTION, PACIFISM, CONSCIENTIOUS OBJECTORS, AND RELATED INFORMATION

Abrams, Grace, and Fran Schmidt, 1972. Learning peace. Philadelphia, PA: Jane Addams Peace Association. (Social studies curriculum.)

Angell, Robert C., 1969. Peace on the march; transnational participation. NY (and London): Van Nostrand. (The effect, on foreign policy, of transnational participation—a sociological factor including study/teaching/residence abroad, participation in international non-governmental and governmental organizations, etc.)

Beitz, Charles R., and Theodore Herman (eds.), 1973. Peace and war. San Francisco: Freeman. (Section on peace includes readings on world government, reforming the state system, domestic change, civilian defence and non-violence, and industrial action and social change.)

Bing, Harold, 1972. The historical and philosophical background of modern pacifism. London: War Resisters' International. (Pamphlet.)

Bloomfield, Lincoln P., and Amelia C. Leiss, 1970. Controlling small wars; a strategy for the 1970s. London: Allen Lane.

Bowett, D. W. (ed.), 1972. The search for peace. London: Routledge & Kegan.

Boyle, Kay, and Justine Van Gundy (eds.), 1972. Enough of dying! NY: Dell (Laurel). ('Compilation of famous *Voices for Peace* including Denise Levertov, Allen Ginsberg, Albert Camus, Malcolm X, etc.')

Brock, Peter, 1970. Twentieth Century pacifism. NY: Van Nostrand. ('. . . best introduction . . . to modern pacifism . . . readable. Thoroughly researched.' Also, companion volumes: *Pacifism in Europe to 1914*, Princeton, NJ: Princeton Univ. Press, 1972. *Pacifism in the United States, from the Colonial era to the First World War,* . . . *Princeton, 1968. Radical pacifists in antebellum America,*. . . . Princeton, 1968.)

Calvert, Robert, 1971. Ain't gonna pay for war no more. NY: War Tax Resistance. ('Everything you'd want to know on war tax resistance.')

Chatfield, Charles (ed.), 1973. Peace movements in America. NY: Schocken. (From 1900 to the 1960s.)

Cook, Blanche W., et. al. (eds.), c. 1970–4. Garland Library of War and Peace. NY: Garland. (327 volumes, including Proposals for peace: a history, 23 v.; Histories of the organized peace movement, 8 v.; Problems of the organized peace movement: selected documents, 10 v.; Peace leaders: biographies and memoirs, 13 v.; Character and causes of war, 41 v.; Political economy of war, 24 v.; Labor, socialism and war, 15 v.; Control and limitation of arms, 18 v.; International organization, arbitration and law, 22v.; International law, 19v.; Kellogg Pact and the outlawry of war, 4 v.; Non-resistance and non-violence, 37 v.; conscription and conscientious objection, 14 v.; Religious and ethical positions on war, 14 v.; Artists on war, 9 v.; Documentary anthologies, 14 v.)

Gandhi, M. K., 1942, 1949. Non-violence in peace and war. 2 Vols. Ahmedabad, India: Navajivan. (And Mystic, CT: Verry.)

Gaylin, Willard, 1970. In the service of their country; war resisters in prison. NY: Viking.

Guinan, Edward, 1973. Peace and nonviolence; basic writings by prophetic voices in the world religions. Paramus, NJ: Paulist-Newman.

(Handbook on . . .), 1968. Handbook on nonpayment of war taxes. 3rd Ed. Cincinatti: Peacemaker.

Held, Virginia, Sidney Morgenbesser, and Thomas Nagel (eds.), 1974. Philosophy, morality, and international affairs. NY: Oxford. ('Discussion of topics like selective conscientious objection, individual responsibility for war crimes, ecocide, genocide, imperialism, and nonviolence.')

Holcombe, Arthur, 1959. Organizing peace in the nuclear age. NY: New York Univ. Press.

Hollins, Elizabeth Jay (ed.), 1966. Peace is possible; a reader for laymen. NY: Grossman. (Broad coverage; 'essays . . . by . . . scientists, . . . economists, etc.')

Hull, William I., 1972. The new peace movement. NY: Ozer. ('Repr. of 1912 ed.' 'Peace Movement in America' Series.)

Hyatt, John, 1972a. Pacifism; a selected bibliography. London: Housmans. (Covers general history, both world wars, Christianity, intentional community, specific actions and practical handbooks; general/Christian/anarchist/American/anthology writings, biography; book and library resources.)

——, 1972b. A pacifist action handbook. London: Youth Association, Peace Pledge Union. ('Practical information on vigils, pickets, individual activity, study groups, etc.')

Joyce, James A., 1959. Red Cross International and the strategy of peace. Dobbs Ferry, NY: Oceana.

Kale, Roy A., 1974. Machinery for peace in the Seventies; a plan and a program for achieving world peace. Hicksville, NY: Exposition.

Lapp, John A. (ed.), 1969. Peacemakers in a broken world. Scottdale, PA: Herald Press. (Many of the 12 papers were first presented in a series of Mennonite 'Peacemaker Workshops'.)

(Learning peace . . .), 1974? Learning peace; ain't gonna study war no more. (From: War Resisters League, NY.) ('A resource unit for teachers, parents and discussion groups.')

Leeds, Christopher, Kenneth Edwards, and Richard Zipfel (eds.), 1975. Peace book 1975. Bristol, England: Student Christian Movement. ('Comprehensive source books for peace workers and educators.')

Martin, David A., 1965. Pacifism; an historical and sociological study. London: Routledge. (Especially, British historical/religious/political experience. Bibliography.)

Melko, Matthew, 1973. 52 peaceful societies. Oakville, Ontario: CPRI.

Melman, Seymour, 1970. The defense economy; conversion of industries and occupations to civilian needs. NY: Praeger.

Miller, William D., 1973. A harsh and dreadful love; Dorothy Day and the Catholic Worker movement. NY: Liveright (Norton).

Montessori, Maria, 1975. Education and peace. Chicago: Regnery.

Murty, K. S., and A. Bouquet, 1960. Studies in the problems of peace. NY: Asia.

Muste, A. J., 1967. The essays of A. J. Muste. NY: Simon & Schuster. (Compiled by Nat Hentoff.)

Network to End War, 1974? Workbook to end war. Baltimore, MD: American Friends Service Committee. ('American resource book on peace work and education. . . . Lots of useful information.')

(Peacemakers . . .), ????. Peacemakers. NY: Harper. (New York Times Resource Library.)

Pickus, Robert (See section on KEY ITEMS, in the first section of this bibliography.)

Polner, Murray (ed.), 1972. When can I come home? A debate on amnesty for exiles, antiwar prisoners and others. Garden City, NY: Anchor.

Prasad, Devi, 1971. They love it but leave it; American deserters. London: War Resisters' International. (Analysis; situation in various countries; publications.)

Prasad, Devi (ed.), 1972. 50 years of war resistance; what now? London: War Resisters' International.

Prasad, Devi, and Tony Smythe (eds.), 1968. Conscription; a world survey of compulsory military service and resistance to it. London: War Resisters' International.

(The pursuit of . . .), 1975. The pursuit of peace; a book of current knowledge and interests for group study. London (Drayton House, Gordon Street, WC1H OBE): NASU. (Miscellaneous broad-spectrum anthology.)

Randle, Robert F., 1973. The origins of peace: a study of peacemaking and the structure of peace settlements. NY (and London): Free Press/Collier-Macmillan.

(Report from . . .), 1968. Report from Iron Mountain on the possibility and desirability of peace. Harmondsworth: Penguin. (Semi-official report originally intended for 'unnamed government administrators of the highest rank'.)

Sampson, Ronald, 1973. Tolstoy; the discovery of peace. London: Heinemann. ('The nature of people's obligation to the state . . .'; 'traces the change in attitudes toward war'. Discussion includes Joseph de Maistre, Stendahl, Alexander Herzen, Pierre Joseph Proudhon, Tolstoy, and also covers a religious understanding of power.)

Schlissel, Lillian (ed.), 1968. Conscience in America. NY: Dutton. ('. . . documentary history of conscientious objection from 1757-1967.')

Sharp, Gene, ????. Non-violent action; an introductory outline for study groups. London: Friends Peace and International Relations Committee. (Also available from the Committee are about 20 pamphlets, by various authors, on related topics.)

Sommerville, John, 1975. The peace revolution; ethos and social process. Westport, CT (and London): Greenwood. (Articulate discussion of atomic-era requirements in 'politics, economics, education, morality, life-style'.)

Stanford, Barbara, 1976. Peacemaking; a guide to conflict resolution for individuals, groups, and nations. NY: Bantam.

Underhill, Hugh, ????. Pacifism—an introductory perspective. London: Peace Pledge Union. (Pamphlet.)

Wittels, Mike, and Jerry Kinchy, 1975. Advice for conscientious objectors in the armed forces. 3rd Ed. Philadelphia: Central Committee for Conscientious Objectors.

Wittner, Lawrence S., 1969. Rebels against war; American peace movement, 1941-1960. NY: Columbia Univ. Press.

PENAL REFORM

Buckley, Marie, 1974. Breaking into prison; a citizen guide to volunteer action. Boston, MA: Beacon.

Deming, Vinton, Ruth Kilpack, Jim Silver, Francis Spicer and Bill Stanton III, 1973? The county jail; a handbook for citizen action. (From WRL, 339 Lafayette St., NY 10012). (Pamphlet.)

Goldfarb, Ronald, 1975. Jails. Garden City, NY: Anchor/Doubleday. (Careful, readable documentation of prisons—especially American ones—and their effect on people, including suggested major changes and law reforms.)

Greenberg, David F., 1970. The problem of prisons. Philadelphia: AFSC (National Peace Literature Service). ('Compelling argument for the abolition of prisons.')

POVERTY ACTION

Bailis, Lawrence Neil, 1974. Bread or justice; grassroots organizing in the Welfare Rights movement. Lexington, MA: Lexington (Heath). (Massachusetts Welfare Rights Organization.)

Brown, Lester, 1974. By bread alone. NY: Praeger. ('world hunger'— 'overview of . . . causes'; 'programs . . . to help'.)

Bull, David, 1970. Action for welfare rights. London: Fabian Society. (Pamphlet.)

Clark, Kenneth B., and Jeannette Hopkins, 1969. Relevant war against poverty; a study of community action programs and observable social change. NY: Harper. (Evaluation of 51 programmes.)

Dolci, Danilo, 1966. Poverty in Sicily. Harmondsworth: Penguin.

Greenwood, Elma, 1967. How churches fight poverty; sixty successful local projects. NY: Friendship Press.

Horowitz, David, 1969. The abolition of poverty. NY (and London): Praeger.

Kurzman, Paul A. (ed.), 1971. Mississippi experience; strategies for welfare rights actions. NY: Association Press.

Lister, Ruth (ed.), 1975. National welfare benefits handbook. 4th Ed. London: Child Poverty Action Group. (Pamphlet.)

Piven, Frances Fox, and Richard A. Cloward, 1971. Regulating the poor; the functions of public welfare. NY: Random/Vintage.

Pollinger, Kenneth J., and Annette C. Pollinger, 1972. Community action and the poor; influence vs. social control in a New York City Community. NY: Praeger.

Raper, Arthur F., 1970. Rural development in action; the comprehensive experiment at Comilla, East Pakistan. Ithaca, NY (and London): Cornell Univ. Press. ('How to help rural families who live at the ragged edge of survival to acquire power—the power of knowledge and of organization—to lift themselves toward a better life'.)

Roberts, Bryan R., 1973. Organizing strangers; poor families in Guatemala City. Austin, TX (and London): Univ. of Texas Press.

Schlesinger, Benjamin, 1966. Poverty in Canada and the United States; overview and annotated bibliography. Toronto, Ontario: Univ. of Toronto Press.

Shipman, George A., 1971. Designing program action against urban poverty. University, AL: Univ. of Alabama Press.

United Nations. Conference on Trade and Development, 1965ff. (Documentation related to developing countries. See Library of Congress, National Union Catalog, author lists, 1968 onwards.) ('A selection of' UNCTAD reports 'is available in Britain from HMSO and in the U.S.A. from the Bookshop, United Nations Headquarters, . . . NY 10017. For . . . information: . . . UNCTAD, Information Service, United Nations Office, Palais des Nations, Geneva, Switzerland.')

(World hunger . . .), ????. World hunger crisis kit; hope for the hungry. Chicago: World Without War Council. ('. . . self-survey, . . . ethical perspectives and obstacles to success . . . , constructive proposals and resources for action.')

PROBLEM-SOLVING, CONFLICT RESOLUTION, CONFLICT THEORIES

Bartos, Otomar J., 1974. Process and outcome of negotiations. NY (and London): Columbia Univ. Press.

Bartunek, Jean M., Alan A. Benton, and Christopher D. Keys, 1975. 'Third party intervention and the bargaining behavior of group representatives.' Journal of Conflict Resolution 19: 532-57.

Bernstein, Merton C., 1968. Private dispute settlement. NY (and London): Free Press/Collier-Macmillan.

Brickman, Philip, 1974. Social conflict; readings in rule structures and conflict relationships. Lexington, MA (and London): Heath.

Curle, Adam, 1971. Making peace. London: Tavistock. ('Situations and . . . methods' for peaceful relationships—at inter-cultural and other levels.)

——, 1972. Mystics and militants; a study of awareness; identity and social action. London: Tavistock. ('. . . types of unpeaceful relationship and . . . peacemaking techniques by which such relations can be transformed . . .')

Deutsch, Morton, 1973. The resolution of conflict; constructive and destructive processes. New Haven, CT (and London): Yale Univ. Press. (Theoretical essays, research papers, summary, bibliography.)

Hoglund, Bengt, and Jorgen W. Ulrich (eds.), 1972. Conflict control and conflict resolution. Copenhagen: Munsgaard.

Hollaway, Otto, 1975. Problem solving; toward a more humanizing curriculum. Philadelphia: Franklin Publishing Co.

Jandt, Fred, 1973. Conflict resolution through communication. NY: Harper.

Leeds, Christopher A., 1974. Teaching of conflict studies. London (12 Gower St.): Politics Association. (Pamphlet.)

Marwell, Gerald, and David R. Schmitt, 1975. Co-operation; an experimental analysis. NY (and London): Academic Press.

May, Rollo, 1974. Power and innocence; a search for the sources of violence. London: Souvenir. (Covers psychological, social, and other sources.)

Miller, Gerald R.; and Herbert W. Simons (eds.), 1974. Perspectives on communication in social conflict. Englewood Cliffs, NJ: Prentice-Hall.

Mudd, Stuart (ed.), 1967. Conflict resolution and world education. Bloomington, IN (and London): Indiana Univ. Press. (Also includes selected bibliography and list of organizations.)

Nicholson, Michael, 1970. Conflict analysis. London: English Universities Press. (Covers research, aggression and war, bargaining and game theory, coalitions, international crises, simulation.)

Nye, Robert D., 1973. Conflict among humans; some basic psychological and social-psychological considerations. NY: Springer.

Palomares, Uvaldo, and Ben Logan, 1975. A curriculum on conflict management. La Mesa, CA: Human Development Training Inst.

Randolph, Lillian L., 1973. Third-party settlement of disputes in theory and practice. Dobbs Ferry, NY: Oceana.

Rapoport, Anatol, 1974. Conflict in man-made environment. Harmondsworth: Penguin.

Rubin, Jeffrey, and Bert R. Brown, 1975. The social psychology of bargaining and negotiation. NY (and London): Academic Press.

Sampson, Ronald V., 1966. The psychology of power. NY: Vintage.

Shaftel, Fannie R., and G. Shaftel, 1967. Role-playing for social values; decision-making in the social studies. Englewood Cliffs, NJ (and London): Prentice-Hall. (Pamphlet. Psychodrama-type roleplaying as an educational technique.)

Spergel, Irving A., 1969. Community problem solving; the delinquency example. Chicago (and London): Univ. of Chicago Press.

Swingle, Paul (ed.), 1970. The structure of conflict. NY (and London): Academic Press. (Based largely on empirical/theoretical social psychology.)

Varela, Jacobo A., 1971. Psychological solutions to social problems; an introduction to social technology. NY (and London): Academic Press. (Personnel selection, persuasion, group problem solving, conflict resolution, toward a new social system; bibliography.)

Walton, Richard E., 1969. Interpersonal peacemaking; confrontations and third party consultation. Reading, MA (and London): Addison-Wesley.

PROTEST, CIVIL DISOBEDIENCE, AND REVOLUTIONARY ACTION—GENERAL

Bedau, Hugo (ed.), 1969. Civil disobedience; theory and practice. Indianapolis, IN: Pegasus.

Berrigan, Daniel, Barbara Deming, James Forest, Staughton Lynd, and others, 1969? Delivered into resistance. (From WIN, 503 Atlantic Ave., Fifth Floor, Brooklyn, NY 11217).

Bromley, Ernest (ed.), 1971. Handbook on nonpayment of war taxes. 4th Ed. South Acworth, NH: Greenleaf Books.

Buckman, Peter, 1970. Limits of protest. London: Gollancz. ('. . . Description of advanced industrial society, . . . possibilities for changing it,' and alternative ways of living.)

Calvert, Peter, 1970. Study of revolution. Oxford: Oxford Univ. Press. (Readable analyses and examples, such as sources of conflict, Quaker Meeting, roleplaying, labour relations. Selected bibliography.)

Carter, April, 1973. Direct action and liberal democracy. NY: Harper.

Crawford, Curtis (ed.), 1973. Civil disobedience; a casebook. NY: T. Y. Crowell.

Dellinger, Dave, 1970. Revolutionary nonviolence. Indianapolis, IN: Bobbs-Merrill. ('. . . selected essays from 1943 to the present, including first-hand accounts of Cuba, mainland China, North and South Vietnam.')

Deming, Barbara, 1971. Revolution and equilibrium. NY: Grossman. ('A series of studies of nonviolent action and its possibilities.')

——, 1974. We cannot live without our lives. NY: Grossman. ('. . . acute perception of present-day political realities; . . . the anarchist/pacifist/feminist world she envisions . . .')

Douglass, James W., 1972. Resistance and contemplation; the way of liberation. Garden City, NY: Doubleday. ('. . . how resistance and contemplation are complementary aspects of the nonviolent way to political and spiritual freedom.')

Dove, Tom (ed.), 1970. Law and political protest; a handbook to your political rights under the law. NY: World Without War.

Easlea, Brian, 1973. Liberation and the aims of science; an essay on obstacles to the building of a beautiful world. London: Chatto and Windus/Sussex Univ. Press.

Fortas, Abe, 1970. Concerning dissent and civil disobedience. Newly Rev. Ed. NY: Signet. ('Defines the limits and scope of lawful civil disobedience'— recent American examples.)

Friedman, Leon, 1971. The wise minority; an argument for draft resistance and civil disobedience. NY: Dial.

Giffin, Frederick C., and Ronald D. Smith (eds.), 1971. Against the grain; an anthology of dissent. Bergenfield, NJ: Mentor.

Goldwin, Robert (ed.), 1971. On civil disobedience; essays old and new. London: Rand McNally/Eurospan.

Gowan, Susanne, George Lakey, William Moyer, Richard Taylor, 1976. Moving towards a new society. Philadelphia: New Society Press.

Gray, Francine du Plessix, 1970. Divine disobedience; profiles in Catholic radicalism. London: Hamilton. (Communitarian, anti-conscription, etc.: Emmaus House, the Berrigans, Mendez Arceo, and Ivan Illich.)

Greaves, Bernard (ed.), 1971? Scarborough perspectives. London: Young Liberals. (Pamphlet. '. . . six short essays': 'Greaves . . . talks of 'urban complexes'. . . . Lawry Freedman . . . on capitalism, . . . 'Liberals in the Anarchist Camp'. . . . Gordon Lishman . . . on Community Politics, . . . how do we achieve democracy?—Victor Anderson . . . Lastly, Peter Hain writes on 'Alternative Movement'.')

Gusfield, Joseph R. (ed.), 1970. Protest, reform and revolt; a reader in social movements. NY (and London): Wiley.

Halpert, Stephen, and Tom Murray (eds.), 1972. Witness of the Berrigans. NY: Doubleday.

Harris, David, 1970. Goliath. NY: Baron. ('. . . vision of the future which must be acted on now in your personal life-style and on the nonviolent process of making change which will inevitably define what you achieve.')

Illich, Ivan D., 1973a. Celebration of awareness; a call for institutional revolution. Harmondsworth: Penguin.

——, 1973b. Tools for conviviality. NY: Perennial Library.

——, 1974. Energy and equity. NY: Perennial Library.

Jezer, Marty, et. al., 1976. The power of the people; active nonviolence in the U.S. Culver City, CA: Peace Press (Robert J. Cooney, ed.).

Kent, Edward (ed.), 1971. Revolution and the rule of law. Englewood Cliffs, NJ (and Hemel Hempstead, England): Prentice-Hall.

Kerry, John, and Vietnamese Veterans Against the War, 1971. New soldier. NY: Macmillan. (David Thorne and George Butler, eds.)

Krassner, Paul, 1971. How a satirical editor became a Yippie conspirator in ten easy years. NY: Putnam.

Lakéy, George, 1972. Strategy for non-violent revolution. London: Housmans. (Pamphlet.)

——, 1973. Strategy for a living revolution. NY: Grossman/Freeman. ('Gives a clear understanding of nonviolence as an effective means for developing a mass movement for change.')

Leggett, John C., 1973. Taking state power; the sources and consequences of political challenge. NY: Harper.

Macfarlane, Leslie J., 1971. Political disobedience. London: Macmillan. (Also includes an annotated bibliography on theory, nonviolent resistance, protest, revolution, and violence.)

McReynolds, David, 1970. We have been invaded by the 21st Century. NY (and London): Praeger. ('. . . collection of short essays and articles written during the 60's . . . when kids started protesting and going to jail for civil rights, . . . resisting the war, resisting the system.')

Mayer, Milton, 1969. On liberty; man v. the state. Santa Barbara, CA: Center for Democratic Institutions. ('. . . general outlook. . . . pacifist libertarian.')

Meyers, William, and Park Rinard (eds.), 1972. Making activism work. NY (and London): Gordon. (Examples in education, health, housing, environment, transportation, law and justice, foreign policy, the economy, quality of life, and media.)

Nearing, Scott, 1972. The making of a radical; a political autobiography. NY: Harper. ('Summarizes a lifetime . . . dedicated to teaching the good life and to opposing war, conscription, and an economy based on greed and waste.')

Noell, Chuck, and Bob Levering, 1973? Nonviolent direct action as a strategy for social change. (From WRL, 339 Lafayete St., NY 10012). (Pamphlet.)

(Nonviolent revolution . . .), 1970? Nonviolent revolution. San Francisco (1360 Howard St., 10012): WRL/West. ('Carefully compiled study kit of essays and training guides.')

Oppenheimer, Martin, 1969. Urban guerrilla. Chicago: Quadrangle. ('. . . strategy of nonviolent guerrilla revolution.')

O'Rourke, William, 1973. The Harrisburg 7 and the new Catholic Left. NY: Apollo.

Ostergaard, Geoffrey, and Melville Currell, 1971. The gentle anarchists; a study of the leaders of the Sarvodaya Movement for Non-violent Revolution in India. London: Oxford Univ. Press. (Also includes a selected bibliography of about 375 items.)

Roberts, Ron E., and Robert Marsh Kloss, 1974. Social movements; between the balcony and the barricade. Saint Louis, MO (and London): Mosby.

Sale, Kirkpatrick 1973. SDS; ten years toward a revolution. NY: Random. (HIstory of Students for a Democratic Society, an American radical organization active in the 1960s.)

Schechter, Betty, 1963. Peaceable revolution. Boston: Houghton Mitflin. (Secondary school text. Thoreau, Gandhi, American civil rights.)

Schumacher, E. F., 1973. Small is beautiful. NY: Harper. ('. . . on the necessity of decentralization.')

Servan-Schreiber, Jean-Jacques, and Michel Albert, 1972. Radical alternative. NY: Dell (and London: Macdonald, 1970). (French economic/social/political study.)

Sharp, Gene, 1970. Exploring nonviolent alternatives. Boston: P. Sargent.

Sibley, Mulford Q., 1969. Revolution and violence. London: Peace News/Housmans. (1st Ed., 2nd reprint.)

——, 1970. Obligation to disobey. NY: Council on Religion and International Affairs.

Smith, Michael, and Kenneth Deutsch, 1972. Political obligation and civil disobedience; readings. NY: T. Y. Crowell.

Tolstoy, Leo, 1968. Writings on civil disobedience and non-violence. NY: Signet.

Uphaus, Robert W. (ed.), 1971. American protest in perspective. NY (and London): Harper. (1776 to 1970. Some of the writers represented are Thoreau, Emerson, Du-Bois, James Baldwin, Norman Mailer, Martin Luther King, Jr. (Letter from Birmingham Jail), Eldridge Cleaver.)

Useem, Michael, 1973. Conscription, protest, and social conflict; the life and death of a draft resistance movement. NY (and London): Wiley.

Van Den Haag, Ernest, 1972. Political violence and civil disobedience. NY (and London): Harper. (Clear brief introduction and analysis.)

Verkuyl, Johannes, and H. G. Schulte Nordholt, 1974. Responsible revolution; means and ends for transforming society. Grand Rapids, MI: Eerdmans.

Vuglen, Stephen M., 1968? National liberation movements; communist conspiracies or political realities? Flanders, NJ: O'Hare Books.

War Resisters' International, 1972. WRI statements; a selection of statements and resolutions from the WRI, 1963–July 1972. London: WRI. (Compiled by Sandra Goldsmith.)

Zwiebach, Burton, 1975. Civility and disobedience. Cambridge, England: Cambridge Univ. Press.

Zwisohn, Van, Jim Forest, and David McReynolds, 1973? 1776 or 1984. (From WRL, 339 Lafayette St., NY 10012). (Pamphlet. 'Three essays on possible paths toward nonviolent revolution and the positive aspects of America's own tradition.')

PROTEST EXAMPLES AND BACKGROUND — AGAINST AMERICAN INVOLVEMENT IN THE VIETNAMESE WAR

Cohen, Carl, 1971. Civil disobedience; conscience, tactics, and the law. NY (and London): Columbia Univ. Press.

Ferber, Michael, and Staughton Lynd, 1971. The resistance. Boston: Beacon. ('. . . first attempt at writing a history of the Resistance movement.)

Fernandez, Benedict J., 1968. In opposition; images of American dissent in the Sixties. NY: Da Capo.

Hayden, Tom, 1971. Trial. London: Cape. Account of the Chicago conspiracy trial, 1969–70, carries with it an articulation of changes sought in society.)

Klare, Michael T., 1972. War without end; American planning for the next Vietnams. NY: Knopf.

Melman, Seymour (ed.), 1968. In the name of America; the conduct of the war in Vietnam by the armed forces of the United States as shown by published reports, compared with the laws of war binding on the United States Government and its citizens. NY: Clergy and Laymen Concerned about Vietnam.

Taylor, Clyde (ed.), 1973. Vietnam and black America; an anthology of protest and resistance. Garden City, NY: Doubleday.

PROTEST EXAMPLES AND BACKGROUND — CHAVEZ/UNITED FARM WORKERS/AMERICAN FARM LABOUR

Day, Mark, 1971. Forty acres; Cesar Chavez and the farmworkers. NY: Praeger.

Dunne, John Gregory, 1967. Delano; the story of the California grape strike. NY: Farrar, Straus & Giroux. (Clear background, description, and analysis.)

Fodell, Beverly, 1974. Cesar Chavez and the United Farm Workers; a selective bibliography. Detroit: Wayne State Univ. Press. (Comprehensive annotated list of several hundred items—among them, nearly fifty bibliographies on this and related topics!)

Fusco, Paul (photographer) and George D. Horwitz, 1970. La Causa; the California grape strike. NY: Macmillan.

Levy, Jacques E., 1975. Cesar Chavez; autobiography of La Causa. NY: Norton.

Lewels, Francisco J., Jr., 1974. The uses of the media by the Chicano movement; a study in minority access. NY (and London): Praeger.

London, Joan, and Henry Anderson, 1970. So shall ye reap. NY: Crowell. (Careful, articulate history of the movement to organize California migrant labour; brief annotated bibliography.)

Matthiessen, Peter, 1973. Sal si puedes; Cesar Chavez and the new American revolution. Rev. Ed. NY: Random House.

Pitrone, Jean Maddern, 1971. Chavez; man of the migrants. Staten Island, NY: Society of St. Paul (Alba House).

Taylor, Ronald B., 1975. Chavez and the farm workers. Boston, MA: Beacon.

Terzian, James P., and Kathryn Cramer, 1970. Mighty hard road; the story of Cesar Chavez. NY: Doubleday.

Yinger, Winthrop, 1975. Cesar Chavez; the rhetoric of nonviolence. Hicksville, NY: Exposition-University Book. (Analysis of speeches, etc.; excellent classified bibliography of about 200 items, partially annotated, 1959-70).

PROTEST EXAMPLES AND BACKGROUND— GANDHIAN/INDIAN

Alexander, Horace G. 1969, What has Gandhi to say to us? London: Friends Peace and International Relations Committee. (Pamphlet.)

Brock, Guy Clutton, and Molly Clutton Brock, 1972. Cold comfort confronted. London: Mowbray. (Account of a Rhodesian multiracial cooperative farm, 1965-70.)

Fischer, Louis, 1954. Gandhi; his life and message for the world. NY: Mentor.

——, 1965. The life of Mahatma Gandhi. 2 Vol. Bombay: Bharatiyavidya Bhavan. (And Macmillan, 1962).

Gandhi, Mohandas Karamchand, 1968. The selected works of Mahatma Gandhi. 6 Vol. Ahmedabad: Navajivan.

——, 1969. Collected works. . . . 2nd Rev. Ed. New Delhi: Publications Division, Ministry of Information and Broadcasting, Government of

India.

——, 1970. The Ghandhi reader; a sourcebook of his life and writings, edited by Homer A. Jack. NY: AMS.

——, 1971. Selected writings of Mahatma Gandhi. London: Fontana. (Selected by Ronald Duncan.)

——, 1972a. All men are brothers. Chicago: World Without War Publications. ('Autobiography and selections on peace, democracy, poverty and nonviolence.' Also, 2nd Ed., 1969, Columbia Univ.)

——, 1972b. Gandhi; selected writings. Selected . . . by Ronald Duncan. NY: Harper.

(Also, a variety of books by and about Gandhi are available from Housmans, 5 Caledonian Rd., London N1 9DX, and from Good Boox, Realbox 455X, 10B Mt. Auburn St., Cambridge, MA 02138.)

Horsburgh, H. J. N., 1972. Mahatma Gandhi. Working/London: Lutterworth Press.

Lanza del Vasto, 1974. Gandhi to Vinoba; the new pilgrimage. NY: Schocken.

Muste, A. J., Joan Bondurant, Mulford Sibley, G. Ramachandran, et. al. 1971? Gandhi; his relevance for our times. (Notice in *WIN*, 15 October 1971, as being available from WRL, 339 Lafayette St., NY 10012).

Ostergaard (See above, under 'PROTEST, CIVIL DISOBEDIENCE, , , ,')

Shriman, Narayan, 1970. Relevance of Gandhian economics. Ahmedabad: Navajivan Publishing.

PROTEST EXAMPLES AND BACKGROUND — MARTIN LUTHER KING

Bennett, Lerone, 1968. What manner of man; a biography of Martin Luther King, Jr. 3rd Rev. Ed. Chicago: Johnson.

Davis, Lenwood G., 1969. I have a dream; the life and times of Martin Luther King, Jr. Chicago: Adams Press.

Ezekiel, Nissim (ed.), 1969. A Martin Luther King reader. Bombay: Popular Prakashan. (Collection of writings and speeches.)

King, Coretta Scott, 1969. My life with Martin Luther King, Jr. NY: Holt.

King, Martin Luther, Jr., 1967a. Trumpet of conscience. London: Hodder & Stoughton.

——, 1967b., Where do we go from here: chaos or community? NY: Harper.

Lewis, David, 1970. Martin Luther King; a critical biography. NY: Praeger. (Singularly articulate and thorough.)

Miller, William Robert, 1968. Martin Luther King, Jr.; his life, martyrdom and meaning for the world. NY: Weybright and Talley.

Muller, Gerald Francis, 1971. Martin Luther King, Jr.; civil rights leader. Minneapolis: Denison.

Power, Jonathon, 1976. Martin Luther King; a reassessment. London: Catholic Commission for Racial Justice and the Fellowship of Reconciliation in Great Britain and Ireland. (Pamphlet.)

Slack, Kenneth, 1970. Martin Luther King. London: SCM.

Smith, Kenneth L., and I. G. Zepp, 1974. Search for the beloved community; the thinking of Martin Luther King, Jr. Valley Forge, PA: Judson Press.

Westin, Alan F., and Barry Mahoney, 1974. The trial of Martin Luther King. NY: Crowell. (Emphasizes legal and judicial aspects of relevant protest action.)

Williams, Daniel T. (Compiler), 1970. Eight Negro bibliographies. NY: Kraus Reprint Co.

PROTEST EXAMPLES AND BACKGROUND — OTHER SPECIFIC PLACES

American Friends Service Committee, 1970. Search for peace in the Middle East. Rev. Ed. Greenwich, CT: Fawcett. ('Concrete proposals based on a 2-year international survey.')

(Amnesty International . . .), 1975. Amnesty Internationsl report on torture. NY: Noonday Press.

Arrowsmith, Pat (editor), 1972. To Asia in peace; the story of a nonviolent action mission to Indo China. London: Sidgwick & Jackson.

de Kadt, Emmanuel, 1970. Catholic radicals in Brazil. London: Oxford Univ. Press.

Deloria, Vine, 1974. Behind the trail of broken treaties; an Indian declaration of independence. NY: Delacorte. (American Indian.)

Doctor, Adi H., 1967. Sarvodaya; a political and economic study. London: Asia Publishing House. ('The art and science of mobilising the physical, economic and spiritual resources . . . of society in the service of the general good.')

Dowd, Douglas F., 1974. The twisted dream; capitalist development in the United States. Cambridge, MA: Winthrop.

Duff, Peggy, 1971. Left, left, left; a personal account of six protest campaigns, 1945–65. London: Allison & Busby.

el-Asmar, Fouziel, 1975. To be an Arab in Israel. London: Frances Pinter. ('. . . autobiography by an Israeli-Arab poet . . . who believes in the possibility of Jews and Arabs residing together . . .' and suggests political and social changes.)

Greene, Felix, 1970. The enemy; notes on imperialism and revolution. London: Cape. ('. . . imperialism and how it works; well-documented.')

(India and . . .), 1973. India and the Nagas. London: Minority Rights Group Report No. 17. (Pamphlet by Neville Maxwell.)

Keim, Albert N. (ed.), 1975. Compulsory education and the Amish. Boston: Beacon. (American 'Supreme Court ruling on a minority's right not to conform.')

Lanza del Vasto, Joseph Jean, 1971. Return to the source. London: Rider (and NY: Pocket Book).

——, 1974a. Gandhi to Vinoba; the new pilgrimage. NY: Schocken.

——, 1974b. Make straight the way of the Lord; an anthology of the philosophical writings . . . NY: Knopf.

——, 1974c. Principles and precepts of the return to the obvious. NY: Schocken.

——, 1974d. Warriors of peace; writings on the technique of non-violence. NY: Knopf. (This and the preceding four volumes 'comprise the key writings of the 72-year-old disciple of Gandhi, leader of the nonviolent movement in France and founder of the Community of the Ark.')

Mangione, Jerre (See below, under the section 'SOCIAL ACTION'.)

Mumford, Dave, and Martin Everett, 1973? Development briefing. London: National League of Young Liberals. ('A do-it-yourself guide to education and action on third world problems.')

North American Congress on Latin America, 1970. NACLA research methodology guide. NY: NACLA.

Page, Joseph A., 1972. The revolution that never was; northeast Brazil, 1955 1964. NY: Grossman.

PARC (compiler), 1971. Appalachia's people, problems, alternatives; an introductory social science reader. Vol. 1. Morgantown, W VA (Route 8, Box 292K): Peoples Appalachian Research Collective.

Rawlinson, Roger, 1976. The battle of Larzac. New Malden, ' Surrey: Fellowship of Reconciliation. (Pamphlet. Campaign of French farmers against expansion of a military camp. Plus short bibliography.)

RADICAL PERSPECTIVES; ALSO, ANARCHISM

Benello, C. George, and Dimitri Roussopoulos (eds.), 1971. The case for participatory democracy; some prospects for the radical society. NY: Grossman.

Bookchin, Murray, 1971. Post scarcity anarchism. Palo Alto, CA: Ramparts Press. ('Ecology and Revolutionary thought' and other essays.)

Deutsch, Steven E., and John R. Howard (eds.), 1970. Where its at;

radical perspectives in sociology. NY (and London): Harper. (A number of the papers exemplify research/analysis in the service of non-violent social change.)

Dorman, Michael, 1974. Confrontation; politics and protest. NY: Delacorte. (Secondary school text.)

Estrin, Marc (ed.), 1971. Recreation; a radical theater approach to life. NY: Dell.

Heather, Nick, 1970. Radical perspectives in psychology. London: Methuen.

Horowitz, David (ed.), 1971. Radical sociology; an introduction. San Francisco (and London): Canfield/Harper.

Horowitz, David, et al., 1972. Counter culture and revolution. Philadelphia: Philadelphia Book Co.

Horowitz. Irving Louis (ed.), 1964. The anarchists. NY: Dell.

Levitt, Morton, and Ben Rubenstein (eds.), 1971. Youth and social change. Detroit, MI: Wayne State Univ. Press.

Lynd, Staughton, and Gar Alperovitz, 1973. Strategy and program; two essays toward a new American socialism. Boston: Beacon. ('. . . offer important models for a more rational world through better leadership and decision-making.')

Milliband, Ralph, and John Saville (eds.), 1975. The socialist register 1975. London: Merlin Press. ('Survey of movements and ideas.')

Shatz, Marshall S. (ed.), 1971. The essential works of anarchism. Toronto (and London): Bantam.

Walter, Nicholas, 1971. 'Anarchist classics.' Peace News (10 September): 3.

Ward, Colin, 1973. Anarchy in action. London: Allen and Unwin.

Weissman, Steve, et al., 1974. The trojan horse; a radical look at foreign aid. San Francisco: Ramparts Press.

RESEARCH — SOCIAL AND PEACE

Armistead, Nigel (ed.), 1974. Reconstructing social psychology. Baltimore: Penguin. ('Is social psychology about people or not?')

Banner, David K., et al., 1975. Evaluating social action programs. Cambridge, MA: Ballinger.

Boasson, Charles, 1971. A prologue to peace research. Jerusalem: Israel Universities Press (and London: North-Holland).

Carson, Robert, 1973? A collection of readings on peace research and war/peace subjects for Canadian high schools. Oakville, Ontario: Canadian Peace Research Institute.

(Check list . . .), 1973? Check list of information sources. London: Community Development Project, Home Office. (Pamphlet. '. . . to provide neighbourhood information centres with details of where they can get information on such problems as planning and the environment, social security, the law, welfare rights, consumer problems and housing.')

Clark, Peter A., 1972. Action research and organizational change. London: Harper. (Mainly as related to collaboration between researchers and organizational managers.)

Cook, Blanche (ed.), 1969. Bibliography on peace research in history. Santa Barbara, CA: ABC-Clio.

Dedring, Juergen, 1976. Recent advances in peace and conflict research; a critical survey. Beverly Hills, CA (and London): Sage.

(Investigators handbook . . .), 1975. Investigators handbook. London: Community Action. (Pamphlet. '. . . comprehensive guide to sources of information on companies, organisations and individuals.')

Kelman, Herbert C., 1968. A time to speak; on human values and social research. San Francisco, CA: Jossey-Bass.

Kumar, Mahendra, 1968. Current peace research and India. Atlantic Highlands, NJ: Humanities.

Lakey, George, 1970. Exploring nonviolent action; a guide to research. London: Housmans. (Pamphlet.)

Lees, Ray, and George Smith (eds.), 1975. Action-research in community development. London: Routledge.

Newcombe, Hanna, and Alan Newcombe, 1969. Peace research around the world. Oakville, Ontario: Canadian Peace Research Institute. ('A comprehensive survey of fundamental studies and theories, including action research, theoretical conclusions, policy recommendations, research recommendations, and 626 basic references.')

(Peace Research . . .), 1967 onward, Peace Research Reviews. Oakville, Ontario: Canadian Peace Research Institute. ('. . . series of . . . monographs, with extensive bibliographies.')

Pruitt, Dean G., and Richard C. Snyder (eds.), 1969. Theory and research on the causes of war. Englewood Cliffs, NJ (and London): Prentice-Hall.

Rossi, Peter H., and Walter Williams (eds.), 1972. Evaluating social programs; theory, practice, and politics. NY (& London): Academic Press.

Smith, David H., 1974. Voluntary action research. Lexington, MA (and London): Lexington/Heath.

(SSIE . . .), . . . Washington, DC: Smithsonian Science Information Exchange (Room 300, 1730 M Street, NW). (Descriptions of research based on a computer file of about 200,000 current projects. Request complimentary booklets describing SSIE services in social sciences and in behavioral sciences. Just a few of the topics represented are: citizen community participation, co-operatives, ecology, environment, health, housing, minorities, poverty, problem solving and conflict resolution, research, social change, social service.)

Tripodi, Tony, 1974. Uses and abuses of social research in social work. NY (and London): Columbia Univ. Press.

US . . . Library of Congress, 1973. A directory of information sources in the United States. Social sciences. Rev. Ed. Washington, DC: National Referral Center, Science and Technology Division, Library of Congress.

Wehr, Paul, and Michael Washburn, 1976. Peace and world order systems; teaching and research. Beverly Hills, CA (and London): Sage.

Weinberg, Meyer, 1970. Desegregation research; an appraisal. 2nd Ed. Evanston, IL: Integrated Education Associates (Phi Delta Kappa).

Wilcox, Leslie D., Ralph M. Brooks, George M. Beal, and Gerald E. Klongham, 1972. Social indicators and monitoring; an annotated bibliography. Amsterdam (and London): Elsevier. (Over 600 abstracts.)

SOCIAL ACTION

Benewick, Robert, and Trevor Smith (eds.), 1972. Direct action and democratic politics. London: Allen and Unwin.

Camara, Helder, 1971a. Race against time. London: Sheed and Ward.

——, 1971b. Revolution through peace. NY (and London): Harper.

——, 1972. Structures of injustice. London: Justice and Peace Commission. (Pamphlet.)

Carter, April, 1973. Direct action and liberal democracy. London: Routledge.

Curle, Adam, 1972. Mystics and militants; a study of awareness, identity and social action. London: Tavistock.

DeCocq, Gustave A., 1969. Citizen participation; doomed to extinction or last foothold of democracy? Leyden, Netherlands: Sijthoff. (Dutch, Danish, German, and British activity for social welfare.)

Dellinger, Dave, 1975. More power than we know; the people's movement toward democracy. NY: Doubleday/Anchor. ('. . . chronicles of the peace movement . . .' '. . . definitive prescription for nonviolent revolution.' '. . . movement tactics, past and future.')

Gamson, William A., 1975. The strategy of societal protest. Homewood, IL (and London): Dorsey. (Empirical study of the experiences of over 50 'American voluntary groups that, between 1800 and 1945, have challenged some aspect of the status quo'.)

Gerlach, Luther P., and Virginia H. Hine, 1970. People, power, change; movements of social transformation. NY: Bobbs-Merrill.

Gowan, Susanne, George Lakey, William Moyer, and Richard Taylor,

1976. Moving toward a new society. Philadelphia: New Society Press. ('. . . criteria for a healthy society, . . . the environmental crisis, how US corporations exploit the Third World,' and American 'domestic problems.')

Hall, Christopher, 1974. How to run a pressure group. London: Dent.

Hessel, Dieter T., 1972. A social action primer. Philadelphia, PA: Westminster.

Jacobs, Jenny, Sheila Rose, and Jim Schrag, 1974? Organising macro-analysis seminars. London: Friends Peace and International Relations Committee. ('. . . group techniques to . . . put social problems into a comprehensive economic and social . . . perspective.')

Lane, Peter, 1973. Radicals and reformers. London: Batsford. (Illustrated text describes about nine successful campaigns for radical change in England, from about 1700 to the present.)

Mangione, Jerre, 1972. The world around Danilo Dolci; a passion for Sicilians. NY (and London): Harper. (Personal observations of Dolci's work for social reform in Sicily.)

Pezzuti, Thomas A., 1974. You can fight city hall and win. Los Angeles, CA: Sherbourne.

Pym, Bridget, 1974. Pressure groups and the permissive society. Newton Abbot, Devon: David and Charles. (Also includes topical bibliography.)

Quinley, Harold E., 1974. The prophetic clergy; social activism among Protestant ministers. NY (and London): Wiley. ('Based on a survey of 1580 parish ministers in California.')

Rivlin, Alice M., 1971. Systematic thinking for social action. Washington, DC: Brookings. (Emphasis on programmes of the American government.)

Ross, Donald K., 1973. Public citizen's action manual. NY: Grossman. (Covers consumer practices; health care; discrimination in employment, education, etc.; taxation, lobbying, organization. About 20 other books related to Ralph Nader's American study groups are also available — various authors.)

Society of Friends. Young Friends Central Committee, 1972. South Africa. London: Friends House. ('. . . how Young Friends can help to promote change . . .')

Sommers, Tish, 1972. How to change things around you — even if you never thought you could. NY: McKay.

Tallman, Irving, 1976. Passion, action, and politics; a perspective on social problems and social problem solving. San Francisco: Freeman.

(Weapons for . . .), 1970. Weapons for counterinsurgency. Philadelphia: National Action Research on the Military Industrial Complex. ('. . . manual for organizing local projects to protest aspects of the military-industrial complex.')

Wooton, Graham, 1975. Pressure groups in Britain: 1720–1970: an essay

338   LIBERATION WITHOUT VIOLENCE

in interpretation with original documents. London: Allen Lane.

Youngdahl, Benjamin E., 1966. Social action and social work. NY: Association Press.

SOCIAL CHANGE

Beitz, Charles, and Michael Washbum, 1974. Creating the future; a guide to living and working for social change. NY: Bantam.

Brode, John, 1969. Process of modernization; an annotated bibliography on the sociocultural aspects of development. Cambridge, MA: Harvard Univ. Press (and London: Oxford Univ. Press).

Carkhuff, Robert R. 1971. The development of human resources; education, psychology, and social change. NY (and London): Holt, Rinehart and Winston.

Eisenstadt, Samuel N., 1966. Modernization; protest and change. Englewood Cliffs, NJ: Prentice-Hall.

Flacks, Richard, 1972. Youth and social change. Chicago: Markham. ('. . . youth culture and . . . politicization . . . during the 1960's . . . and . . . youth as an agency of change.')

Jackson, John N., 1972. The urban future; a choice between alternatives. London: Allen and Unwin.

Kohr, Leopold, 1973. Development without aid. Llandybie, Carms, Cymru, UK: Christopher Davies.

Morris, Robert, and Robert H. Binstock, 1966. Feasible planning for social change. NY (and London): Columbia Univ. Press.

Postman, Neil, and Charles Weingartner, 1971. The soft revolution; a student handbook for turning schools around. NY: Dell.

Pringle, P., 1969. Great ideas in social reform. Oxford, UK: Pergamon.

Simpson, Dick, and George Beam, 1975. Strategies for change; reflections for effective citizens. Chicago: Swallow.

Thomas, D. Woods, Harry R. Potter, William L. Miller, and Adrian F. Avenie (eds.), 1972. Institution building; a model for applied social change. Cambridge, MA: Schenkman. (Examples of agricultural colleges in the 'developing countries'; taxonomy and analysis; real world applications.)

Unnithan, T. K. N., 1956. Some problems of social change in India in relation to Gandhian ideas. Groningen, Netherlands: Wolters. (Sociological and other analyses; bibliography.)

Zaltman, Gerald, Philip Kotler, and Ira Kaufman, 1972. Creating social change. NY (and London): Holt, Rinehart and Winston.

Zaltman, Gerald, et. al., 1973. Processes and phenomena of social change. NY (and London): Wiley.

SOCIAL SERVICE

Balshaw, Barbara J., 1969. The importance of caring; a handbook on community service. Royston, Hertfordshire: Priory.

Biddle, William W., 1968. Encouraging community development; a training guide for local workers. NY (and London): Holt.

Demone, Harold, and Dwight Harshbarger (eds.), 1973. Handbook of human service organizations. NY: Behavioral Publications.

Demos, George D., and Bruce Grant, 1973. An introduction to counseling; a handbook. Los Angeles: WPS.

(A directory of . . .), 1976. A directory of Church of England social services. London: Church of England Committee for Social Work and the Social Services.

(Directory of . . .), 1975. Directory of social and health agencies of New York City. NY (and London): Columbia Univ. Press for the Community Council of Greater New York.

Drezner, Stephen M., and William B. McCurdy, 1973. A planning handbook for voluntary social welfare agencies. NY: Family Service.

Hershey, Cary, 1973. Protest in the public service. Lexington, MA (and London): Lexington. (Mainly in an American context, including objections to involvement in the Vietnamese war, inadequate programmes of social welfare, etc.)

Hobman, David, 1971. Who cares? A guide to voluntary and full-time social work. Oxford, UK: Mowbrays.

Jones, Howard (ed.), 1975. Towards a new social work. London: Routledge.

Mathews, Gordon, 1974? Nowhere to go. Canterbury, Kent: The Cyrenians. ('Radical guide to social services for single homeless people.')

Mays, John, Anthony Forder, and Olive Keidan (eds.), 1975. Penelope Hall's social services of England and Wales. 9th Ed. London: Routledge.

(More books . . .), 1973. More books on the social services. London: National Council of Social Service. (Pamphlet.)

O'Sullivan, Maeve, 1972. Let the client choose; non-directive casework — fact or fallacy? London: Bedford Square Press of the National Council of Social Service. (Pamphlet.)

Philips, Andrew, 1975. Charitable status. London: Inter-Action/Writers and Readers. ('. . . registration', acceptability, 'tax advantages and constraints on activities.')

Schulman, Eveline D., 1974. Intervention in human services. Saint Louis, MO (and London): Mosby/Kimpton.

Shertzer, Bruce, and Shelley C. Stone. 1974. Fundamentals of counseling. 2nd Ed. Boston (and London): Houghton Mifflin.

(Social services . . .), 1975. Social services year book. London: Councils and Education Press.

Zax, Melvin, and Gerald A. Specter, 1974. An introduction to community psychology. NY (and London): Wiley. (Programmes in schools and colleges, clinics, etc.)

SONGS AND POETRY, ETC.

Denisoff, R. Serge, 1973. Songs of protest, war and peace; a bibliography and discography. Rev. Ed. Santa Barbara, CA (and Oxford, UK): ABC-Clio.

Glazer, Tom (collector), 1972. Songs of peace freedom and protest. NY: Fawcett/World.

Morgan, Robin, 1972. Monster. NY: Random. (Poems.)

STUDENT/YOUTH ACTIVISM

Altbach, Philip G. (ed.), 1970. Student revolution; a global analysis. Mystic, CT: Verry (and Bombay: Lalvan). (International coverage.)

Erlich, John, and Susan Erlich (eds.), 1970. Student power, participation and revolution. NY: Association Press.

Keniston, Kenneth, 1973. Radicals and militants; an annotated bibliography of empirical research on campus unrest. Lexington, MA (and London): Lexington. (Meticulous summary and evaluation of over 300 American empirical studies.)

Owens, B. D., and Ray B. Browne, 1970. Teach-in; viability of change. Bowling Green, OH: Bowling Green Univ.

Sampson, Edward E., Harold A. Korn, and Associates, 1970. Student activism and protest; alternatives for social change. San Francisco, CA: Jossey-Bass. (Also includes a review of recent research.)

Schaflander, Gerald M., 1972. Passion, pot, and politics. Boston, MA: Little, Brown. (Also, comprises Part 2 of: Seymour Martin Lipset and Gerald M. Schaflander, *passion and politics; student activism in America*; Boston MA: Little, Brown, 1971.)

Smith, David Horton, 1973. Latin American student activism; participation in formal volunteer organizations by university students in six Latin cultures. Lexington, MA (and London): Heath.

(Student protest . . .), 1968. Student protest bibliography. Vancouver, BC: University of British Columbia.

VOLUNTEERS

Carkhuff, Robert R., 1969. Helping and human relations; a primer for lay and professional helpers. Vol. 1: Selection and training. Vol. 2: Practice and research. NY (and London): Holt, Rinehart and Winston.

Central Bureau for Educational Visits and Exchanges, 1974. Volunteer work abroad, medium and long term, a directory of organisations. London: Central Bureau . . . (Pamphlet.)

(Directory of . . .), 1973. Directory of alternative work. Rewritten Ed. Birmingham, UK: Uncareers.

Hobman, David, 1969. A guide to voluntary service. London: HMSO.

Jerman, Betty, 1971. Do something! A guide to self-help organisations. London: Garnstone.

Loeser, Herta, 1974. Women, work, and volunteering. Boston: Beacon.

London Council of Social Service, 1971. Someone like you can help; opportunities for voluntary social service in London. London: London Council of Social Service.

Moorhead, Caroline, 1975. Helping; a guide to voluntary work. London: Macdonald and Jane's.

Morris, Robert C., 1973. Overseas volunteer programs; their evolution and the role of government in their support. Lexington, MA (and London): Heath. (International guide to official programmes.)

National Council of Social Service, 1975. Voluntary social services; directory of organisations and handbook of information. Rev. Ed. London: Bedford Square Press.

Schindler-Rainman, Eva, and Ronald Lippitt., 1975. The volunteer community; creative use of human resources. 2nd Ed. Fairfax, VA: NTL Learning Resources.

Sladen, Christopher, 1973. Getting across; a publicity primer for voluntary organisations. London: Bedford Square Press.

Smith, David Horton, 1975. 'Voluntary action and voluntary groups.' Annual Review of Sociology 1.

Stenzel, Anne K., and Helen M. Feeney, 1968. Volunteer training and development; a manual for community groups. NY: Seabury.

Thomas, Michael, 1971. Work camps and volunteers; the P.E.P. study of international work camps in Britain and British work-camp volunteers, London: Political and Economic Planning Broadsheets.

United Nations Conference on the Environment, Stockholm, 1972. 50 million volunteers; a report on the role of voluntary organisations and youth in the environment. London: HMSO.

Varah, Chad (ed.), 1973. The Samaritans in the '70s; to befriend the suicidal and despairing. London: Constable.

ABOUT THE CONTRIBUTORS

'MUTHUKUMARASWAMY ARAMVALARTHANATHAN, for short M. Aram, was born in Tirunelvelly . . . He took his Master's degree in English from the Madras University, after which he went to the USA and obtained his PhD in educational psychology from the Ohio State University. Returning to India he was appointed Professor in the Ramkrishna Vidyalaya at Coimbatore . . . After a year he became the Principal of the Vidyalaya and held that post with distinction for eight years, i.e., until he joined the Delhi-Peking March in 1963. That was his first contact with the non-violence movement . . .' Then 'he worked as Secretary of the Asian Regional Council of the World Peace Brigade . . .' Subsequently, 'Dr Aram went to Nagaland at my invitation, and as long as I was actively associated with the peace work and the Kohima Peace Centre, Dr Aram was my most valued colleague.'—Jayaprakash Narayan.

HERBERT H. BLUMBERG received a doctorate from the Johns Hopkins University. In 1969 he joined the University of London (Institute of Psychiatry) and he currently lectures in psychology at the University of London Goldsmiths' College. He was a research associate at the Center for Nonviolent Conflict Resolution (Haverford College) and was present among those at the Friendly Presence. A. Paul Hare and he co-edited *Nonviolent Direct Action; American Cases, Social-psychological Analyses.* He has authored or co-authored about thirty articles on nonviolent action, surveys of drug use, social research methods, and other topics in social psychology.

JOAN BONDURANT has written widely on nonviolence, political problems in India, and other topics. She received a PhD from the University of California, Berkeley, in 1952. She has been a Research Political Scientist at the Institute of International Studies, and a member of the Department of Political Science at the University of California, Berkeley. At present she is Professor of Comparative Politics at the University of the Pacific.

HELDER CAMARA is archbishop of Olinda and Recife in the North-East of Brazil. 'He has won a worldwide reputation by his devotion to the poor and his eloquent advocacy of the demands of the underdeveloped countries of the world. This dedication has characterized his career as a priest since his ordination in 1931. He was auxiliary bishop of Rio de Janeiro from 1952 to 1964 and worked particularly with young people and the poor. He was the first vice president of the Latin American Bishops' Conference from 1955 to 1965. He is the author of a number of books.'

FRANK CARNEY was a student at Haverford College at the time of his experience with the Antillean Institute of Social Science.

APRIL CARTER was Secretary of the Direct Action Committee Against Nuclear War from 1958 to 1961 and helped to organize the Sahara Protest Team. During 1961 she acted as European Co-ordinator of the San Francisco to Moscow March and she served on the editorial staff of *Peace News* from 1961-2. She studied politcs at the London School of Economics from 1962-5, lectured in political theory at the University of Lancaster 1966-9, and was a part-time tutor in the social sciences for the Open University from 1971-6. She is now a lecturer in politics at Oxford University. Her peace movement activities include helping to organize the visit of A. J. Muste, Bishop Ambrose Reeves and Rabbi Feinberg to Hanoi in January 1967; demonstrating in Budapest as part of the War Resisters International protest in four Warsaw Pact capitals against the invasion of Czechoslovakia in 1968; and chairing the Campaign for Nuclear Disarmament 1970-1. Publications include a chapter in Adam Roberts (ed.) *The Strategy of Civilian Defence* (1967); and two books on *The Political Theory of Anarchism* (1971) and *Direct Action and Liberal Democracy* (1973)

NARAYAN DESAI, son of Mahadev Desai, Gandhi's secretary, was born on Christmas Eve, 1924, in Gujarat, Western India. He spent the first twenty years of his life in Gandhi's Ashrams at Sabarmati and Sevagram, where, without going for any formal education, he had trained under the guidance of his father working in Gandhi's secretariat. Now, after years of teaching in a Gandhian School of Basic Education in a tribal village of Bhoodan Padatatra (walking on foot demanding donations of land for the landless), of writing books and editing journals on peace, of founding and supervising peace centres, he is among the servants of the nonviolent revolution led by Acharya Vinoba Bhave. Since 1962, as secretary of Shanti Sena, he has been on the frontiers of the peace movement in India: on the India-China border in 1962, in Calcutta, Ahmedabad and Bhivandi during the riots and in the refugee camps on the Bangladesh borders. His deep interest and experience in training for nonviolence has taken him to many places in Asia, Africa, Europe, and America.

A. PAUL HARE, born in Washington, DC, in 1923, took his PhD in sociology at the University of Chicago, and is currently Professor of the Department of Sociology at the University of Cape Town. He has been visiting professor at the University of Ibadan (Nigeria) and Makerere University (Uganda) and professor at Haverford College in Pennsylvania. He is the editor (with

E. F. Borgatta and R. F. Bales) of *Small Groups; Studies in Social Interaction,* the author of *Handbook of Small Group Research,* and has been editor of the journal *Sociological Inquiry.* He co-edited (with Herbert H. Bumberg) *Nonviolent Direct Action; American Cases, Social-psychological Analyses.* He was director of the Center for Nonviolent Conflict Resolution at Haverford College and, under a grant from the National Institute of Mental Health, principal investigator for the Nonviolent Action Research Project. His experience includes work with a number of the projects described in this volume. He spent some weeks visiting the Shanti Sena and took part in third-party activity with Narayan Desai after one riot in India. He was present as part of the Friendly Presence. In 1971 he made frequent visits to Kent State under the NIMH grant for research on nonviolence and gave a graduate seminar on nonviolence as a visiting member of the Sociology Department. He was part of the research team covering the Culebra action and was on hand when the first Omega Team crossed into Bangla Desh. He played a part in developing and co-ordinating the projects for Curacao and Cyprus.

MARTIN LUTHER KING, JR., was internationally known for his work in the American civil rights movement. The many awards he received include the Nobel Peace Prize. Like Gandhi before him, he was assassinated while leading a movement to extend human rights by nonviolence.

FRED OVSIEW was born in New Jersey in 1949. He graduated from Haverford College in 1971, Phi Betta Kappa with Honours in Philosophy. After spending two years doing community mental health work, he entered the Medical School of the University of Pennsylvania, to finish in 1977. His experience at the First Annual Antillean Institute of Social Science in Curacao took place in 1970, between his last two years of college.

DEVI PRASAD was born in Dehra Dun, India, in 1921. After studying Fine Arts at Vishvabharati, Rabindranath Tagore's University at Shantiniketan in Bengal, he founded and directed the Art School in Sevagram — a community founded by Gandhi to put into practice his ideas on education, self reliance, village development, and the equality of religions. In 1962 Devi Prasad came to England with his family to become General Secretary of the War Resisters' International, which he was until 1972 when he became chairperson for three years. Since 1972 he has been working in his own art and pottery studio in London and travelling to bring news to one another of various groups around the world working nonviolently for change. He has been editor of Nai Talim (an educational journal of the Gandhian movement); council member of the International Confederation for Disarmament and Peace; and since 1967 a member of the board of directors of Peace News. He has lectured in nonviolent politics (e.g. at Bryn Mawr and Haverford Colleges, in Pennsylvania) and written widely, including *Child Art and Education; Collected Essays on Education; Conscription, a World Survey; They Love It, But Leave It—American Deserters; Fifty Years of War Resistance, What Now?; Problems of Development;* and *Gramdan, the Indian Land Revolution.*

ROGER RAWLINSON. Born 27 January 1918. (English father, French mother.) Received most of his education in France. Married, two sons. Professional photographer. As a convinced anti-fascist, served in the British army in the Second World War (including four years in the Middle East). Later took the pacifist position and developed a strong interest in Gandhian nonviolence, which he saw as a better way of fighting injustice and repression and of establishing a peaceful social order. Active in the peace movement since 1948, particularly in the Peace Pledge Union. Also, member of the Fellowship of Reconciliation. He started writing about the Larzac 'Battle' through his interest in the French nonviolent Community of the Ark which had a strong influence on the conduct of the struggle. He visited the region a number of times to obtain on-the-spot information, tape recordings, and photographs.

JAMES L. SCHRAG lives in the Philadelphia Life Center, a social change training and action community. 'I do nonviolence training and political education work with two collectives of the Philadelphia group of the Movement for a New Society, including co-authoring the manual *Organizing Macro-analysis Seminars* in its American and British editions. I have an MA in sociology from the University of Michigan (1967).' The article on Wounded Knee 'was written soon after my return to Philadelphia from the third party intervention efforts at Wounded Knee. It was written for Peace News at the request of John Hyatt, PN staff member who was in Philadelphia at that time.'

LYLE TATUM is a 57 year old Quaker with a life-time of experience as a peace activist, including participation in numerous nonviolent direct action projects. He has worked for a number of peace and Quaker organizations including Philadelphia Yearly Meeting and the American Friends Service Committee.

CHARLES WALKER is a veteran organizer and trainer for nonviolent action projects, in the US and elsewhere. He has served as staff member for pacifist organizations, edited the book *Quakers and the Draft*, was secretary for the Gandhi Centenary Committee USA. For four years he was Director of Field Studies for the Nonviolent Action Research Project at Haverford College. The first draft of the article on nonviolence in East Africa was prepared for a study on nonmilitary peacekeeping, 'A world peace guard', commissioned by the Cyprus Resettlement Project. 'Access to the World

Peace Brigade papers enabled me to revise and expand it as a preparatory paper for the International Conference of Peace Researchers and Peace Activists, Noordwijkerhout, the Netherlands, July 1975.'

ELLEN WILKINSON 'worked for eight months on Cyprus before the 1974 Greek-Turk conflict. A work camp project with Cypriot-Turk and Cypriot-Greek students provided the information contained in my writing.' 'I graduated from the University of Denver with a BA in English literature and French in 1972. Since then I have worked for the Friends Peace Committee as a fieldworker, the Daily Local News as a reporter, The Central Committee for Conscientious Objectors (since October 1974), and freelance as a cartoonist in Philadelphia.

INDEX

The index contains name and subject entries in a single alphabet. Consult Key Sources (page 290) as well as the index. For a title index to the bibliographic guide, see Nonviolent Liberation (cited on page 288, above). Name entries include surnames plus initials. The same author may be indexed in slightly different places, depending on the initials shown on different works. Nearly all punctuation is omitted from index entries. Most acronyms, such as UK, are alphabetized as if they were words.

INDEX 357